THE PERSECUTORY IMAGINATION

English Puritanism and the Literature of Religious Despair

JOHN STACHNIEWSKI

CLARENDON PRESS · OXFORD
1991

Oxford University Press, Walton Street, Oxford OX2 6DP
Oxford New York Toronto
Delhi Bombay Calcutta Madras Karachi
Petaling Jaya Singapore Hong Kong Tokyo
Nairobi Dar es Salaam Cape Town
Melbourne Auckland
and associated companies in
Berlin Ibadan

Oxford is a trade mark of Oxford University Press

Published in the United States
by Oxford University Press, New York

British Library Cataloguing in Publication Data
Stachniewski, John
The persecutory imagination: English Puritanism and the
literature of religious despair.
1. English literature. Influence of Puritanism
I. Title   820.9
ISBN 0–19–811781–7

Library of Congress Cataloging in Publication Data
Stachniewski, John.
The persecutory imagination: English Puritanism and the
literature of religious despair / John Stachniewski.
Includes bibliographical references and index.
1. English literature—Early modern, 1500–1700—History and
criticism.   2. English literature—Puritan authors—History and
criticism.   3. Puritans—England—History—17th century.   4. Future
punishment in literature.   5. Persecution in literature.
6. Calvinism in literature.   7. Despair in literature.   I. Title.
PR435.S7   1990   820.9' 382—dc20   90–4643
ISBN 0–19–811781–7

Typeset by Cambrian Typesetters, Frimley, Surrey
Printed and bound in
Great Britain by Biddles Ltd,
Guildford and King's Lynn

To my parents

ACKNOWLEDGEMENTS

I have been enormously fortunate in my friends, who have met my frequent whingeing during the writing of this book with more tolerance than it deserved. I am very grateful, also, to the colleagues and friends who read drafts of individual chapters and made valuable comments on them. They include Paul Dawson, Gerald Hammond, Keith Hanley, David Palmer, and Patrick Swinden. It is hard to measure out gratitude but for their extraordinary willingness to volunteer their time I would like especially to thank Roger Holdsworth and David Pirie. Roger's sharp eye for infelicitous expressions and daft ideas has performed the work of a benign censor, and David, who went meticulously through earlier versions of most chapters, combined critical insight with warm encouragement in a way only he knows. I have benefited greatly from discussions with both of them.

The deepest intellectual influence on me, I hope, has been the teaching and critical example of John Carey. I thank him both for this influence and for the scholarly advice and kind personal support he has unhesitatingly and generously provided. Graham Midgley was also most kind and helpful to me when I embarked on postgraduate work in Oxford. Finally I would like to record specific thanks to Keith Thomas, who gave me invaluable advice about historical sources, and, snowed under though he was, found time to make helpful suggestions about my first chapter. May I make emphatic the conventional saver that none of the people mentioned here has anything to do with the weaknesses that remain (or reappeared) after their assistance or in spite of their influence.

Two people without whom it is doubtful I would have completed this book are Joanna Steven and my mother. Joanna rescued me from my own slough of despond; and my mother laboured tirelessly, or so she heroically made it appear, over the typing and re-typings. My love to both.

NOTE: Chapter 5 incorporates material from my article 'Robert Burton's Use of John Abernethy's *A Christian and Heavenly Treatise*', *Neophilologus*, 62 (1978), 634–6; and Chapter 6 is adapted and developed from my 'John Donne: The Despair of the Holy Sonnets', *ELH* 48 (1981), 677–705. I am indebted to the original publishers for permission to use this material.

CONTENTS

LIST OF ILLUSTRATIONS

ABBREVIATIONS

The following abbreviations have been adopted for periodicals:

ELH	*Journal of English Literary History*
ELR	*English Literary Renaissance*
JEGP	*Journal of English Germanic Philology*
LRB	*London Review of Books*
MLR	*Modern Language Review*
MP	*Modern Philology*
P&P	*Past and Present*
PMLA	*Publications of the Modern Language Association of America*
RES	*The Review of English Studies*
SEL	*Studies in English Literature 1500–1900*
SIR	*Studies in the Renaissance*
SP	*Studies in Philology*
SS	*Shakespeare Studies*

TEXTUAL NOTE

In quotations the use of 'i' and 'j' and 'u' and 'v' has been modernized, abbreviated words have been expanded, and indisputable misprints have been corrected. Some of the more unwieldy titles have been given in short form. Unless stated otherwise the place of publication is London.

INTRODUCTION

THIS book has two main purposes: to examine the role of a specific cultural phenomenon in the construction of seventeenth-century subjectivities; and to show how the dynamics of major literary texts can be effects of the pressures exerted by a collective imagination, to which the organizing intelligence of individual artists is largely subordinate. I begin by quoting C. S. Lewis's pugnacious remarks when he turned to speak of 'the original Protestant experience' in *English Literature in the Sixteenth Century*:

> The very word *experience* perhaps makes clear the angle at which I approach it. Some social or economic historians treat the Reformation solely from the point of view of their own disciplines, regarding its spiritual and even its intellectual side as mere epiphenomena; perhaps as 'rationalizations' by which men explained to themselves behaviour whose real causes were of quite a different kind. Fortunately there is no need to discuss the correctness of this view: for even if it were wholly correct it would not much concern the historian of literature. His business is with the past not as it 'really' was (whatever 'really' may mean in such a context) but with the past as it seemed to be to those who lived in it: for of course men felt and thought and wrote about what seemed to be happening to them. The economic or social historian's 'appearances' may be the literary historian's 'facts'. We want, above all, to know what it felt like to be an early Protestant.[1]

Beside this I place an observation in a review written by the historian Blair Worden:

> Our temptation is to soften the Puritan mentality and, as we suppose, to humanize it . . . Possibly Wallington's literary gifts were unequal to the communication of those more cheerful and creative features of Puritan (and Calvinist) faith which our time has emphasized. Yet we err if we neglect the darknesses of Puritanism, at least in its 17th-century form. The volume of despair engendered by Puritan teaching on predestination is incalculable . . . Social and economic explanations of Puritanism have collapsed, and we do not know how to replace them. In what sense can it have been in anyone's *interest* to subscribe to Wallington's spiritual anxieties, to sit, as he did, through 19 long sermons in a week, to endure

[1] C. S. Lewis, *English Literature in the Sixteenth Century Excluding Drama* (1954; paperback edn. 1973), 32.

endless fasts, to rise in the middle of the night for meditation and suffer agonies of self-reproach for dozing beyond the appointed hour? Puritanism roams the highway of our history, and before we could 'explain' it we would need to have the measure of the beast.[2]

Lewis and Worden entertain a similar objective: to understand the experience of early English protestants. Both indicate scepticism towards materialist approaches to such understanding. The literary critic is confident that the experience is transparently on show in the literature protestants produced about themselves. The historian is honestly puzzled by their behavioural patterns. Lewis (in another passage) stresses the 'buoyancy' of the early protestants, seeing grimmer aspects, specifically doubt of election, as belonging mainly to 'fiction'.[3] Worden, writing much more recently, notes an over-concentration on happier features and proposes that a steadier gaze be directed towards the darker ones as a precondition of adequate explanation. Their periods differ somewhat; so too do the objects of their attention. Lewis is talking primarily of Elizabethan leaders of the Reformation, invigorated by the novelty of the ideas they were bringing from the Continent, and of their influence after Marian persecution. Worden is thinking of ordinary people who lived with Calvinist ideas and puritan habits which were woven into their consciousness as received orthodoxy.

As the title of my book confesses, I am with Worden in believing that the brighter side of protestantism has attracted disproportionate attention. There are a number of reasons for this emphasis. First, committedly Christian literary critics and scholars such as Lewis, naturally well represented in this area, are given to seeing the essence of their faith as unchanging, so that they are guided by an inclination to read their own religious experience back into the past, fleshing this out with the historical accidentals. This procedure is evident both with those who associate their own faith with the tradition that begins, or reasserts itself, at the Reformation and with those (one thinks for example of T. S. Eliot, Helen Gardner, and Louis Martz) of High Church sympathies who wish to stress continuity of faith through the Christian millennia. Sometimes the work of these

---

[2] Blair Worden review of Paul S. Seaver, *Wallington's World: A Puritan Artisan in Seventeenth-Century London* (1985), *LRB* (23 Jan.–6 Feb. 1986), 16–17.

[3] *English Literature in the Sixteenth Century*, p. 34.

critics benefits from sympathetic engagement with their subject; the drawback, however, is that where such engagement is frustrated by the text the stubborn material tends to be edited out, or at least pushed to the margin. Doubt of election is usually treated as an aberration of minor significance which in any case had more to do with the pathology of those afflicted with it than with the religious culture itself.

Secular-minded literary critics as a rule have limited interest in the theological content of religious writing and, usually under the influence of liberal humanism, have been polite to Christianity, attending most to the enduring aesthetic and moral values that writers are seen to sift out of it and integrate with their presumed artistic purposes. Reverence for the artist is an unscandalizing displacement of more explicitly metaphysical reverence. Many literary historians (their lens firmly positioned over literature in relation to its own history) resemble the Christian critics in their idealist search for evolving traditions, for the communings of inspired minds across the centuries, so there is a tendency again to strip texts as far as possible of what are seen as their epiphenomenal trappings. Alan Sinfield's *Literature in Protestant England 1560–1660* (Beckenham, 1983) and William Empson's more specifically focused *Milton's God* (Cambridge, 1961) are the only critical books I know which take a sustained interest in the rebarbativeness of Christianity in this period.[4] Harder to classify, but needing mention since I found it highly suggestive when conceptualizing this book, is Erich Fromm's *The Fear of Freedom* (1942), a psycho-social interpretation, written in the shadow of Nazism, of authoritarian ideologies in modern history, including the protestantism of Luther and Calvin. Taking as his primary object the characteristic adjustments of the psyche to post-medieval social formations, Fromm seems to me refreshingly independent of the sight-lines the more identifiable disciplines

---

[4] Other critics bring in Calvinist cruelties more incidentally: most trenchantly, I think, John Carey in *John Donne: Life, Mind, and Art* (1981) and Wilbur Sanders in *The Dramatist and the Received Idea: Studies in the Plays of Marlowe and Shakespeare* (Cambridge, 1968). See also James D. Boulger, *The Calvinist Temper in English Poetry* (The Hague, 1980); Jonathan Dollimore, *Radical Tragedy: Religion, Ideology, and Power in the Drama of Shakespeare and his Contemporaries* (Brighton, 1984); Robert G. Hunter, *Shakespeare and the Mystery of God's Judgements* (Athens, Ga., 1976); Paul R. Sellin, 'The Hidden God: Reformation Awe in Renaissance English Literature', in R. Kinsman, ed., *The Darker Vision of the Renaissance: Beyond the Fields of Reason* (Berkeley, 1974).

tend to establish. Recent 'new historicist' work has dealt, too, with relations of power, but it is the practices of power centred on the court, along with strategies of resistance to state power, with which it has been mainly concerned. The power exercised through the religious culture has been treated incidentally.

Historians have also inclined towards an up-beat reading of the protestant story. Those of a Weberian bent have wanted to show how protestant ideas shaped and speeded economic progress and the self-confidence of the bourgeoisie. Those more attracted to the Marxist perspective attribute to religious ideas the disguised function of rationalizing and securing the interests of contending socio-economic groups (eventually classes), so that for them too only ideas offering adherents some form of positive reinforcement move into frame. A humanistic Marxist like Christopher Hill, who assigns a positive role in history to deliberate human agency, is interested in the adaptability of protestantism to anti-authoritarian, egalitarian purposes. To convey this it is, naturally, the energizing, revolutionary potential amongst the common sort, especially of apocalyptic visions of an imminent transformation of society, that is the strand of protestantism picked out. While the experience of persecution is an important part of this story, the resilience of the radicals measures the righteous conviction and solidarity that sustained them. Of course Hill is far too knowledgeable to neglect the authoritarian aspect, with its concomitant despair;[5] but it is subordinated. Revisionist historians, resisting what they see as teleological explanation—whether idealist or materialist—argue that the great magnet to historians of the seventeenth century, the Civil War, resulted from a concatenation of events which had no necessary determinants. Perhaps in consequence of this, recent emphasis has fallen, as Margo Todd observes, 'more on activities than on ideas'. 'We now know', she says, 'what puritans did, as urban magistrates and churchwardens and clergymen and gentlemen, but the theoretical underpinning for their actions has received scant attention.'[6] More scanted still

[5] See especially the chapter 'Sin and Hell' in *The World Turned Upside Down: Radical Ideas during the English Revolution* (1972; Harmondsworth, 1975). Hill associates Calvinism with competitive individualism and social discipline in some contexts and with radical resolve in others. I admire his social contextualizing of similar ideas, and differ mainly in the socio-theological nexus to which I give prominence.

[6] Margo Todd, *Christian Humanism and the Puritan Social Order* (Cambridge, 1987), 3.

(since, after all, a good deal has been written about ideas at the level of polemics) has been the consideration of how, provided with their ideas, puritans felt, how their subjectivity was organized.

The first part of the book addresses itself, then, to the lacuna, to what it felt like to be an early protestant—but more the Worden than the Lewis variety. To my mind Lewis's sharp division between the social and economic and the spiritual and intellectual dimensions of life, even if restricted to the purposes of the literary historian, is itself a piece of 'rationalization'. It decontaminates a presupposed world of ideal essences, not by arguing for its primacy but by bracketing the material world as if it did not exist at all, as if a life of feeling could go on altogether in its absence. Relating theology to social and economic dimensions of experience does not, however, require, as Lewis implies, a translation from one set of terms into another but broader receptivity to the language of the texts themselves and the history they help to constitute. The notion that theology is separable from social and economic factors is, ironically, one that developed only in the eighteenth century[7]—so Lewis was himself introducing an anachronistic perspective by denying their connection in experience. To know, moreover, what it felt like to be a protestant it is not enough to précis what a contemporary says about experience since the pressure towards certain forms of description was intense; it is necessary to follow clues, supplied by the text's own language, to areas of recalcitrance to the official gloss.

Insistence on the relevance of material conditions need not, however, imply that religious ideas must be understood as rationalization of an interest; as Worden indicates, this is an unhelpful thought in the face of the behaviour he describes. What such behaviour rather suggests is the enwebbing of a hapless body and mind in a symbolic system. The punishing routine it imposed on the London turner Nehemiah Wallington and countless others derived from a discourse, promulgated from the pulpit, in which they learnt to construct their identity, their sense of themselves, and from which there was therefore no escape. The question then becomes, why was this discourse, especially in

[7] See below, p. 73.

its repellent aspects, so successful in putting roots down in the community? What gave it purchase on the psyche? The answer is complex and requires many levels of explanation. But a part of such explanation depends, I think I can show, on recognizing that making sense of social and economic circumstances can be negative, against one's interest, as well as self-serving. The negative aspects of Calvinism tended to bond with negative aspects of the social and economic milieu, in particular the severity of parental discipline and the menacing volatility of the economy for the lower to middle orders of society from the late sixteenth to the mid-seventeenth century. Religious ideas have powerful effects when they seem to answer to specific social circumstances, and these circumstances can make painful explanations seem most credible to the imagination. Even where such linguistic reinforcement of negative intuitions is finally overcome, or converted into positive terms, the trace of the former experience and its linguistic encoding remains influential.

The locus for examining the construction of subjectivities—or the process of 'subjectification', to use a term prompted by Foucault which points to the collaboration of internal with external agencies of control through the medium of discourse[8]— is most obviously autobiography. Seventeenth-century spiritual autobiographies exhibit, often very rawly, the way in which conceptions of the self developed through the interaction of available vocabularies and the social processes to which a human being was subjected. Much commentary on these works to date has seemed to me distorted by presupposed writerly intentions (the implementation of which is then taken as the critic's brief): either to display literary gifts, or to exhibit conformity to approved spiritual formulae, or to edify the flock of believers and would-be believers, or a combination of these. Whatever role such intentions may have played, commentary based on them is limited by the common assumption of a unitary authorial presence consciously and autonomously stamping particular

[8] Paul Rabinow uses the term in the introduction to his edition of *The Foucault Reader* (Harmondsworth, 1986), 11. I prefer it, as a translation of Foucault's *assujettissement*, to R. Hurley's 'subjectivation' (*The Use of Pleasure: The History of Sexuality* (Harmondsworth, 1987), ii. 27) because it better suggests his idea of self-objectification. See also Michel Foucault's essay, 'The Subject and Power', appended to Hubert Dreyfus and Paul Rabinow, *Michel Foucault: Beyond Structuralism and Hermeneutics* (Chicago, 1982).

significances on the work. In fact both the narrating subject and the subject of the narration are moving targets of analysis; the language of the text implicates the author in conflicts in the description of the self so that there can be no aloof controlling consciousness. While the quest for stability (itself culturally imposed) is clearly one dynamic in the text it is pitted against other forces which are far from submissive to authorial intention. These forces are nucleated in the collective projection of the Calvinist God. It is this communal construct, whose presence was not solicited by any individual but nevertheless had potent effects inside the psyche, that my book's title, the persecutory imagination, identifies. What most of us would regard as a fiction (and are therefore perhaps prone to underestimate) was an unignorable reality to the spiritual autobiographers which, they supposed, reserved all autonomy to itself. It invaded the most intimate thought processes where in many cases, by the power vested in it by collective belief, it actively persecuted its host. Consequently the narrative shape of certain of the autobiographies, and their linguistic manœuvrings, are largely dictated by the pressures it exerted.

But it is not only in the autobiographies that the persecutory imagination had a shaping role. *The Pilgrim's Progress* evolves under similar pressures, except that here the psychic persecution is more fully amplified in its social dimensions. Bunyan's allegory provided the aptest literary vehicle for the persecutory imagination, uniting the physical, psychological, and social levels on which it was simultaneously experienced. Again the intensive analysis of a single text seems to me productive because it supersedes, exposes the restricted vision of, earlier intentionalist readings rather than merely doing something different with texts (abstracting bits and pieces to make up a super-text more to the critic's taste—a danger in application of the proper recognition of intertextuality). Marjorie Levinson, who takes new historicism to the Romantic period, speaks of 'the interdeterminations of psychic and social forms';[9] to 'psychic' and 'social' I would want to add 'literary'. My analysis of *The Pilgrim's Progress*, as of *Grace Abounding* and Richard Norwood's 'Confessions' in the foregoing

[9] Marjorie Levinson, *Wordsworth's Great Period Poems: Four Essays* (Cambridge, 1986), 13.

chapters, addresses itself to psychic and social interdeterminations to which the form of the text—its structure and narrative evolution—is germane. The medium of the interdeterminations is of course language, so full attention goes to the peculiar linguistic culture, and consequently shared perceptual, discursive, and literary habits, out of which my object texts emerge. I try to explain, in other than the mystical terms of Parnassan inspiration (and its post-Coleridgian variants), why it is that Bunyan describes *The Pilgrim's Progress* as an involuntary creation.

The focus shifts, after the Bunyan chapters, away from texts soaked in puritan culture to the question of how far Calvinist discourse obtruded itself on earlier writings—selected for their range of both genre and mode of assimilating the discourse—by canonical authors no one would call puritan. Here literary criticism is catching up with the comparatively new recognition by historians that Calvinism was, in the late decades of the sixteenth century and throughout James's reign, the orthodoxy of the Church of England. Prior to the rise of Laud (shortly after the accession of Charles I) adherence to Calvinist theology was not equated with puritanism. The church was run by Episcopalian Calvinists. Generally speaking, therefore, Christianity to English people of this era meant Calvinism.

Robert Burton, an encyclopaedically minded Oxford don, is a test case for the influence of Calvinist discourse as there are strong signs in *The Anatomy of Melancholy* of resistance to its construction of experience. The final section of the work, on religious despair, is the site of conflict between competing languages for understanding experience: the medical-humanist, which will just about harmonize with mollified elements of pre-Reformation Christianity, and the Calvinist, which is uncompromisingly exclusive. The task of dismantling the Calvinist–puritan vocabulary and replacing it with another proves unachievable, even systematically unthinkable, partly because the authority of the first discourse maintains its status as an accurate description, but more fundamentally because the experience is generated by the words themselves, inheres in them, and is not a detachable entity receptive to alternative explanation. By closely monitoring interlocked but mutually repelling discourses as the sequence of sentences unfolds it is possible to see how Burton's own mind, as expressed by the flux of his writing, is held captive by the very discourse from whose effects he apparently wishes to free people. Revisions of the *Anatomy* interestingly continue into the period when Calvinism began to be politically disfavoured, so the text's negotiations with the changing conditions complicate understanding of the ideological pressures and state power structures governing the appropriation or rejection of discourses. As with my other chapters an attempt is made to understand the text's relationship to Calvinist discourse in ways that relate to the social situation of the author.

While Burton positions himself in relation to his material as a commentator, and so helps to map Calvinism on to the contemporary social scene, John Donne's 'Holy Sonnets' provide a more intimate record of the tentacles it could extend into an individual psyche. In my analysis of the 'Holy Sonnets' I have felt obliged by the controversial nature of my interpretation to confront other views, especially those of Helen Gardner, from the start. I aim to show that interpretations based on the idea of sequence are both mistakenly premissed and given to distortion along predetermined lines; the way will then be clear to examine discrete poems as produced under the press and screw of the persecutory imagination. The doctrinal presence of Calvinism and the despair constructed by the poems (which turn constantly against the poet-speaker) seem to me, though superficially surprising, finally incontrovertible. These findings go against the biographical grain—the assumption of a unique individual trajectory—in terms of which religious influence is usually understood. And they disfigure the effectively disseminated picture of a cultured élite loftily untouched by protestant vulgarities. When one looks, though, to the prevailing theological vocabulary at the time of composition in concert with the social predicament from which the poems were articulated, the dominant self-understanding they project becomes more credible.

As a psycho-drama, *Doctor Faustus* places mental conflict in a social context (albeit an expressionist one), and therefore invites treatment after the public and private facets of my subject respectively exhibited by Burton and Donne. The play also represents an attempted defiance of the God Marlowe's society had imagined for itself; and for that reason its cultural significance is best understood once that God's power has been fully gauged. With *Doctor Faustus* once again, though Calvinist readings have this time been touted, they are not generally accepted. So I try to establish the case that the play dramatizes specific and exclusive Calvinist dogmas. The chapter's aim is not, though, to abstract a theology from the play—as if the dramatist had put it in; it is rather to explore the culture in which it inheres, and by which Marlowe's own imagination was constrained. The play has often been pared down in criticism to a grandiose fable of humanism versus Christianity, or of the infinite potential of man trapped in finite space and time. I understand the consciousness invested in Faustus rather as a passionately detailed concentration of literal contemporary experiences of subjectivity in a theological culture so repressive that it created the rebel state of mind it reprobated. In this way the seemingly arid theological abstractions like predestination to damnation, divine calling, and prevenient grace to repent can assume the socially concrete meanings to which their credibility was attached. In grasping the exaggerated ordinariness of Faustus it helps, I think, to look at parallels in the consciousness of one of the play's spectators; and to consider the somewhat sadistic relationship the play cultivates with its audience.

My last chapter concentrates on Milton's Satan. *Paradise Lost* converses with both puritan and humanist traditions, belongs to the end of the period covered by this study, and enjoys unparalleled status as a criticism of contemporary English culture and society. Structurally, then, this analysis cements my two parts. I have tried throughout to resist looking at protestant experience teleologically, as a preparative to secular enlightenment on the one hand and comfortable bourgeois providentialism on the other, since only a resolutely synchronic approach seems to me to clamp the structures of feeling obtaining in the period probed. The Milton chapter is in a sense, therefore, a concession to the pressure to conclude a narrative and present a liminal moment. But only in a sense; for while Milton's work, especially *Paradise Lost*, is seen to mark a conscious advance from Calvinism's construction of social and psychological experience, less consciously it too contends with the powerful drag of inherited imaginative patterns. The Satan Milton creates is the receptacle into which much of that experience is diverted; but the old-style puritanism which contributes a great deal, I argue, to the imaginability and creation of this Satan implicates God along with him, so spreading itself throughout the epic and confusing its system of values. Too extrinsic a history-of-ideas approach freeze-frames Milton's Arminian pronouncements and gives a spurious stability and absoluteness to that apparent stance. Milton has Calvinist-puritan habits of mind which survive his active rejection of doctrines which helped to form them. The way in which Milton's work develops the idea of purpose—both negatively and positively—appears to me to be shaped by Calvinist culture; and the imaginative vitality with which this idea had been imbued helped, given his bearings in a changing social and political order, to propel him (and others, like Adam, who seize their exiguous opportunity) towards a limited form of emancipation from the authoritarian deadlock in which Satan/ God remains.

Ritually, anyone who writes a book with 'puritanism' in its title has a go at defining it. So I will introduce my first chapter with a brief description of the puritanism with which I will be concerned. Puritans, for my purposes, were people whose minds appear to have been captured by the questions whether or not they were members of the elect, and how the life of an elect (and elect community), in contradistinction to that of a reprobate, should be ordered. In principle they took a literalist view of the Bible and were either vociferous and vigorous in their attempts to purify the Church of England of perceived accretions to the practices of the primitive church or split off into sects which they thought conformed to these more closely. Such preoccupations ramify into political attitudes, even political theory, but in this book my attention to these is restricted to their impact on the personal issues most puritans themselves felt bound to consider paramount. The species can be roughly dated (if Lollard forerunners are ignored) from the 1560s, when the returned Marian exiles hit their stride in the Church of England and began to promote the idea of a godly commonwealth throughout the country and when, indeed, the term 'puritan' began to circulate.[10] A crystallization of the puritan tradition in the theological sense occurred in 1589 when William Perkins, a Calvinist divine at Christ's College Cambridge, published a work

[10] D. M. Palliser, *The Age of Elizabeth: England under the Later Tudors 1547–1603* (1983), 337.

entitled *A Treatise Tending unto a Declaration whether a Man Be in the Estate of Damnation or in the Estate of Grace: And if he Be in the First, how he May in Time Come out of it: If in the Second, how he Maie Discerne it, and Persevere in the Same to the End.* 'This treatise', says church historian R. T. Kendall, which, like Perkins's other works, stresses soteriology rather than ecclesiology, 'inaugurated a new era in English theology.' Perkins's doctrine of faith acquired credal authority at the Westminster Assembly of Divines (1643–9).[11]

This definition of puritanism, like any other, is open to objections. It largely ignores the radical end of the 'puritan' spectrum, or at least subsumes it to an aspect of puritan belief which may be seen as marginal to the radicals' historical significance. And it creates a problem in distinguishing between puritans and pre-1630 Church of England Calvinists. My defence on the first point is that a good deal of attention has been given to the radicals in the last couple of decades; and that the kind of puritanism I explore directly involved, so far as we can tell, a much larger proportion of the population. There is therefore some value, I hope, in seeing how radical figures relate to this more culturally dominant puritan experience, though it is in the nature of my emphasis that they remain on the periphery of my study.

The second point is tricky, and will be taken up again in the chapter on Burton. Mine is a cultural and psychological rather than an institutional or political definition of puritanism, and the cultural *Geist* does not respect fixed boundaries. There was a powerful community of theological belief embracing puritans and Episcopalian Calvinists. And there were shades of enthusiasm for further reformation of the church. As my conjunction in one study of Bunyan and other sectarian autobiographers with such figures as Burton and Donne indicates, I am concerned to show that Calvinist obsessions did not confine themselves to the puritan strongholds (though this is where they were most intensively cultured), but infiltrated the mental life of the nation. Most simply one can say that Calvinist theology was orthodoxy; the call for immediate and large-scale reform of ecclesiastical and

---

[11] R. T. Kendall, *Calvin and English Calvinism to 1649* (Oxford, 1979), 1; see also Peter Toon, *The Emergence of Hyper-Calvinism in English Nonconformity 1689–1765* (1967), 26.

political structures was not. Often puritans identified themselves by promoting the second along with the first. But they also tended to be associated with zealous insistence on the Calvinist predestinarian tenets some churchmen sought to dilute by discreet underemphasis. It was this insistence that gave colour to Laud's retrospective attempt to stigmatize all Calvinists as puritans. The happiest title most puritans could agree on for themselves was 'the godly'.

An end-date for puritanism is more problematic since in various guises (eighteenth-century dissent, nineteenth-century evangelicalism) the tradition had a vigorous afterlife. There are some writers, William Cowper for example, who are throwbacks to the tradition at its height. But as a cultural and political force, securely rooted in the theology of Calvin, which either did or threatened to control English mores and government, puritanism was dealt its death-blow at the Restoration. By the time Bunyan refers to the term, nostalgically, in 1680[12] the movement may be split roughly into two groupings: sectaries like Bunyan who retained puritan beliefs but had forfeited any pretensions to their national ideological hegemony and belonged to a cultural backwater, and the increasingly affluent middle sort who, more confident in general of their ability to hold or improve their position in the world, made their peace with the Restoration and allowed the ferocity of their parents' religion to subside. Of those who had acquiesced in the Restoration, some conformed to the reconstituted Church of England. Others looked instead to comprehension of their moderate Presbyterianism in the national church; and when this failed to materialize, and the Act of Toleration finally put an end to physical persecution, occupied a fairly comfortable alternative culture in which they appear to

[12] John Bunyan, *Grace Abounding and the Life and Death of Mr. Badman*, ed. G. B. Harrison (1928), 278. Further references to *Mr. Badman* are to this edition and embodied in the text. In fact, the sort of people common parlance dubs 'puritan' seem, from the late 1640s, to have used the term affectionately to refer to stouter forebears (see Patrick Collinson, 'A Comment: Concerning the Name Puritan', *Journal of Ecclesiastical History* 31 (1980), 483–8, 487). An autobiographer, Jane Turner, in 1653 reviews her introduction many years previously to 'some who were then called Puritans' (*Choice Experiences of the Kind Dealings of God, before, in, and after Conversion: Whereunto is added a Description of True Experience* (1653), 12). There is a clear sense of identification with a tradition, part of which was to suffer the opprobrium of the term 'puritan'; at the same time denominational identity—Presbyterian, Baptist, etc.—acquires greater immediacy.

have developed an increasing interest in their worldly prosperity. Sweeping statements as these are, to which many individual exceptions (such as Milton) may be found and many questions addressed, they merely indicate the waning of puritanism's star, not its instant eclipse.

One more generalizing word about the critical stance informing this book. What I favour is a greater anthropological detachment, a willingness, undistracted by the need to reverence the individual artist or honour a heritage, to enter another culture and understand its patterns of ideas, values, and practices at different social levels.[13] Literary critics have privileged, though potentially misleading, access to these patterns since the linguistic concentration of most texts we are used to calling literary on the representation of human experience (whether fictional or actual) allows us to look out at the world through something like the perceptual grid with which people in the seventeenth century inhabited their institutional structures. No doubt for this reason social historians draw increasingly on material more traditional historians used to cordon off, under deep suspicion, as 'literature'. In promoting the idea of literary criticism as immanent anthropology I recognize the objection that we cannot put in abeyance the linguistic grid through which we in our turn make sense of the world. And I see no point in seeking to conceal, by a wholly impersonal tone, the reflexes of my own value system. Anthropological detachment is not meant to imply pretended objectivity but a suspension of interest in the various trajectories by which English culture is thought to have developed. To a degree at least I think we can consciously resist assimilation of the past to the present and commute between the two perspectives without ambitions to align them in ways that suit our own preferred values. Confronted with a phenomenon as bizarre as belief in the Calvinist God, I find that the temptation to claim this bit of the past as some kind of legacy recedes in favour of a naïve intellectual curiosity: how, socially and psychologically, did people live with these ideas?

[13] It is encouraging to find this call for an 'anthropological' criticism in the introduction to Stephen Greenblatt's thoughtful and influential book, *Renaissance Self-Fashioning* (Chicago, 1980), 4. I agree too with the kind of anthropological emphasis he favours: 'anthropological interpretation must address itself less to the mechanics of customs and institutions than to the interpretive constructions the members of a society apply to their experiences.' See also Alan Sinfield, 'Against Appropriation', *EC*, 31 (1981), 181–95.

Part I

1
English Puritanism and the Social Reality
of Religious Despair

THEOLOGICAL BASIS

John Calvin, Theodore Beza, and William Perkins are, says Christopher Hill in *Puritanism and Revolution*, 'often cited as the trinity of the orthodox'.[1] Beza succeeded Calvin as Moderator of the Genevan Church and Perkins became the most influential English Calvinist. Calvin himself was England's most published author between 1548 and 1650. From 1574 to 1587 there were fifteen editions of *The Institution of Christian Religion*. And by 1600 there had been ninety editions of works by him. From the last two decades of the sixteenth century the *Institution* was required reading at both Oxford and Cambridge University.[2] Calvin's fame was almost univocally celebrated by English protestants. Robert Bolton called him, typically, 'that great and incomparable glory of the Christian World, blessed *Calvin*'.[3] But even retroactive father of Anglicanism and champion of Episcopalian church government, Richard Hooker, hailed him, presumably without Francophobic irony, as 'incomparably the wisest man that ever the French church did enjoy, since the hour it enjoyed him'.[4] The chief manifestation of the esteem in which he was held, however, was that, as Charles and Katherine George point out, his phrases were constantly re-echoed.[5]

On the face of it Calvin's theology does not differ greatly from Luther's or Augustine's, both of whom believed in the pre-destination of the elect. Luther stressed the impotence of the

---

[1] Christopher Hill, *Puritanism and Revolution: Studies in Interpretation of the English Revolution of the Seventeenth Century* (1958), 216.

[2] See F. J. Brenner, *The Puritan Experiment: New England Society from Bradford to Edwards* (New York, 1976), 18–19; R. T. Kendall, *Calvin and English Calvinism to 1649* (Oxford, 1979), 52; Norman Pettit, *The Heart Prepared: Grace and Conversion in Puritan Spiritual Life* (1966), 65.

[3] Robert Bolton, *Instructions for a Right Comforting Afflicted Consciences* (1631), 123.

[4] Richard Hooker, *Of the Laws of Ecclesiastical Polity*, Books 1–4, ed. Ronald Bayne (1907), i. 79.

[5] Charles and Katherine George, *The Protestant Mind of the English Reformation (1570–1640)* (Princeton, 1961), 35.

human will. In fact it was his central disagreement with Erasmus.[6] Impotent as he had agonizingly felt to contribute to his own salvation he regarded 'God's secret decree,' says Max Weber, as 'most definitely the sole and ultimate source of his state of religious grace'.[7] Moreover he saw despair prior to salvation, based on the recognition of impotence, to be the condition of the reception of grace. Only in this state of abject terror, which he called *Anfechtung*, could the gratuitousness of God's gift be sincerely apprehended and so appropriated by faith alone. He was fascinated by *Anfechtung*, about which he planned to write a book. This is one of many descriptions of the experience:

When he is tormented in *Anfechtung* it seems to him that he is alone: God is angry only with him, and irreconcilably angry against him: then he alone is a sinner and all the others are in the right, and they work against him at God's orders. There is nothing left for him but the unspeakable sighing through which, without knowing it, he is supported by the Spirit and cries, 'Why does God pick on me alone?'[8]

There were casualties of this prescribed paranoia—people who entered the state of despair and failed to surface from it because they could not achieve the conviction of divine mercy. Yet, another quotation will suggest why Luther's teaching tended not to induce terminal despair:

That the God who is full of goodness and mercy should of his own will harden men, leave them and damn them as though he delighted in such eternal torments of the miserable: to think thus of God seems iniquitous and intolerable . . . I myself have been offended more than once even to the abyss of despair, nay so far as even to wish that I had not been born a man; that is before I knew how beautiful that despair was, and how near to Grace.[9]

The sense of God's anger, even the emotional reflex questioning the justice and character of God, was the flashpoint of conversion; and the constant insistence on this connection naturally tended to overlay the negative experience with the promise of release. In

    [6] See Gerhard Ebeling, *Luther: An Introduction to his Thought*, trans. R. A. Wilson (1970), 217–18.

    [7] Max Weber, *The Protestant Ethic and the Spirit of Capitalism*, trans. T. Parsons, intro. Anthony Giddens, 2nd edn. (1976), 102.

    [8] Quoted by Gordon Rupp in *The Righteousness of God: Luther Studies* (1953), 107; see also p. 106 n.   [9] Quoted ibid. 282.

spite of its personal importance to him, moreover, Luther pushed
the doctrine of predestination into the background as he became
increasingly involved in the practical politics he was precipitated
into as head of his church. 'With Calvin,' says Weber, 'the
process was just the opposite': predestination assumed increasing
importance in his theology.[10] And it was predestination with a
difference: double predestination. In this teaching God decreed
who was to be reprobate as explicitly as he decreed who was to be
elect.[11] It was this explicitness about the inescapably doomed
majority of mankind which contributed most to typical patterns
of religious experience.

Calvin's thought in the *Institution*, the matrix for English cases
of despair, proceeds along binary lines. Unlike any major
theologian before him Calvin habitually specifies the corollary of
God's action on the predestined elect, the experience the
predestined reprobate can expect. His reason for doing this
appears to be the central tenet of his theology: absolute divine
sovereignty. Nothing could coerce, alter, aid, or hinder God's
purposes. This meant that everything that appeared to have
these effects had to be systematically reinterpreted. He aggressively opposed, on this basis, the softening of predestination into
foreknowledge whereby the decrees became the effect of God's
prevision of how people would behave (*Inst.* 3. 21. 5). But
there were also specific consequences for his view of the
reprobate. Defiance and defection gave an illusion of human
autonomy so both had to become effects of prior exclusion.
Anyone who failed to respond to the preaching of the Word had
been 'geven into this perversnesse' (*Inst.* 3. 24. 14). And anyone
who, after living amongst the faithful with every appearance of
being saved, deserted the faith or grew lax had been the recipient
not of saving grace but of 'common' or 'temporary faith' (*Inst.* 3.
2. 12; 3. 2. 11–12; 3. 24. 8): it had always been qualitatively
different from the real thing. If, on the other hand, God had
elected you, his grace could not be resisted (*Inst.* 2. 3. 13–14; 3.
23. 14).

---

[10] See *Protestant Ethic*, p. 102.

[11] See John Calvin, *The Institution of Christian Religion*, trans. T. Norton (1561),
3. 21–4. Further references will be to this edition, abbreviated as *Inst.*, and embodied
in the text. Where a more modern translation is clearer I have adduced the
alternative phrasing in square brackets from *Institutes of the Christian Religion*, trans.
H. Beveridge (Edinburgh, 1863).

While these dogmas dealt very satisfactorily with any form of opposition it is also evident why they should have disturbed would-be believers. Anyone's faith might be common or temporary or—another Calvinist idea—an unconscious pretence (e.g. *Inst.* 3. 2. 10; 3. 2. 12). Moreover, since grace was supposed to arrive with irresistible force, uncertainty as to whether one was an authentic recipient had alarming implications. So the question around which anxiety circled for the individual was, 'How do I know I am saved?' Calvin's own answer to this question when put to him in an attack on predestinarian dogma was: 'If Pighius asks how I know I am elect, I answer that Christ is more than a thousand testimonies to me.'[12] This certainly conveys his own assurance but it was not much use to others. He does not explain what form these testimonies take.

Recurrently in the *Institution* Calvin ignores the anxieties he is creating. Worse than this, he even asserts that to experience such anxieties may be a sign of reprobation. While encouraging a necessarily introspective search for the operation of the Holy Spirit in the would-be Christian's life he at the same time warned that 'If thou consider thy self, there is certaine damnation' (*Inst.* 3. 2. 24). While there may be a theological distinction between these scanning practices, it is clear that experientially the difference is between the sanguine and the diffident—and Calvin made diffidence itself a trap for the reprobate: a diffident assessment of your spiritual prospects was probably an accurate one. On the question of temporary faith, even R. T. Kendall (himself a time-warped Calvinist) admits that Calvin 'seems not to have anticipated the dilemma this teaching could create . . . he comes short of any concrete counsel to a weak believer who may wonder if his faith is but temporary.'[13] But it distorts Calvin's theology even to suggest that the lack of counsel was an omission. Those who discreetly passed over biblical predestination so as not to 'trouble weake soules' claimed a circumspection superior to God's (*Inst.* 3. 21. 4). If temporary faith, an aspect of that predestination, troubled people then that was all part of the plan. Calvin was coolly conscious that very few would be saved and it was clear to him that the damned would be partly composed of

---

[12] John Calvin, *Concerning the Eternal Predestination of God*, trans. and ed. J. K. S. Reid (1961), 130.
[13] *Calvin and English Calvinism*, p. 22.

those who wanted to be or at some point thought they were saved.

Calvin criticized Augustine (who influenced him, and Luther, more than any other theologian) for omitting to speak of the effect of the law (the divine moral code under which everybody stood condemned) on the reprobate as well as the elect. It is a criticism which could equally have been levelled at Luther who, apart from seeing the law as in general entailing damnation for those who do not heed the gospel, considers only its productive effect in preparing for the reception of grace. Typical of the alarming attention Calvin paid to the psychology of the reprobate is his assertion that

> this first office of the lawe is not idle even in the reprobate also. For thoughe they goe not thus farre forwarde with the children of God, that after the throwinge downe of their fleshe they bee renued and florishe againe in the inwarde man, but amased with the firste terroure do lie still in desperation. (*Inst.* 2. 7. 9)

But the elect too, he says, 'yf he do not by and by regenerate them, he keepeth them by the workes of the lawe under feare, until the tyme of his visitation' (*Inst.* 2. 7. 11). The experience then from which your all-important spiritual category was to be deduced was ambiguous. Both reprobate and elect were liable to fear of condemnation under the law and an indefinite time might elapse for an elect individual before God chose to make his visitation. And even if this seemed to take place a conviction of being 'renued . . . in the inwarde man' was imperative; experiential verification of that kind of phrase cannot have been easy.

In general, the crucial distinctions were those most difficult to apply to experience. The ambiguities become most evident in Calvin's discussion of reprobation; in fact he admits and attempts to resolve some of them in the following passage:

> for thoughe none receive the light of faith, nor do truely feele the effectuall working of the Gospell, but they that are foreordeyned to salvation: yet experience sheweth that the reprobate are sometime moved wyth the same feeling that the elect are, so that in their owne judgement thei nothing differ from the electe . . . not that they soundly perceave the spirituall force of grace and assured light of faith: but bicause the Lorde, the more to condemne them and make them inexcusable, conveieth himselfe into their mindes so farre forth, as his goodnesse maie be tasted without the spirit of adoption. If any object,

that then ther remaineth nothing more to the faithfull whereby to prove certainely their adoption: I answere that thoughe there be a great likenesse and affinitie betwene the elect of God, and them that are endued with a fallinge faith for a time, yet there liveth in the elect onely that affiance which Paule speaketh of, that thei crie with full mouthe, Abba, father . . . In the meane season the faithfull are taught, carefully and humbly to examine them selves, least in steede of assurednesse of faith, do creepe in carelesse confidence of the flesh. Byside that, the reprobate do never conceive but a confused feelinge of grace, so that they rather take holde of the shadowe than of the sounde bodie, bicause the holy Spirite doth properly seale the remission of sinnes in the elect onlye, so that they applye it by speciall fayth to their use. (*Inst.* 3. 2. 11)

The passage puts a premium on confidence; this was the key to election:

And that [assurednesse] can not be, but that we muste needes truely feele and prove in our selves the swetenesse thereof. And therefore the Apostle out of fayth deriveth assured confidence, and out of it agayne boldenesse . . . Which boldnesse procedeth not but of assured confidence of Gods good will and our salvation. Whiche is so true, that many times this word faith is used for Confidence. (*Inst.* 3. 2. 15)

A true believer 'with confidence glorieth that he is heyre of the kyngdome of heaven' (*Inst.* 3. 2. 16): a truly miraculous state of mind in the imaginative ambience Calvin's theology fostered. It was this required confidence that tended to split puritan communities, at their extremities at least, into obnoxious prigs (the Jacobean stage type) and quaking obsessives. Equally the theological demand for sincerity in rather large claims for interior experience was what foregrounded the problem of hypocrisy (with which, especially in literature, the nonconformist tradition has commonly been associated).

Calvin's interest in the reprobate ramified beyond the in-authenticity of their faith. There was an important relationship between God's sovereignty, predestination, and the operation of providence. 'Let us note,' he said, 'that God has decreed for us what he means to make of us in regard to the eternal salvation of our souls, and then he has decreed it also in respect of this present life.'[14] By dogmatizing about God's treatment of the reprobate on this side of the grave Calvin encouraged the idea

---

[14] Quoted by François Wendel in *Calvin: The Origins and Development of his Religious Thought*, trans. P. Mairet (1963), 268.

that predestination worked itself out in the everyday detail of life. He faulted Augustine, once more, for attributing the blindness and hardness which brings doom on the reprobate to prescience rather than the operation of God himself. Just as God exerted his power in the elect so equally were the reprobate governed by his providence and forced to serve him (*Inst.* 2. 4. 3; 1. 18. 2). Consequently he thought it important, especially in adversity, 'to understand whereunto the chastisementes have respect, wherwith God correcteth us for our sinnes, and howe much they differ from those examples wherewith he pursueth the wicked and reprobate with indignation' (*Inst.* 3. 4. 31). The experiences differed solely in virtue of the divine attitude they were judged to convey. 'For the order of playne teachyng, let us cal the one kinde of judgement, the judgement of Revenge, the other of Chastisement' (*Inst.* 3. 4. 31). The afflictions of the reprobate were 'a certayne entrie of hell, from whense they doe alredy see a far of their eternall damnation' and rather than benefiting or being reformed by them, they were 'prepared to the most cruell hell that at length abideth for them' (*Inst.* 3. 4. 32). Sickness, pestilence, famine, and war he called 'the curses of God' just like 'the judgement of eternall death . . . when they are layed upon menne to this ende, to be instrumentes of the Lordes wrath and vengeance agaynst the reprobate' (*Inst.* 3. 4. 34). But although inimical providence could spell eternal punishment, propitious circumstances were no more comforting: 'For he dothe not therefore shewe himselfe mercyfull unto them,' explains the remorseless Calvin, 'for that he havyng trucly delivered them from death, dothe receyve them to his savegarde, but onely he discloseth to them a present mercie' (*Inst.* 3. 2. 11). In fact all providential data lent themselves to consistent interpretation either in the light of God's love or his hatred. Double providence was the mechanism of double predestination.

That Calvin conceived of the experience of the reprobate as a foretaste of hell indicates the intensity of the despair for which his theology provided. Indeed he impatiently dismissed those who, like preachers of the late medieval church, concentrated their terrorizing eloquence on the physical torments of hell as having 'crassae imaginationes'.[15] Hell, as for Luther, was essentially

[15] D. P. Walker, *The Decline of Hell: Seventeenth-Century Discussions of Eternal Torment* (1964), 62.

psychological. It was the pain of eternal rejection by God. And since rejection could be communicated to the reprobate in this world, hell was the literal experience of the despairing reprobate. That Calvin believed this and took trouble to make people feel it to be true measures the extremism of his theology. The reprobate were as incapable of arousing his sympathy as the devils. They were objects of God's glorification and their mental torment provided a stimulating spectacle of his judgemental power.

Calvin's emphasis on predestination has, over the past couple of decades, been questioned. J. F. H. New argues that he consistently discouraged speculation on the question, omitted the doctrine when presenting the main points of his theology, and only wrote about it when forced into controversy.[16] And R. T. Kendall claims that it was Beza who distorted English Calvinism by stressing predestination and self-inspection for signs of elect or reprobate identity.[17] Viewed from an experiential perspective these are misleading or pedantic claims. New will not find a predestinarian divine who omits to discourage speculation about God's decrees on the basis that their rationale is impenetrable by human reason and that seeking to penetrate God's secrets is itself a sign of reprobation. This was (dishonestly) considered a different matter from observation of the symptoms of the decrees (see *Inst.* 3. 24. 4). And the influence of the *Institution* is the influence of its completed form, which includes lengthy discussion of predestination. Calvin was, it is true, more interested in divine sovereignty than predestination but such was his understanding of the former that, as we have seen, it unignorably entailed the latter.

Kendall argues that while Calvin linked the predestinarian decrees to Christ's redemptive sacrifice and usually discussed them in relation to the reception of grace, Beza subordinated Christ's work to the decrees, arguing that Christ died only for the elect. Clearly what drove Beza and the English puritans to linger on predestination, however, were the implications of Calvin's theology. As Calvin's successor at Geneva Beza would not have got away with what seemed to people at the time significant departures from this; and English puritans certainly believed

---

[16] John F. H. New, *Anglican and Puritan: The Basis of their Opposition 1558–1640* (1964), 16.   [17] *Calvin and English Calvinism*, pp. 55–76 *et passim*.

their theology accorded with Calvin's. If Calvin had, like Luther (and Augustine), merely extrapolated from the experience of passivity in conversion the idea of being chosen, it would have been possible to subordinate the idea of predestination to that of the redemptive power of Christ, because it would only be in the reception of grace that predestination would impinge on experience. But where the corollary of elect experience was constantly pointed up the attention of all but the most tough-minded was bound to swerve to the question of whether they were to be granted faith, whether they had been predestined to salvation or damnation. The distinction Kendall labours is not one that would make an obvious difference to would-be believers. Either they were damned because God's prior decree meant that Christ had not died for them (Beza); or, although Christ's death was sufficient to atone for their sins, they had been denied the faith to benefit from this, not being of the elect (Calvin). Either way the explicitness of the doctrine of reprobation made for despair.

It was Calvin not Beza who through Norton's translation of the *Institution* introduced the term 'reprobate' to England in its meaning of 'rejected by God' (see *OED* 'reprobate' a. 3). It was Calvin who made this experience imaginatively so available that his own ingenuous assurance of the testimonies of the Holy Spirit that he was elect became increasingly hard to come by. Thinking always from the divine viewpoint, he considered the experience of the reprobate with complete detachment. There was no doubt, from the divine viewpoint, about who was and who was not elect. And Calvin's interest was solely in how God executed his decrees both in the external world and in individual experience. His apparent intention was not to provoke terror but to explain the terror that the reprobate, given that they suspect they are reprobate, must feel. Assuming that the authentic elect had total confidence he did in fact encourage contemplation of God's decree of reprobation. Discouraging speculation about God permitting the Fall (which Beza did venture) he commended 'the other part, showing that God chose out of the condemned race of Adam those whom He pleased and reprobated whom He willed' as 'much more fitting for the exercise of faith'.[18] Such meditation

---

[18] Quoted by P. Toon, *The Emergence of Hyper-Calvinism in English Nonconformity 1689–1765* (1967), 13.

on (not, of course, questioning of) predestination enhanced the sense of divine sovereignty.[19] His obsession with the idea that God effected everything made him unaware of the extent to which his own theology might affect the nature of religious experience and unaware that individuals might be more likely to doubt their election if experiences resembling each other closely (as he himself conceded) could point to polarized spiritual destinies.

It was, then, Calvin's expectation that the elect would simply concentrate on Christ whose gift of faith they would receive with simple confidence. This after all had been his own experience. Unlike Luther's his had been 'a sudden conversion'[20]—and an experience free from the menace of the theology he was to develop. Beza and Perkins were aware that the possibility of reprobation was bound, in practice, to be distracting. They therefore ministered to the anxiety by conceding the priority of the predestinarian decrees and setting about detailing ways of knowing, by introspection, into which spiritual category you fell. In doing this they were moreover sanctioned by statements Calvin himself made when, for example, he opposed the error of elevating faith in such a way that it appeared independent of the election which it fulfilled: 'we shall kepe the best order, if in sekyng the certaintie of our election, we sticke fast in these later signes, whiche are sure witnessinges of it' (*Inst.* 3. 24. 3–4). And along with signs of election Calvin had supplied the idea of 'markes' of reprobation, counterparting 'vocation and election', by which God revealed 'what jugement abideth for them' (*Inst.* 3. 21. 7; see also 3. 23. 13). So it is not surprising that in spite of his caution against introspection 'Calvinist and covenanting neo-Calvinist alike', as Patrick Collinson says, 'were prone to train the sensitive organ of conscience on their daily lives for signs of encouragement or warning.'[21] By formalizing the signs which distinguished the elect from the reprobate Beza and Perkins certainly did not allay anxiety. They erected a structure for it to occupy. But the foundation was Calvin's linked concerns in the *Institution*: divine sovereignty, reprobation, and its providential outworking.

---

[19] See Wendel, *Calvin*, p. 270.
[20] See Kendall, *Calvin and English Calvinism*, p. 21.
[21] Patrick Collinson, *The Elizabethan Puritan Movement* (1967), 435.

SOME EVIDENCE

There are perhaps six sources of evidence for the contention that Calvinism and puritanism were conducive to despair and that this was both a widely recognized and widespread phenomenon in England at least from the late sixteenth century. One is the frequency with which puritan divines address the problem of despair. Then there are firsthand records in diaries and autobiographies. References to cases of despair can be found in a variety of non-puritan, often medical, sources. Recriminations were exchanged by protestants and Catholics on the question. Later works (at least from the outbreak of the Civil War), sometimes by writers still within the puritan tradition, attack puritan theology for producing despair. And finally there is the evidence from literary texts.

The treatment of despair by divines will, along with the medical literature on despair, be mainly considered in the chapter on Burton, which examines his role as counsellor in the context of religious and medical traditions. It may simply be observed that the numberless published treatises or sermons on predestination or signs of election virtually without exception speak about despair, generally in order to distinguish the despair of the reprobate from its potentially misleading simulacrum in the pre-conversion experience of the elect. Charles I in 1628 forbade all but bishops and deans 'at the least' to preach on 'the deep points of predestination, election, reprobation, or universality, efficacity, resistibility, or irresistibility of God's grace'.[22] These were the issues which fanned despair. The Ordinance was a measure of the prominence they had achieved. They were the rallying call to Calvinist zealots, their shibboleths of theological soundness. Yet that preaching about these issues had more practical than polemical purposes and effects is evidenced most forcefully by the spiritual autobiographers (who will also be examined later). To quote just one victim who generalizes helpfully to connect up the practical effects with the ubiquitous preaching (and to comment on the efficacy of Charles's Ordinance): John Crook, speaking about London in the 1630s, writes of

---

[22] 'The Directions concerning Preachers' in *Documents Illustrative of English Church History*, ed. H. Gee and W. J. Hardy, 4th edn. (1921).

the ministers then commonly preaching by marks and signs, how a man might know himself to be a child of God, if he were so, and how it would be for him, if it were not so, which made me sometime to conclude I had saving grace, and by and by conclude, I was but a hypocrite.[23]

Autobiographical evidence for the connection between typical protestant preaching and despair is hard to resist since the despair is expressed in terms of the theological categories described in the works of the puritan divines; but three objections to it might be raised. One, to be considered when discussion broadens out from theology, is that theology merely interpreted a pre-existing mood in which these autobiographers shared. Another is that their despair is factitious, mainly formulaic, its purpose being to dramatize the significance of conversion by exaggerating the then and now. My analysis in the next two chapters seeks to refute this. A third is that the autobiographies, although fairly large in number (over 200 extant[24]), may be representative of no one but their authors, the writing of autobiography being itself related to a propensity to despair. Refutation of this (which does not involve denial of a connection between despair and autobiography) requires the remaining sources of evidence. Literary evidence is also deferred. Though far more extensive than that provided by the texts I analyse it is not quantitative in nature.[25] It is the effects on visualization of the world that literature attests and these can best be shown in the structure as well as the detail of the individual works.

In considering Catholic and protestant charges and counter-charges the most reliable evidence can be gleaned from the case protestants advanced in their defence. That Catholics considered religious despair, sometimes leading to suicide, as a protestant scandal from which their polemic could benefit is attested in England as early as events referred to in Foxe's *Acts and Monuments* (popularly known as *The Book of Martyrs*). Foxe is clearly indignant at the charge and accuses Catholics of rigging the evidence. John Randall, whom Foxe describes as 'my

---

[23] John Crook, *A Short History of the Life* (1706), 10.

[24] See the bibliography to Owen C. Watkins, *The Puritan Experience* (1972).

[25] For some sense of the extent of literary treatment of religious despair in the Jacobean drama see Rowland Wymer, *Suicide and Despair in the Jacobean Drama* (Brighton, 1986), chs. 1–4.

kinsman', apparently committed suicide while a young scholar in Christ's College Cambridge in about 1531:

at the last, after four days, through the stench of the corpse, his study door being broken open, he was found hanged with his own girdle within the study in such sort and manner that he had his face looking upon the Bible, and his finger pointing to a place in Scripture whereon predestination was intreated of.

Foxe had no imaginative difficulty in concluding that somebody (he suspected Randall's tutor, Wyer) had murdered him in order to make an educative theological point:

Surely this matter lacked no singular and exquisite policy and craft of some old naughty and wicked man, whatsoever he was that did the deed, that it should seem the poor young man through fear of predestination to be driven to despair; and that the young men being feared through that example should be kept back from the study of the Scriptures as a thing most perilous.

If one accepts Foxe's inference (which is not easy), the incident at least indicates that Catholics considered the connection between predestinarian teaching and despair a vulnerable area in protestantism well worth exploiting. And if he is wrong, his presentation of the case still reveals more than that a solitary protestant dramatically despaired of his salvation. Foxe himself evidently considers the connection of protestantism with despair on imputation Catholics would wish to make. He is clearly on the defensive.

This is apparent, too, in his retort to Bishop Gardiner's reported criticism of 'the following and profession of the gospel [as] a doctrine of desperation'. Gardiner made the charge after the suicide by drowning of Judge Hales. Foxe parries by saying that 'The stinking end of Gardiner proveth popery and not the gospel to be the doctrine of desperation.' The claim that Gardiner on his death-bed 'said that he had denied with Peter, but never repented with Peter—and so both stinkingly and unrepentantly died' looks certain, however, to be a fabrication.[26] The story gives protestant readers the multiple satisfaction of Gardiner (the leading persecutor of protestants under Mary)

[26] John Foxe, *The Acts and Monuments*, ed. J. Pratt, 4th rev. edn. (1877), iv. 694; viii. 635.

acknowledging protestantism as the true religion, confessing his own wickedness, and still being damned. As neat as it is improbable. Besides, if true, it would be as a protestant not a Catholic that Gardiner would have died. Foxe's claim based on this case amounts to no more than that if a Catholic rejects Catholicism and recognizes that in opposing protestantism he has opposed Christ he may despair. This is a weak reply to the charge that protestants despair as a result of their subscription to protestant theology. Once again the issue has Foxe, uncharacteristically, on the defensive.

Such defensiveness, even when taking the form of counter-attack, is typical of protestants in this area of controversy with Catholics. Supplementing her own early autobiography, the biography of Katherine Brettergh was, we gather from its prefaces, published because Lancashire Catholics had, as Patrick Collinson says, 'spread a tale of the failure of protestant faith *in extremis*'.[27] It is in a way a curious retort since, although Katherine Brettergh eventually pulled through to serenity, even euphoria, about her spiritual state, she experienced prolonged despair before doing so. Catholics, less accustomed to these agonies prior to assurance of salvation, might well have considered that the presentation of this case as a triumphant refutation helped to confirm the justice of their charge. Again, though, the motive for recording and publishing this woman's experiences indicates a defensive posture among protestants. Lay records also suggest that Catholics were shocked by tormented protestants. Diarist Edward Trench, who stayed with a friend in the house of a Dutch Papist, 'labour'd exceedingly under great Terrours and Sorrows for *Sin*; having many bitter Pangs and long Agonies, with plenty of Tears and Cries'; yet he seems to have been affronted when the Catholic 'charg'd our *Religion* as uncomfortable'.[28]

Calvinists consistently showed themselves to be unable or unwilling to step momentarily outside their theological assumptions in order to determine empirically the volume of despair the

[27] Patrick Collinson, ' "A Magazine of Religious Patterns": An Erasmian Topic Transposed in English Protestantism', *Studies in Church History*, 14 (1977), 223–49, p. 241; see also K. Brettergh, *A Brief Discourse of the Life* (1606).

[28] *Some Remarkable Passages in the Holy Life and Death of the Late Reverend Mr. Trench: Most of them Drawn out of his own Diary* (1693), 25.

two religions produced. When Perkins considered the Catholic doctrine that grace was universally offered he denied that it could yield comfort on the grounds that it lacked credibility.[29] Since God was the author of protestant theology Perkins saw himself as merely awakening people to their plight. The therapeutic success for which he was famed was judged as though the despair to which they had been reduced was a given. Since, moreover, only the elect were meant to recover, and the despair of the reprobate counted for nothing, Calvinists could claim total success. Despair was not for Perkins an isolable psychological phenomenon, an evil in itself to the eradication of which he should apply himself.

Calvinist imprisonment within revealing theological assumptions is exhibited by Theodore Beza's reply (appended in translation to Perkins's most influential treatise) to the charges of the Catholic Andreas:

First, for the place of Scripture which he alledgeth, namely, that *God is greater than our hearts.* It is so farre from comforting an afflicted conscience, that it will rather drive him to despaire . . . And for the other place, when as a man doubteth of his salvation, and feeleth no testimonies of faith in himselfe . . . what comfort think you, can he have in these words, *Hee that beleeveth and is baptised, shalbe saved?* For he would rather reason contrarily thus: I indeed am baptised, yet for all that I believe not, and therefore my baptisme is not availeable, I must needs be condemned.[30]

The second text whose comforting effect Beza disputes implies the reliance of Catholics on the authority of the church's institutions, especially the sacraments, to relieve them of the subjective sense of guilt and unworthiness. Beza's reply assumes the subordination of the sacrament of baptism to the testimony of the individual conscience. Indeed sacraments which feel ineffectual give further evidence of reprobation. (Puritans particularly stressed St Paul's warning that taking communion unworthily constituted eating and drinking damnation to oneself.) In Beza's protestant view, then, reminding people who doubt their salvation that they have been baptized intensified their despair; no one effectually baptized as one of the elect would

---

[29] William Perkins, *The Works* (Cambridge, 1605), 122.

[30] *An Excellent Treatise of Comforting such as are Troubled about their Predestination: Taken out of the Second Answere of M. Beza to D. Andreas*, trans. and rpt. in William Perkins, *A Golden Chaine, or the Description of Theologie* (1591), sig. X2^v–3^r.

subsequently have doubts of election. Beza's response to the first text is still more revealing. To the Catholic Andreas God being greater than our hearts meant that God could love people who hated themselves and who projected their self-hatred on to him. God's greatness lay in his greater mercy, his greater capacity for forgiveness. But this is not at all how Beza conceives of God's greatness. God's greatness invokes for him the idea of God's power and the mystery for mankind of his decrees of election and reprobation. Contemplating God's greatness, Beza is betrayingly aware, will further afflict the conscience because it is a reminder of his capacity to hate and to damn without comprehensible motives.

The most frequent protestant counter-charge on the subject of despair was drawn from Catholic opposition to the protestant doctrine of assurance. Gervase Babington diagnoses what was an important element in the protestant protest against priestly tyranny at the time of Luther:

For the heart of man and woman ever desiring and wishing some certaine safetie, some comfort and hope touching the life to come, and being beaten from the sweet promises of Christ by these men, and taught, that they must ever feare and doubt assurance, being presumption, straight it turneth it selfe to outward, and thinkes of workes to be done, and gifts to be given, to winne eternall life by . . . And when, not even all, in the Agonie of Death yeeld any comfort, but still the Soule feareth, and is perplexed, then have they Purgatorie to put them in hope of: which being subject (as they say) to their Prayers and Offices, shall surely be overcome by the same, and they there-hence delivered joyfully, if they will give and bequeath liberally.[31]

Catholicism was not, then, a joyous religion. Even from Babington's onslaught, however, inferences can be made which suggest that protestantism could make things still worse. The complaint, for instance, that Catholics deprecated certainty of salvation is accurate but the angle from which the Catholic position is viewed tells us as much about the protestant standpoint as about Catholic doctrine. People who were certain they were destined to salvation would, Catholics thought, abuse their resulting freedom from moral obligation. No one, according

[31] Gervase Babington, *Comfortable Notes upon the Bookes of Numbers and Deuteronomie. With an Exposition of the Catholike Faith: Or, the Twelve Articles of the Apostles Creed*, in *The Workes* (1615), 216.

to them, could be saved by faith alone so salvation could not, while there was still time to commit mortal sin, be assured. It was a system which kept the faithful on tenterhooks and which delivered them into the power of the church. But it was by the same token a system which mitigated the arbitrariness of who was and who was not saved.

As for purgatory, this was, it is true, a terrifying prospect. A. G. Dickens adduces a medieval description of purgatory—'the long prison-sentence which the average man must anticipate'— to refute the

many idealisers of medieval religion [who] have supposed that the equally inscrutable Deity of the Calvinists represents some sinister novelty, or that fifteenth-century religion had a childlike gaiety and optimism reminiscent of some sweet group of saints by a Sienese master.[32]

One need not, however, make medieval Catholicism appear so agreeable in order to insist on the sinister novelty of Calvinism. Purgatory could not induce despair because it lacked an essential condition, permanence. The doctrine also avoided polarizing human destinies in the arbitrary and inscrutable manner of Calvinism. There was a comprehensible relationship between offence and punishment and it was at least possible to think of oneself as an average person, more or less in the same boat as one's average neighbours. Then again, throughout life there were opportunities to improve one's prospects, and this worked against the fatalism which Calvinism produced.

Even the withholding of certainty of salvation was a moderating attitude, since, as we have seen, the psychological difficulty of securing assurance in a milieu where damnation was statistically much more probable tended to plunge people into a more terrible despair than anything they had suffered when such confidence was not expected of them. So while complaining at an inhumane aspect of Catholic doctrine protestants were actually indicting their own extremism, their typical desire for polarizing those who were certain of salvation and would be saved and those who lacked such assurance and were heading for hell. There were protestants, like Richard Hooker, who virtually ignored the damned in their discussion of theology and who could fairly see

[32] A. G. Dickens, *The English Reformation* (1964), 19.

the Catholic denial of certainty as purely negative, recommending instead the confident seizure of 'the naked promise of God'.[33] But most late sixteenth- and early seventeenth-century Church of England preachers, including Babington, were enthusiastically Calvinist and their objection to Catholic opposition to their doctrine of assurance was, like so much of Calvinism, two-edged: supportive to the sanguine and murderous for the melancholy.

When Babington attacks the Catholic denial of the doctrine of assurance he quotes the relevant canons of the Council of Trent, which read:

If any man shall say, That to the obtaining of the remission of sinnes it is necessarie that every one should beleeve certainely, and without doubting or wavering, in respect of his owne infirmitie, that his sinnes are forgiven him, let that person be accursed;

and

If any man shall say, That a man borne againe and justified, is bound by his faith to beleeve that he certainely is of the number of the elect, let him be accursed.[34]

It is clear from the phrasing of the anathemata that in so far as foreseeable psychological consequences can have been a motivation in framing doctrines the concern here is with protecting peace of mind. There is a recognition of the difficulty involved in obligating people to feel certain of forgiveness and certain of election, on pain of their denial. Like Perkins, Babington reveals that he is so attuned to the idea of predetermined elect and reprobate categories that he is incapable of seeing this problem. Catholics belonged to a tradition of social incorporation so that despite their fearful enumeration of the damned their theology tended to address all their parishioners as belonging, potentially, to the category of the saved.

If one looks to Counter-Reformation estimates of the number to be saved, they are as glum as those of protestants. Arthur Dent generalizes Calvinist estimates: 'Some thinke one of an hundred, some but one of a thousand shalbe saved.'[35] William Perkins asserted that 'howsoever all men do desire to beare this name; yet very few are indeed true and sound Christians: for not one of an hundred can rightly invoke the name of God.'[36] The Jesuit,

[33] 'Sermon on the Certainty and Perpetuity of Faith in the Elect', in *The Laws*, i. 8.
[34] *Comfortable Notes*, p. 216.
[35] Arthur Dent, *The Plaine Mans Path-Way to Heaven* (1601), 290.
[36] *Works*, p. 906.

Thomas Wright, opined still more drastically that 'for one that goes to heaven, almost a million goes to hell.'[37] And the most widely read Catholic writer in England, Robert Parsons, affirms 'that he damneth so many thousandes for one that he saveth'.[38] A late puritan writer makes the fair point, therefore, that the paucity of the elect was 'not only the judgment of a few peevish censoreous Puritans'.[39]

Such estimates do not necessarily, however, have a profound emotional impact. These Catholic writers were, first of all, addressing themselves to Catholics and potential converts in a protestant country. They state their statistics, moreover, not as cold scientific observation but as a persuasive to diligence. Unlike Calvinists, Catholics did have free will. God used all means, according to Parsons, to convert those who end up in hell, so the implication of his statistics for the balance between God's justice and mercy is less dismaying than in Calvinism. God, Parsons quotes from the Bible, 'desireth al men to be saved' and, unlike Calvinists who hedged this text with qualifications (see *Inst.* 3. 24. 16), Catholics took it simply to mean that the damned were people with free will who 'will not accept of his mercy offered'. God 'offereth his mercie most willinglie and freelie to al, but useth his justice onelie upon necessitie (as it were;) constrained thereunto by our obstinate behaviour'.[40] That last phrase, in particular, giving people a form of power over God, would never do for protestants. For Catholics, then, the imaginative picture of God as predominantly merciful remains emotionally possible despite the huge statistical imbalance between the saved and the damned; fatalism is once more eschewed.

In Catholic meditation, too, the sombreness of many of its characteristic subjects is offset by the extent to which the will is able to assert its final mastery over them. 'Luther', says Harbison,

came out of his spiritual struggle convinced that man's sinfulness is inherent, that he cannot save himself, and that only a merciful God can save him. Loyola came out of his struggle believing that both God and

---

[37] Thomas Wright, *The Passions of the Minde* (1601), 321.
[38] Robert Parsons, *A Christian Directorie Guiding Men to their Salvation* (1585), i. 806.
[39] Giles Firmin, *The Real Christian, Or a Treatise of Effectual Calling* (1670), 235.
[40] Parsons, *Christian Directorie*, i. 806.

Satan are external to man, that man has the power to choose between them, and that by the disciplined use of his imagination—vividly picturing to himself, for instance, the horrors of hell and the sufferings of Christ—he can so strengthen his will as to make the choice for God. Where Luther and Protestantism ended in a belief in predestination and the utter sovereignty of God, Loyola and the Catholic Church insisted upon man's free will and his power to cooperate with God—even, according to Loyola, to the point of influencing the course of the battle between the armies of God and of Satan by his choice. Luther denied man's free will; Loyola glorified it and set out to discipline it by the use of imagination. The record of his method [is] *Spiritual Exercises*.[41]

Catholic preoccupation, in meditation, with subjects such as death, the last judgement, and hell should not then be confused with the despairing anticipation of these terrors to be found among puritans. While puritans internalized hell, equating it with the psychological experience of severance from God's mercy and the elect community, Catholics tested the strenuousness of their wills by summoning external spiritual enemies and wrestling with them.

Counter-Reformation pastoral theology was certainly influenced by the reforms it countered. The phraseology writers like Parsons use is frequently picked up from their adversaries. For instance he considers the question 'How a man may judge or discerne of him self, whether he be a true Christian or not'. This is not a question to which the church addressed itself before the Reformation; it is imbued with Calvinist determinism. But while Parsons latches on to the phraseology with which his English audience will be familiar, he soon reveals that the concession to alien modes of thought is only apparent. He goes on to stress the importance of right living as the necessary accompaniment of faith and attacks 'this wicked opinion of only faith'. He borrows the puritan rhetoric of self-examination ('we must examine the truth of our faith, by consideration of our lyfe') but his explicit concern is that readers should improve their lives in order to prove the genuineness of their faith, not that they should inspect their present lives for evidence of the possession or lack of faith or grace.[42] Parsons recognizes, then, in his own choice of language that Calvinism has unignorably shifted theological discourse; yet

---

[41] E. Harris Harbison, *The Age of Reformation* (New York, 1955), 83–4.
[42] Parsons, *Christian Directorie*, i. 298, 316, 319.

he battles against the implications that inhere in it, insisting on the principles which dissociated Catholicism from a deterministic view of experience. Loyola, in his seventeenth 'Rule for Thinking with the Church', even felt compelled to warn against speaking too much of grace in case this should encourage the heresy 'whereby liberty be taken away'.[43]

The best-known case of Calvinist despair, which passed into puritan mythology, was that of Francis Spira, a lawyer from near Padua who recanted his Calvinist beliefs to save his family from torture and then suffered terrible guilt which turned into an unshakeable, seven-year-long conviction that he was a reprobate. He died in despair, possibly by his own hand. His mental torments were recorded, by eyewitnesses, in several versions (the drama of despair was destined to attract numerous spectators wherever it was played out), and one of these has a preface by Calvin himself.[44] Nathaniel Bacon's English version, published in 1638, went through eleven editions before the century ended.[45] Catholics, too, related tales of apostates who suffered agonies of remorse; and their cautionary value to persecuted adherents to either religion is evident.[46] So the situation does not by itself convey a distinctively Calvinist despair. The case was taken up, though, by puritan writers and treated, like that of Judas, as a type of reprobate despair which need not result from ostensible betrayal. Richard Baxter complained that 'the reading of Spira's case causeth or increaseth melancholy for many.'[47] Bunyan for instance believed he conformed to Spira's type after a purely internal betrayal of Christ. The book rubbed salt into his freshly wounded mind.[48] John Crook, another Bedfordshire man, wrote an autobiography similar to *Grace Abounding* in which he records

---

[43] Cited by William H. Halewood, *The Poetry of Grace: Reformation Themes and Structures in English Seventeenth-Century Poetry* (1970), 86.

[44] In Matteo Gribaldi, *A Notable and Marvelous Epistle*, trans. E. Aglionby (1550).

[45] Nathaniel Bacon, *A Relation of the Fearefull Estate of Francis Spira, in the Yeare 1548* (1638).

[46] See, for example, the tragic fate of Francis Marsh in William Weston, *The Autobiography of an Elizabethan*, trans. P. Caraman (1955), 178–84. This young Oxford undergraduate suffered agonies of remorse after attending a Church of England service. Even so, it was, if the Catholic reporter is to be believed, protestant divines who harried him to his death.

[47] Richard Baxter, *Christian Directory* (1673), 312.

[48] John Bunyan, *Grace Abounding to the Chief of Sinners*, ed. Roger Sharrock (Oxford, 1962), 163. Further references will be to this edition and embodied in the text. References will be to paragraph numbers except where pages are indicated.

how he was plunged into despair by reading the life of Spira.[49] A
15-year-old girl feared, after reading Cotton Mather's sermons,
that she 'should go to Hell, like Spira, not Elected'.[50] At the end
of the century a work entitled *The Second Spira* was published and
still sold so well that it was followed by another eyewitness's
account of the case.[51]

Spira's spectacular despair naturally got into popular compila-
tions of God's judgements such as Thomas Beard's *Theatre of
Gods Judgements* and Edmund Rudierd's *The Thunderbolt of Gods
Wrath against Hard-Hearted and Stiff-Necked Sinners*.[52] The appeal of
these records of punitive interventions directed at reprobate
individuals was not restricted to the semi-literate, however. It
was on the basis of evidence from Dr Beard, his Huntingdon
schoolmaster, that Cromwell made his first parliamentary speech
moving the censure of Bishop Neile. And when Beard's testimony
was no longer required Cromwell told him he could now get on
with the important task of enlarging the third edition of his
Theatre.[53] (Even sophisticates like Francis Bacon had called for
this kind of work.[54]) Spira's case exerted a fascination over highly
respected preachers too. Robert Bolton excitedly declared that
Spira 'became a spectacle of such spirituall misery and woe to the
whole world, that there is not any thing left unto the memory of
man more remarkable'.[55] It was Spira's exemplification of
reprobate experience rather than anything special to apostates
that gripped the puritan imagination. Preachers added him to
biblical types of reprobate despair—Cain, Esau, Achitophel, and
Judas.[56] The original accounts are full of disputation with Spira
whose tenacious arguments for the certainty of his damnation

[49] Cited by William York Tindall, *John Bunyan, Mechanick Preacher* (New York, 1934), 27.
[50] Quoted by Lawrence Stone, *The Family, Sex and Marriage in England 1500–1800* (New York, 1977), 174.
[51] J. S., *The Second Spira: Being a Fearful Example of an Atheist, who had Apostasized from the Christian Religion, and Dyed in Despair at Westminster, Decemb. 8, 1692* (1693); N. L., *The Second Spira: Being a Fearful Example of F. N. an Atheist* (1693).
[52] Thomas Beard, *The Theatre of Gods Judgements* (1597), 62–4; Edmund Rudierd, *The Thunderbolt of Gods Wrath* (1618), 19.
[53] *Oliver Cromwell's Letters and Speeches*, ed. Thomas Carlyle (1897), i. 64–7.
[54] See Walker, *Decline of Hell*, p. 102.
[55] *Instructions*, p. 18; see also pp. 19, 81–2.
[56] See for example John Sheffield, *A Good Conscience the Strongest Hold* (1650), 296; John Abernethy, *A Christian and Heavenly Treatise containing Physicke for the Soule* (1615), 400.

overwhelm those of his well-wishers. More impressive than self-interested claims to elect experience, this 'seven years monument of Gods Justice' served puritan preachers well;[57] it and cases like it seemed to verify their theology.

Examples of individuals who were as dramatically self-accusing as Spira abound. Autobiographical records of this state of mind will be explored in the next chapter, but there are also numerous second-hand reports. Foxe includes in *Acts and Monuments*, despite his rebuttals of the Catholic association of protestantism with despair, the case of John Glover who for five years endured the 'boyling heates of the fire of Hell'.[58] Puritan preachers frequently cited cases known to them. William Perkins speaks for example of a Master Chambers who on his death-bed 'grievously despaired, and cryed out that he was damned'.[59] Since Chambers had been a keen puritan for many years Perkins was eager to consider him elect and casuistically latched on to his desire for faith as a hopeful sign. In doing so he overrode both his own principle that only the individual's conscience can determine the state of his soul and his own conditions, including assurance of salvation, for membership of the elect.[60] The resolute insistence by despairing Christians, in Spira's vein, that their own judgement of their spiritual estate could not be gainsaid was particularly frustrating to preachers whose pastoral instinct was to minister to souls in distress. Robert Bolton tells us of his own spiritual mentor Thomas Peacock, fellow of Brasenose College, Oxford from 1594, who despaired on his death-bed in 1611 in spite of the prolonged ministrations of John Dod, Henry Airay, and other puritan notables. In fact he rebuked his counsellors' reassurances that they would pray for him: '*Take not*, replied he, *the name of God in vaine, by praying for a Reprobate*.'[61] Thomas Goodwin, one of the Westminster divines, speaks more generally of the type:

---

[57] Thomas Shepard, quoted by George Swinnock in *Heaven and Hell Epitomized. The True Christian Caracterized* (1663), 63.

[58] Cited by Bolton in *Instructions*, p. 85.   [59] *Works*, p. 500.

[60] At one moment 'The desire of grace, is grace it self'; at another the reprobate 'Doth confesse his sin. V. Acknowledgeth God to be just in punishing sin. VI. Desireth to be saved' (*Works*, pp. 492, 117).

[61] *Instructions*, pp. 85–6. See also Edward Bagshawe, *The Last Conflicts and Death of Mr. Thomas Peacock* (1646).

I have observed some who have set all their wits awork to strengthen
all arguments and objections against themselves, and who have bin glad
if they could object any thing which might puzzle those who have come
to comfort them; if they could hold argument against themselves: as if
they were disputing for the victory only.

He stresses the inaccessibility of their minds to the 'skilfullest and
strongest comforters'.[62]

Henry Jessey, biographer of the despairer Sarah Wight, also
generalizes about the 'poor soules, that are perswaded they are
reprobates, that are assured of it upon certain grounds, (as they
judge;) and that they are damn'd, and in Hell already; that never
any in their case was, or can be saved'. The language he uses—of
being 'perswaded' and 'assured' 'upon certain grounds'—is
precisely that used by the inverse cases of those who believed
themselves to be elected. It was difficult to question the
assurance of one group when the assurance of the other was
thought to be unassailable. Sarah Wight seems to have derived
grim satisfaction from the extremity of her torments. Jessey
recounts her meeting with a young woman in Lawrence Poutney,
where she was attending a lecture. Their conversation is worth
recording for the insight it gives into the bizarre place despair
occupied in puritan culture:

Mris *Sarah* saw one walk about and about in a sad habit, and went to
her, and asked *how shee did*, shee answered; In as sad a condition as ever
was any. *Mris Sarah, None is in a Condition like to mine.* So they sate
together; and after that, they went together, and spake further of their
sad conditions: each counting their own state the worse.

Their dialogue, on a second meeting, is reproduced:

Mris A. said, The Lord knows that knows all things, that I would rather
then all the world, that I were in your condition.

Mris Sarah W. answ. *But if you knew how desperate my condition is, you would
be afraid to change place with me, for you know not my sad sorrows. None in the
world can compare with mine. Except that you would desire to be in hell, you would
not desire to be in my condition.*

Mris A. I must be damn'd.

---

[62] Thomas Goodwin, *A Childe of Light Walking in Darknes: Or a Treatise Shewing the
Causes, by which the Cases, wherein the Ends, for which God Leaves his Children to Distresse of
Conscience* (1636), 186–7.

Mris S. *I am damn'd already, from all eternitie, to all eternitie: its not to doe, but tis done already.*

Mris A. I was a great professor, but I was but an hypocrite, and an hypocrites hope shall perish.

Mris S. *I have bin an hypocrite, a revolter, a backslider.*

Mris A. I know it shall be well with you.

Mris S. *As well as it was with* Judas, *who repented and hang'd himselfe: which I must do, before I shall be free from these torments.*

At their parting, for a farewell, Mris A. said, I think I shall perish ere I see you againe.[63]

This edifying contest in ultimate one-downmanship, appropriately located at a puritan lecture, cannot easily be dismissed as lunacy. The women speak a shared language, not the uncommunicative private languages of obsessives. And that language emerges directly from a religious system which provides a rational basis (given the fundamental assumptions on which Calvinist theology relies) for their view of themselves. Moreover, Jessey, who recounts the conversation, does not consider the interlocutors insane. Hypocrites, meaning not those who deliberately deceived with a pretence of religion but those who mistakenly laid claim to membership of the elect, were a frequently discussed group whose existence nobody of Calvinist persuasion questioned. Backsliders, a puritan neologism,[64] constituted another well-known class of spiritual derelicts. Identification with Judas was commonplace (Bunyan details the mental convulsions this could lead to), and was effectively encouraged by the double typology of elect and reprobate experience Calvinist preachers discovered in the Bible. And the conviction of being 'damn'd already' was an experience the doctrine of reprobation had made possible. Spira's 'verily desperation is hell it selfe' was constantly reiterated.[65] Jessey's narrative tone indicates his participation in Sarah Wight's theological assumptions and suggests how far the puritan culture had assimilated the practical consequences of Calvin's stress on reprobation as a foretaste of hell.

[63] Henry Jessey, *Grace Advanced by the Spirit of Grace in an Empty Nothing Creature, Viz. Mris Sarah Wight* (1647), sig. A2^v–A3^r, pp. 44–5.
[64] Marinus van Beek, *An Enquiry into Puritan Vocabulary* (Gröningen, 1969).
[65] Bacon, *Francis Spira*, p. 89; also, for example, Bolton, *Instructions*, p. 19.

More evidence in Jessey's work of the currency of despair in puritan mythology is supplied by casual anecdote. He has an aside, for example, on 'that famous Mris Honeywood' who took a Venice glass and 'said shee was *as sure to be damn'd, as that was to break*; and therewith threw it from her to break it; yet it brake not'. Sarah Wight's mother also, it is mentioned, had been 'in deep terror and great distraction of Spirit'. After her recovery Sarah herself held a regular day clinic for despairing women. One young woman typically announced: 'Hee'l save them he hath chosen, but I am none of them.'[66]

It is perhaps more than coincidence that a large number of the reported cases of despair concerned women. The mental doctor Richard Napier had ninety-one patients 'doubtful of salvation' or 'tempted to despair of salvation'—and that despite his own well-publicized hostility to puritanism, which would have repelled most of those who had submitted themselves to the authority of puritan preachers. Of these seventy-two were women.[67] Divines, moreover, seem to have been kept particularly busy by them. The renowned Thomas Hooker, of whose own 'agonies' Cotton Mather speaks,[68] went in 1618 to Esher in Surrey as chaplain to Francis Drake's household where his main role was as counsellor to Joan Drake. The noble lady was convinced, like innumerable others, that she had committed the unforgivable sin against the Holy Ghost and it took all Hooker's energies over a long period and the assistance of the celebrated John Dod and the young John Preston to recover her from her conviction that she was damned.[69] Robert Bolton appears to have thought the frenzied victim of despair was typically a woman. Setting out to deny the charge that puritan religion drives the melancholy to distraction, he impersonates his opponent's views that 'Her so much reading the scriptures, and such poring upon precise bookes . . . hath made her starke mad: *The Puritane is now besides herselfe, etc.*'[70]

The attraction of puritanism to women must in many ways have resembled its attraction to other socially deprived groups

[66] Jessey, *Grace Advanced*, p. 11, sig A8ᵛ, p. 61.

[67] Michael MacDonald, *Mystical Bedlam: Madness, Anxiety, and Healing in Seventeenth-Century England* (Cambridge, 1981), 22–3, 31, 220–2, Appendix D.

[68] Pettit, *The Heart Prepared*, pp. 93–4.

[69] See G. H. Williams, 'Called by Thy Name, Leave us not: The Case of Mrs. Joan Drake, a Formative Episode in the Pastoral Career of Thomas Hooker in England', in *Harvard Library Bulletin*, 16 (1968), 111–28, 278–300.

[70] *Instructions*, pp. 199–200.

(as we find it, say, in the dispossessed Bunyan); it offered the replacement of a worldly hierarchy by a spiritual apartheid. It was possible to trump the authority of men based on the education they had monopolized. Henry More, writing on enthusiasm, also thinks of a woman as typifying puritans' intellectual intransigence: argue with one, he says, and 'she will look upon it as a piece of humane sophistry, and prefer her own infallibility or the infallibility of the Spirit before all carnall reasonings whatsoever.'[71] And John Earle, in his *Micro-cosmographie* (1628), does 'A She-Precise Hypocrite', who has similar exasperating traits, the unintended honour of being his only woman character (save a few ribald lines on 'A Handsome Hostess').[72]

Jane Turner, to move from a hostile, external, male view to the view from the inside, was 'conscious to my self of some extreme in minding truth as it relates to the inward man'.[73] (George Eliot could still warn two centuries later of the tendency of women to 'live too exclusively in the affections'.[74]) While detecting anarchistic risks in this elevation of private spiritual experience, Turner nevertheless remained defiantly sure that 'things merely historical or traditional will vanish and come to nothing'.[75] It was natural to people lacking not only physical, historical, and social power but the prospect of such power to place stress on experience which seemed to belong to a dimension independent of its exercise and which could be taken as a foretaste of liberation from historical contingency. In one or two women writers— Anna Trapnel for example—the value placed on interior experience, personal vision, married up (as it did for lower-class male radicals) with excited expectation of an apocalyptic leap out of the squalid prison history represented to them into a transformed millennial society whose imaginative immediacy was only heightened by their persecution by reigning powers.[76]

---

[71] Henry More, *Enthusiasmus Triumphatus: Or, a Discourse on the Nature, Causes, Kinds, and Cure, of Enthusiasm* (1656), 57.

[72] John Earle, *Microcosmography: Or a Piece of the World Discovered in Essays and Characters*, ed. H. Osborne (n.d.), 72–4, 97.

[73] Jane Turner, *Choice Experiences of the Kind Dealings of God* (1653), 157.

[74] *The George Eliot Letters*, ed. Gordon S. Haight et al. (New Haven, 1954–78), v. 106.   [75] *Choice Experiences*, p. 196.

[76] Anna Trapnel, *Strange and Wonderfull Newes from White-hall: Or the Mighty Visions Proceeding from Mistris Anna Trapnel* (1654); *Report and Plea, or, a Narrative of her Journey from London into Cornwal* (1654).

But the acquisition of such spiritual confidence was an arduous affair.

To people burdened by their culture with feelings of inferiority, and inhabiting the segregative theological milieu I have been describing, the unassailable authority of the individual conscience could more easily support despair than divine afflatus. Even in their despair, however, a triumphant note is often struck, as was evident in Sarah Wight's dialogue with her rival. Anna Trapnel found that she 'could not relish' the doctrine of free grace, which she considered 'a cold, lean, poor discovery; I being under the flashes of hell, I delighted in the thunderings of the Law'.[77] Hannah Allen, in similar mood, laid claim to 'worse Sins than the Sin against the Holy-Ghost' and dubbed herself 'the Monster of the Creation'; *'in this word,'* she confesses, *'I much delighted.'*[78] Perhaps there was a kind of relish in holding out for their damnation. They were flatteringly surrounded by educated men of the church who tried to win them over by their arguments but who ultimately had to admit defeat. Certainly the feeling of being different, a form of individualism, informs all their testimonies. They gained a sense of worth, socially denied to them, by wallowing in their worthlessness. But it was a grotesque form of compensatory masochism, and the overwhelming impression is pathetic. When Sarah Wight asked a despairing maid she tried to console why she saw herself as reprobate and was tempted to commit suicide, the girl replied: 'Sometimes this, because I am not as others are: I do not look so, as others do.'[79]

Another despair-prone group, less likely to attract sympathy, were future preachers. Their attitude to the experience was decidedly ambivalent. Passage through a period of torment seemed to bestow a certificate of profound spirituality in a religious movement in which the personal spiritual credentials of divines were seen as paramount: their preaching was supposed to be based on the understanding gained from personal intercourse with the Almighty. A preacher's authority could therefore be enhanced if his own passage into the faith had been a dramatic tussle. It was said of Robert Bolton that 'the Lord ran upon him

---

[77] Anna Trapnel, *A Legacy for the Saints* (1654), 4.
[78] Hannah Allen, *Satan's Methods and Malice Baffled* (1683), 42–3.
[79] Jessey, *Grace Advanced*, p. 123.

as a *Giant*, taking him by the neck and shaking him to Pieces.'[80] John Cotton, who went on to become a celebrated New England preacher, had been deeply disturbed by Perkins's preaching while an 18-year-old at Cambridge, and admitted secret relief at his death.[81] Many of those who made names for themselves as preachers passed through long periods of dire despair before they gained assurance. They generally made sure they gave others the same medicine.

Included among these are Thomas Shepard, his father-in-law Thomas Hooker (both notoriously harsh), John Rogers of Dedham, and Daniel Rogers (whom Giles Firmin would have pitied had he not done so much to disturb the minds of others[82]). They attached great value to the ordeal they had undergone. Their theology reflected their sense of the kudos of despair in its (un-Calvinist) emphasis, studied by Norman Pettit, on 'preparation' as intrinsic to the experience of salvation.[83] But they also exhibited personal pride. Thomas Hooker proclaimed his own anguished conversion and implicitly associated himself with the famous cases he listed where 'the Lord must come down from heaven and break open the door by strong hands, by awakening his conscience, that all the country rings of him.'[84] More impartially Giles Firmin, who wrote to restrain the excessive severity of his co-religionists, confirms the view that '*Great sinners, and men of great parts, great spirits, whom God intends to make of great use, these are the men, the persons, who usually, if not always, meet with great bruisings, terrors, fears, and sorrows.*'[85] One of the most curious anecdotes about puritan spiritual leaders is that reported by Fuller on the death of William Perkins. He was said by some to have died 'in the conflict of a troubled conscience, just like Master Chambers about whom he has discoursed'. On his death-bed he cried out 'Mercy Mercy,' 'which some standing by

---

[80] Samuel Clarke, *The Marrow of Ecclesiastical History* (1650), 489.
[81] Kendall, *Calvin and English Calvinism*, p. 76.
[82] Firmin, *Real Christian*, sig. A.4.
[83] *The Heart Prepared*. Calvin, a sudden convert, had exclaimed: 'Away, then, with all the absurd trifling which many have indulged in with regard to preparation' (*Inst.* 2.2.27). Puritan reintroduction of the idea did not help peace of mind—as Luther's *Anfechtung* paradoxically could—because terror under the law could also be a reprobate experience.
[84] Thomas Hooker, *The Soules Preparation for Christ* (1632), 180–1.
[85] *Real Christian*, p. 75.

misinterpreted for despair'.[86] It is a stark demonstration of the inescapability of the dark shadow of puritanism. Its most renowned leader may have been engulfed by it at his death. Even if Perkins remained confident, the interpretation some placed on his cry indicates how readily the idea of despair could spring to the puritan mind.

So extreme was the religious despair undergone by many that it commonly gave rise to suicidal temptations, suicide attempts, and even actual suicides. It was widely believed in the early seventeenth century in England that the problem of suicide was reaching epidemic levels. A leading puritan preacher, William Gouge, supposed 'that scarce an age since the beginning of the world hath afforded more examples of this desperate humanity, than this our present age, and that in all sorts of people, Clergie, Laity, unlearned, Noble, Female, young and old'.[87] The connection between religious despair and suicide was, moreover, constantly made.[88] Perkins, speaking of desperation, instances Saul, Achitophel, and Judas as suicides each of whom was 'out of all hope of the pardon of his sinnes' and coolly adds: 'this makes many in these daies to do the like.'[89] Thomas Adams inveighs against 'distrust of Gods mercy' which

causeth a man to break that league of kindnesse which he oweth to his owne flesh; and offers to his hand engines of his owne destruction: evermore presenting his mind with halters, swords, poisons, pistolls, ponds: disquieting the heart . . . till it hath advised the hands to imbrue themselves in their owne bloud, to the incurring of a sorer execution from the justice of God.[90]

The first published book solely on suicide was written by the puritan John Sym, in 1637. Treating religious despair as the major cause, he describes the state of mind in which he supposed

---

[86] Quoted by Hill, *Puritanism and Revolution*, p. 217 n. 5.

[87] Quoted by S. E. Sprott, *The English Debate on Suicide from Donne to Hume* (Urbana, 1961), 32.

[88] Susan Snyder points out that the connection between religious despair and suicide was rarely made in medieval theology. Augustine and Aquinas assumed that the motive for suicide was to minimize divine punishment by curtailing a life of sin (the inducement Despair uses in Book I of *The Faerie Queene*) and by executing judgement on oneself ('The Left Hand of God: Despair in Medieval and Renaissance Tradition', *SIR* 12 (1965), 18–59, p. 50).   [89] *Works*, p. 643.

[90] Thomas Adams, *Mystical Bedlam: Or the World of Mad-Men* (1615), 43.

suicide occurred. Guilt and the expectation of punishment, he said,

overcharges the wounded *conscience*, when withall a man apprehends himselfe to bee wholly destitute of true *grace*, and deserted and forsaken of God; given over to a reprobate sense; *whereby* he cannot rest, but is comfortlesse, and at last is swallowed up of utter desperation; living as if he were continually in *hell*, sensibly feeling, as he thinks, the flames and tortures of the damned, in his conscience: *For* ease out of which estate, men many times kill themselves, hoping to mend themselves by change; although it be but, as skipping out of the frying-pan into the fire.[91]

That callous application of a domestic proverb indicates again the extent to which Calvinists could shield themselves with dogma from a decently human response to misery. It was commonly employed—by Joseph Hall, the character writer, for example: suicides, 'like unto those fondly impatient fishes, that leap out of the pan into the flame, have leapt out of this private hell that is in themselves, into the common pit'.[92] Suicides were generally presumed to be reprobates and their deaths were viewed as judgements of God. Indeed Beard added a chapter on suicides to the second edition of his *Theatre of Gods Judgements* in 1612.

Whether contemporaries were right to believe that suicides were on the increase does not matter much. A literature on suicide, which S. E. Sprott traces from Donne to Hume,[93] testifies at least to a heightened awareness of the problem. This need not have been stimulated by a dramatic statistical increase (though suicide does seem to have been more rare in medieval England, and Durkheim has famously associated protestantism with high rates of suicide[94]). Some religious despairers did kill themselves; innumerably more contemplated doing so. Evidence of widespread temptation may have been the main reason for growing sensitivity to the problem. A large proportion of the cases of despair recorded in diaries, autobiographies, and

[91] John Sym, *Lifes Preservative against Self-Killing* (1637), 218.
[92] *Heaven upon Earth and Characters of the Vertues and Vices*, ed. Rudolph Kirk (New Brunswick, 1948), 92; also, for example, Abernethy, *Treatise*, p. 133.
[93] See n. 87.
[94] See P. E. H. Hair, 'A Note on the Incidence of Tudor Suicide', *Local Population Studies Magazine and Newsletter*, 5 (1970), 36–43, esp. p. 41; Emile Durkheim, *Suicide: A Study in Sociology*, trans. J. A. Spaulding and G. Simpson, ed. G. Simpson (1968).

elsewhere include temptations to commit suicide. A typical example taken at random is Anna Trapnel:

And I was damn'd, one set a part for destruction, and I was strongly tempted to destroy my self . . . I have been waked in the night by the devill for this very purpose, and directed where to have the knife, and what knife I should take; and these assaults followed me not seldom, but very often.[95]

Katherine Brettergh was used by Robert Bolton as an exemplum of an elect who had been the victim of powerful suicidal impulses so as to encourage similarly afflicted members of his congregation.[96] And suicidal temptation was a discussion point for Sarah Wight and her visitors.

Certainly the practical determination of aspiring suicides varied. Thomas Shepard was tempted to brain himself against walls but refrained from experiment.[97] Hannah Allen put (as she thought poisonous) spiders in her pipe and smoked them. Disappointed by failure she later planned a coach ride to a remote wood where she could quietly expire but—a fastidious monster—was deterred by the coachman's foul language.[98] George Trosse was unsubtle in seeking assistance. Filled with 'grievous Horror and Anguish, with great Anxiety and sinking Despair', he

went forth into the *Outward Room* with my *Cloaths* hanging about me, and some of them off. As I was going out, I met an antient *Servant-Maid*; (A Sight doubtless frightful to Her) and in a distracted manner cry'd out, *I have committed the Sin against the Holy Ghost, and I must necessarily be Damn'd.* I begg'd she would lend me a *Pair of Scissors* to cut off my Hair; but she fearing a *worse Use* (as I suppose) would be made of them than I pretended, refus'd my Request.[99]

Lack of nerve and ineptitude do not lessen the anguish producing the wish. The temptations generally seem real enough.

What is staggering is that people in despair of salvation, believing what they believed, should have attempted suicide at all. S. E. Sprott thinks 'Despair of holiness and incorrigibility of

---

[95] *Legacy for the Saints*, pp. 2–3.   [96] *Instructions*, p. 84.
[97] Thomas Shepard, *Autobiography*, ed. Nehemiah Adams (Boston, 1832), 24–8.
[98] *Satan's Methods*, pp. 32–3, 45.
[99] George Trosse, *The Life* (Exeter, 1714), 49–50.

inspiration are the heart of the Puritan problem of suicide.'[100]
The first of these makes one think of Spenser's Red Cross knight,
whose characterization not only absorbs Calvinist theology but
harks back, too, to medieval ideas of saintliness. But puritan
records do not suggest frustration with moral effort; nor did
victims express the belief that they were inspired to execute
themselves. They seem rather to have found life so unbearable
that they did not believe hell could be worse. Wight's biographer,
like Sprott, tries to make easier sense of her urge: at times she
believed

> there was no heaven; nor no hell, but in our Conscience; and that she
> was *damn'd already* . . . and therefore if she could but dispatch this life of
> hers, there was an end to her sorrows. A subtle deceit of the old Serpent!
> Hence she often attempted *wickedly* to destroy her selfe; as by *drowning*,
> *strangling*, *stabbing*; seeking to beat out her *eyes*, and *braines*; wretchedly
> bruising and wounding her selfe.

Yet Sarah Wight herself is quoted as saying, '*I thought hell* to
come, could not be worse than what I *felt*.'[101] Belated Calvinist
William Cowper also thought that hell could not be so bad since
at least it could not include the pain of suspense. His suicide
attempt only failed because the garter he was hanging himself
with snapped. When he fell to the ground he thought he had
dropped into hell.[102] Richard Capel, a divine, generalized in
1633 that 'he that is once out of hope, wil desire to see the worst
as soon as may be, and so leape into their own death.'[103] They
embraced death on the basis of their conviction that no greater
torment was possible.

Many actual suicides resulted from religious despair.
Cambridge was notorious for them in the 1580s and 1590s, the
period of its greatest domination by puritan preaching.[104] This
adds significance to the relief of the tormented young Cotton
when Perkins died. Suicide did on occasion follow promptly on
sermons. Winthrop, in his Journal, mentions a man who killed
himself after 'being wounded in conscience at a sermon of Mr.

---

[100] *Debate*, p. 52.   [101] Jessey, *Grace Advanced*, pp. 7, 70.
[102] William Cowper, *The Autobiography* . . . *Or an Account of the Most Interesting Part of his Life* (1835), 16, 24.
[103] Richard Capel, *Tentations: Their Nature, their Danger, their Cure* (1633), 324.
[104] James D. Boulger, *The Calvinist Temper in English Poetry* (The Hague, 1980), 116.

Shepard's', presenting the fact as an admiring testimony to the preacher's powerful delivery.[105]

Gruesome tales abounded across the nation. One—free from the possibility of publicity-seeking embellishment—must suffice. London turner and diarist Nehemiah Wallington, himself a multiple failed suicide who copied Spira's story into a notebook, wrote at immense length about his troubled conscience, 'The Marke that I am a Child of God', the distinction between 'the saints' trials and the reprobates' despair', and so forth, reported to himself on a case in his neighbourhood. Early one June morning in 1635 Mr Monk 'run forth in his shirt very bloody, flourishing his sword in his hand and leapt into the Thames (at Botolph's Wharf) and hit himself on a boat'. Slipping a rope someone threw round him he dived to the bottom but was dragged up by the watermen's boat-hooks and taken home, where 'he did roar most hideously, crying that he was damned, and he had prayed often, and God would not hear him . . . He lay crying very strangely and hideously till the next Wednesday, and then he died.'[106] Wallington's fascination was not merely idiosyncratic. Such cases provided a macabre intimacy, a frisson of identification, to the many who were similarly tempted. Another drowning decorated the cover of a twopenny chapbook titled *The Danger of Dispair*.[107]

Countless other cases of temptation to suicide and attempted or actual suicide could be cited (for his lugubrious purposes Wallington alone was able to fill a notebook with them). They do not provide us with statistics but both the cases recorded and the frequency of puritan comment on the subject gives a powerful indication of the atmosphere of the puritan culture in which this pressure towards suicide existed. In spite of the horrific deterrent (the deed itself guaranteed damnation) S. E. Sprott believes that the predestinarian temptation to suicide was, in the 1640s, 'the pre-eminent aspect of the problem of suicide'.[108] And Michael MacDonald remarks in his study of Sir Richard Napier's medical

---

[105] See David Leverenz, *The Language of Puritan Feeling: An Exploration in Literature, Psychology, and Social History* (New Brunswick, 1980), 55.

[106] See Paul S. Seaver, *Wallington's World: A Puritan Artisan in Seventeenth-Century London* (1985), 21–4, 199–203, 60.

[107] Samuel Pepys's collection of 'small godly' books, *Penny Godlinesses*, Pepys Library, Magdalene College, Cambridge, 13, 247–70.

[108] *Debate*, p. 49.

THE
𝕯𝖆𝖓𝖌𝖊𝖗
OF
DISPAIR,
Arising from a
Guilty Conscience.

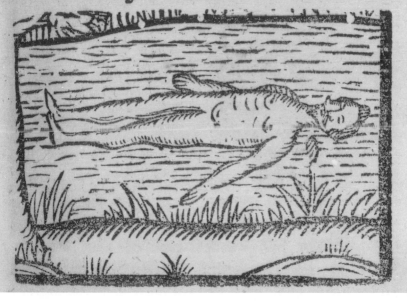

practice that 'The resolution to kill oneself was routinely equated with the temptation to despair of God's mercy and to abandon all hope of salvation.'[109] As the case of William Cowper shows, the problem persisted into the eighteenth century although in a society where the legatees of strict puritanism were a derided minority the cultural claustrophobia in which such suicidal despair was ubiquitous had dispersed. The experience had become eccentric to the dominant ideology and therefore, except to the individual affected, less significant. Isaac Watts, who belonged to the puritan tradition, attributes suicide, in 1726, to 'the Sceptical Humour and growing Atheism of the Age, with the Disbelief of a future State and of all the Terrors of another World'.[110] The religious suicide appears to have faded from prominence. Suicide had become the luxury of those who could disbelieve in hell.

It is difficult to grasp the experiential actuality of puritanism. Much (too much) comment has simply refused to face Calvinist extremism, to inhabit imaginatively its assumptions about the world. As good a critic as Helen White can shrink from what she herself observes to be prominent in seventeenth-century devotional literature: 'The burden of despair, doubled by the conviction that that very despair was a sign of God's disfavour, must have weighed crushingly on many a poor soul but for the saving grace of the practical sense of the Englishman.'[111] It is a curious lapse into Anglophile irrationality. Certainly extreme despair was not confined to England. While Luther spoke of it as rare Calvin not unnaturally saw a good deal of it.[112] The Dutch poet, Dirk Camphysen, to take another example at random, spoke of the belief in doom to eternal torment as a cause of suicide: 'Of this', he says, 'there are not a few examples, and some of them known to me personally.'[113] It is not clear what Helen White can mean, however, by practical sense: perhaps that the English knew at some intuitive level that Calvinism was untrue and therefore undermined its logical consequences. For this view no justification is, however, offered. I have tried to cite

[109] MacDonald, *Mystical Bedlam*, pp. 133–4.
[110] Quoted by Sprott, *Debate*, p. 117.
[111] Helen C. White, *English Devotional Literature (Prose) 1600–1640* (Madison, 1931), 208.
[112] See Rupp, *Righteousness of God*, p. 114; and, for example, *Inst.* 3. 2. 15.
[113] Quoted by Walker, *Decline of Hell*, p. 90.

individual cases which suggest—by the way in which they are treated—that they are the visible tip of a cultural phenomenon of large dimensions. Cambridge divine John Overall found, on visiting his Epping parish in the 1590s, that many parishioners were distressed because 'they could not be persuaded that Christ died for them.'[114] This was the humdrum reality of provincial life.

The last source of evidence for the prevalence of religious despair in puritan culture lies in the criticism of Calvinism and its effects which became vociferous in the late 1640s and persisted into the eighteenth century. The lack of any serious doctrinal challenge to Calvinism prior to 1630 meant that it presented virtually unbroken ideological cloud cover to the popular imagination. Unable to disseminate a critical attitude to Calvinism as such, preachers and writers could at best set a humane example; they could not erect a theoretical defence of humaneness. Richard Hooker, for example, steered his interpretation of scripture towards an affirmation of the faith of the religiously anxious. He took the example of Habakkuk and asked 'Whether he did by this very thought, *the law doth fail*, quench the Spirit, fall from faith, and shew himself an unbeliever, or no? The question is of moment; the repose and tranquillity of infinite souls doth depend upon it.'[115] Hooker is clearly aware of addressing himself to an audience which belongs to a culture in which a momentary blasphemous thought can be taken as evidence of reprobation. He takes a biblical antecedent and attempts tactfully to hinge on it reasons for optimism among his anxious readership. But he appears unable to go further than this to challenge the theological teaching that there were signals of divine hostility to be discovered or that there existed a class of would-be Christians who had been forsaken by God.

Even puritan writers could be critical of excessive severity but only in the context of total acceptance of the theology from which the severity sprang. Thomas Goodwin, in a treatise published in 1636 called *A Childe of Light Walking in Darknes*, observes that 'the opinions whereby some do measure what strictnesse is essentiall

---

[114] Quoted by H. C. Porter, *Reformation and Reaction in Tudor Cambridge* (Cambridge, 1958), 285.

[115] 'Sermon on the Certainty and Perpetuity of Faith in the Elect', *Laws*, i. 5.

to the being in the state of grace are often too severe and rigid.'[116]
And Richard Sibbes warns fellow divines against

making those generall and necessary evidences of grace which agree not
to the experience of many a good Christian, and lay salvation and
damnation upon those things that are not fit to beare so great a waight,
whereupon men are groundlessly cast down lower by them, than they
can hastily be raised up againe by themselves or others.

Nevertheless Sibbes confesses that his own emphasis on the need
to evacuate all self-belief can be dangerous: 'It is dangerous (I
confesse) in some cases with some spirits, to press too much, and
too long this bruising; because they may die under the wound
and burthen, before they be raised up again.'[117] He seems to
indicate here that he too knows of those who have been driven to
suicide: if it were merely a figurative death of the old self to which
he refers he would approve, since this was the condition of
spiritual rebirth. He is, moreover—as he seems aware—out of
line with his confrères in his warning; they generally stress the
folly of bending the Word of God to the needs of experience.[118]

It was only after the outbreak of the Civil War that significant
numbers of those encompassed by puritan culture began to break
ranks and set up independent religions. Christopher Hill
observes a decisive shift:

The Calvinist emphasis on predestination and discipline had tried to
carry hierarchical social subordination and national thought-control
over into the modern world: the breakdown of Calvinism in the middle
decades of the seventeenth century witnessed to the failure of this
attempt.[119]

A good example of surfacing resentment against the spiritual
witchhunt set afoot by the puritan stress on hypocrisy is the
anonymous work, *Tyranipocrit Discovered*. It 'attacked the doctrine
of predestination', says Hill, 'because it led to "the quintessence
of hell, I mean despair" '.[120] It was the spiritual tyrant who
posed as a Christian minister, not the anxious believer, who

[116] *Childe of Light*, p. 74.
[117] Richard Sibbes, *The Bruised Reed and Smoking Flax* (1630), ed. P. A. Slack
(Menston, 1973), 72, 37.
[118] See, for example, Arthur Dent, *The Plaine Mans Path-Way*, p. 32.
[119] Christopher Hill, *Society and Puritanism in Pre-Revolutionary England* (1964), 496.
[120] Christopher Hill, *The World Turned Upside Down: Radical Ideas during the English
Revolution* (1972; Harmondsworth, 1975), 173.

needed to be unmasked. One of the most rasping critics of despair-inducing theology was Gerrard Winstanley who, with others, saw puritan doctrine as a tool of oppression in much the way that Luther had perceived the practices of the Catholic Church. Drawing on the medical terminology which alone, in the seventeenth century, offered an alternative interpretation of religious melancholy, Winstanley describes how theology preys on a state of mind:

> But if the passion of sorrow predominate, then he is heavy and sad, crying out, *He is damned, God hath forsaken him, and he must go to Hell when he dys, he cannot make his calling and election sure*: And in that distemper many times a man doth hang, kil, or drown himself: so that this divining Doctrine, which you call *spiritual and heavenly things*, torments people always when they are weak, sickly, and under any distemper.[121]

The bitten-off anger in Winstanley's writing on this subject conveys an outraged humanity and contempt which has at last come through; the strength of feeling is commensurate with the duration and efficiency of its suppression. There are few heterodox autobiographies to be found in which unbearable predestinarian despair did not energize the development of a new religion, one that could be literally lived with.[122] 'And many', admitted Richard Baxter, 'turn Hereticks . . . some of them that were long troubled get quietness and joy by such changes of their Opinions, thinking that now they are in God's way.'[123]

But it was not only people as heterodox as Winstanley or the Ranters who joined the new chorus of condemnation of a theology which had long gone unchallenged. Of those who remained firmly within the puritan-Presbyterian tradition perhaps the most significant critic is Richard Baxter himself. Baxter recognized from pastoral experience that his religion was driving people to suicide: 'And when it cometh to extremity, they

---

[121] Gerrard Winstanley, *The Law of Freedom in a Platform* in *The Works*, ed. G. H. Sabine (Cornell, 1941), 568.

[122] For some examples of their despair, see George Fox, *A Journal or Historical Account of his Life, Travels, Sufferings, etc. in the Work of the Ministry* (1694), 38; Jacob Bauthumley, *The Light and Dark Sides of God* (1650), extracted in Norman R. C. Cohn, *The Pursuit of the Millennium* (1957), 339; Laurence Clarkson, *The Lost Sheep Found* (1660), 8; Richard Coppin, *Truths Testimony* (1655), 9; Lodowick Muggleton, *The Acts of the Witnesses* (1699), 14–15, 17–25.

[123] Richard Baxter, *Preservatives against Melancholy and Overmuch Sorrow: Or the Cure of Both by Faith and Physick* (1713), 21.

are weary of their Lives, and strongly followed with Temptations to make away themselves, as if something within them were either urging them to drown themselves, or cut their own Throats, or hang themselves, or cast themselves headlong, which alas too many have done.' He realized too that this trouble resulted from the quest for signs of election or reprobation. He came into contact with innumerable despairers. One he mentions in his autobiography, James Nalton, used to say, 'I can no more pray than a post! If an Angel from Heaven would tell me that I have true Grace, I would not believe him.' Baxter estimated that 'some Two or Three in a Week, or a Day, come to me in the same Case': 'they think that God hath forsaken them, and that the Day of Grace is past.' And usually, into the bargain, 'they are afraid lest they have committed the unpardonable Sin against the Holy Ghost.' Recollecting his early Christian life he mentions a friend who considered that 'such as Bolton were too severe, and enough to make men mad.' But it took a good many direct encounters with tragic victims before Baxter began to suspect that his theology caused needless distress. He came to see how easily people could be trapped by the processes of introspection. Protestant teaching had led them 'to spend their dayes in enquiring after signs of their sincerity'.[124]

Baxter admits in his *Reliquiae* that this critical attitude was a late development. He had himself spent seven years in frenzied search for signs of his own salvation, 'examining my Sincerity'. His reaction to sermons on heaven and God's attributes was, 'Every body knoweth this, that God is great and good, and that heaven is a blessed place; I had rather hear how I may attain it.'[125] The dismissiveness reveals how little such claims for God impinged on his experience. Talk about God's goodness was blague; it was his caprice in determining the elect that occupied young Baxter's mind.

For many years he inflicted on others the theological emphasis from which he suffered, unable to escape the grooves along which, in the first half of the century, the puritan mind invariably travelled. He peddled the customary titles up till the Restoration: *The Right Method for a Settled Peace of Conscience* (1653), *A Sermon of*

---

[124] *Preservatives*, pp. 22–3; *Reliquiae Baxterianae: Or Mr. Richard Baxter's Narrative of the Most Memorable Passages of his Life and Times*, ed. Matthew Sylvester (1696), 431; *Preservatives*, pp. 18–19; *Reliquiae*, p. 4.   [125] *Reliquiae*, p. 129.

Judgement (1655), *A Treatise of Conversion* (1657), *Of Saving Faith* (1658), *Directions and Persuasions to a Sound Conversion* (1658), *A Sermon of Repentance* (1660), *The Vain Religion of the Formal Hypocrit* (1660). This is not to say he was unconcerned by casualties. He revised *The Saints Everlasting Rest,* for example, to include for 'men's comforts' 'a more exact inquiry into the nature of sincerity'.[126] But then Perkins and the rest had also been assiduous 'Physicians of the Soul',[127] while declining to modify the theology that brought in their patients. Baxter was caught, on the one side, by the sensed imperative to reinstate a perception of God as loving and just and, on the other, by the constraints placed on such movement by his own need to associate himself with the traditional puritan orthodoxy in which he had been nurtured. This tension produced both doctrinal embarrassment and, increasingly, a shift in emphasis.[128] *Gods Goodness Vindicated* (1671), for example, expresses his awareness that God's image needed cleaning up. At least one despairer credited his recovery to this book. He 'had fallen into deep melancholy, feeding it daily with the thoughts of the number that will be damned, and tempted by it to constant blasphemy against the goodness of God, who could save them, and would not, but decreed their damnation.'[129]

Baxter was himself rebuked for promoting anxiety, by Giles Firmin in *Real Christian* (1670). Firmin's attack on the cruelties of puritan theologians stems, like much criticism of Calvinism from the middle of the century, from bitter personal experience. For 'many years I found trouble my self', he confesses, clearly

---

[126] Richard Baxter, *The Saints Everlasting Rest* (1649; 7th edn. 1658), sig. C3ʳ; see also Pt. III, ch. 11, pp. 443 ff.

[127] See William Haller, *The Rise of Puritanism* (New York, 1938), ch. 1.

[128] Baxter was criticized by contemporaries for apparent oscillation between Calvinism and Arminianism (see N. H. Keeble, *Richard Baxter: Puritan Man of Letters* (Oxford, 1982), 22). In what I regard as the crucial point—the arbitrariness of election—he remained a Calvinist. The so-called 'middle way', represented by the 'hypothetical universalism' of John Davenant, which distinguished between 'sufficient' and 'efficient' grace, merely rephrases Perkins's 'effectuall calling' and 'calling not effectuall'. Retaining the doctrine of total depravity Davenant and Baxter continued to believe that any non-elect individual was incapable of responding to 'sufficient' grace; so 'sufficient' was a dishonest casuistry which did not materially affect the position of the anxious parishioner (see William M. Lamont, *Richard Baxter and the Millennium* (1979), 136–49, and Perkins's 'Table', below, pp. 164–5).

[129] Quoted by Amy L. Reed, *The Background of Gray's 'Elegy': A Study in the Taste for Melancholy Poetry 1700–1751* (Columbia, 1924), 24.

resenting the impediments to peace of mind placed in his way by revered puritan expositors. He writes sarcastically of the direction of their preaching effort: 'To undeceive these *nominal* Christians, hath been the labour of the Pulpit and the Press. Our works being something different from the ancient Fathers, they laboured to convert *Heathens*, we to convert *Christians*.' Like the later Baxter he saw that the demands made on believers led to large-scale self-disqualification: 'I observed some eminent Divines, while they declared, what was required to make a *sound Believer*, have made such Requisites as trouble *many*, and cut off most of the sound, with the unsound Christians.' The divines he selected for detailed criticism included Perkins, Shepard, Daniel Rogers, and Baxter. The first three of these were leading puritan figures whose theology had not been criticized from within puritan ranks. Firmin's criticisms centre on their 'preparation' theology, their views of what must be undergone before genuine conversion can occur:

That abundance of Christians have a long time doubted of, and argued against the truth of their union with Christ, for want of their sensible experience of these preparative works, which they have learned and read, is well known to him who hath had any inward converse with Christians, if his own experience be not a witness of it: How many years have some Christians here stuck, and could not answer or help themselves.

Summing up Rogers and Shepard, he says: 'here is enough to sink a poor Christian, that if a man feareth terribly he shall be damned, and useth diligently all means whereby he may be saved, this is but a way of *self-love*, and a way to Hell; *self* must be hated.' Shepard and Hooker required the believer 'to be quiet without Gods love, without manifestation of grace, to be content though God will never work grace, to be content to be disposed of by Christ to Hell and damnation.' Some Christian mystics, St John of the Cross for example, appear to have perverted their minds in this way with some deliberateness. But making it a mandatory phase of preparation for salvation was devilish sadism. To those Firmin is criticizing, however, the pain caused was immaterial. Shepard's retort to the assertion that many 'have proved themselves good Christians without such compunction' was, Firmin was aware, an easy one: '*Many thousands are miserably deceived about their estates by this one thing, of crooking and wresting Gods Rule to Christians experiences.*'[130] Such divines had no concern about the numbers of would-be Christians to be sacrificed to dogma. Diminution of the elect always accorded with numerical expectation.

Actually, when Firmin's own views are inspected they too are orthodox enough in puritan terms. His own book is after all called *Real Christian*. He accepts the distinction between nominal and real Christians which he criticizes in Thomas Shepard's *Sound Believer* (1645) and others, asserting that 'the number of *Real Christians*, is but small, whatever those, who are called Christians, think.' Since sound believers 'are but few in comparison of the unsound, take them all in all' his only complaint is that 'if you exclude them who have not this assurance [that Christ is theirs], you will leave a pitiful remnant indeed.'[131] Essentially, then, his views (and Baxter's) were as morally disgusting as those they attacked (the majority of mankind was still going to hell and was predestined to do so).[132] This may be qualified if one considers that experientially, for those who submitted to its authority, their preaching aimed at more benign effects. Perhaps in judging an ideology more attention should be given to its functioning within the community adhering to it than to theoretical tenets which can be emotionally obsolescent—merely vestigial discursive habits. Firmin is useful as a barometer of change because he remained firmly in the puritan tradition. His attack on the severity of earlier preachers is more striking evidentially than attacks by outsiders such as Winstanley. Firmin writes in 1670 in a different cultural climate. Many people were growing sceptical of Christianity and many more had bidden Calvin good-night. It began to seem less necessary to ferret out the insincere within the puritan fold when dissent was so open. Baxter and Firmin obviously thought they were taking a personal stand in deprecating former rigours, but they were in fact responding to wider ideological changes. They needed to woo a recoiling public. Moreover, an empirical regard for what conduced to human happiness had made inroads into their own minds, as Firmin reveals when he can take stock of the

---

[130] *Real Christian*, sig. Cl^v, pp. 1, 207, 6, 7.   [131] *Real Christian*, pp. 227, 191.
[132] For the argument that Baxter wavered between a Calvinist and Arminian position on predestination, see Joan Webber, *The Eloquent 'I': Style and Self in Seventeenth-Century Prose* (Madison, 1968), 115–27.

fact that outsiders look on the ways of God 'as good for nothing else but to make men mopish and sad'.[133]

In reply to Firmin Baxter agreed with criticism of Perkins, proposed further correction of Shepard, and confessed of his own earlier work: 'And I find what long agoe I found, that I was too blame that I observed no more, the weakness and danger of melancholy persons'.[134] What one sees here, as in Winstanley's observations, is the growing authority of a medical discourse. A late work, written in about 1683, *Preservatives against Melancholy and Overmuch Sorrow: Or the Cure for Both by Faith and Physick* (1713), reflects a developing consensus that religious melancholics ought to be regarded as psychologically disturbed. No doubt the ten years Baxter spent working as a doctor helped him towards this view. Yet to allow authority to this interpretation the theological climate had to be a milder one. In persisting pockets of strict Calvinism blindness to the effects of theology can still be found in the nineteenth century. The author of the preface to Cowper's gruelling *Autobiography* (1835) is confident that it 'will disprove the oft-repeated calumny,—"That religion tends to melancholy," by shewing that the absence of religion may make men melancholy, but the fruits of righteousness are "peace and joy in the Holy Ghost" '. But Baxter, whom Hill places in the mainstream of puritan thought with Perkins *et al.*,[135] manages to remain in touch with prevailing values in his society by mollifying his theology. The 'theory and terminology for popular attacks on the Puritans came largely', says John F. Sena, 'from medical treatises of the seventeenth and eighteenth centuries'.[136] These treatises were ideologically peripheral in the first half of the seventeenth century, as analysis of Burton's *Anatomy of Melancholy*, will show. That the same, on the whole equally unscientific, kind of works began to attract the respect even of 'puritans' suggests that they were symptoms not causes of a changed outlook.

Religious despair was not, in origin at least, a psychological disorder (although it is revealing that people increasingly

---

[133] *Real Christian*, p. 69.

[134] Richard Baxter, *The Duty of Heavenly Meditation Reviewed . . . at the Invitation of Mr. Giles Firmin's Exceptions: In his Book Entitled 'The Real Christian'* (1671), 1, 27.

[135] *Society and Puritanism*, p. 29.

[136] John F. Sena, 'Melancholic Madness and the Puritans', *Harvard Theological Review*, 66 (1973), 293–309, p. 307.

thought it was). It was a rational response to unchallengeable tenets—a product far more of nurture than of nature. And Baxter's *Preservatives* would just have been a new style of cant had the medical diagnosis not been accompanied by a theological shift. Of the doctrines Baxter rejects in this work the most significant is the demand for assurance: 'if none should have *Comfort*, but those who have *Assurance* of their *Sincerity* and *Salvation*, Despair would swallow up the Souls of most, even of true Believers.'[137] The literal implication of this is that the majority of those who took their religion seriously in the preceding era, in which assurance was a condition of salvation, were consumed by despair. He may have been right.

THE SOCIAL COMPOUND

There are many factors besides theology to which the religious despair of the puritan period is related and while it is not my business to determine their interrelations as cause and effect the experience of religious despair will be only partially understood as it shows itself in literature unless they are brought into the discussion. In what follows I will deliberately stress negative aspects of the social environment. There were clearly counter-vailing influences, both in social and economic organization and in puritan thought and mores, but my emphasis is guided by the question how this society succeeded in being so fertile a breeding ground for the kind of despair documented above.

Historians have often made suggestive remarks on the extension of religious despair beyond a purely theological context. Michael Walzer, for example: 'Now it is probably not true that Calvinism *induced* anxiety; more likely its effect was to confirm and explain in theological terms perceptions men already had of the dangers of the world and the self.'[138] Or Perry Miller (without specific reference to despair): 'But as long as it [puritanism] remained alive, its real being was not in its doctrines but behind them; the impetus came from an urgent sense of man's predicament, from a mood so deep that it could never be completely articulated.'[139] While Walzer especially is

---

[137] *Preservatives*, p. 37.
[138] *The Revolution of the Saints: A Study in the Origins of Radical Politics* (1966), 308.
[139] Perry Miller, *The New England Mind* (Cambridge, Mass., 1939), 4.

illuminating about the interaction of Calvinism and social and
political history such comments elide easily into more misleading
formulations. Helen White speaks of 'that despair of his salvation
which was the form the self-disillusionment of the times so often
took in the souls of the religious'.[140] In their massive work on
melancholy Klibansky, Panofsky, and Saxl attribute to religion,
in the latter half of the sixteenth century—a traumatic period of
transition—a counteractive, palliative purpose: 'the very strength
of the emotional pressure made Melancholia a merciless reality,
before whom men trembled as before a "cruel plague" or a
"melancholy demon", and whom they tried in vain to banish by
a thousand antidotes and consolatory treatises.'[141] Those who
write primarily about theology can make similar points. Norman
Pettit says of puritanism, for example, that 'no other system of
spirituality so concerned itself with problems of fear, doubt and
despair. None has so closely described the struggles of the
interior life.'[142]

All these observations suppose the pre-existence of anxiety, a
mood, self-disillusionment, Melancholia, problems of fear, doubt,
and despair. Certainly Calvinism did not grip the popular psyche
solely in consequence of the political accidents that led to its
importation, still less by virtue of Calvin's intellectual brilliance.
It clamped itself on to English social conditions partly as an
instrument of social discipline and—this is what made its
disciplinary function effective—partly as a persuasive rationalization of them. Some of the above comments make Calvinism
seem very innocent, however. White assumes self-disillusionment
to be ubiquitous, without explaining what illusions about
themselves people had entertained; Calvinism merely mediates
this for the religiously disposed. Klibansky *et al.*, attuned to the
iconographic emphasis of their study, personify the evil, 'Melancholia', assuming that religion must address itself to consolation,
and so, like White, foreclose discussion of the intermeshed social
and religious character of their subject. Pettit makes the
assumption that the struggles of the interior life are constant in a

[140] Helen White, *The Metaphysical Poets: A Study in Religious Experience* (New York,
1956), 114.
[141] Raymond Klibansky, Erwin Panofsky, Fritz Saxl, *Saturn and Melancholy: Studies
in the History of Natural Philosophy, Religion and Art* (Cambridge, 1964), 233.
[142] *The Heart Prepared*, Preface.

human nature which is constant through history and through the idioms available at any time for its expression. Like the others he does not acknowledge that the linguistic materials made available for the expression of despair helped to determine the experiential product. Calvinism fitted a historical sensibility and, in the process of articulation, directed and modified it, as does any ideology. From the point of view of the people subjected to it there was no prior mood; Calvinism and their social conditions existed in imaginative compound.

R. H. Tawney describes the movement away, in the sixteenth century, from an agrarian economy in these terms:

It was a society in rapid motion, swayed by new ambitions and haunted by new terrors, in which both success and failure had changed their meaning . . . To the immemorial poverty of peasant and craftsman, pitting, under the ever-present threat of famine, their pigmy forces against an implacable nature, was added the haunting insecurity of a growing, though still small, proletariate, detached from their narrow niche in village or borough, the sport of social forces which they could neither understand, nor arrest, nor control.[143]

In the theses of both Weber and Tawney this period of insecurity was succeeded by the growing self-confidence of an ascendant commercial class whose members tended to equate material with spiritual well-being. This is where the emphasis of their studies falls since they, like subsequent economic historians, address the still-disputed question of the relationship between protestantism and the rise of capitalism. The issue dividing them (was protestantism an incentive or a rationalization?) aligns their focus. They scrutinize the period of transition primarily for explanatory clues to the evolution of English class structure and economic organization. So although Tawney, for example, recognizes the new experience of being the sport of incomprehensible social forces his concern is not with structures of feeling prevailing at different cross-sectional historical moments. This teleological perspective is aided, in the case of Weber, by conceptualist use of the term 'protestant'. If a distinction is made between Calvinism or puritanism and middle-class dissent, disregarding the fact that the first evolved into the second, a different picture emerges. The switch of perspective is usefully

---

[143] R. H. Tawney, *Religion and the Rise of Capitalism* (1922), 137.

suggested by D. W. Howe who argues that 'When Capitalism most flourished, Calvinism declined.' Theologically Calvinism declined amongst commercially prosperous classes, not just after 1660 in England but amongst the economically secure and socially contented Genevan patricians and elsewhere. By detaching Calvinism from protestantism it is possible to see that it is the period of transition itself, the period of insecurity, to which Calvinism addressed itself most pertinently. 'The explanation for the decline of Calvinism', Howe maintains, 'must be sought beyond the disputations of theologians and philosophers in the profound transformation of Western society during early modern times.'[144] Equally explanation of its reign needs to be found beyond, as well as within, the theology itself.

Christopher Hill puts the positive side of the pertinence of Calvinism to England's transitional economy:

There was no salvation in the old priestly magic, because that no longer gave them [small producers] any sense of control over the world of economic fluctuations in which they now had to live. Only an assertive self-confidence could do this, and that was so novel that it must seem to come arbitrarily from outside.

But the negative tie-up with despair ('In this society the few who climbed the social ladder did so at the expense of their neighbours') is the logical correlate which historians have lacked the motivation to explore. In exemplification of his point about self-confidence Hill quotes lines from Donne's 'Batter my heart' ('Take me to you, imprison me, for I | Except you enthrall me, never shall be free | Nor ever chaste, except you ravish me') which express the *inability* to acquire confidence.[145] More stress

[144] Daniel Walker Howe, 'The Decline of Calvinism: An Approach to its Study' in *Comparative Studies in Society and History*, 14 (1972), 306–27, pp. 323, 308. See also Christopher Hill's observation that 'Arminianism became popular among the victorious patrician class in the big cities of the Netherlands after the revolt; predestinarian theologies descended the social scale after the English revolution' (*Milton and the English Revolution* (1977), 274).

[145] Christopher Hill, 'Protestantism and the Rise of Capitalism', reprinted in *Change and Continuity in Seventeenth-Century England* (1974), 92. I should point out, however, that Hill remains the only historian to have given detailed attention to cases of religious despair, in the chapter 'Sin and Hell' in *The World Turned Upside Down*; in his just-published biography of Bunyan, while his emphasis remains upbeat, he both adds to these examples and makes suggestive observations about the relationship between predestinarian belief and social conditions (*A Turbulent, Seditious, and Factious People: John Bunyan and his Church* (Oxford, 1988), 20, 68, 172, 184–5).

should fall perhaps—Hill's own statement suggests it—on the improbability of gaining the miraculous confidence which, as the first section showed, was the key to Calvinist salvation. Once the middling sort acquired a reliable sense of being in a prosperous groove, once they had grasped the new economic principles and were able to play a more deliberate role in determining their future, their theology appears to have adjusted itself. Before this collective assurance was gained, however, Calvinist theology reflected the sense of helplessness in the face of powers which overrode individual will and decision; co-operation with them, like attempts to contribute to salvation, was as likely as not to backfire.

In an unprecedentedly fluid society large numbers of people, especially among the poorer classes, were seen to be the victims of forces over which they had no control and which offered them no chance of success. Others were swept to social and economic improvement. Experience of these apparently arbitrary forces made predestination a credible explanation, universal availability of salvation a remote fantasy. Perhaps this is why William Perkins was able to toss aside the apparently reasonable view that the doctrine of universal grace would do more to ease minds than his predestinarian preaching: 'I appeale to the judgement of all men, whether there is in this manner of consolation, any great comfort to the conscience afflicted. *Christ died for all men*: Thou art a man: Therefore Christ died for thee.'[146] In the conscience (sensibility) of the victim of despair the offer of salvation to all failed to fit the apprehended facts of life. Perkins appeals (doubtless unconsciously) to the conditions of life with which theological abstractions fused.

In the sixteenth and seventeenth centuries belief in God was not voluntary. There were questions only of what God was like; and the first impulses to build up a picture came from the surrounding social reality he was thought to dispose. The social and economic forces people experienced were seen to be actuated by a deliberate will; a personality lay behind them. Hence the understandable paranoia (our word) of individuals who felt circumstances conspired against them. One of Calvin's favourite topics was the unpredictability of life. 'In long self-indulgent

---

[146] *Works*, p. 122.

ruminations,' says Walzer, 'he dwelt on the uncertainties of existence; disaster, he insisted, is always imminent.'[147] His understanding of providence, which meant that unpredictable events were in fact not just foreseen but decreed, offered a bulwark against the misery such uncertainty must otherwise provoke.[148] But of course for those to whom providence was, or seemed, hostile the misery was intensified.

How major upheaval really was in the sixteenth and seventeenth centuries is now a matter of controversy (see Appendix) but there is at least small doubt that contemporaries believed it was extensive and that they reacted strongly to their belief. The strength of their reaction is largely attributable, it seems, to deeply rooted assumptions about the rightness of social stasis. Changes in land economy gave the impression that 'the society of fixed hierarchical status was . . . giving way before a new and apparently destructive force.'[149] More generally, D. M. Palliser comments, 'The emphasis on order and degree won general acceptance; yet there was also widespread agreement that social mobility was wreaking havoc with traditional distinctions of status.' (Palliser ends his chapter on 'Society and Social Change', it may be added, passing on 'a salutary reminder that the glitter of the successfully mobile, the Cecils and the Shakespeares, should not blind us to the misery of Humphrey Gibbons ['who he?' being the point] and of many like him.')[150] When Shakespeare's Ulysses famously laments the effects of the loss of degree it is, both in the speech and in its context, the violation of the ideal not the ideal itself which is put across.

Long ago (1933) L. C. Knights linked seventeenth-century melancholy in literature to the loss of economic and social stability:

In the economic and social organization of the State the early seventeenth century was a period of transition. The relatively stable medieval society had decayed, and the new economy was not yet understood . . . by 1600 neither the new aristocracy nor the new

---

[147] *Revolution of the Saints*, p. 34.

[148] See K. V. Thomas, *Religion and the Decline of Magic* (1971), 81.

[149] Arthur B. Ferguson, *The Articulate Citizen and the English Renaissance* (Durham, NC, 1965), 285.

[150] *The Age of Elizabeth: England under the Later Tudors 1547–1603* (1983), 83, 94.

commercial classes had altogether adjusted themselves to the changed conditions.[151]

Members of these classes felt insecure because they were unused to the principles or unprinciples of competition. Rather than sharing in group expectations for the future—or indeed group disasters like famine or plague—individuals felt exposed to personal treatment by the powers that be. This is reflected in the Calvinist emphasis on a personal relationship with God where the personhood of God is enhanced by the unpredictability of his behaviour and his use of providence as a medium of communication. As Sibbes said: 'God doth not put things into a frame, and then leave them to their owne motion, as wee doe *clocks*.' God acted unpredictably 'to shew his own *soveraignty*, and to exercise our *dependance*'. There was, he said, 'a mystery not onely in Gods *decree* concerning mans eternal estate, but likewise in his *providence*, as why he should deale unequally with men, otherwise equall'. This-worldly unpredictability and inequity patterned out divine dispositions. In spite of the mystery, however, '*Providence* hath a language' which must be attended to.[152]

An imaginative picture of God formed which absorbed the feared amoralism of the new society: 'for men are not to imagine,' said Perkins, 'that a thing must first be just, and then afterward that God doth will it: but contrariwise, first God wils a thing, and thereupon it becomes just.'[153] On to God was projected the fear that conventional moral-social values were no longer meaningful; that, as Ulysses says (in a speech whose brittle pomposity and strained appeals to cosmic laws suggest aristocratic terror of dispossession),

> Force should be right—or rather, right and wrong,
> Between whose endless jar justice resides,
> Should lose their names, and so should justice too.
> Then everything includes itself in power,
> Power into will . . .[154]

The character of God could no longer be fixed by the proportionate analogy of being fostered by the idea of the Great

[151] L. C. Knights, 'Seventeenth-Century Melancholy', in *The Criterion*, 13 (1933–4), 97–114, p. 110.
[152] Richard Sibbes, *The Soules Conflict with it selfe, and Victory over it self by Faith* (2nd edn. 1635), 270, 273, 280, 292. [153] *Works*, p. 496.
[154] *Troilus and Cressida*, ed. Kenneth Palmer (1982), I. iii. 116–20.

Chain. His attributes—love, reason, justice—could no longer be counted on because whatever meaning the words might have for him was beyond human comprehension. What God did became just because he had the power to do it. This view of God paralleled developments in political thought. James I took an absolutist view of his power and Thomas Hobbes later theorized the conservative reaction to the threat of chaotically competing individuals, which included portraying the ruler as unanswerable to his subjects for the justice of his treatment of them.[155] In the same way Calvin thought it was not 'mete that the wil of God should come downe into controversie among us' concerning the justice of his decrees (*Inst.* 3. 23. 5). Paradoxically, the displacement of monarchy could itself produce the feeling of exposure to raw power. Marvell expresses this in a way that extrapolates a metaphysical principle ('The force of angry heaven's flame') from what seemed to him a new *Machtpolitik*:

> Though justice against fate complain,
> And plead the ancient rights in vain:
> But those do hold or break
> As men are strong or weak.[156]

The brute facts of history must be deemed the vehicle of a higher, though incomprehensible, providential justice than that familiarized through historic, but merely human, institutions. The connection between the new God and the new society was made explicit by those more hostile to the parliamentary cause. In *The Civil War*, for example, Abraham Cowley accused the king's enemies of making their Calvinist God in their own image:

> Why doe yee thus th'old and new *Prisons* fill?
> When thats the onely why, because you will!
> Fain would you make God to thus *Tyrannous* be,
> And damne poor men by such a *stiffe decree*.[157]

At the same time as reflecting and intensifying fear of exposure to morally inexplicable personal treatment puritanism fully participated in the attempt to curb the very changes that seemed

---

[155] Thomas Hobbes, *Leviathan*, ed. C. B. Macpherson (Harmondsworth, 1968), pt. II, ch. 18.

[156] 'An Horatian Ode', *Andrew Marvell: The Complete Poems*, ed. Elizabeth Donno (Harmondsworth, 1972), 56, ll. 37–40.

[157] Ed. Allan Pritchard (Toronto, 1973), ll. 551–4.

to be producing this alarm. Like Tudor governments they wanted to push people back into their holes. 'The psychology of a nation which lives predominantly by the land', says Tawney, 'is in sharp contrast with that of a commercial society . . . In the former the number of niches into which each successive generation must be fitted is strictly limited; movement means disturbance, for, as one man rises, another is thrust down.'[158] Tawney goes on to show how Tudor Councils aimed to prevent social dislocation by restraining individual initiatives. The dislocation of individuals from well-defined social roles and the authoritarian response this produced is boldly explained by Lawrence Stone:

In the 16th century and earlier, the standard world view was that all individuals in society are bound together in the Great Chain of Being, and all are interchangeable with each other. One wife or one child could substitute for another, like soldiers in an army. The purpose of life was to assure the continuity of the family, the clan, the village or the state, not to maximise the well-being of the individual. Personal preference, ambition and greed should always be subordinated to the common good.

The second view, which developed in the sixteenth and seventeenth centuries, was that each individual thinks of himself as unique, and strives to impose his own will on others for his own selfish ends. The result is a Hobbesian state of nature, the war of all against all, which can only be brought under control by the imposition of stern patriarchal power in both the family and the state.

The third view, which developed in the late seventeenth and early eighteenth century, was that all human beings are unique. It is right and proper for each to pursue his own happiness, provided that he also respects the rights of others to pursue theirs. With this important proviso, egotism becomes synonymous with the public good.[159]

In the intermediate phase the nascent individualism was, Stone shows, combated by a repressive patriarchalism on familial, legal, and political levels—but this also occurred in religious experience. In records of religious experience, moreover, it becomes clear that the potentially anarchic view individuals had of themselves as unique could be far from a carefree self-affirmation. Stone earlier remarks on the two strands of thought

[158] *Religion and the Rise of Capitalism*, p. 166.
[159] *Family, Sex and Marriage*, pp. 257–8.

('the secular Renaissance ideal of the individual hero as expressed in the autobiography of Cellini or the essays of Montaigne; and religious introspection arising from the Calvinist sense of guilt and anxiety about salvation') in which the concept of the uniqueness of the individual apparently originated; and it is the Calvinist strand which he finds to be dominant in England before 1660.[160] Self-awareness as an individual was often identical with the pain of exclusion. People were unable to shake their own minds free of the stern patriarchal power which punished impulses to autonomy. Both the imaginative impact of society's competitive squeeze and of the imposition of stern patriarchal power need to be considered.

When human beings do not fill or feel able to accept an allotted social niche or when the niches society offers are themselves unstable they are forced to consider both their uniqueness and the nature of the forces controlling their destinies. Responses to lonely exposure could of course differ, as literature suggests. To the extent that the *picaro* represents a social reality—Arnold Kettle sees the growth of trade, enclosures, and other social developments as throwing him up—he portrays the possibility of buoyantly manipulating fate. 'The *picaro* or rogue', says Kettle, 'was the social outcast, the man rejected by and rejecting feudal society and its morality.'[161] The Dick Whittington myth exerted a strong fascination. And wily exploitation of the unpredictable is a constant theme of stage comedy. Closer, perhaps, to social reality, however, was the stage malcontent. The difficulty of assimilating people to roles amongst the educated classes—dramatized for example in Webster's Flamineo and Bosola—is anxiously attested by Francis Bacon's warning to James I in 1611 about the dangers of over-education. An excess of grammar schools has resulted, he argues, in

> there being more scholars bred than the State can prefer and employ, and the active part of that life not bearing a proportion to the preparation, it must needs fall out that many persons will be bred unfit for other vocations, and unprofitable for that in which they were bred up, which fill the realm full of indigent, idle and wanton people, who are but materia rerum novarum.[162]

[160] *Family, Sex and Marriage*, p. 225.
[161] Arnold Kettle, *An Introduction to the English Novel* (1951), i. 23.
[162] Quoted by L. C. Knights in 'Seventeenth-Century Melancholy', p. 105.

Yet beneath the satire and cynicism even of a Bosola there are suggestions of a despair which naturally assumes a religious formulation. Antonio sums him up:

> You would look up to Heaven, but I think
> The devil, that rules i' th'air, stands in your light.

This glosses Bosola's earlier grumbling acceptance of Ferdinand's murky employment; the money will, he says, 'take me to hell'. Driven, as he sees it, to break human bonds by unemployment he later bears Antonio out: 'That we cannot be suffer'd | To do good when we have a mind to it!'[163] Deprivation of the opportunity to live a good (socially integrated) life matched the Calvinist doctrine of total depravity. The reprobate could not do good or repent ('look up'); their circumstances did not allow it. God, as we will see in later chapters, left them to the devil—a social role performed obviously enough in this play by the Duke.

There were those then, no doubt, who were psychologically tough enough to ride their vicissitudes. Some autobiographers displayed such confidence (Lord Herbert of Cherbury, equipped by birth with aristocratic *superbia*, is an extreme example). Paul Delany persuasively attributes the rise of autobiography to 'the spur to increased self-awareness' provided not by the fortunes of one class but by 'the unprecedented general social mobility of the period'. There was a need to pin down personal identity (except for those who, wedded to one occupation all their lives, tended to produce medieval style records of their activities).[164] But the spiritual autobiographer responded antithetically to the *picaro* or the self-assertive autobiographer, buckling to an overwhelming destiny and seeking the dissolution of independent selfhood with which sin and guilt were equated. Calvinism's stress on the depraved will was one way of making sense of individualism— the way that best justified beating it down.

So widespread, it seems, was the problem of finding suitable employment that Bacon concluded gloomily: 'They are happy men whose natures sort with their vocations.'[165] Puritans were at least as concerned about both confusion of degree and the poor fit

[163] *The Duchess of Malfi* in *John Webster: Three Plays*, ed. D. C. Gunby (Harmondsworth, 1972), 2. 1. 98–9; 1. 2. 190; 4. 2. 357–8.

[164] Paul Delany, *British Autobiography in the Seventeenth Century* (1969), 19, 15–16, *et passim*.

[165] Quoted by L. C. Knights in 'Seventeenth-Century Melancholy', p. 111.

between men's natures and their vocations as other spokesmen of Elizabethan and Jacobean society. Perkins, for instance, deplores the way in which increased liberty for the individual had led to subversion of the social hierarchy: 'And it is a common abuse of the libertie in our dayes that the meane man will be in meate, drinke, apparell, building as the gentleman; the gentleman as the knight; the knight as the Lord or Earle.'[166] D. M. Palliser agrees with M. M. Knappen that late Elizabethan puritanism's economic teaching was 'practically indistinguishable from the traditional teaching of the medieval Church, and was indeed "ultra-conservative and eventually futile".'[167] The chief way in which puritan ideology appears to have resolved the contradiction between the recognition—at a spiritual level—of a process of social polarization in a changing economy and the demand for social order and maintenance of the concept of degree was by developing the idea of the calling beyond its previous ecclesiastical sense.

Lawrence Sasek summarizes Perkins's views on callings:

each man has a particular calling, or vocation, such as that of a magistrate, minister, master, servant, father, child. One person can fit into several particular categories; his calling is not so much a classifiable occupation as a particular role in society, and Perkins' main concern was to emphasise the need for a particular calling, a definite 'state or condition of life in the family, in the Commonwealth or in the Church'. The same emphasis governs his first rule: 'Every person of every degree, state, sex, or condition, without exception must have some particular calling to walk in.' His second rule is concerned with social unrest: 'Every man must judge that particular calling, in which God hath placed him, to be the best calling for him.' Then follow . . . rules which relate the particular calling to the general: 'Every man must join the practice of his personal calling with the practice of the general calling of Christianity.'

As stated here, this concept of the calling may not appear distinct from medieval degree. Individual identity should be absorbed by an unchanging role in society and the faithfulness with which this role is performed is closely related to spiritual reward. 'Essentially,' says Sasek, 'the concept of a particular calling seems designed to

---

[166] *Works*, p. 648.
[167] *The Age of Elizabeth*, p. 348.

enforce a feeling of moral responsibility, to encourage social stability, to maintain an institutionalized society, and to discourage vagabondage and adventurism in economics or politics.'[168] Indeed if Perkins's statement had been made in the medieval period, apart from the new use of the word calling, it would be perfectly in keeping with orthodox social teaching. In the medieval period it was not possible to sever social, economic, political, and religious duties. 'When the age of the Reformation begins,' says Tawney, 'economics is still a branch of ethics, and ethics of theology; all human activities are treated as falling within a single scheme, whose character is determined by the spiritual destiny of mankind.'[169] In fact until the development of the concept of 'Indifferentism' in the eighteenth century, according to which economic activity lay outside the sphere of religion, economics continued—as the idea of the calling, sermonizing about usury, and so forth show—to be embraced by religious teaching. Since, however, the economic conditions to which Perkins is addressing himself were different from those obtaining in the medieval period, so too his concept of the calling, though resembling that of degree, acquired a different meaning.

Aquinas wrote that

The goodness of any part is considered in comparison with the whole; Hence Augustine says (Conf. III) that *unseemly is the part that harmonises not with the whole*. Since then every man is a part of the state, it is impossible that a man be good, unless he be well proportionate to the common good: nor can the whole be well consistent unless its parts be proportionable to it.[170]

By the time Perkins wrote, however, this social integration, with all members (except for a small proportion of rebels and unfortunates) filling their ordained niche, is no longer possible. The concept of the calling insists on the social stability and cohesion which for Aquinas is an ideal for the whole of society in circumstances where this can only be partially achieved. Weber argues that the doctrine of the calling (extending beyond the priestly vocation) originates with Luther and is stressed under

[168] Lawrence A. Sasek, *The Literary Temper of the English Puritans* (New York, 1969), 110–12.   [169] *Religion and the Rise of Capitalism*, p. 278.
[170] Thomas Aquinas, *Summa Theologica*, trans. Fathers of the English Dominican Province (1911–25), pt. II (First Pt.), Qu. 92, Art. 1.

Calvin.[171] It was clearly the very disintegration of society into atomic individuals (before an individualist ethos had developed) which required this explicit doctrinal emphasis. For all that the idea of a calling may eventually have stimulated the development of the capitalist ethos, and certainly underwent modification, it clearly arose as a reactionary response to the same menace of social disorder about which the crown was anxious.

What is crucially different from medieval degree is that the economic calling is as selective as a means of establishing security and contentment as is the spiritual calling of the elect. Furthermore the two were explicitly linked by Calvin and his followers. The *OED* defines 'calling' sb. 9 as 'The summons, invitation, or impulse of God to salvation or to his service; the inward feeling or conviction of a divine call; the strong impulse to any course of action as the right thing to do.' The next definition is 'Position, estate, or station in life; rank [Founded on 1 Cor. vii. 20 . . . L *vocatione* where it stands for the condition or position in which one was when called to salvation; but afterwards often mixed up with sense 9, as if it meant the estate in life to which God has called a man.]' It was not only the word calling that did double service in order to link secular and spiritual spheres. The words 'estate' and 'condition' could equally be used in spiritual and secular contexts with the effect of blurring the distinction between them.

Anthony Giddens, condensing Weber's account of the calling, says that

On the pastoral level, two developments occurred: it became obligatory to regard oneself as chosen, lack of certainty being indicative of insufficient faith; and the performance of 'good works' in worldly activity became accepted as the medium whereby such surety could be demonstrated. Hence success in a calling eventually came to be regarded as a 'sign'—never a means—of being one of the elect.[172]

Understandably again the economic historian states one half of the case, the half relating to the emergence of a new economic ethos. But when Giddens says 'it became obligatory to regard oneself as chosen' he seems to assume that this way of regarding

---

[171] See Anthony Giddens's introduction to Weber's *Protestant Ethic*, p. 4.
[172] *Protestant Ethic*, p. 5.

oneself was always an available choice. Just as economic success could not simply be chosen, however, nor could membership of the elect. We recall Bacon's remark that 'They are happy men whose natures sort with their vocations' together with Perkins's that 'Every man must judge that particular calling, in which God hath placed him, to be the best calling for him.' One can see how, especially in the middle ranks of society, contemporaries' confidence in their work (generated by the conviction that God had specifically called them to do it) combined with the industry with which it was carried out (the means of demonstrating election) might have led to the production of surplus value and thus to capitalism. Equally, however, the anxiety arising from the inability to secure employment which felt appropriate was, as a result of the doctrine of the calling, intensified by the presumptive evidence of reprobation it supplied.

Apart from economic historians' indifference to the corollary of the self-confidence the doctrine of callings could promote, they also tend to inspect it in the light of results which were not envisaged by its original proponents. Sasek rightly says that an effect Perkins had in mind was to discourage adventurism in economics. The eventual equation, in the decadence of puritanism, of economic and spiritual prosperity is one from which he would have completely dissociated himself. To understand the constructions seventeenth-century people placed on their experience it is necessary to hold in tension the reactionary impulse in puritan preaching and the self-approving uses to which the theology came, amongst some social groups, to be put. As it was preached by the likes of Perkins at the beginning of the seventeenth century the doctrine of callings helped to arm a vigorous rearguard action against irreversible social change, emphasizing the need for those things which were no longer reliably generated by society's infrastructure: in particular fixed roles within a stable hierarchy. As will be shown in my analysis of the autobiography of Richard Norwood in the next chapter, this meant that when economic forces flung people out of their expected niche their insecurity was preyed on by a sense of guilt and rejection.

The doctrine of the calling embodies the awareness of puritan ideology (how consciously this was held by puritans themselves is another question) that the new economic laws were as arbitrary in their distribution of favour as divine laws: 'as one man rises,' says Tawney, 'another is thrust down.' People were entirely passive and helpless in both economic and salvific processes. The puritan preparedness to consider as rejected by God those who had no control over their circumstances is indicated in their attitude towards the city poor, a group which had greatly increased as a result of population growth, enclosures, and other effects of market forces in the agrarian economy. Perkins gives prominence in the dedication for his *Treatise of the Vocations* to his condemnation of 'all wandering and straggling persons'. The Poor Law 'for the restraining of beggars' is, he says, 'an excellent statute' which is 'never to be repealed' since it is 'in substance the very law of God'.[173] Lacking a calling, they also lacked an indispensable sign of election or spiritual calling. Tawney speaks of the 'frigid scepticism' with which contemporaries responded to the view 'that distress was the result, not of personal deficiencies, but of economic causes, with its corollary that its victims had a legal right to be maintained by society . . . Like the friends of Job, it saw in misfortune, not the chastisement of love, but the punishment for sin.'[174]

So while the religious system built in the arbitrariness of success (you had to be called), it also condemned failure. Moreover the elision of social-economic and moral-spiritual failure tended to reach beyond vagrants to wage labourers and indeed to anyone insufficiently educated (or versed in the Word) to be eligible for salvation. In theory God could call people to the meanest work; but then work could only be dignified as a calling if it was united with the informed piety required by the general calling. No doubt this had its (unconscious) ideological uses. While on the one hand there was genuine alarm at a perceived crisis of order, on the other the ability to view as presumptively reprobate not only vagrants but illiterate labourers was conveniently desensitizing for employers. Perhaps the attitude to the first group paved the way, psychologically, for that to the second. Surplus, and consequently exploitable and expendable, labour was as necessary to the evolving economic system as the idea of reprobation apparently was to the new religious system.

---

[173] *Works*, p. 910.
[174] *Religion and the Rise of Capitalism*, pp. 264–5.

The essence of mercantilism, say Fletcher and Stevenson, 'was the doctrine of the utility of poverty: a nation's wealth and power depended on large numbers of badly paid labourers who should be habituated to drudgery. Mercantilism encouraged the gentry to suppose that, within the longstanding notion of social hierarchy, there was a basic division between rich and poor'[175]— as there was now, within that notion, a basic division between the elect and the reprobate. Respectability (which tended to require privileges such as education) became, in the course of the seventeenth century, a criterion bisecting especially village communities and overtaking hierarchical gradations (on which it also fed) as a means of social orientation.[176] The poor, whether vagrants or barely subsisting labourers, were in many parishes dehumanized by the assumption on the part of the respectable godly that they were, by and large, reprobates—irredeemable and therefore unabusable. Yet it would be wrong to assume from this a clean separation between those who preened themselves with Calvinist theology, while wielding it to enforce moral restraint on those below them, and those who fell victim to it.[177] Few could, in the period from 1590 to 1660, have total confidence in their economic future. And while avoidance of poverty may have been a necessary it certainly was not a sufficient condition of salvation. The religious system operated semi-autonomously in the mind.

Surplus selfhood unaccommodated to the divine scheme could certainly be evident in the higher as well as the lower echelons of society. 'The standing pool', writes Richard Steele, 'is prone to putrification: and it were better to beat down the body and to

---

[175] A. J. Fletcher and J. Stevenson, edd., *Order and Disorder in Early Modern England* (1985), 13.

[176] See David Underdown, *Revel, Riot, and Rebellion: Popular Politics and Culture in England 1603–1660* (1985), 20.

[177] Margaret Spufford warns against 'the emphasis on "puritanism" as an instrument of social control' because it 'leads in no time at all into a simplified equation of puritanism with social control'. Equally to be avoided, I think, is a simplifying reaction to such a distortion which sees moral and social attitudes as stemming from 'the relationship of the individual with the being he thought to be exterior, whom he described as "God" ' ('Puritanism and Social Control?' in Fletcher and Stevenson, *Order and Disorder*, p. 43). The phrase 'he thought to be' looks suitably detached; but of course if 'God' was not really (or unmediatedly) an exterior reality he was a communal discursive construct—and that recognition takes one back to the social circumstances which were involved with his construction.

keep it in subjection by a laborious calling, than through luxury
to become a cast-away.'[178] And William Perkins simply denounced idle gentlemen who 'live in no calling'.[179] A striking
exemplum for their admonitions can be found in a tragic incident
involving a younger son. Younger sons of the gentry were, Joan
Thirsk points out, 'the only competitors from this class in the
labour market'. They could have found work but the necessity
was irksome when they compared their lot with that of elder
brothers. And furthermore 'the habit of working for a living was
not ingrained in younger sons of this class.' The younger son of
Sir George Sondes, Freeman, received a good education but
refused suggested careers as a lawyer or merchant. He ended up
murdering his elder brother, George. Just before his execution
Freeman identified the cause of his action, offering himself as a
caution to all gentlemen to read the Bible regularly and pray
daily; and to parents not to 'suffer their sons to live in idleness
(which exposes a man to temptation) but to employ them in
some honest public calling'.[180]

In the period when puritanism was at its height, then, the new
sense of the uniqueness of the individual was, above all, a source
of anxiety. Post-medieval economic instability and social mobility
forced people to consider their uniqueness, since existence, for
many, was not explained by a clear function in a social organism.
This is not of course to say that everyone's role in post-medieval
society was equally problematic or even that there is a constant
correlation between those who were economically insecure or
dislocated and those who experienced a spiritual anxiety framed
by Calvinist discourse. But where the correlation does exist, as it
often does, the mutual confirmation of identity from both spheres
of life seems to touch the quick of puritan ideology, and the sense
of self puritans made articulate becomes most expressive.

Secular calling was generally associated by puritan divines
with spiritual calling. Puritanism responded to and in some ways
fostered individualism, as we know. In the end, as William
Haller says, puritan preachers tried 'to adapt Christian morality

---

[178] Richard Steele, *The Tradesman's Calling, being a Discourse concerning the Nature, Necessity, Choice, etc. of a Calling in General* (1684), 20.

[179] *Works*, p. 907.

[180] 'Younger Sons in the Seventeenth Century', in *History: The Journal of the Historical Association*, 54 (1969), 358–77, pp. 367, 368, 372.

to the needs of a population which was being steadily driven from
its old feudal status into the untried conditions of competition
between man and man in an increasingly commercial and
industrial society under a money economy'.[181] Before this
adaptation occurred, however, stress fell on individual exposure
to a providence under which spiritual destiny, whether salvation
or damnation, had to be worked out in fear and trembling.
Puritanism consequently encouraged empiricist induction rather
than deduction from general social and religious laws. The
adjective 'special' or 'particular' was predicated of providence
when its purpose was to express God's will to an individual.
Similarly calling was 'particular', picked out for each person by
God. In another sense, though, the calling was one of several
features of puritanism which counteracted individualism. Individualism in the sense of awareness of independent selfhood was
stimulated by puritan preachers but the purpose of this was (as
they thought synonymously) to stimulate a sense of radical
sinfulness and helplessness. Once this was done, those who were
to be saved would then have their sinful selfhood eclipsed by a
new identity as members of the community of the elect. The
calling was one way of losing the painful sense of separate
identity by submerging it in an area of the divine purpose. 'The
Lord commands every one of us, in all the actions of life,' said
Calvin, 'to regard his vocation. For he knows with what great
inquietude the human mind is inflamed.'[182] Bits of independent
identity which were not accounted for by functions performed, in
family life, at work, or during religious observance, caused
problems of introspection and anxiety which were traits of the
reprobate. Hence the necessity of believing one's calling to be
that designed by God: economic and spiritual insecurity were
resolved in the absorbing performance of social and religious
roles.

A last point should be made concerning the mirroring of
puritan theology and domestic social history. Puritan theology
may be linked to what Lawrence Stone calls the reinforcement of
patriarchy, in train since about 1480. External checks on
patriarchal power declined, he argues, as kinship ties and
clientage weakened. 'The period from 1530 to 1660 may', he

---

[181] *Rise of Puritanism*, p. 117.
[182] Quoted by Leverenz, *Language of Puritan Feeling*, p. 135.

writes, 'be regarded as the patriarchal stage in the evolution of the nuclear family.' Particularly in pious upper-class households in the seventeenth century, he says, 'the power of the head of the household was oppressive in its completeness.'[183] Stone is not concerned with the parallel oppressive completeness of the power of the Calvinist God who, like the father in the nuclear family, gained some of his awesome power by freeing himself from the constraints of a wider social system into which he had been incorporated. But not only is the parallel self-evident, Calvin and his followers pressed it themselves. 'Calvin', writes Michael Walzer, 'radically deemphasised the natural affective aspects of fatherhood, and dramatically stressed its authoritarian features.'[184] And Walzer's claim that the father became legal sovereign with power of life and death over his children-subjects is literally borne out by Calvin's stipulation of the death penalty (never implemented in Calvin's Geneva, but made legislatively operative in Connecticut and Massachusetts in the 1640s) for disobedience to parents.[185] 'For they are monsters and not men,' he declared, 'that breake the authorite of parentes with dishonore or stubbornesse. Therefore the Lord commaunded all the disobedient to their parentes, to be slaine, as men unworthy to enjoye the benefite of lighte' (*Inst.* 2. 8. 36). William Perkins said 'the father hath authority to dispose of his child':[186] his power could no more be appealed against than God's.

Walzer is surely correct, then, to say that 'the defence of secular repression and the assertion of "the claims of God" are so closely woven together that it is extremely difficult to disentangle them.'[187] The two sources of power and oppression were associated—as the next chapter will show—in the imagination of the victims of despair. No ideological outlet existed for feelings of protest or resentment against the power of father, father-surrogates, or God. And this could nurture an intolerable tension in individuals between their expanding self-awareness and the submissiveness demanded of them. Clearly there was a relation-ship, as the phrase itself suggests, between 'the reinforcement of

[183] *Family, Sex and Marriage*, pp. 218, 155.
[184] *Revolution of the Saints*, p. 49.
[185] See *Family, Sex and Marriage*, p. 175.
[186] Quoted by Walzer, *Revolution of the Saints*, p. 191.
[187] Ibid. 46.

patriarchy' and the existence of forces which threatened the social order. Not least among them was the growing self-awareness and impulse to autonomy which finally achieved a measure of toleration. In the early seventeenth century, however, opposition to it in the family and in religion was at its most violent.

There has been some questioning of the degree to which puritanism was authoritarian, theologically and in the home. Perry Miller says that 'If we today insist upon supposing that their philosophy was an absolute authoritarianism, we ought to be very much disconcerted by their continual appeals to experience and reason, appeals which, from our point of view, imply assumptions altogether at variance with those of the creed.'[188] But Miller's picture of puritanism is mainly shaped by the New Englanders' increasingly mellow version of it in which God's sovereignty was explicitly moderated by covenant theology. Appeals to experience and reason can, moreover, take many forms. Reason, says Calvin, should tell us not to be inquisitive about the reason for God's decrees. He means by it prudence. And while, like Calvin, English puritans were interested in experience, it was not for its own sake but for what it revealed about God's purpose. This did not mitigate authoritarianism either. More recently David Leverenz has claimed that far from paternal conduct being equated with divine, the craving of puritans for an all-powerful father-God was owing to the weakness and insufficiency of real fathers.[189] Leverenz's contention is based, though, on few examples, and again he goes to New England for most of his evidence. As we shall see from the spiritual autobiographies, English (and Scottish) puritans were frequently the victims of extreme bullying treatment. And this was compounded by the oppression of remoter economic forces.

It is later in the century that a reaction set in against paternal heavy-handedness, and puritan parents appear to have turned as kindly as any. As Stone says:

It cannot be proved conclusively that in reality the powers of fathers over children . . . in the upper and middle ranks . . . became greater than they had been in the middle ages. But this seems a plausible

---

[188] Perry Miller, *Errand into the Wilderness* (Cambridge, Mass., 1956), 70.
[189] *Language of Puritan Feeling*, pp. 11, 50–69.

hypothesis, given the fact that patriarchy for its effective exercise depends not so much on raw power or legal authority, as on a recognition by all concerned of its legitimacy, hallowed by ancient tradition, moral theology and political theory.

Stone also remarks on the contrast between complaints of parental severity in the late seventeenth century and the opposite protest against particularly maternal indulgence in the eighteenth.[190] The very articulation of this protest in the late seventeenth century furthermore indicates that the legitimacy of such unrestrained power had come to be questioned. It is doubtful whether anyone could, before the Civil War, have generalized as John Aubrey does about childhood at that time: 'The child perfectly loathed the sight of his parents, as the slave his Torturer.'[191] In the first half of the seventeenth century such was the strength of belief in the right of fathers to exercise absolute power that this seemed no more opposable than the omnipotence of God which it closely resembled: 'the husband and father for a time became the family despot, benevolent or malign according to temperament and inclination, lording it over his wife and his children.'[192] In Richard Leigh's indignant words in 1675:

> In *arbitrary Families*,
> Which seem *Domestique Tyrannies*,
> *Parents*, with *Turkish Rigour* sway.[193]

The literary articulation of religious despair will, then, be understood in the light of the various contexts sketched for it. Paramount, since it provides both the language in which despair was publicized and the theoretical framework in terms of which it was consciously apprehended, is theological discourse itself. But theology will itself be poorly understood if it is considered apart from other areas of experience in which it was believed at the time to be fully concerned. Differently placed writers variously register an emotional and intellectual congruity between their theological comprehension of the world and their own social

---

[190] *Family, Sex and Marriage*, pp. 151, 439.

[191] A. Powell, *John Aubrey and his Friends* (1963), 278.

[192] *Family, Sex and Marriage*, p. 158.

[193] Richard Leigh, 'The Union of Friendship', in *Poems*, ed. H. Macdonald (Oxford, 1947), 50.

construction within it. I have therefore pointed up historical conditions of the early seventeenth century which most strikingly answer to aspects of Calvinist-puritan theology bearing on despair. These are all in one way or another connected with the economically and socially transitional character of the period. First there is the post-feudal liberation of market forces to which various kinds of social dislocation are relatable, from enclosures to surplus education of the socially ambitious classes. Segregation of the principles believed to operate in economic and religious spheres had not yet occurred so that the alarming unpredictability of the market and its, at times, socially devastating effects were reflected in Calvinism, where the place of individuals in the divine scheme was worked out in the course of life in direct encounters with cosmic powers. They were not sheltered by a social network to which they were automatically assimilated—the family, the stratified community, the church—from exposure to the forces which controlled their destiny, from a God unanswerable to any human moral values who gradually disclosed his *ad hominem* purposes through providence. Because of their impotence to predict or control their destiny they felt predestined to a successful or unhappy end. It does not much signify that only some people experienced this exposure to capricious economic forces directly or that those who did were not necessarily the ones who held to the corresponding theology. What is important to an understanding of the collective, persecutory imagination is that the correspondence existed and that the common ground between theology and economic conditions was mutually reinforcing.

More directly related to economic transition are what on the individual psychological level Freud termed reaction formations. The doctrine of callings and the general reinforcement of patriarchy were reactionary attempts to re-establish a disappearing social cohesion. The doctrine of callings was a transmutation of medieval degree, aiming at individuals what for Aquinas was a practicable model for the whole of society. Not having a secular calling you could accept as designed for you by God was, in a mobile society where unsettledness was commonplace, presumptive evidence that the same was true spiritually. Again the same principles obtained in both spheres. It was 'their first assumption', says Tawney, 'that the ultimate social authority is the will of God.'[194] The reinforcement of patriarchy was another aspect of the repressive clampdown, an attempt to reassert social control at the level of the household. Fathers could seem to the child as emotionally remote and as physically menacing as the Calvinist God and their severity could provoke similar questions about the ambivalence of love and hate, acceptance and rejection, in a relationship prosecuted on principles of power and submission.

[194] *Religion and the Rise of Capitalism*, p. 279.

2
Patriarchs, Providence, and Paranoia: Subjectification and Autobiographical Narrative

MY aim in this chapter is to relate to each other the determining circumstances which seem to me, in the context of puritan culture, to co-operate in the production of both conceptions of selfhood and their inscription in autobiographical narrative. I set about this task against the scholarly background of much 'softening' and 'humanizing', to pick up Blair Worden's terms, of 'the Puritan mentality'. The manner in which puritan culture constituted human beings as subjects corresponds in some ways to Michel Foucault's concept, 'subjectification'. The authorities in that culture—the preachers and their books, and then, in the domestic arena, fathers and their surrogates—used what Foucault calls 'dividing practices', both in their constant discursive segregation of the godly from the ungodly and, more subtly, by inducing the replication of that division within the individual consciousness. Their stress on exclusion (reprobation) proved to be a manipulative tool of devastating efficacy, reaching inside the mind to structure its activity and especially its reflections on itself. The individual was thus drawn to participate in the process of self-formation. 'There are two meanings of the word *subject*,' says Foucault: 'subject to someone else by control and dependence, and tied to his own identity by a conscience or self-knowledge. Both meanings suggest a form of power which subjugates and makes subject to.'[1] The discourse of Calvinism was the power source into which spiritual autobiographers were plugged; and its disciplinary shocks were administered by the agency of both authority figures and the mental processes they had trained to deputize for them. Offenders were not simply disciplined or frightened back into line, however; they were offered an alternative discourse, that of the reprobate, in which a

---

[1] 'The Subject and Power', in H. Dreyfus and P. Rabinow, *Michel Foucault: Beyond Structuralism and Hermeneutics* (Chicago, 1982), 208, 212.

sense of self, however unwelcome, could, and frequently did, inhere.

In the second half of the chapter I move on from the general survey of pressures bearing on the process of self-formation and the shaping of spiritual autobiography to a close study of the narrative evolution of the 'Confessions', and subjectivity, of Richard Norwood. Here I bring into play the economic conditions which fused, in the medium of Calvinist discourse, with experience of patriarchs in the imaginative projection of a persecutory providence. It was in negotiation with this projection—indeed in recalcitrance to, rather than compliance with, approved mental states and behavioural patterns—that the sense of self as a continuous and distinct entity seemed to acquire decisive reality.

Samuel Clarke eulogized William Perkins, 'the dominant influence in Puritan thought for the forty years after his death'[2], in these terms:

He was an excellent Chirurgeon at the jointing of a broken Soul, and at stating of a doubtfull conscience, so that the afflicted in spirit came far and near to him, and received much satisfaction, and comfort by him. In his Sermons he used to pronounce the word *Damn* with such an Emphasis, as left a dolefull Echo in his auditors ears a good while after: And when hee was Catechist in Christ's College, in expounding the Commandments, he applied them so home to the conscience, as was able to make his hearers hearts fall down, and their haires almost to stand upright.[3]

This did not seem to contemporaries an absurd statement. Robert Bolton—'a son of Thunder' who was also 'a sweet son of Consolation' 'sought to far, and near' for his 'excellent Art in relieving afflicted consciences'[4]—was quite right, given shared doctrinal premises, to criticize 'Daubers' who preached 'of being carried to Heaven in a Bed of Downe' and congratulate preachers like himself for being 'Plain-Dealers'.[5] It is much odder to find modern commentators uncritically transmitting their ideology.

William Haller adopts the first phrase of Clarke's encomium

---

[2] Christopher Hill, *Puritanism and Revolution: Studies in Interpretation of the English Revolution of the Seventeenth Century* (1958), 216. (Perkins died in 1602.)

[3] *The Marrow of Ecclesiastical History* (1650), 851.   [4] Ibid. 490–1.

[5] *Instructions for a Right Comforting Afflicted Consciences* (1631), 147–8, 149.

on Perkins to cue his own description of him as 'indeed a kind of sixteenth-century William James' who provided 'the descriptive psychology of sin and regeneration'.[6] Roger Sharrock, who repeats both Clarke and Haller, finds this 'descriptive psychology' 'all very English and empirical'.[7] Owen Watkins cites Clarke again, apparently sharing his admiration, on Thomas Wilson whose auditors heard 'not so much Words as Thunderclaps' when he 'opened the curses of the law'. Yet he then presents as freak-show exhibits terrorized victims for whom 'a monomania concern with their own doom conditioned every response'.[8] On the one hand 'curses of the law' are treated respectfully as though they had some transcultural reality; on the other seeing devils and so forth requires a switch of register. Haller is even more startlingly one-sided. 'There can be no question', he says, 'that the chief service of the preachers before 1640 was . . . to build up the courage and self-confidence of the people. The prime temptation of the devil was timidity, confusion and despair. Sinners had to be helped out of the slough of despond.'[9] In the first sentence the modern idea of self-confidence is invoked (whereas confidence in self was the last thing the puritans saw themselves as encouraging[10]); in the second the devil is brought in to mystify the preachers' destructive effects in just the way they found him convenient (Perkins's prototypical Christian, Eusebius, is made to report that 'the divell . . . in fearfull manner cried in my eares, that I was a reprobate, his child: that none of Gods children were as I am.'[11]) If it was the preachers, and not God, who rescued people, it was the preachers, not the devil, who plunged them into the slough. When Christian thrashes around in the Slough of Despond it is a theologically induced experience. One form of manipulation has been noted. Would-be believers

---

[6] *The Rise of Puritanism* (New York, 1938), 92.

[7] Roger Sharrock, *John Bunyan* (1954), 20; see also his 'Spiritual Autobiography in *The Pilgrim's Progress*', *RES* 24 (1948), 102–20; and the introduction to *Grace Abounding*, p. xxviii.

[8] *The Puritan Experience* (1972), 8, 67. [9] *Rise of Puritanism*, p. 155.

[10] Despair of self was a precondition of the reception of grace, as it had been for Luther. Vavasor Powell sees it as an encouraging sign, for example, when he has lost all self-confidence (*The Life and Death of . . . with some Eulogies and Epitaphs by his Friends* (1671), 45; see also Perkins, *The Works* (Cambridge, 1605), 456; Bolton, *Instructions*, p. 197). 'Self-confidence' was indeed a puritan coinage but it carried an entirely negative sense: see M. van Beek, *An Enquiry into Puritan Vocabulary* (Gröningen, 1969).

[11] *The Works* (Cambridge, 1605), 458.

themselves, under the power of suggestion, brought observations into line with authorized specifications for the elect. 'Seen by the light of the word,' says Haller, 'as they read it in the holy book and heard it expounded from the pulpit, their own lives fell under their gaze into the pattern set by Paul.'[12] Such massaging of experience does of course occur. William James quotes Jonathan Edward's account of the process (the operation, that is, of a prescriptive not descriptive psychology):

> Very often their experience at first appears like a confused chaos, but then those parts are selected which bear the nearest resemblance to such particular steps as are insisted on; and these are dwelt on in their thoughts, and spoken of from time to time, till they grow more and more conspicuous in their view, and other parts which are neglected grow more and more obscure. Thus what they have experienced is insensibly strained, so as to bring it to an exact conformity to the scheme already established in their minds.[13]

The sociologist Bryan R. Wilson says much the same about members of modern sects, who 'bring their reasons for conversion into conformity with group expectations, gradually eliminating idiosyncratic elements and reiterating in-group justifications'.[14]

What Haller (and, for example, Louis Martz who says that those who looked for marks of election were likely to find them[15]) overlooks is the binarism of the puritan account of experience. The set of steps derived from St Paul—subdivisions of vocation, justification, sanctification, and glorification—was paralleled by another, so the resultant experience was not easy conformity to the programme of election but the anxious honing of a sense of identity against extreme opposed paradigms of human destiny, one of which was being actualized. Reprobation was always an influential possibility. How, otherwise, could it even be rumoured that puritan supremo William Perkins despaired on his death-bed? Haller says that 'the very titles of many of William Perkins' sermons yearn eloquently over the troubled soul', giving as an

[12] *Rise of Puritanism*, p. 91.

[13] Quoted by William James in *The Varieties of Religious Experience* (1902), 200.

[14] Bryan R. Wilson, 'Becoming a Sectarian: Motivation and Commitment' in *Studies in Church History*, 15 (1978), 481–506, p. 505.

[15] Louis L. Martz, *The Poetry of Meditation: A Study in English Religious Literature of the Seventeenth Century*, 2nd edn. rev. (New Haven, 1962), 162; M. M. Knappen, *Tudor Puritanism* (Chicago, 1939), 348, 393–5; Weber, *The Protestant Ethic and the Spirit of Capitalism*, trans. T. Parsons, intro. A. Giddens (1976), 114–15.

example 'A Case of Conscience, the greatest that ever was: how a man may know whether he be the child of God, or no'.[16] It was above all Perkins, however, who made the 'or no' of this grimly absorbing test-yourself exercise alive to the imagination—even to his own.

Preachers wrapped people who were drawn into puritanism's cultural ambit in theological barbed wire. They were, said George Fox, 'Men of cruel visages and of long teeth'.[17] John Phillips, Milton's nephew, apostrophized victims of the Presbyterian clergy:

> Vain foolish people, how are ye deceived,
> How many several sorts have ye received
> Of things called truths, upon your backs laid on
> Like saddles for themselves to ride upon![18]

They exerted, through the reprobate alternative, a dual discipline over the mind (which negotiated its painful way between them): the danger of hypocrisy and the danger of rejection. Laying claim to signs of election when they were inauthentic could produce a more ineluctable despair than confession to the feeling of rejection. And both—uncertainty of the authenticity of religious experiences or acknowledgement that the most real experience was the sense of rejection—gave probability to a reprobate interpretation.

The existence of the reprobate paradigm made the signs of election themselves treacherous. Arthur Dent helpfully gives the plain man 'Seven infallible signes of salvation'. They are 'Assured faith in the promises', 'Sinceritie of heart', 'The spirit of adoption', 'Sound Regeneration, and Sanctification', 'Inward Peace', 'Groundednesse in the truth', and 'Continuance to the end'. None of these can be found 'truly' in a reprobate.[19] If at any moment the mysterious forms of confidence on which these signs rely seemed to desert believers they would fall prey to Perkins's idea, derived from Calvin,[20] of 'A calling not effectuall' which had

---

[16] *Rise of Puritanism*, p. 155.

[17] *A Journal or Historical Account of his Life* . . . (1694), 86.

[18] *Satyr against Hypocrites* (1655), reprinted in Christopher Hill, *Milton and the English Revolution*, Appendix 2, p. 487.

[19] *The Plaine Mans Path-Way to Heaven* (1601), 259.

[20] While Kendall thinks it important that Perkins got the term '*ineffectual* calling' from Beza (*Calvin and English Calvinism to 1649* (Oxford, 1979), 7) it is clearly present

produced 'A yeelding to Gods calling' succeeded, according to God's plan for the reprobate, by 'Relapse'. Perkins's 'Table', prefixed to *A Golden Chaine* (and reproduced below, pp. 164–5), which he invites people to look at for a simple understanding of theology, draws the mind back through these steps to their origin: 'The decree of Reprobation' leading to 'Gods hating of the Reprobate'—the actual persons, that is, whose identity as reprobates he had decreed. The medieval idea that God hates the sin but loves the sinner was first rejected by Luther, and then by Calvinists.[21] So the immediate inference from any loss of assurance was the feeling of being an object of God's implacable hatred. Perkins's 'Table' exposes the absurdity of the stern warnings preachers issued against probing 'the secret and hidden counsell of God',[22] which began the chain of cause and effect people were taught to examine. They were told to consider *whether* they were objects of God's hatred and this was the chief cause of anguish even if it did not produce the reckless question *why*.

The lexicon of reprobate experience in puritan literature is capacious, reflecting its significance. The subdivisions in Perkins's 'Table' give some idea of this and they are supplemented by the captions on Bunyan's *Mapp* (see below pp. 196–7). As well as experiencing 'A yeelding to Gods calling' Perkins's reprobate are capable of 'Penitence' and 'Zeale'. Phases indicated by Bunyan are similarly snared with ambiguity. *'conviction(s) for sin(ne)'* appears under both election and reprobation. The reprobate have *'desires after life'* and *'some tasts of Life'*; but while the elect gain in *'confidence'* the reprobate soul *'groweth secure'*. The elect *'Soul is cast down'* and tempted to despair; the reprobate soul, by supposed contrast, completes its preparation for hell with *'the sinne against the Holy Ghost'* which gives rise to *'a certain fearfull looking for Judgment'*. Although Bunyan's terms are biblical quotations they are stacked up in a way that gives them a cumulative impact their original contexts do not support. The

---

avant la lettre in, for example, *Inst*. 3. 2. 11–12: though the reprobate do not 'truely feele the effectual working of the Gospell,' God may 'enlighten some with a present felyng of his grace'. See also *Inst*. 3. 21. 7 and 3. 24. 8.

[21] See J. S. Whale, *The Protestant Tradition: An Essay in Interpretation* (Cambridge, 1959), 23.

[22] Richard Greenham, *The Workes*, 2nd edn. (1599), 440.

apparent clarification offered by Perkins's 'Table' and Bunyan's *Mapp* masks terrifying ambiguities.

Like most of the rest of the church-going population spiritual autobiographers could not have avoided books of signs like Dent's *Plaine Mans Path-Way to Heaven*: 'Almost every puritan preacher of note', says Owen Watkins, 'produced a similar work.'[23] And the predictable response to the development of signs of reprobation as well as those of grace (the ones Watkins notices) is attested both in the phrases autobiographers appropriate to describe their experience and in explicit references to books and sermons. Laurence Clarkson consulted 'the ablest Teachers in *London* . . . unto whom I daily referred, if possible, to get assurance of Salvation', but the failure of his quest was exacerbated by books by Thomas Hooker 'which so tormented my soul, that I thought it unpossible to be saved; however I labored what in me lay, to finde those signs and marks in my own soul.'[24] Michael Wigglesworth concluded after reading Henry Scudder's deceptively titled *The Christians Daily Walke in Securitie and Peace* (1627) that he had sinned the unforgivable sin against the Holy Ghost. Hugging the barbed wire he 'was in some measure contented though I should be damned'.[25] James Fraser, chancing on Thomas Shepard's *Sincere Convert*, 'went after Dinner thro' the Fields, and read that Book all through; and the Power of God was present: And reading what Lengths Hypocrites might come . . . and the great Difficulty of saving Conversion, I was wounded through and through; my Condition was now worse than ever, and I was brought to . . . Despair.' Years later he realized that 'truly most Mens Fears and Doubts proceed from mistaken Marks given in Books.' At that time reading Richard

---

[23] *Puritan Experience*, p. 11. Margaret Spufford's survey of popular literature finds that the negative emphasis of 'small godly books' would 'certainly have tended to accentuate, rather than alleviate' widespread 'chronic religious anxiety'. While providing useful documentation and comment this survey also tends to blame 'some psychological types', a 'type of worrier', for susceptibility; and the discussion ends with this consoling formulation: 'The doubter who feels himself without faith must therefore wait patiently, continuing to ask God for that gift which it is undoubtedly His intention to bestow.' Yet the passage she had just quoted offers no such theological guarantee (*Small Books and Pleasant Histories: Popular Fiction and its Readership in Seventeenth-Century England* (1981), 207, 210, 211).

[24] *The Lost Sheep Found* (1660), 8.

[25] *The Diary of Michael Wigglesworth 1653–1657*, ed. Edmund S. Morgan (New York, 1965), 101.

Baxter did nothing to allay his anxieties.[26] Baxter himself 'got all
the Books that ever I could buy which lay down Evidences and
Marks of true Grace, and tended to discover the Difference
betwixt the true Christian and the Hypocrite or Unsound: I liked
no Sermon so well as that which contained most of these
Marks.'[27] Examples could be multiplied.

Much anxiety centred on the idea of hypocrisy. Preachers
inserted it into the mind by ventriloquism: 'I feare oftentimes
least my profession of religion should bee onely in truth meere
hypocrisie'; 'our hearts may conclude our selves hypocrites';
'sometimes I feare that all is but in hypocrisie in mee.'[28]
Autobiographers chimed in. Oliver Heywood feared 'lest I be not
yet gone beyond the hypocrite'; James Fraser was 'a Formalist',
'not sincere'; 'the Devil came in and told me *I was a Hypocrite*,'
said an anonymous convert, '*and that the Hypocrites Hope would
perish*'; 'No Hypocrite', people sought to reassure Thomas
Halyburton, 'is able to counterfeit that Language in such a Case
as you are in. Laurence Clarkson shows how pressure to evince
signs of grace could induce actual hypocrisy: drying in the midst
of secretly prepared 'extempore' prayer, he 'came off like a
hypocrite as I was, which so seized on my soul, that I thought for
my hypocrisie damnation would be my portion.'[29]

For all their crocodile tears, through the idea of hypocrisy the
preachers had their parishioners trapped in masochistic dependence on them. Goodwin speaks, for example, of 'that seeming
neere similitude which hypocrisie holds unto the truth and power
of grace'.[30] Similarities are often so great, said Perkins, 'that none
but Christ can discerne the sheepe from the Goates, true
Christians from apparent Christians'. It was no good believing
'generally in a confused manner'. Many are elect 'in their own
thinking', yet in truth they are not perswaded so: for they are
deceived'. Those who 'truly believe' had to possess a 'special
trust and confidence . . . a special assurance that we are adopted,

---

[26] James Fraser, *Memoirs of the Life* (Edinburgh, 1738), 44–5.

[27] *Reliquiae Baxterianae*, ed. M. Sylvester (1696), 195.

[28] Perkins, *Works*, p. 457; Goodwin, *A Childe of Light Walking in Darknes* (1636), 45;
Timothy Rogers, *The Righteous Mans Evidence for Heaven* (1619), 27.

[29] Oliver Heywood, *His Autobiography, Diaries, Anecdote and Event Books*, ed.
J. H. Turner (Brighouse, 1882), i. 147; Fraser, *Memoirs*, pp. 22, 26, 28; Charles Doe,
ed., *A Collection of Experience of the Work of Grace* (1700), 17; Thomas Halyburton,
Memoirs of the Life, 2nd edn. (Edinburgh, 1715), 213; Clarkson, *The Lost Sheep Found*,
p. 6.   [30] *Childe of Light*, p. 61.

and in the favour of God'.[31] It is cheering to know that leading purveyors of these ideas, like Perkins, could impale themselves on them. John Bradford, eminence of the first wave of English Calvinists, seems to have lost the buoyancy C. S. Lewis attributes to the early protestants and concluded himself a hypocrite.[32] The combination of the unconscious nature of hypocrisy and the imperative nature of assurance (which Watkins wrongly says was not mandatory in puritan circles[33]) was—a modern perspective is bound to add—compounded by the dubious reality of all the claimed experience of God. It must have been hard work tending off the idea of hypocrisy when the form of the requisite assurance was the experience of a *'heart-ravishing voice'* calling out *'thou art a Child of God, thy sins are pardoned.'*[34] Worry about the reality of religious experience may be gauged by the frequency with which autobiographers call on the devil to account for atheistic doubts by which they are assailed.[35]

It was not only the fear of not being elect with which autobiographers contended: it was, too, the imaginative impact of the idea of being loathed and daily victimized by an all-powerful deity. A double reaction resulted: on the one hand a feeling of total self-alienation (because the justice of the ruler of the universe—the ultimate patriarch—seemed axiomatic (see *Inst.* 3. 23. 5)); on the other a sometimes irrepressible reflex of hatred and defiance. 'In these Bonds,' writes George Trosse, 'I came to have *direful Apprehensions* of the Wrath of God: I was hereupon prompted to *bite off my Tongue,* and (which I desire to mention with *Trembling*) *spit it in the Face of God.'*[36] The parenthetic delay, ostensibly excusing the repetition, allows mimetic expulsive force to the burningly remembered blasphemous urge. Blasphemy was often experienced as the spurting into consciousness of an impulse of hatred under the high pressure of authoritarian repression. This was generally followed by despairing prostration. Thomas Halyburton found that 'The Wrath of

---

[31] *Works*, pp. 431, 426, 510, 115–16.
[32] See Goodwin, *Childe of Light*, p. 45; Lewis, *English Literature in the Sixteenth Century Excluding Drama* (1973), 34.   [33] *Puritan Experience*, p. 11.
[34] Robert Bolton, quoted by Firmin in *The Real Christian* (1670), 197.
[35] For example, Doe, *Collection*, p. 17; J[ane] Turner, *Choice Experiences of the Kind Dealings of God, before, in, and after Conversion* (1653), 25; Fraser, *Memoirs*, p. 119; John Rogers, *Ohel or Beth-shemesh, a Tabernacle for the Sun* (1653), 428.
[36] *The Life* (Exeter, 1714), 70.

God was dropp'd into my Soul' after his 'Spirit sometimes rose in Quarrellings against God' with the result that 'I could not but justify him, if he had destroyed me.'[37] Merciless punishment often took the form of the conviction of having sinned against the Holy Ghost.[38] Rushing to the assistance of those tormented by the thought, Richard Capel concluded his attempt to distinguish between this sin and blasphemy: 'neither is it in the wit of every man, to say, where the difference lies betwixt them.'[39] If horrified self-condemnation led to despair of God's mercy victims had still more probably snookered themselves into the sin against the Holy Ghost since despair was the commonest interpretation. Chirurgeon Perkins was soothing about this: 'The Elect cannot commit this sinne: and therefore they who feele in themselves a sure testimonie of their election, neede never to despaire.'[40]

Autobiographers were not preoccupied by particular sins for themselves. They always saw them as symptomatic. What was significant about the sin against the Holy Ghost, as Bunyan makes clear in *Grace Abounding*, is that God should have chosen particular individuals to commit it (157). It was a touchstone of spiritual identity. Although this is how the books of signs encouraged people to think about sin, their doing so could further compound self-condemnation. 'I mourned for Sin,' says Fraser, 'not because it offended God, but because of the Consequents of it; and this made me conclude I was not sincere.' This thought possessed him 'for the Space of three Years almost'.[41] Sins were not primarily wicked deeds: Sin was rather an engulfing sense of being rejected and hated. Perkins said of the reprobate: 'their best actions are sins.'[42] This is how autobiographers felt. God seemed impossible to please. Richard Norwood struggled with what he calls 'a heathenish and harsh conceit of God'.[43] John Rogers bewails 'these *hard thoughts* I had of God!' James Fraser constantly exhorts himself to 'Put a good Construction on God's Ways' and practises this by assuring himself that it is Satan who 'represents God as a hard Master . . .

---

[37] *Memoirs*, pp. 65, 64, 65.   [38] For example, Fraser, *Memoirs*, pp. 28–9.
[39] *Tentations: Their Nature, their Danger, their Cure* (1633), 275.
[40] *Works*, p. 118; see also Capel, *Tentations*, p. 274.   [41] *Memoirs*, p. 28.
[42] Quoted by K. T. Kelly in *Conscience Dictator or Guide: A Study in Seventeenth-Century English Protestant Moral Theology* (1967), 84.
[43] *The Journal of Richard Norwood Surveyor of Bermuda*, ed. W. F. Craven and W. B. Hayward (New York, 1945), 75. Further references will be embodied in the text.

as One that commands and requires Duties, as tyrannical Rulers make Laws to entrap the Subjects . . . and requiring such Exactness, or else not at all to be accepted.'[44] 'No doubt', says Baxter

> it is the death of our heavenly life, to have hard and doubtful thoughts of God; to conceive of him as a hater of the creature (except onely of obstinate Rebels), and as one that had rather damn us, then save us, and that is glad of an opportunity to do us a mischief, or at least hath no great goodwill to us: This is to put the Blessed God into the similitude of Satan . . . When in our vile unbelief . . . we have drawn the most ugly picture of God in our imaginations, then we complain, that we cannot love him, and delight in him. This is the case of many thousand Christians.[45]

'Labour to have and keep . . . charitable Thoughts of God: Fix a lovely Character of God in thy Heart,' Fraser urges himself.[46] Failure was not through want of trying.

The sense of divine rejection was often related to feelings about fathers, father-surrogates, or the social hierarchy. Frequent, often discriminatory or arbitrary, beatings; banishment from the father's presence and the threat of being disowned; guilt-feelings arising from lack of filial affection or hatred as a reaction to punishment; the desire to escape from paternal anger; the knowledge that paternal power circumvented any infantile plot: in all these experiences God and actual fathers seem to have been imaginatively conflated. In tribute to Robert Bolton's influence over his children Samuel Clarke says: 'hee verily believed that none of them durst think to meet him at the great Tribunal in an unregenerate state.'[47] It might be supposed that Bolton's children would in the circumstances have more pressing worries; it is only if their father had been absorbed into a picture of God that the statement can make sense. Many of the autobiographies support the suggestion.

John Rogers also had the misfortune to be the son of a well-known puritan preacher. After his father's sermons he was 'almost in the *bottomelesse abysmes* of *torments*: I took the *Bible* to

[44] *Ohel or Beth-shemesh*, p. 428; *Memoirs*, pp. 276, 287.
[45] *The Saints Everlasting Rest* (1658), 683.
[46] *Memoirs*, p. 261.
[47] *Marrow of Ecclesiastical History*, p. 493.

look these *Scriptures*, read them over and over and over again, but the more I *read* the more I *roar'd* in the *black gulf* of *despair*.' He did not dare confide his fears but

prayed, *fasted*, mourn'd, got into *corners*, yea many times (being I was *ashamed* to make my case known), I have run into *barnes*, *stables*, *house or office*, any where (pretending as I had *businesse*) on purpose to *pray*, sigh, *weep*, knocking my *breast*, curse that ever I was born; wishing I were a *stone*, any thing but what I was, for *fear of hell* and the *devils*.

Rogers *père* practised the cruelty he preached so that the domestic regime reinforced the lessons of the pulpit:

Besides great outward *afflictions* which I met with, were of much force to *bring* me into this *condition*, being often (and doubtlesse I might deserve it too too much) beaten, bruised, turn'd out of doors, whirl'd and kickt about, hardly and unkindly used; at which times I should sometimes be *tempted* to *murther my self*, sometimes think I could not belong to *God*, for then he could not endure to see me thus used and *afflicted*, and yet I *flie* to him, and pray, and pray, and pray, but as good speak to a post, for I am not relieved.[48]

Beatings, says Levin Schücking in *The Puritan Family*, seem 'to have constituted the most essential part of education.' This may be an exaggeration. Not all fathers and schoolmasters were equally ferocious. Yet considering the general sparseness of external detail in the spiritual autobiographies beatings do seem to occupy a prominent place in them, and therefore in the mind of the child at least. And the cultural foreignness of a society in which a respected spiritual leader can offer this as a vignette of marital harmony must be acknowledged: the wife, says Daniel Rogers, 'holdes not his hand from due strokes, but bares their skins with delight, to his fatherly stripes'.[49] Adam Martindale's best schoolmaster, at the age of 7, was 'humourous and passionate, and sometimes in these moods he would whip boys most unmercifully for small or no faults at all'. Another would return to the schoolroom drunk and lay about him so that 'those that had ropt [romped and fought] and plaid all the time of his absence, and those that had followed their businesse, and were ready to give him a good account, were, in a manner, in the same

[48] *Ohel or Beth-shemesh*, p. 426.
[49] Levin Schücking, *The Puritan Family: A Social Study from the Literary Sources*, trans. B. Battershaw (1969), 75.

predicament. In a word, innocence and dilligence would not secure us from his fury.' Martindale formed an impressive view of the extent of patriarchal power (sensibly managing, as a rule, to displace its operation on to others). Brother Hugh, 'growing wild and unmanageable', married a Papist and disappeared to Ireland. This was 'so much to my father's dissatisfaction, that we had reason to beleeve we should never see him againe, as accordingly it proved': he promptly died as is the custom, observes Martindale, with 'disobedient children'. Martindale was much struck too by his sister's smallpox: formerly proud of her good looks she acquired a face 'so swelled that scarce any forme of a visage was discernible'. God, he previously noted, 'hath great varietie of rods in store' to punish those who 'remaine stubborne and unhumbled'.[50]

James Fraser tried ingenious methods of making himself too ill to go to grammar school so as to avoid the whippings he almost daily received there. His attitude to punishment was, however, less simple than this suggests. Normally disciplined at home by his guardian he worried most when beatings stopped: as the guardian's religious zeal abated he lost interest in restraining original sin in his charge. Yet Fraser was, he says brightening,

not altogether left by God . . . by Reason of the tyrannical Rigidity of a certain Schoolmaster I had, who delighted in the Scourging of Children, and would ofttimes pick Quarrels with me and scourge me for little or no Faults at all; so that every Day almost I was sure to be scourged, carry and do as I liked; which made my Life grievous and a Burden to me.[51]

One such tyrant turned to beating his breast: 'What man fearing God', asked Richard Kilby, 'can find in his heart to play the tyrant among Gods tender children, reviling, buffeting, striking, scourging . . . as if they were . . . limmes of the Devill, no man can with a safe conscience so cursedly use a beast, as I in word and deede have used my schollers.'[52] The answer, of course, is that he found in his heart what an authoritarian ideology had put there. It was the puritan view that children (since even elect children were as yet unregenerate) were limbs of

[50] *The Life of Adam Martindale Written by Himself*, ed. Richard Parkinson (1845), 14, 25, 21–2, 23, 18, 10.   [51] *Memoirs*, pp. 19–20.
[52] Richard Kilby, *The Burthen of a Loaden Conscience* (Cambridge, 1608), 85–6.

Satan. Oliver Heywood had fond childhood memories of himself
as 'a limb of satan'. 'I cannot remember', he muses, 'the time or
age, state or place wherein I was free from sin or perpetrating
thereof, what peevishnes, untowardnes, stubbornes,' and so on.
Improving on St Paul he concludes that 'when I was a child I
spake as a child, yea rather like a devil incarnate.' When tempted
to 'over-love' his own children on account of their outward
beauty he checks himself with the thought of their 'inward
deformity'.[53] Leah Marcus sees belief in original sin as a
stimulant to greater intimacy with children and concern for their
education.[54] It may be that amongst the artisan and yeoman
classes the doctrine of total depravity was assimilated to a less
punitive tradition of child-rearing. But it is hard to see how it can
have made for less severity and a number of autobiographies and
other sources reveal that it could sanction more. Increased
interest in the moral and spiritual welfare of children was not
necessarily a boon from the point of view of the child. 'The world
is too too ful', lamented Kilby, 'of petty tyrants.'[55] They seem
populous enough in the autobiographies to believe him.

More striking, however, than the brutal treatment actually
meted out is the extent to which punishment was masochistically
internalized. Kilby's inability to avoid transmitting the punitive
code to the next generation is made more understandable by his
own continued entrapment in it. 'When I was a child,' he says,
'and first began to understand and speake, then was the
foundation laide of all my miserie. Because I was not by and by,
entered into the faith, and feare of God, but the Devill had leisure
to take full possession of my heart.' He attributes experience of
'the terrible wrath of almightie God' to the feeling that 'I
horriblie dishonoured my father and mother even from my birth
untill they were dead, and buryed. Therefore I could never take
good roote in any place whithersoever I came.'[56]

This kind of inflation of guilt-feelings towards parents (mothers
included) appears to have been common. Michael Wigglesworth
assigns the cause of his suspected reprobation ('my spot is not the

---

[53] *Autobiography*, i. 153, 154, 146.

[54] *Childhood and Cultural Despair: A Theme and Variations in Seventeenth-Century Literature* (Pittsburgh, 1978), 55.

[55] Richard Kilby, *Hallelu-iah: Praise Yee the Lord, for the Unburthening of a Loaden Conscience* (Cambridge, 1618), 97.   [56] *Burthen*, pp. 1, 37.

spot of Gods children') to his 'want of natural affection to my father, in desiring the continuance of his life'.[57] Sarah Wight was precipitated into four years of despair by telling her mother that a hood she had lost was at her grandmother's house. Offering up the moral of her case she says: 'For if they knew the terrors that I have felt, the terrors of Hell, for sinning against light, against God, and against a Parent . . . if they knew what it is to have God hide his face, and be as an enemy, they would *not presume.*' Recovery was sealed by adding her mother's forgiveness to that of God.[58] When Nehemiah Wallington remembered filching small sums of money from his father a dozen years previously he 'thought that the tiles would fall down from the house and knock out my brains, and I thought as Cain did that everyone that meeteth me would kill me.' It was only when his father had reluctantly received his fourfold restitution and 'told me he had forgiven me' that his spiritual trouble lifted: 'Oh, the lightness of heart, Oh, the peace of conscience and the joy of the spirit I had then.'[59] George Trosse, whose father died young intending him to follow a lawyer's calling, lost money in trade and returned, in his early twenties, to the parental home. Angered by loss of his mother's favour he came home drunk one night, knelt down to receive her blessing, and fell flat on his face. He awakened next morning to years of torment.[60]

The oppressiveness of authority figures, from parents to God, gave rise, in Thomas Halyburton's phrase, to 'Hatred of my Reprovers'.[61] Yet ideological conditions denied children access to the devastating insight Richard Baxter was to advance: 'I saw that he that will be loved, must love; and he that rather chooseth to be more *feared* than *loved*, must expect to be hated, or loved but diminutively: And he that will have *Children*, must be a *Father*: and he that will be a Tyrant must be contented with Slaves.'[62] Children therefore took on themselves the entire blame for the 'unnaturalness' of their feelings towards parental figures, saw

[57] *Diary*, p. 17.
[58] Jessey, *Grace Advanced by the Spirit of Grace in an Empty Nothing Creature* (1647), sig. A7, p. 25.
[59] Quoted by P. S. Seaver, *Wallington's World: A Puritan Artisan in Seventeenth-Century London* (1985), 29–30.
[60] *Life*, pp. 4, 37, 45 ff.   [61] *Memoirs*, p. 12.
[62] Quoted by Webber in *The Eloquent 'I': Style and Self in Seventeenth-Century Prose* (Madison, 1968), 125.

them as symptoms of reprobation, and found themselves still less able to love a God who seemed bent on magnifying punishment to a factor of infinity. 'But as the persuasion of the fatherly love of God is not faste rooted in the reprobate,' said Calvin, 'so do they not soundely love him agayne as his children' (*Inst.* 3. 2. 12).

Escape was impossible. Caught out for a prank he thought undetectable the boy of Fraser's narration fathers the man who exclaims: 'O how mighty are Folks when they walk with the Lord!'[63] Puritan parents were advised, when beating children, to tell them that it was against God that they had sinned.[64] This may be one reason why the hand of God is so vigorous a presence in the autobiographies. Preachers made much of this analogy. 'And as other Fathers shew their anger by whipping the bodies of their children . . . So, for the like reason', said Thomas Goodwin, 'may God shew his anger, and chastise his children by lashing their spirits.'[65] God's circumvention, like the father's to the small child, was total: 'his *hand* can reach thee and avenge him on thee every moment.'[66] Martindale warns himself that it was 'a presumption to conclude we shall escape God's hand, because others are freed that are under like circumstances; God being bound to no rule but his owne good pleasure.'[67] Those who felt the punitive hand of God on them were tormented by the knowledge that escape was impossible: 'withdraw thine hand from me,' Richard Kilby had uselessly begged, 'and let me die.'[68] 'Oh that thou wouldst let go thy Hand,' longed the Second Spira, 'for ever forget me, and let me fall into my first nothingness again.'[69]

'Over each one of us', says Freud, explaining the appeal of religion, 'there watches a benevolent Providence which is only seemingly stern and which will not suffer us to become a plaything of the over-mighty and pitiless forces of nature.'[70] Things were less simple for the puritan. There was a genuine ambivalence as to the attitude behind the sternness. This appears to have its counterpart once more in the child's sense of

---

[63] *Memoirs*, p. 61.   [64] See Schücking, *The Puritan Family*, p. 76.
[65] *Childe of Light*, pp. 23–4.
[66] Swinnock, *Heaven and Hell Epitomized* (1663), 123.
[67] *Life*, p. 23.   [68] *Hallelu-iah*, p. 103.
[69] J. S., *The Second Spira* . . . (1693), 24.
[70] *The Standard Edition of the Complete Psychological Works of Sigmund Freud*, trans. J. Strachey *et al.* (1953–74), xxi. 19.

paternal hatred. Lawrence Stone comments on the physicality of treatment of children in this period (fondling as well as beating)[71] and this seems to have fed into ambivalent feelings about the governing attitude of an interventionist God; so Goodwin suggests:

If dandled in Gods lap afore and kist, now to be lasht with terrors, and his sharpest rods, and on the tendrest place, the conscience . . . how bitter is it to them! Once they say . . . their hearts were welcomed, their heads stroakt . . . But now *God is a terrour to them* . . . Once they never lookt to heaven but they had a smile; now they may cry day and night and not get a good look from him.

Goodwin reassures anyone prone to misconstrue God's intentions on the basis of such treatment that he 'whips thee with the same rod of his immediate wrath and displeasure, wherewith he lasheth those *that* are cut from his hand'.[72]

The other way in which paternal hostility could be inferred was banishment from his presence. 'The possibility of being left alone', points out Erich Fromm in *The Fear of Freedom*, 'is necessarily the most serious threat to the child's whole existence.'[73] It might seem in such a world, on the contrary, a blessed relief. This was not entirely so, however. Because of the father-God's protective-punitive ambivalence it was, as Fraser's gratitude for punishment suggests, a desperate feeling to be left alone: in large part, of course, because it boded the worst of all punishments, but also because of the masochistic dependence which developed in this authoritarian atmosphere. The patriarch developed in the child's mind into the guarantor of ultimate safety owing to his demonstrated power. Michael Wigglesworth asks apprehensively: 'wil he fall upon my neck and kiss me?' Yet punishment would have been almost as relieving: 'why hast thou not', he chillingly suggests to God, 'pluck't away from me by some sad stroke my dearest ones?'[74] Donne's plea 'O thinke mee worth thine anger, punish mee'[75] expresses a common feeling.

[71] The Family, Sex and Marriage in England 1500–1800 (New York, 1977), 167.

[72] *Childe of Light*, pp. 171, 40.

[73] *The Fear of Freedom* (1942; paperback, 1960), 16.

[74] *Diary*, pp. 13, 9.

[75] 'Good friday, 1613. Riding Westward', in *The Divine Poems*, ed. Helen Gardner, 2nd edn. (Oxford, 1978), 31. Further references to Donne's religious poetry will be to this edition and will be embodied in the text.

Neglect was exclusion, and exposure. '*It is a fearfull thing*', says Donne, '*to fall into the hands of the living God*; but to fall out of the hands of the living God, is a horror beyond our expression, beyond our imagination.' The claim may seem suspiciously politic but, amazing as it is, contemporaries appear to have been capable of feeling that 'when all is done, the hell of hels, the torment of torments is the everlasting absence of God, and the everlasting impossibility of returning to his presence.'[76] Anna Trapnel was 'perswaded that I was for ever shut out from the presence of God, which weight I could hardly bear, it was so burdensome, that I still cryed out, what shall I do?'[77]

No historian to my knowledge has examined the incidence of the 'casting off' of children in the seventeenth century. Yet it would seem both from fictional literature and autobiography to have been a common threat and not infrequent occurrence. Richard Norwood, whose case will be considered in detail, believed his father had 'cast me off' ('Confessions', p. 31). Martindale's brother was disowned. So too was John Rogers. To add just one more example, the Quaker Thomas Ellwood feared 'provoking my Father to use Severity towards me: and perhaps to the casting me utterly off'.[78] (His elder brother had been cast off already.) The emotional correspondence of this ultimate insecurity with spiritual anxiety easily suggests itself. Severe treatment might be (though hard for the child to believe) the chastening of the beloved; or it could be the prelude to being 'cut from his hand'. Once again Thomas Goodwin—who himself spent nearly seven years searching for signs of divine favour—supplies the emotional root and analogy:

and God takes the liberty that other fathers have, to shut His children out of his presence, when he is angry: and it is but *for a moment*; that is, in comparison of *eternity*; though happily it should be thus with him during a mans whole life; and he therefore takes liberty to do it, because he hath such an eternity of time, to reveale his kindnesse in; time enough for kisses and embraces, and to poure forth his love in.[79]

---

[76] *The Sermons of John Donne*, ed. G. R. Potter and E. M. Simpson (Berkeley, 1953–62), v. 266, 260. Further references to Donne's sermons will be to this edition and will be embodied in the text.

[77] *A Legacy for the Saints* (1654), 3.   [78] *The History of the Life* (1714), 46.

[79] Thomas Goodwin, *The Works . . . To which is Prefix'd an Account of the Author's Life from his own Memoirs* (1704), p. xv; *Childe of Light*, p. 13.

The theological term for this potentially lifelong (but to God, consolingly, momentary) anguish was 'desertion', on which Perkins wrote a treatise. The problem with desertions from the point of view of the deserted was that they seemed permanent, and what was worse the spiritual variety commonly were, as Perkins makes clear.[80] Goodwin thoroughly confuses the position by suggesting that God's 'dispensations of *desertion* . . . towards them already *regenerated*' are the inverted image of his '*visitations* towards *such* as often *attaine not to regeneration*'. He finds an analogy for this which seemed to please him: 'The needle of Gods favour and love *varying* as much (that I may so allude) towards Hell in their *Compasse* who shall be saved: as it doth heavenward in the other, many of whom arrive not thither.'[81] More in sorrow than anger he then remarks on the '*jealousies* and suspitions' people harbour towards God (Donne frequently reproaches himself for this[82]): and once suspicion is aroused they are 'apt to draw a misinterpretation of all Gods dealings with [them] to strengthen that conceit'.[83]

It was the ambiguity of providence, whose possible malevolence was as alive to the imagination as its hoped-for benevolence, which impelled the strenuous review of life a spiritual auto-biography often expresses. 'As all things wrought together for the best, and to do good to them that were called, according to his purpose,' says Bunyan in *Grace Abounding*, adding a typical Calvinist corollary to a Pauline text (Rom. 8: 28): 'so I thought that all things wrought for my dammage, and for my eternal overthrow' (157). 'I had a bad Construction of God and all his Ways to me, inasmuch as I thought God did in Wrath take away my Terrors,' confesses James Fraser. He comments on 'the Sadness of this Providence'—of his (Satanically inspired) picture of God

as One who had been watching all my Lifetime to do me Evil, that had been deluding me with Frames of Spirit, and that was now manifesting that hid Displeasure against me which he bore this long Time, and let me see he would take Vengeance on me. I thought, or apprehended, God's Wrath and Prejudice was more at my Person than Faults.

[80] *Works*, p. 496.   [81] *Childe of Light*, pp. 28–9.
[82] See, for example, *Devotions upon Emergent Occasions*, ed. John Sparrow (Cambridge, 1923), pp. 28, 31.   [83] *Childe of Light*, p. 42.

'Prayers unanswered', he is still firmly reminding himself on page 256, 'are not a Sign of Hatred.' It comes as a shock, and a revelation, when the tortured Fraser effuses:

The calling to Mind and seriously meditating on the Lord's Dealings with me . . . has done me very much Good, cleared my Case, confirmed my Soul of God's Love and my Interest in him, and made me love him. O what Good hath the Writing of this Book done me! . . . Scarce any Thing hath done me more Good.[84]

That writing these harrowing pages made him feel better speaks unwritten volumes for the sense of persecution which inhabited his imagination in daily life. It also exposes the main motive for autobiography however: to put if possible a good construction on a providence that often felt malevolent. A life described one of two narratives and the aim was to construct a narrative governed by a teleology of election, love, acceptance which could convincingly subordinate, while accounting for, all the evidence of experience that seemed to document a narrative governed by a teleology of reprobation, hatred, rejection. The sense of ultimate success or ultimate failure as the controlling principle of experience, the inability to see a variegated picture or to accept life as a communal actuality, not a story in the mind at all, is perhaps a cultural legacy for which an amalgam of protestantism and capitalism is to be thanked.

Critics of the spiritual autobiography have taken the view that the primary motives for writing were 'didactic and self-advertising'.[85] The godly man, says Delany, 'recounts his experiences for the encouragement and edification of his fellow-seekers after holiness'. Along with this goes a tendency to assume that the sense of sin and despair are being exaggerated. This is how Delany sees Richard Kilby's *The Burthen of a Loaden Conscience*: 'in the confession of his many sins Kilby reinforced the drama of his spiritual conflicts by proclaiming that it still lay in the balance whether he was to be saved or damned.' He then quotes Kilby's note 'To the Printer' which, he says, 'takes up this theme':

I protest before God, that nothing be mitigated concerning me; by turning *I am*, into *I was*, etc. It is very needefull for a man to know what

---

[84] *Memoirs*, pp. 60, 119–20, 277.
[85] L. D. Lerner, 'Puritanism and the Spiritual Autobiography', in *The Hibbert Journal*, 55 (1956–7), 373–86, p. 377.

he is. I know none but my selfe, I judge none but my selfe; I intreate others to give me leave to judge my selfe, because I feare the judgement of God, and would perswade people to feare God, that they may escape his judgement, and obtaine his mercies.[86]

Delany's reading of this statement misplaces the work in a foreign context of literary self-consciousness. Kilby's self-presentation as a probable reprobate may well add drama but it is much more difficult to believe that this is why he writes as he does than that he is telling the truth: he would scarcely have risked his salvation for a literary effect. He prefers to face the Scylla of divine rejection rather than allow himself to be sucked into the Charybdis of hypocrisy. Fastidious sincerity alone provides him with a chance of future release. 'And if I vary concerning some experiences in this,' says Anna Trapnel for similar reasons, 'in respect of doubting, and questioning union after sealing, it is my own experience, I must not record anothers experience; it may be some may scruple at it, and therefore I thought fit to mention it.'[87] Jane Turner was at first deterred from writing at all 'fearing lest through forgetfulness . . . I might possibly write something which was not, which I would not by any means willingly do; this I discerned to be a temptation for fear of hypocrisy.'[88] The wretched Michael Wigglesworth, on the other hand, moralizes on his folly in 'affirming that for truth which I doubt or am not certain of'.[89]

Kilby explains his scrupulosity: 'Believe verily . . . you are alwaies in the sight of God. He searcheth out your thoughts and affections: he hearkneth to your words, he vieweth your behaviour, and writeth up all in a booke, with purpose to judge you.'[90] Since God was the real author of the book of his life nothing could be gained by falsifying his own version. At Judgement Day the two would be examined together to see if they tallied. 'The *books* are opened,' says George Swinnock, 'both for Gods *omniscience* and *mans conscience*, by which all men are to be tryed for their everlasting lives and deaths.'[91] 'What is it,' asked the awed John Sheffield, 'to keep thy *soul-book*, to keep *Gods book*,

[86] *British Autobiography in the Seventeenth Century* (1969), 56.
[87] *Legacy for the Saints*, p. 12.
[88] *Choice Experiences of the Kind Dealings of God, before, in, and after Conversion* (1653), 4.
[89] *Diary*, p. 17.   [90] *Burthen*, p. 2.
[91] *Heaven and Hell Epitomized*, p. 131.

to keep this *Dooms-day-book*?'[92] William Perkins was privy even to procedure at the divine bar. First everyone would 'give an account of all the actions done in this life. Secondly . . . shall everie worke that they have done, be made manifest, even the most secret workes of all.' God was able to do this because he 'hath bookes of record, wherein all mens thoughts, and words, and deedes . . . are inrolled.' These books were 'first of all the infinite knowledge and providence of God: secondly the consciences of men, to testifie to our doings.' He thought it imperative 'to take a fore-hand reckoning of our selves', bringing the account into line with conscience (which could detect cheating) and with the apparent 'tracks and footsteps', as John Sharp later puts it, 'of a Divine over-ruling Providence'.[93]

Naturally the usual objective was to wrestle experience convincingly into the shape of election. Oliver Heywood marvels 'that god should make that the time of love which I thought was a time of loathing'. And he writes to steady this wobbly assurance: 'to make my calling, and election sure, not in itselfe, but to my selfe'. The first reason he gives for his relation is 'to lay open more carefully and convincingly my posture and gestures' so as to avoid being 'accursed by god in old age'.[94] Halyburton suggests mournfully to himself that writing his *Memoirs* 'may, at least, be of great use to my own confirmation'; he plainly needed 'confirmation' since his editors report that on his death-bed he called out: 'My Evidences are much clouded indeed.'[95] In a weak moment Vavasor Powell lent his diary to a distant friend so that he was left sweating with horror as he examined himself afresh on his sick-bed.[96] Even Kilby hoped his unsparing honesty would qualify him for the reception of grace; and so it turned out: ten years later he was able to publish a happy sequel.[97]

That autobiographers sought assurance from writing does not, however, justify scepticism about former or persisting gloom. Owen Watkins quotes Goodwin's observation that the Holy Spirit 'writes first all graces in us, and then teaches our consciences to read his handwriting,'[98] but neglects his eloquent

[92] *A Good Conscience the Strongest Hold* (1650), 234.
[93] *Works*, p. 937; John Sharp, *A Sermon Preach'd before the King and Queen at Whitehall the 12th November* (1693), 9.   [94] *Autobiography*, i. 135, 134, 151.
[95] *Memoirs*, pp. 57, 171.   [96] *The Life and Death*, pp. 12–13.
[97] *Hallelu-iah: Praise Yee the Lord, for the Unburthening of a Loaden Conscience.*
[98] *Puritan Experience*, pp. 11–12.

expression of the difficulty of fixing interpretation of a book whose contents change under the reader's gaze. The devil, Goodwin says, 'can turne downe that columne in the leaves of our hearts, wherein grace, or any thing that may comfort is written, and turn over only, and hold our eyes fixt to read nothing but that other wherein our *Errataes* and sins are written'.[99] In that autobiographers went the length of committing the book of conscience to paper they may, indeed, have been especially afflicted by the threat of reprobate content (which writing aimed to disarm). But they were merely formalizing an exercise other puritans considered incumbent on them and performed under the same pressures. 'Experience', says Powell,

is a Copy written by the Spirit of God upon the hearts of beleevers . . . And when Christ is with-drawne within the vaile, and the wings of faith clipped, and the flouds of temptation over-flow, and over-whelme the poore distressed doubting, despairing and drowning soule: this barke keepes, and holds up the soules-head above water, till the Arke returne.[100]

But, as Powell found, unless experience was objectively transcribed it could not be relied on to keep believers afloat.

The relationship between double providence and the production of autobiographical narrative can only be properly gauged over the course of a single work. At the cost therefore of thinning the generalizable evidence, especially—since every case differed—that concerning social and economic circumstances, I am singling out Richard Norwood's 'Confessions'. (The chapter on *Grace Abounding* will amplify some of the points.) A neglected document of the puritan imagination in any case, Norwood's autobiography also offers incidental advantages as a case study. First, it was unpublished—plainly by choice since Norwood did publish other works, on military fortifications, navigation, and trigonometry, as well as one on a pious subject.[101] So he escapes any version of the charge that he was writing for public effect. Second, it was written between 1639 and 1640 (when Norwood

---

[99] *Childe of Light*, p. 116.

[100] Vavasor Powell, *Spirituall Experiences of Sundry Believers* (1652), sig. A2^v.

[101] See *DNB*; Norwood's *Trigonometrie* (1631) made a modest contribution to English science (see Nicholas Tyacke, 'Science and Religion at Oxford before the Civil War', in D. Pennington and K. V. Thomas, edd., *Puritans and Revolutionaries: Essays in Seventeenth-Century History Presented to Christopher Hill* (Oxford, 1978), 87).

turned 50). Predating the spate of autobiographies which appeared in the 1650s it is therefore largely independent of generic constraints (formulaic expression of experience, the force of precedent in structuring the work and selecting relevant material). Its contents belong, moreover, to the first three decades of the century, supplementing the case that the persecutory imagination bound up with Calvinism and puritan culture had a continuous life from Perkins to Bunyan. Norwood was, for much of his life, a loner who moved through a variety of social milieux; and again this confers documentary value on his record: the language of puritan culture pervaded his mind in spite of the fact that his nomadic existence detached him from any closed community in which such linguistic saturation might be assumed.

Norwood's example shows us that ideology need not be, in any meaningful sense, chosen by the individual; rather a nexus of beliefs takes root in the personality, shapes the subject, because the psychic soil is prepared by social circumstances. His record, in particular his persuasive recreation of the constructions placed on experience in childhood, enables us to follow the interaction between available language and social process in the evolution of the subject.

Edmund Gosse observes in *Father and Son*: 'precisely as my life ceases to be solitary it ceases to be distinct.' It is not merely that his recollection grows indistinct; his life itself ceases to be a distinct (bounded and perceptible) object. The idea of a continuous inner self presumes a consciousness of estrangement from its social world (the inception of which at the age of 6 Gosse remembers with brilliant distinctness). Curiously, the solitary life Gosse recalls is represented by 'scenes in which my Father and I were the sole actors within the four walls of a room'.[102] The solitariness of the puritan autobiographer was also relational: not so much aloneness as alienation. The feeling of aloneness was associated with that of rejection. Identity split into social actor, a self-protective conformist unpersuaded of his or her sincerity, and a guilty inner rebel who ascribed recalcitrance not to subjection to humiliating treatment and unreasonable expectation but to personal unworthiness. The sense of being discriminated

---

[102] Edmund Gosse, *Father and Son* (Harmondsworth, 1949), 157, 28–34.

against focused the self as the object of discrimination and stimulated too the fantasy of an ego-ideal who would be favoured and accepted.

Norwood reports his parents' 'severe disposition and carriage towards me', justifying it in the usual terms as 'suitable to that mass of sin and folly which was bound up in my heart' (p. 4). Two other areas of alienating social experience were inseparable, even in his young mind, from Calvinist ideology. School, a half-way house, connected home (confirming the punitive character of authority—he has a general memory of 'sharp and grievous stripes' (p. 7)) with wider society (impressing on him the remoter forces which could conspire against him).

A pathetic incident at his elementary school suggests the dominant pattern experience assumed for him from a young age:

There came a gentlewoman, a stranger, one day to visit my dame, and we (the scholars) being at play and she sitting at the door, I merely out of pride ran before her with all my might that she might see how fast I could run, thinking she would praise me for it, and just as I came against her, fell and broke my face sorely, that I think I could not rise again till my dame came and took me up and paid me well for it.

It is little wonder, since he was extrapolating from the conduct of more immediate authority figures, that he found God's love for him hard to credit. Assured of it by the same schoolmistress, his private self had responded: 'I thought it no small matter to be beloved of God, but I doubted much whether that were so or how they could know it was so' (p. 7). In themselves such early incidents might perhaps have receded into insignificance, but they were compounded by remoter sources of discrimination.

The nature of the Norwood family's decline was a common story. The 'Confessions' records economically forced moves from Stevenage to Berkhampstead to Shutlanger to Stony Stratford. Reaching the first of these in his narration, Norwood comments on his father:

it was great losses which he sustained that had brought him thither; for having been brought up from his youth as a gentleman, when afterwards he was married he took a farm at Stevenage . . . and whether through his unskilfulness in that course of life, or otherwise, I know not, but he had very great losses in sheep and otherwise. (p. 11)

Contrasting them with the fortunate few who gained advancement D. M. Palliser speaks of the many who 'had to struggle
hard to maintain their social position, often by moving geographically to avoid dipping downwards socially, while others
were less fortunate still and sank into obscurity'. The period
between Norwood's birth in 1590 and 1620 witnessed the most
widespread decline and loss of land in particular.[103] But
Norwood did not, for that, suffer the effects any less acutely. On
the contrary they took on for him dark ideological tones which
would not have impinged on his mental world had not a more
general need for explanation of a social phenomenon been felt.
One notes the still-baffled phrase 'or otherwise, I know not'. It is
an early example of a gawkily insistent integrity in Norwood's
style, a refusal to be crisply overdecisive. Norwood has no
language in which to speak about the market forces which were
transforming land economy; but he is intuitively right not to
plump for his father's incompetence, while at the same time the
cultural habit of attributing failure to personal guilt is registered.
As in many a literary childhood it was at school that declining
family fortune made its deepest mark on his imagination.

The child's sensitivity to social discrimination was attached to
a grammar-school rival, Adolphus Speed—'a gentleman's son'—
towards whom he had ambivalent feelings:

I thought though I was before him in learning, yet God had endued him
with sundry gifts and virtues which I had not, and that he was much in
the favour of God but that I was not, or not so much, and this jealousy
possessed me for the most part, yet I loved him very well. I did also
much reverence and affect my master there, though I scarce knew it
then, fear more prevailing. And though I then thought him to be more
sharp and severe towards me than to others, yet doubtless he did affect
me very tenderly, as was manifest by his frequent commendations of
me. (p. 11)

Measuring himself against Adolphus strengthened his sense of
rejection: his works could not make him acceptable while
Adolphus was the incarnation of the grace he lacked. The wistful
honesty—'yet I loved him very well'—suggests that the rival
(whose gains were his losses) was also an alternative self. The

---

[103] *The Age of Elizabeth: England under the Later Tudors 1547–1603* (1983), 93–4. See
related discussion of the decline of Bunyan's family in chapter 3.

favour of God comes naturally into play and elides easily into what is a repeated recollection of his master's apparently discriminatory treatment (see also p. 5). His inferences build on the earlier doubt of God's love for him.

Autobiographical narrative, it begins to emerge, is being constructed within the autobiographical narrative. A story takes shape in the child's mind based on the idea of rejection. It was well fed with pertinent external detail. Knowing that the family had to leave Berkhampstead Richard found himself in competition with Adolphus for a maintenance scholarship at the school, to which academic merit seemed to entitle him. But the school's patroness Lady Paget intervened (Norwood later learns that Mr Speed was her steward) to award to Adolphus 'that maintenance which was before moved and intended for me'. Norwood's rueful (and apparently contemporaneous) reflections readily fit the shapes Calvinist theology provided:

And he surely was fitter for such a happy condition, being of a tender, gentle, and sweet disposition (so far as I could then judge) but I . . . of an aspiring mind . . . and possessed with much inward pride and vanity of mind, and yet on the contrary (as a just punishment of the former) as often subject to a very dejected and despairing mind without any very notable cause for either. (p. 12)

On a grandee's caprice or discrimination, irrespective of his efforts, Norwood's identity as a reject was reinforced. The word 'condition', like 'estate', carries double reference to social and spiritual senses. As a young man of 20, for instance, he 'thought it a blessed condition to live and especially to die in the favour of God' (p.35). That his father was, as he keeps stressing, 'much decayed in his estate' (pp. 6, 30, 31), moreover, is not unrelated to Norwood's spiritual legacy. He observes of his 17-year-old self: 'I was always (to my best remembrance) convinced in my thoughts that I was in an evil estate' (a conviction which proved particularly agonizing when he lay on his sick-bed expecting the arrival of devils) (p. 68). Deprived of affection and gentlemanly prestige (Adolphus was a 'gentleman's son'; the woman he had wanted to impress with his running was a 'gentlewoman') the child was bound, in an educational environment which nurtured ambition and a society which Lawrence Stone points out observed one essential social division, between those who were

gentlemen and those who were not, to have an aspiring mind.[104]
But induced self-denigration was his dominant attitude so that
his own mind administered punishment (which his adult self still
thinks 'just'). Mental lashings were the more impressive for the
ideological invisibility of their actual source. No other explanation
for his mind turning on its owner with such viciousness was
available to him than that a spiritual power could usurp it for
punitive purposes.

Norwood's re-creation of the feelings of a child, on his
impending departure from school, can scarcely be matched in the
seventeenth century. He has a reason for remembering: they
contribute to the providential narrative, fidelity to which is
imperative:

Surely God made me sensible of the misery ensuing when I came from
Berkhampstead, for my schoolmaster there, being as I conceived
something sharper to me than to my fellows, when I knew I must
shortly go from him I thought I would then be even with him, for I
purposed then to carry myself very cheerfully without any sign of grief
at departure, that so he might see I did not love him. But as the day
grew nearer, qualms of grief and dismay began to seize on my heart, and
much more when that woeful day was come and that my master called
me aside, giving me good admonitions, and I to take my leave of him
and my fellows. Then my heart was ready to break and my eyes to gush
out abundantly with tears. And not without cause, for from that time
forwards I went no more to school to any purpose . . . but passed my
time in a more fruitless and dissolute manner. (pp. 5–6)

When that dismal day came that I must depart I had sundry thoughts,
as to hide myself in some corner near the school, etc. but I thought all
would be in vain; I should then be sent away with disgrace. So I
departed with a most sorrowful heart, sprinkling the way with tears.
(p. 12)

The boy's plucky but failed attempt to disguise his feelings
reveals the masochistic dependence on ambivalently punitive
authority (is it, or is it not, vindictively motivated?) which works
itself into a permanent feature of Norwood's identity. In the
second passage the quasi-biblical 'hide myself', 'depart', and
'sprinkling the way with tears' evoke expulsion from Eden (after
Adam and Eve 'hid themselves from the presence of the Lord'

---

[104] Lawrence Stone, *The Crisis of the Aristocracy 1558–1641* (Oxford, 1965), 49.

(Gen. 3: 8)). His aspiring mind receives due punishment. He does not leave school but is banished by a well-orchestrated providential campaign.

Keith Thomas observes of providence as an interpretative tool: 'there was no way in which the theory once accepted could be faulted.'[105] This holds for persecution as well as protection. Norwood's life (as it evolved, and not merely in laundered retrospect) turned into a (sometimes allegorical) narrative exegesis of the sense of identity induced by his childhood. *Déclassé* (at 15 he became a fishmonger's apprentice) and lumbered with feelings of persecution, he found, even in ostensibly pleasant events, confirmation of his alienated selfhood. He remembers distinctly (because of the *then* split between social actor and narratorial spectator) a puritan widow allowing her children to play with him on account of his 'sober and serious countenance and carriage. But I thought they were deceived, whatsoever my countenance did promise; I knew the disposition of my heart was otherwise' (p 13). By this time he was frequently engaged in reading such forbidding works as Arthur Dent's *Sermon of Repentance*, which must have fortified a cumulative reprobate logic.[106]

Realizing the hopelessness of his position—the impossibility, that is, of bringing his sense of interior identity into tolerable relationship with his outward social functions—Norwood tried to dissolve the discrepancy by estranging himself physically. Heading eventually for Rome (ideologically the remotest spot on the globe) he completed his alienation by feigning Catholicism and taking the sacraments. The narrative is strangely divided between practical exigency (he begs his way, with seeming aimlessness, from place to place; pretending to be a Catholic serves the purpose of obtaining a pass into Rome) and a generally relegated, always implicit, sense of the spiritual significance of his actions. The two levels cannot be conveniently assigned to the subject of the narration and the narrating subject respectively. Since there was no apparent material gain in going to Rome (he thought he would have to beg there too) and since

---

[105] *Religion and the Decline of Magic* (1971), 82.

[106] Arthur Dent, *A Sermon of Repentance: A Very Godly Sermon, etc.* (1583). There were at least twenty-one impressions of this work by 1638. Dent was, of course, the popular puritan author who influenced Bunyan.

he then 'conceived [his] dissembling' to be 'very offensive to
God' it seems that he was making a courageous bid for
autonomy: 'And then did I now as it were bid adieu to parentage,
education, friends, country, religion.' A bolder statement of
individualism could scarcely be framed, but a corrective retrospect hastily adds:

But miserable and foolish man, I understood not the many dangers of
soul and body whereinto I cast myself and how every step I went, as it
was further from my native country so it led me and alienated my heart
farther from God, from religion, and from a desire to return. (p. 22)

Norwood is not primly rebuking his unregenerate self here but
pityingly anticipating the psychic turbulence he was running
into. Posing as a Catholic, he says,

grieved me exceedingly, and being much perplexed in mind with
objections on both sides, and in consideration of my forlorn condition,
and no longer able to contain myself I went aside out of the way into the
standing corn (being harvest time) and there wept abundantly till I
think I was something distracted. (p. 21)

The interesting phrase is 'on both sides', as is 'alienated . . . from
a desire to return' in the previous quotation. Reduced to beggary
(the lowest 'condition' of all), anguished, and alone on the one
side, he leaves us to infer what the objections were *on the other side*.
Objections to return were evidently weightier. Destitution
abroad measures the unbearableness of self-alienation in England.

Now 'resolved for Rome', Norwood found in the psychic forces
which preyed on his conscious mind the evidence of the
illusoriness of his autonomy. Hostility spilt out, as he travelled,
from his unconscious on to the external world. His suppressed
conscience was projected on to passers-by whose staring so riled
him that he 'was ready to fall on some of them to do them a
mischief'. Unable to withstand their gaze he hid himself till
nightfall: 'and so travelled by night and hid myself for the most
part by day and went through byways for several nights' (p. 22).
Developing the narrative of his life into a kind of natural allegory
(an aspect of the puritan imagination my chapter on *The Pilgrim's
Progress* will explore) he wishes futilely to hide from God, whose
agents the peering strangers have become. Night travel both
symbolizes the wish to black out the part of his mind that
condemns him, and fulfils it, to the extent that the punitive

attitude has been passed on to the strangers (who can neither see nor be seen by him). Once again Norwood's record defies critical assumptions about an after-the-event overlay of piety; the paranoid providential reading of events was already inscribed in his mind, dictating not just interpretation but conduct. The inefficacy of his wish-fulfilling subterfuge soon discovered itself, moreover, in a way that both conforms to Calvin's diagnosis of reprobate behaviour and succeeds in being unimpugnably idiosyncratic.

Calvin applauded the

revengement of Gods majestie, which doeth somuch the more vehemently strike their consciences as they more labor to fly away from it: They do in dede loke about for all the starting holes that maie be, to hide themselves from the presence of the Lord [and again efface it from their mind], but whether they wil or no, they are still holden faste tied For howsoever sometime it [conviction] semeth to vanish away for a momente, yet it ofte returneth againe, and with new assaulte doeth runne upon them: so that the reste whiche they have, if they have any at all, from torment of conscience, is much like to the slepe of drunkardes or phrenetike men, which even while they slepe do not quietely reste, because they are at every momente vexed with horrible and dredfull dreames. (*Inst.* 1. 3. 2)

Conviction with new assault ran upon the mind of the fleeing Norwood (who had tried to efface God from it by concealing himself) in the form of dire horrific dreams which he calls 'the mare'. It was, like his childhood despair, 'a just judgment of God for my wilful blindness and apostacy contrary to my own conscience and contrary to that light and those principles . . . planted in me' (p. 27). Travelling by night did not defeat God's more intimate agents. The long arm of paternal providence reached out and struck him the more vehemently for the resolute bid for freedom. Often in these terrible nightmares he found himself in hell and 'Usually in my dreams methought I saw my father always grievously angry with me' (p. 26).

The mare, says Norwood, 'seldom . . . left me without nocturnal pollutions' (p. 26). At the risk of getting tangled in psychoanalytic speculation it is worth saying that these too had a role in shaping Norwood's narrative. Male guilt often fastened on masturbation and wet dreams. Because they were secretly shaming and virtually inevitable (as sin was for the graceless) they were apparent reprobate symptoms particularly difficult to argue away. Michael Wigglesworth is forever wringing his hands over his nocturnal pollutions and Richard Kilby, 'before God a most ougly monster, and a detestable loathsome wretch', thought of resorting to '*Origens* remedy' (self-castration) for his masturbation.[107] Perkins, the author most frequently cited by Norwood, treats 'nocturnall pollutions' and masturbation as sins against the Commandment, 'Thou shalt not commit adultery.'[108] It is typical of the acted allegory of Norwood's life that, instead merely of dreaming of castration as the punishment for his spunky travels, he actually took a knife to bed with him (so as to deal with a nasty furry little animal that kept crawling on his belly during the mare). Norwood blames this near self-mutilation ('it was God's mercy that I had not by this means slain myself') on 'the wily fiend' (p. 26) but it seems no coincidence that he connects this experience with his return to England. The mare abated on the way (and recrudesced, moreover, when he resumed his voyaging); nocturnal emissions ended (p. 27). The drive to self-assertion was forced, it appears, to retreat before the threat of emasculation (or death). Geographical distance could not purchase freedom when patriarchal authority was so fully internalized that he could become the agent of his own punitive destruction.

This is perhaps an apposite moment at which to contrast *Robinson Crusoe*. In his chapter 'The Transition to Fiction', in *Defoe and Spiritual Autobiography* (New York, 1971), G. A. Starr ignores crucial differences between the anonymous Private Gentleman's autobiography, on which he mainly relies, and the novel. The Gentleman is afflicted by 'trouble of mind' and suicidal temptations on which he reflects: 'I smarted the more, I'm confident, for the neglect of paternal Advice; let the Rebellious consider it, and know assuredly, God may be a slow, but will be a sure Avenger of any Degree of such unnatural Contempt.'[109] This looks back to Norwood rather than forward to Crusoe, whose experience of horror at rebellion against patriarchal authority is reduced to the vestige of a superseded ideology. So far as superficial parallels go (running off from

---

[107] *Diary*, pp. 6, 50, 80–1, 93; *Burthen*, p. 52.   [108] *Works*, p. 59.
[109] *An Account of Some Remarkable Passages in the Life of a Private Gentleman* (1708), 134–5.

home, spatial-spiritual equations, adventurism) Norwood's 'Confessions' resembles *Robinson Crusoe* more closely than does the Gentleman's *Account*. That it was written seventy years earlier undermines the thesis that the characteristics of *Account* express a literary process of metamorphosis into the novel, and makes more credible the view that the novel was fostered by larger forces (which at the same time, indeed, transformed the structures of feeling typical of later autobiographies[110]). The spiritual autobiography of the seventeenth century supplies merely a structural skeleton. The religion which animated it has died.

Owen Watkins is reminded, when Norwood takes to hiding by day in Italy, of Crusoe 'whose life on the island has often been interpreted as a symbol of the loneliness that is the price of a developed self-consciousness'.[111] But Crusoe never experiences this acute alienation from other people. Watkins also cites Norwood's feeling, when cast away on an island near Bermuda for five days, that 'it was one of the greatest punishments in the world, yea I thought it was one of the greatest punishments in hell.' Crusoe does not, after a period of adjustment, find physical isolation so terrible either. Norwood himself remarks how odd it is that, apt to 'retire myself much from company', he should feel these terrors of solitude (p. 54). What the paradox points up again is his enslavement to a definition of himself in relation to a patriarchal figure. He is not so much alone as, in the puritan term, a 'castaway',[112] a reject. Crusoe is able to make the most inimical circumstances favour him and thereby secure divine approval.

Donald Davie asks: 'Which is the more characteristically Calvinist response—Cowper's seeing the solitude of Alexander Selkirk as the worst of all possible privations, or Defoe's Crusoe exulting in it, as the condition of his autonomy?'[113] Characteristically (though not in Cowper's case) the responses belong to different eras. Crusoe's reflects the increased confidence in management of the future made possible to the bourgeoisie by

---

[110] See Delany, *British Autobiography*, p. 79, for reference to smug autobiographies such as Joseph Lister's and Gervase Disney's which, characteristically, appear from the beginning of the eighteenth century.

[111] *Puritan Experience*, p. 78.   [112] See van Beek, *Puritan Vocabulary*.

[113] Donald Davie, *A Gathered Church* (1978), 9.

economic betterment and comparative predictability. Corres-
pondingly the psychological distinction is between masochistic
dependence on authority (the feeling of rejection) and the
confident grasp of life's controls. While Crusoe identifies his
'original sin' as rebellion against his father in the form of 'not
being satisfy'd with the station wherein God and nature has
plac'd' him, his vagrant temperament is quickly seen as the
condition of his success. He becomes a father to Man Friday, a
king with his own subjects, is implicitly compared even to God as
deliverer, turns himself into the conscious agent, rather than the
victim, of providence, and returns to England to find his father,
and the reproof he embodied, defunct.[114] While Crusoe leaves a
securely middle-class home, impelled by self-confidence—a self-
improving adventurist, only vestigially sinful—Norwood leaves a
degraded home and truncated education, driven by self-
alienation—condemned already and bound, whatever course he
takes, to confirm his reprobation. Crusoe's God is the God of
bourgeois dissenters; Norwood's God is the God of anomic
puritans.

Contrast with Crusoe helps to clarify Norwood's reasons for
not returning to England, of which this passage prompts
understanding:

> once or twice for a short time my heart did relent a little and had some
> thoughts and purposes to return into England and to settle myself I
> cared not in how mean a calling so I might have the favour of God and
> turn away his displeasure, which I conceived lay heavily upon me, but
> these purposes were not constant but soon vanished again. (p. 27)

The idea of the calling is at the heart of Norwood's adult sense of
his reprobation. Crusoe's discontent with his station can be
breezily conveyed because social and spiritual attitudes have
shifted. God helps those who help themselves. But Norwood is
spiritually condemned for being a social misfit. Perkins laid it
down that 'as soone as ever a man begins to looke towards God,
and the wayes of his grace, he will not rest till he find out some
warrantable calling.'[115] It is not difficult to see why Norwood
could not feel he was called to be a fishmonger: it was discrepant

---

[114] Daniel Defoe, *Robinson Crusoe*, Everyman (1945), 142, 152, 175, 179, 185, 202.
[115] Quoted by Robert S. Michaelsen in 'Changes in the Puritan Concept of Calling
or Vocation', in *the New England Quarterly*, 26 (1953), 315–36, p. 320.

with his background. Yet, said John Cotton, a man 'should stoop
to any work his calling led him to . . . if it appears to be his
Calling, faith doth not picke and choose, as carnall reason will
doe'.[116] Failure to be satisfied, to 'settle' himself in whatever
occupation he undertook, was also a sign of reprobation—so
while Norwood's pious wish to settle himself in a mean calling is,
in his menacing circumstances, understandable, so too was his
reluctance to turn back. In the volatile economic conditions of
the period feeling settled was far from easy. Even the anxiously
diligent and modest artisan Nehemiah Wallington can report, in
middle age, that 'my murmuring and discontent with my
calling . . . is a great project of the devil to bring me to misery.'[117]

The knowledge that no good purpose could be served by
returning to a calling with which he could not be contented was
counterparted, for Norwood, by his fear of fake conversion. His
father came into this. His minatory dream presence had been a
response to Norwood's sense of primal disobedience based on the
belief that, as Perkins had declared, the first filial imperative was
'in the choice of a lawfull calling, wherein the child is to be
ordered and appointed at the discretion of the parent'.[118] In an
attempt on his return to England to assuage guilt, or turn away
God's pursuing displeasure, Norwood wrote his father a penitent
letter. Receiving what seems to have been a kind reply he put it
to one side, convicted by it of his own hypocrisy. As with the
puritan widow interior awareness was at odds with his conformist
self: 'I am not the man my father takes me to be.' He lacked the
'childlike affection, and desire of reformation' (p. 32) his letter
had pretended. He had 'forsaken the calling wherein my parents
had placed me, and betaken myself to another course of life
[initially at sea] without and against their liking and without any
due calling or encouragement from God' (p. 16). His feelings had
developed and accreted under the impression that his father had
'cast me off'. A lachrymose letter and forgiving words in reply
were not enough to dissipate these, so that his own rockbed
disposition testified against the authenticity of his repentance.

[116] *The Puritans: A Sourcebook of their Writings*, ed. Perry Miller and Thomas H.
Johnson (New York, 1963), i. 323.

[117] Quoted by Seaver, *Wallington's World*, p. 124.

[118] *Christian Oeconomie: Or a Short Survey of the Right Manner of Erecting and Ordering a
Familie, according to the Scripture*, trans. T. Pickering (1609), 147.

An actual father, however mellowed, exercised no control over the image of himself that stalked his son's unconscious. Unable to credit, and thus embrace, paternal love for the real him, Norwood bracketed remoteness from his parents with apostasy: 'I was much estranged, as in religion so likewise in my affection towards them' (p. 31); 'I am not,' he was acutely conscious, 'as my father thinks of me, a Protestant.' He was particularly sceptical (and continued to be so 'many years after') of the truth of his father's assurance: 'I doubt not but God hath reserved thee to some special good end, if good use be made of his admirable providence' (p. 32).

So long as he was unable to settle in a calling Norwood could not 'settle' (see pp. 34–5) in his faith. Particular (economic) calling and general (spiritual) calling, prerequisite to salvation, were psychologically interlocked. He reacted angrily to a minister, Mr Elton, who lectured him on just the related points— disobedience to parents and forsaking his calling—on which he accused himself. He had small chance of making a go, he protested, of his father's drastically depleted stock. The anger appears to have been fuelled not just by guilt-feelings: 'His words though true,' Norwood admits, 'did touch me very nearly, yet withal I apprehended myself to be contemned of him because I was poor and as it were in a forlorn condition' (pp. 32–3). The two meanings of 'condition' appear to meet here. We cannot know for certain that Norwood was not projecting his own self-dissatisfaction on to the cleric. Probably not, however, since he was much impressed by another minister's attentiveness ('though I was in a poor habit, yet he caused me to sit down by him' (p. 34)). It is at least certain that Norwood could not be spiritually relieved while 'destitute of a calling' (p. 33), and poor. A Calvinist doctrine (one of the Five Points agreed at the Synod of Dort) which particularly bothered him was the perseverance of the saints.[119] The elect, it maintained, never fall away. Since relapse was terminal the possibility of inauthentic conversion was a powerful deterrent. Behaving penitently to his father, adopting a calling, and testing out the possibilities of conversion were of a piece: he was not in a position psychologically (though knowing this was itself a torment to him) to sustain any of them

---

[119] See Kendall, *Calvin and English Calvinism*, p. 1 n. 4.

without hypocrisy: a hypocrisy which would irrevocably damn him. He set sail once more (pp. 35–6; see also pp. 66–7).

Things seemed to improve. While at sea Norwood discovered a talent for the science of navigation and through that God gave him, he reflects, 'a good entrance and settling in that which should afterwards be my calling' (p. 41)—that is mathematics. The good progress he made both redeemed his arbitrarily inflicted failure at school and offered him the prospect of a calling (in its conflated senses). 'It pleased the Lord,' he says, 'to raise me from that poor condition whereinto I had cast myself in my outward estate.' His reported response again elides secular into spiritual in a way that suggests their (then) inseparability for him:

For partly by nature and partly by many accidents that had befallen me I was much inclined to a dejected and despairing mind. But the Lord having given me so good success in my studies, I began to think that the good things which belonged unto others belonged also to me, and what was attainable by others might also be attained by me, if I did diligently use the means. Some glances I had also at some times towards heaven and heavenly things, the Lord inviting and calling me but I found no affection to those things but such a violent stream of affections carrying me another way to evil that it seemed to be altogether in vain to strive against them. (p. 45)

He records here the movement of his mind through three phases. A despairing sense of his continuous selfhood had evolved in accordance with the Calvinist view that an implanted essential nature, in his case reprobate, is reinforced and exposed by an answering divine providence. The absence of theological terms from the opening statement helps us to see as the passage progresses how naturally feelings about himself induced by social experience assumed an intensifying religious meaning. In the new circumstances, since he took every experience to be beamed on to him by God, he immediately extrapolated from his success a new direction for his life in general. By the end of the second sentence he has slipped into puritan discourse: the phrase 'if I did diligently use the means' refers at once to his studies and, since it is a puritan cliché, to the means of his salvation. 'You should thinke thus,' says Henry Scudder, for example (offering a grim variant on Pascal's wager): 'if I doe not use the meanes of

Salvation, I shall certainly perish everlastingly.'[120] Norwood himself later uses the phrase in specifically theological contexts (see pp. 73, 92, 94). It is then a natural progression to observe his glances towards heaven. But turning round the narrative of his life was a less simple affair, as the directional metaphor in the last sentence indicates. He could not rub out his past—both because it would have to become part of a narrative of elect providence and because it had constituted his nature and moulded his feelings. Conscious wishes counted for nothing. He spectated impotently on himself drawn to catastrophe: 'I found myself carried away with a stream of corrupt affections into foul and enormous sins and so conceived myself to be going along in that highway that leadeth unto Hell' (p. 45). Approach to repentance ignited the smouldering deposit of resentment ('corrupt affections' is his self-mystifying phrase) years of felt discrimination had left in the psyche—just as the attempt at autonomy had brought internalized punitive powers leaping to the surface.

Norwood's persisting problem was 'feeling myself destitute of the wedding garment of love' (p. 65). A useful image (again from a common stock of puritan biblical appropriations[121]), it unites his feelings with God's posture towards him: since God has not given him love (or the feeling of being loved) he is denuded of the love he should return. Trapped in this impasse what he most coveted was a 'middle estate' (p. 64) between heaven and hell: freedom from an ideology which forced on him a binary sense of the narrative of his destiny as controlled either by God or, on God's rejection, by the devil; freedom from the necessity, he may perhaps be interpreted to mean, of seeing his life as governed by ultimate success or ultimate failure. The middle estate, which in a secular sense was to develop into a reliable social reality, was not credible for him. In fact because his feelings about God and himself did not improve they followed a gradient of decline: 'To hell I conceived surely I must needs tend,' he concluded,

---

[120] Henry Scudder, *The Christians Daily Walke in Holy Securitie and Peace* (1635), 550.

[121] Oliver Heywood, for example, wanted to 'see whether I have that wedding garment' (*Autobiography*, i. 134). Other autobiographers longed to escape from the polarities protestantism had forced on the imagination: 'For I did not care whether I was Happy,' said Lodowick Muggleton, 'so I might not be Miserable. I car'd not for Heaven so I might not go to Hell, but I could not be sure I should go to Heaven, nor certain I should escape Hell which was a great perplexity to my Mind, not knowing which way to help myself out of God's Hands' (*The Acts of the Witnesses* (1699), 25).

evolving a simile which again reveals the imaginative interpenetration of all levels of his experience: 'I seemed as it were to
be within the ken of it, even as a ship after a long voyage
discovers the place whereunto she saileth.' Traditionally the ship
reaching harbour signified the heavenly haven after life's voyage;
Norwood's experience of seafaring as sinful rebellion invests his
final destination with the opposite meaning—a meaning reinforced by Calvin's promotion of the belief that the afflictions of
the reprobate were 'a certayne entrie of hell, from whense they
doe alredy see a far of their eternall damnation' (*Inst*. 3. 4. 32).
With punctilious qualification which conveys an impression of
raw sincerity Norwood recalls the apprehension that his reprobate
journey neared its end:

I apprehended my race to be almost finished and to be as it were within
the hearing of the screechings and yellings of tormented souls, not by
any sensible noise but as it were an impression of the species of it, as
audible as a sensible noise. (p. 70)

At the age of 26 Norwood underwent an experience of
conversion. Renewed terror had caused him to rebound once
more into submissiveness. He attributes conversion to the
influence of Perkins and Augustine. No doubt such maxims of
Perkins as 'that the right way to goe unto heaven, is to saile by
hell'[122] had a cheering effect but Norwood's more moving
passages seem quite beyond the range of Perkins's influence. He
began to glimpse a different picture of God:

That beam of light of the knowledge of God in Christ which shined into
my heart began to dissolve all those foggy mists of darkness by little and
little. I conceived and understood him to be he who giveth to all things
not only their beings but also their well-beings; whose mercy is over all
his works, who hath a care of all his creatures, giving them food in due
season, filling the hearts of all with food and gladness; who giveth to
everything its grace and comeliness. (p. 74)

His former conception of God is blamed on Satan. Yet, again,
there is no facile narrative U-turn. His heart, he knows, has been
'deeply . . . poisoned and forestalled with a . . . harsh conceit of
God and of his ways, which I can very hardly shake off unto this
day' (p. 75). The imaginatively persuasive puritan God of his

[122] *Works*, p. 457.

imagination had not changed his spots. Seduced into laying claim to faith, he soon fell over the puritan tripwire (the doctrine of perseverance) of which he had earlier been wary (p. 92). It scarcely seems possible, but the reprobate line of his narrative had further yet to travel. As he 'looked back' now he saw himself 'far entered within the gates of hell' (p. 94). Paranoia reached an unprecedented pitch. Satan, he felt, harried him: 'It is hard to express the manner of it, but sometimes he seemed to lean on my back or arms or shoulder, sometimes hanging on my cloak or gown' (p. 93). He even wondered whether he was himself a devil (p. 95). The mare returned and with it the old picture of God as 'hard and unmerciful'. He hated God and 'rage[d] against Him as the damned spirits do' (p. 96). This made him a prime target of the persecutory providence so that he had to dodge the horses and carts aimed at him as he made his way to a minister's house in search of spiritual relief (pp. 98–9).

From the time of his conversion Satan became a vigorous antagonist. This was the only conceivable way of clinging to the possibility of election: God could not, after conversion, persecute an elect. Yet exposure to Satan's persecution suggested that (as he once felt of his father) 'the Lord had or should utterly cast me off'. And the interpretation remained theologically available in spite of the conversion experience since temporary conversion, designedly ineffectual calling, was a fate the Calvinist God allotted to many of those towards whom he felt unfriendly. In his 'blackest thoughts' Norwood continued to infer a malevolent providence which lifted him (in the euphoria of conversion) 'to make my fall the more terrible' (p. 101).

What I have been examining is Norwood's ur-narrative, the narrative his mind appears actually to have composed at every step of his journey through life from the age of around 6. The narrative embracing this narrative looks like an abreactive enterprise. Norwood settled down (marrying at 32), settled in the Bermudas, and settled in his calling as surveyor of the islands. Absorbed by his work and a respected member of a community, he seems to have managed, to a degree, to settle his faith too. He is too honest to deny however (dishonesty would be futile) that he remains 'prone to doubting, distrustfulness, and qualms of despair' (p. 106). He appears to have written his 'Confessions', two decades after its content, in an attempt to release and domesticate the monster in his thought. How successful he was it is impossible to say.

Norwood's narration reveals that it cannot be said that either social factors or theology produced his experience. His mind seems always to have been at the point where they meshed together. In a less excruciating metaphor, they imbued his perception in imaginative compound. Theology relied on feelings of individual exposure and such feelings would not have formed as they did if the personality of the puritan father-God had not been at the back of them. The theologians legislated for paranoia of the type Norwood expresses. Perkins offered readers a model in *A Dialogue of the State of a Christian Man:* exemplary Eusebius recalls: 'I could not sleepe in the night season I was afraid of every thing. If I were in my house: I thought the house would fal on my head: if abroad, I thought every crannic of the earth would open it selfe wider and swallow me.'[123] On the other hand Thomas Beard attributes similar symptoms to the guilt-tortured recipient of divine judgement:

> In what place soever you are, he is alwaies above you, ready to hurle you downe and overturne you, to breake, quash, and crush you in pieces as pots of earth . . . heaven threatneth from above, and the earth which you trample on from below, shaking under your feet, and being ready to spue you out from her face, or swallow you up in her bowels: in briefe all the elements and creatures of God looke a skew at you in disdaine, and set themselves against you in hatred.[124]

Many of the autobiographies, like Norwood's, combine inimical circumstances with a powerful sense of a persecutory will behind them. And their authors were no more adept at distinguishing varieties of paranoia than the divines. John Rogers, for example, hounded out of his parents' home and so ravenous, he claims, that 'I took up the skin of my wasted hand and armes with a resolution to tear it off for *hunger*,' expresses his plight in this analogy:

> see how a *bird* that is escaped out of the hand is hunted up and down by the *boyes*, the doores are shut, the windowes and holes stopp'd to hinder her escape; and see how they hunt her, throw their hats at her, scare her up and down till they think to tire her, and make her fall into their *fingers* again: So did *Satan* set upon me.

[123] *Works*, p. 458.   [124] *The Theatre of Gods Judgements* (1597), 471–2.

Physical misery was compounded by the conviction that it was personal, that he was being hunted. (That he sees Satan, not God, as his persecutor is probably a revision. He thought himself a reprobate and even considered a pact with the devil.)[125] Bunyan sat forlornly on a bench in a neighbouring town: 'and, after long musing, I lifted up my head, but methought I saw as if the Sun that shineth in the Heavens did grudge to give me light, and as if the very stones in the street, and tiles upon the houses, did bend themselves against me, me-thought that they all combined together to banish me out of the World' (187). George Trosse, visited in his despair by an elderly minister, was so convinced 'the House would immediately have fallen down, and have crush'd him and us all' that he 'had so much Charity as to warn him of it'. He was 'a *Bull*', he felt, 'kicking in the *Net* of GOD's *Judgments*'.[126] In all these cases (Bunyan's is about to be examined) the victims were made psychologically vulnerable by their social circumstances of which the interventionist, capricious yet relentless, God of protestant imagining was the unignorable source.

Paranoia could not be acquired entirely to order. Or rather the divines would not have acquired the authority to induce it unless social conditions were somehow receptive to their message. Puritan subjectification relied on the susceptibilities fostered by a heavily patriarchal culture in a vicissitudinous social world. Narrative addressed itself mainly to the paranoid fears which spun their own providential story out of daily events in quest of assurance that these fears were groundless. Autobiographers who lacked a sustained sense of a favouring providence 'carrying a man sweetly forwards as a prosperous gale' had to 'row against wind and tide' (p. 107) in the debilitating belief that their puny efforts had no bearing on the vessel's destination.

[125] *Ohel or Beth-shemesh*, pp. 434, 432, 436.
[126] *Life*, pp. 69, 71.

3

Perceptual Frames in *Grace Abounding*

'I T is not fantastic to assert', writes Q. D. Leavis, 'that it was the Puritan culture as much as Bunyan that produced *Pilgrim's Progress*.'[1] This serves well as an epigraph for the following two chapters, though a quite different view is taken of the culture and the relationship to it of Bunyan's work. I see both *Grace Abounding* and *The Pilgrim's Progress* as produced by the puritan culture in the sense that they mediate and respond to a collective imagination whose persecutory menace they seek to appease.

Bunyan's life and work have a dramatic national backdrop. His childhood coincided with Laud's primateship; he took part in the Civil War on the Parliamentary side; he was converted and began to preach during the Interregnum; and he was either in prison or ministering to his Independent Baptist flock from the time of the Restoration. These political upheavals impressed themselves on him in various ways. As is evident from Part Two of *The Pilgrim's Progress*, the experience away from home in the New Model Army infiltrated his imagination; and doubtless the ideas that army fermented had their influence on him too. Comparative liberty of conscience and freedom of assembly under Cromwell provided the conditions in which he could participate in a religious community independent of, and even assisted by, the state; and it was this puritan milieu that enabled him to project himself as a writer. Physical persecution, from the Restoration on, inevitably shaped his life and outlook. But there is a danger, I think, of looking for too direct a relationship between the great events and the social structures occupied by a rural tinker. The army experience was brief in comparison with the humdrum continuities to which, after all, Bunyan returned apparently unreconstructed. The Bedford separatists did not, during the Commonwealth period, subsist in a utopian vacuum sealed off from entrenched power and property relations. And the sense of persecution Bunyan records in *Grace Abounding* and

[1] Q. D. Leavis, *Fiction and the Reading Public* (1965), 97.

dramatizes in *The Pilgrim's Progress* does not, in spite of the fact that these are prison writings, derive from the experience of political persecution. The chief efficacy of political persecution was, paradoxically, to strengthen the peace of mind Bunyan found so elusive; it is associated, in *Progress* and elsewhere, with exhilaration and triumph. The sense of persecution Bunyan's texts attest has more intimate causes. To say this is not to downplay the impact on Bunyan of the politics of social struggle; rather it is to relocate it in the network of meanings an ordinary seventeenth-century village community could constitute. *Grace Abounding* reveals how Bunyan's modes of perception developed under the pressures of his immediate environment and the ideology which permeated it.

This chapter, therefore, analyses Bunyan's record of the construction of his identity in the cultural context to which the text itself points. Respecting the primacy in the text of theological discourse, I begin by suggesting how the act of writing *Grace Abounding* emerges from the need to overcome the alienated individualism fostered by the doctrine of reprobation. Institutionalized in the Calvinist system, the idea continues to pester the imagination, threatening to displace the elect perception of experience which autobiography strives to reify. The development, from early childhood, of Richard Norwood's sense of identity has already shown how theology could mesh with social experience. In *Grace Abounding*, too, this largely overlooked layer of experience helps, notwithstanding the intense privacy characterizing the record, to explain how the idea of reprobation wedged itself into Bunyan's mind. Like Norwood again, Bunyan acquired belief in his election—and anguish receded—as he began to find his feet in a calling which provided him with an acceptable social identity. Yet an undertow of fundamental doubt persists into the writer's present. By rehabilitating the persecutory imagination in the theological culture in which it developed, assisted by a broader perspective on its ideological basis, we can understand why it was so hard to slough. *Grace Abounding* appears in the end less the quirky document of a religious fanatic than a full imaginative response to a value-laden environment from which release could only be of a qualified and contaminated kind. Erich Fromm distinguishes between two essential types of religious experience:

In societies ruled by a powerful minority which holds the masses in subjection, the individual will be so imbued with fear, so incapable of feeling strong or independent, that his religious experience will be authoritarian. Whether he worships a punishing, awesome God or a similarly conceived leader makes little difference. On the other hand, where the individual feels free and responsible for his own fate, or among minorities striving for freedom and independence, humanistic religious experience develops.[2]

To some extent we observe in Bunyan the development of the first type into the second, a development reflected in Parts One and Two of *Progress*. Bunyan's imagination is, however, so deeply imbued with the thoughts attached to experience of a discriminatory social structure that it is permanently disfigured, permanently engaged in the attempt to exorcize the fears it entertains.

To argue for the shaping role of the reprobate paradigm in the construction of Bunyan's autobiography is to cut across previous commentators who again seem to me guilty of a writing-down of areas of the text under the treacherous guidance of contemporary theological punditry in perverse alliance with modern liberal sentiments and rationalist assumptions. Even W. Y. Tindall, who was the first to acknowledge the need to situate Bunyan's work in its cultural milieu, assumes that in *Grace Abounding* Bunyan is 'exaggerating his symptoms for purposes of ministerial propaganda' and speaks of the 'rigid formula of regeneration, which preachers of every sect were eager to illustrate by their own experience'.[3] Both statements fail to recognize the social reality of religious despair and the persisting doubleness of the experiential paradigm. Emphasis is thrown, trivializingly, on to self-advertisement so that the discipline which constrains the writing—the need to avoid hypocrisy while conquering feelings of rejection—is ignored.

In fact Tindall provides a good basis from his own researches for countering his argument that the purpose of writing a puritan autobiography 'was the advertisement of the author's experience and gifts'. This conclusion is reached from specimens of enthusiastic autobiography such as Arise Evans's weirdly

---

[2] Erich Fromm, *Psychoanalysis and Religion* (1951), 59.
[3] *John Bunyan, Mechanick Preacher* (New York, 1934), 233, 37.

prophetic *Eccho to the Voice of Heaven* (1652) and is then transferred
to Bunyan. But he here sidesteps his own observation that fellow
Baptists such as Henry Jessey and Hanserd Knollys 'failed to
publish the autobiographical products of their enthusiasm, from
which, therefore, they could expect only a posthumous fame'.
Tindall notes, moreover, 'a close parallel to *Grace Abounding*' in
the Bedford Quaker, John Crook's *A Short History of the Life*
(1706), adding that, because it was published posthumously, it
'wants . . . the motive of useful advertisement, and must be
regarded as a memoir'.[4] Bunyan's autobiography resembles
Crook's and belongs to the tradition of Jessey's and Knollys's,
none of which was published by its author, and is quite unlike
Evans's, which was. There is no reason to suppose that Jessey
and Knollys were interested in posthumous fame (they had
better hopes). Therefore unless publication is *ipso facto* self-
advertising *Grace Abounding* appears unlikely to be so.

A more guarded view along similar lines is expressed by Owen
Watkins, who says that 'Bunyan's purpose is didactic', and Paul
Delany, who thinks the work 'designed for the edification of
fellow-Christians'.[5] Christopher Hill, brilliant though he is on
the text's historical connections, has chimed in here, expressing
circumspection about its autobiographical reliability. 'The object
of the work', he warns, 'is to convey a message.'[6] Presumably
publication of a religious work indicates that the author expects
it to be profitable to others, as Bunyan explicitly does, but this
does not establish the primary purpose in writing. Beatrice
Batson offers the only alternative so far suggested, declaring that
'the aim of spiritual autobiography is literary, not propagandist.'[7] But it is not clear what she means by 'literary', and the
claim does not seem to tally with Bunyan's rejection of a higher
style; sincerity rather than literariness was his avowed aim in the
preface: to '*lay down the thing as it was*'.[8] Conscious intention is, in
any case, irrecoverable. What can be profitably investigated are

---

[4] *Mechanick Preacher*, pp. 25, 29, 27.

[5] *The Puritan Experience* (1972), 102; *British Autobiography in the Seventeenth Century*
(1969), 88.

[6] Christopher Hill, *A Turbulent, Seditious, and Factious People: John Bunyan and his
Church* (Oxford, 1988), 65.

[7] E. Beatrice Batson, *John Bunyan: Allegory and Imagination* (1984), 17.

[8] See above, ch. 1, n. 48.

the pressures that seem to exert themselves on the process of writing.

Together with the idea of exaggeration, in Tindall's comment, went that of the formula of regeneration. Here, again, as we saw in relation to the spiritual autobiography, other critics have agreed. In the introduction to his edition of *Grace Abounding* Roger Sharrock applauds Bunyan's 'freedom from rationalization into stock Calvinist formulae' (p. xxxii). He nevertheless supplies the 'clearly defined stages' of regeneration (conviction of sin, calling, justification, sanctification, and glorification) (pp. xxvii–xxviii) and finds that in Bunyan's work, 'All happens in due order as might be approved by a Puritan academic, a Perkins or a Sibbes' (p. xxxii). Because Bunyan is an artist, it is implied, he genuinely recreates 'the life of the soul' which takes the general course charted by the 'great Elizabethan practical Puritans, Richard Greenham, William Perkins, John Dod, and their successors [who] laid the foundations of a descriptive psychology of conversion' (p. xxviii) Apparently it does not occur to him that their description had the effect of prescription, so that what Bunyan genuinely recreates is an experience already informed by their categories. It therefore will not do to notice conformity to the elect categories and to dismiss 'the mental conflicts' as 'grow[ing] out of quibbling misunderstandings about texts' (p. xxxiii). On Perkins's 'Table' the elect phases Sharrock delineates are counterparted by 'Gods hating of the Reprobate', 'A calling not effectuall', 'A yeelding to Gods calling' (which breaks down into 'A generall illumination', 'Penitence', 'Temporarie faith', 'A Tast', and 'Zeale'), 'Relapse' (which breaks down into 'The deceit of sinne', 'The hardening of the heart', 'An evill heart', 'An unbeleeving heart', and 'Apostasie'), 'Fulnes of sinne', and 'Damnation'. These categories, especially their derivation from God's hatred, potently inform Bunyan's imagination too.

Beatrice Batson's recent book succumbs again to one-sided schematization, broken down as: 'Stranger to Grace (sections 1–36), Movement towards Grace (sections 37–229), Advent of Grace (section 230), Discoveries in Grace (sections 231–339).'[9] It is an agreeable process bearing little resemblance to Bunyan's record. Accordingly the author finds an 'indivisible personality'

[9] *Allegory and Imagination*, pp. 13–14.

in the work, which is remarkable in view of the alternation of elect and reprobate selves, the unbearable split between exclusive identities, which is the theme of the narration and the source of its tension.

Bunyan has not, even by the end of the narration, graduated from his reprobate fears. The illusion that he has may be encouraged by his *Account of the Author's Call to the Work of the Ministry* (265–317). But this is a separate narrative which deals with the comparatively external matter of how he became a preacher. He tells us, for instance, that he 'preached what I felt, what I smartingly did feel, even that under which my poor Soul did groan and tremble to astonishment' (276) rather than reliving, in such a context, the substance of these feelings. We know nevertheless that he was still 'sorely afflicted . . . concerning my eternal state' (268). 'The CONCLUSION', which follows both this narrative and the *Account of the Authors Imprisonment* (318–39), brings us up to date with his persisting difficulties: '1. Inclinings to unbelief, 2. Suddenlie to forget the love and mercie that Christ manifesteth, 3. A leaning to the Works of the Law' (pp. 102–3). Experientially the reprobate paradigm kept tangling with or effacing the elect, though naturally Bunyan is as reticent in spelling that out (since theory taught that they were exclusive) as seems to him consistent with veracity.

The minute logicality of the recorded thought-processes by which Bunyan inched his way out of the reprobate impasse when he thought he had sold Christ is too peculiarly exact about the source of his anguish to be capable of invention or significant reshaping whether for propagandist or literary purposes; and it has much more to do with an awareness of God's capacity for hatred and rejection than with a movement towards grace. It takes him over a hundred paragraphs to negotiate his escape (132–235)—a period of nearly two and a half years measured out in logically linked steps, not one of which may be forgotten if, like the pilgrims, he is not to be disqualified as an elect for failing to take, and remember, the correct route. 'If thou miss but one letter in thy evidence,' said Bunyan of the day of judgement, 'thou art gone.'[10] No wonder Powell sweated on his sick-bed

---

[10] *Of the Resurrection of the Dead*, in *The Works of John Bunyan*, ed. George Offor (Glasgow, 1854), ii. 120. References to all works by Bunyan, except those for which other editions have been identified, will be to this edition and embodied in the text.

when his diary was not to hand. The general experience Bunyan records was, moreover, not at all uncommon. Richard Baxter observes:

oft times they are strangely urged, as by something in them, to speak some *Blasphemous word of God*, or to renounce him, and they tremble at the Suggestion, and yet it still followeth them, and some poor Souls yield to it, and say some bad Word against God, and then as soon as it is spoken, somewhat within them saith, now *thy Damnation is sealed, thou hast sinned against the Holy Ghost, there is no hope.*[11]

The consequences of Bunyan's 'bad Word against God', his momentary mental assent to a suggestion that 'did follow me . . . continually' 'for the space of a year' (133)—'*Let him go if he will!*' (139)—should therefore be seen not as exaggeration, nor as pathological idiosyncrasy, but as a product of his culture.

It is the search for accurate recollection and the need to subjugate reprobate perception of himself which are the detectable worried energies working on the labile substance of Bunyan's past. This is not to deny that addressing others was an important awareness. Bunyan lays emphasis in his preface on remembering his own experience for his own benefit and, secondarily, on its potential benefit to his flock:

Wherefore this I have endeavoured to do; and not onely so, but to publish it also; that, if God will, others may be put in remembrance of what he hath done for their Souls, by reading his work upon me. (p. 2)

Like Baxter, he reinforces his own confidence more effectively by helping others: 'And it much increased my Peace when God's Providence called me to the comforting of many others that had the same Complaints: *While I answered their Doubts I answered my own.*'[12] The writing attempted to produce a certificate of assurance, like Christian's, or Christiana's letter, and, since it communicated with the elect community, a guarantee of emancipation from the private alienation it relived.

The autobiography sought to accomplish and attest release from the solitary confinement of despair. It resembled the review of terrifying solitary experience which Christian and Faithful exchange to confirm their exit from the Valley of the Shadow of

---

[11] *Preservatives against Melancholy and Overmuch Sorrow* (1713), 22; see also Goodwin, *A Childe of Light Walking in Darknes* (1636), 115.

[12] *Reliquiae Baxterianae*, ed. M. Sylvester (1696), 9.

Death. By the same token, what the autobiography actually preponderantly contains is agonized isolation. The more firmly Bunyan concludes himself a reprobate the more strongly his isolation is stressed: 'I counted my self alone' (87); 'I went moping into the field' (140); 'Oh! none knows the terrors of those days but my self' (153). As with Norwood it is these experiences of detached consciousness which make his identity distinct, marking off a subject whose life can be continuously narrated. External details get remembered because of the intensity of lonely experience which brands them on to the mind: '*Have you forgot the Close, the Milk-house, the Stable, the Barn, and the like,*' he asks his flock, '*where* God *did visit your Soul?*' (p. 3). Bunyan remembers whether he was sitting at the fireside or on a settle in the street or trudging the road between Elstow and Bedford when he had particular experiences.

Yet the sense of isolation is reinforced when his experiences are located in public contexts—in the game of tipcat, for example, when he was 'put to an exceeding maze' by a voice from the skies: 'Thus I stood in the midst of my play, before all that then were present; but yet I told them nothing' (22–4). The contrast between a social situation and an unbetrayed experience clarifies the separateness and the incommunicability of the spiritual self. This early incident dramatizes how the theology that threatened him drove a wedge between his exterior and interior self, so that in the most ordinary social surroundings ('sitting in a Neighbours House' (113) or 'walking to and fro in a good mans Shop' (174)) his mind is wholly abstracted (assessing his slim chance of inheriting eternal life or punishing himself with self-abhorrence). Nearly all outer detail is subservient to inner event, a mere trace left as a mnemonic for mental states. This spare specificity accommodating intensely private feeling suggests that his consciousness was largely barred from participation in his bodily, social existence; and the feeling of being locked into an incommunicable mind-set appears itself to have exacerbated the experience of suspected reprobation so that he spirals down, or sinks (to use the metaphor he favours), into more impregnable introspection. Nor was alleviation to be gained, Bunyan found, by seeking out those who might understand. On the one occasion when he did disclose his experience his reprobate self-diagnosis received brutally matter-of-fact confirmation: 'I told [an Antient

Christian] I was afraid that I had sinned the sin against the Holy Ghost; and he told me, *He thought so too*' (180)—spiritual succour of a kind Jane Turner reports as commonly dispensed by the saints.[13]

While the autobiography sharply defines the alienated individual it also associates salvation with the ability to break out of isolation. In the body of the autobiography despair is a state of solitary confinement. In the closing paragraphs of the narrative Bunyan had, in spite of the phases of election he should have left behind, been undergoing a typical experience in which 'suddenly there fell upon me a great cloud of darkness, which did so hide from me the things of God and Christ, that I was as if I had never seen or known them in my life' (261). Eventually, he recalls, 'I suddenly felt this word to sound in my heart, *I must go to Jesus*' (262). His mood is transformed and it produces an immediate communicative impulse, which ends his narrative and presages its writing:

Then with joy I told my Wife, O now I know, I know! but that night was a good night to me, I never had but few better; I longed for the company of some of Gods people, that I might have imparted unto them what God had showed me. (263)

The need to communicate emerges as a need to give social reality to his religious experience. Until it is the means of integrating him into the community it remains evanescent, a mere mood or 'frame'.

An earlier experience makes the nature of the autobiographical impulse still more apparent:

Now was my heart filled full of comfort and hope, and now I could believe that my sins should be forgiven me; yea, I was now so taken with the love and mercy of God, that I remember I could not tell how to contain till I got home; I thought I could have spoken of his Love, and of his mercy to me, even to the very Crows that sat upon the plow'd lands before me, had they been capable to have understood me, wherefore I said in my Soul with much gladness, Well, I would I had a pen and ink here, I would write this down before I go any further, for surely I will not forget *this* forty years hence; but alas! within less than

---

[13] *Choice Experiences of the Kind Dealings of God, before, in, and after Conversion* (1653), 6–7.

forty days I began to question all again; which made me begin to question all still. (92)[14]

He needs those capable of understanding him and he needs the authority and permanence of a transcript of his feelings before they can attain objective status and attest his release.

The swings of feeling Bunyan records do not conform to the frequently invoked paradigm of salvation. His assurance of salvation at one moment can be displaced instantaneously by despair at both early and later stages of the narrative. (The double-takes on his identity persist with Christian, too, through to the end of *Progress*.) It is the task of the narrative to manipulate this chequered experience in such a way as to make the reprobate anxieties seem illusory. The narrator is seeking to impose a divine objectivity on experiences which, in the present, seem wholly real. This is why the puritan's narrative of experience was necessary: it was an attempted means of disarming the reprobate threat.

The immediate and probably most important reason for the sudden evacuations of faith Bunyan records was the doubleness of the puritan paradigm. Thomas Goodwin, in *A Childe of Light Walking in Darknes*, seems more perceptive about the kind of puritan experience *Grace Abounding* expresses than some recent commentators who are fixated on the paradigm of election:

A mans heart is like those two-faced pictures, if you looke one way towards one side of them, you shall see nothing but some horrid shape of a devill, or the like; but goe to the other side, and look again, and you shall see the picture of an Angell, or of some beautifull woman etc. So some have lookt over their hearts by signes at one time, and have to their thinking found nothing but hypocrisie, unbelief, hardnesse, self-seeking; but not long after examining their hearts again by the same signes they have espied the image of God drawn fairely upon the table of their hearts.[15]

The experience the puritan kept reviewing was an unstable percept. What was seen depended on the angle from which it was

---

[14] The last phrase is supplied from G. B. Harrison, ed., *Grace Abounding and The Life and Death of Mr. Badman*. Presumably Sharrock decided not to add the phrase to the 1666 version because it seemed pleonastic. See comment below, p. 138.

[15] *Childe of Light*, p. 193. For specimens of such perspective paintings see Ernest B. Gilman, *The Curious Perspective* (New Haven, 1978).

viewed. It was not a question of seeing more of this aspect and less of that; the witty perspective painting presented opposite and exclusive identities. Like Wittgenstein's duck-rabbit the puritan's past and present appeared as wholly one extreme or wholly the other, never a compromise between them. The doubleness of identity was constructed, not from a raw experience naturally possessed of such bipolar ambivalence, but from the interpretative apparatus that structured perception.

Long before Bunyan produced his *Mapp*, probably in 1663, the theology it summarized constituted a grid through which the world was organized. Concern with phases of election, the formula of regeneration, derived from and was subordinated to the strain between the competing teleologies. It was this that governed experience. Bunyan himself uses the word 'frame' on several occasions (for example, 25, 229, 261) in a sense which *OED* (frame sb.6, Mental or emotional disposition or state) dates from 1665. M. van Beek lists it as a puritan coinage.[16] It was a term made necessary by the puritan mode of perception where the entire outlook on the world and the self was controlled by one cast of mind or another. Such alternating frames could not be explicitly equated with election and reprobation (because, according to theory, your elect or reprobate state was inalterable) but they are clearly the subjective counterparts.

This is betrayed when Bunyan exhorts himself not to confuse his 'frame of Heart' (229) with an objective spiritual state or comments sadly on the frame which half-consciously possesses the minds of others, so that they resign themselves to their reprobation (25). Single biblical texts (such as one promising grace and another threatening identification with the reprobate Esau) trigger elect or reprobate trains of thought. His 'diverse frames of Spirit' were, he says, 'still according to the nature of the several Scriptures that came in upon my mind' (212). When, two paragraphs later, the texts finally fulfil Bunyan's wish for them to 'meet in my heart at once' so that he can discover which 'would get the better of me' he finds that 'The Word of the Law and Wrath must give place to the Word of Life and Grace.' The happy outcome enables him to re-express the subjective frames

---

[16] *An Enquiry into Puritan Vocabulary* (Gröningen, 1969). Richard Norwood's unpublished autobiography, written in the years 1639–40, antedates *OED* (p. 51); so also does Anna Trapnel's *A Legacy for the Saints* (1654), 20, 43.

in the objective terms of the teleologies of damnation and salvation (though the confidence generated by this experience does not prevent the reimposition of the reprobate frame (216)). The binary scheme subjected his mind to violent mood swings of which, as in this description, he is the passive recipient.

We see in the writing the attempt to banish the persisting reprobate spectre by wrestling with narrative material which flickers under the gaze. Although the autobiography fixes an elect interpretation, as Bunyan wished he could when he longed for pen and ink, the process of ambivalent review does not end there. Just as the evidence of reprobation could produce a despairing narrative which was then subsumed to an elect teleology, so later experience could cast a reprobate retrospect over that narrative, re-expressing it as delusion (which collapsed into hypocrisy). Richard Baxter speaks in his autobiography of *'having transcribed thus much of a life which God hath read, and Conscience hath read, and must further read'*.[17] Once the questioning of the authenticity or significance of an experience started up it developed its own narrative momentum by requiring a reinterpretation of all experience. This happens to Christian and Hopeful in Doubting Castle although they have already exchanged elect readings of themselves. Bunyan implied the relentlessness of this reappraisal in the phrase: 'I began to question all again; which made me begin to question all still.' The repetitive addition mimes the generation of the vicious circle. The questioning of the assurance he had wanted to capture on paper cannot be passed over as a momentary doubt, rather the whole mind is, as it were, crashed into reverse by it.

As with other autobiographers, while the perceptual frames of election and reprobation dominate imaginative experience they are not adopted arbitrarily. Receptivity can generally be seen to depend on their aptness to the believer's milieu and personal circumstances. Richard Norwood supplied an extreme example of a persecutory imagination produced by the combination of family decline and patriarchal oppression from which the rationalizing and legitimating ideology of Calvinism could at no stage be severed. In *Grace Abounding* the interpretative frames impose themselves fairly relentlessly, ensuring that the conscious

[17] *Reliquiae*, p. 136.

mind perceives all experience as theological. There is no other reality to which to penetrate. But there are indications, especially in the first third or so where they might be expected, of how Calvinism gained its imaginative purchase, or 'fastened on [his] spirit' (23). These prepare us to understand the interpenetration of theology and social conditions in *The Pilgrim's Progress*.

Bunyan's biographer, John Brown, discovered that in the mid-sixteenth century the Bunyans had farmed over nine acres of land around Elstow. John Bunyan's grandfather, who lived until 1641, described himself in his will as a 'Pettie Chapman' (small village trader). Bunyan and his father both worked as tinkers. Reminders of the family's former standing confronted them in the locality. Two fields were still known as 'Bunyans' and 'farther Bunyans'; there was a 'Bunyan's Walk', and part of the parish of Elstow was known as 'Bunyan's End'.[18] Local studies suggest that an 'economic polarization' tended to occur in village life between the 1590s and 1620s producing a dominant group made up of minor gentry and yeomen who saw themselves as the 'better sort'. At the same time there was a pattern of decline of yeomen and smallholders into labourers. To those that had, indeed, more was given. Reasonable insulation from price fluctuations required upwards of fifty acres; then it was possible to profit from high scarcity prices and swallow up poorer neighbours forced into sale.[19] Since Bunyan's family had declined from smallholder status it seems particularly likely that he would be vulnerable to the collective imagination which, as Norwood's experience suggested, registered a congruence between the Calvinist God and arbitrarily discriminatory market forces.[20]

[18] John Brown, *John Bunyan: His Life, Times and Work* (1887), 26, 31, 28.

[19] See D. M. Palliser, *The Age of Elizabeth: England under the Later Tudors 1547–1603* (1983), 77, 94; Keith Wrightson, *English Society 1580–1680* (1982), 32–3; Keith Wrightson, 'Aspects of Social Differentiation in Rural England c. 1580–1660', *Journal of Peasant Studies*, 5 (1977–8), 33–47; David Underdown, *Revel, Riot, and Rebellion* (1985) 20, 28; John Hatcher, 'English Serfdom and Villeinage', *Past and Present*, 90 (1981), 3–39, esp. p. 39. Christopher Hill notes the novel, and resented, development of a sharp division within the peasantry between village élites and a class of permanent poor (*A Turbulent, Seditious, and Factious People*, pp. 16–18).

[20] Hill also remarks on the appropriateness of the idea of predestination to an environment in which people were at the mercy of the market (adding in weather, plague, and war). He returns to the point later, noting 'the great economic divide, in which the lucky few might prosper while the mass of their neighbours were plunged

The pertinence of this family history to *Grace Abounding* is most dramatically apparent where Bunyan's despair is at its most acute and protracted: after his momentary consent to the year-long insistent temptation to 'Sell Christ'. In succumbing to this temptation Bunyan believed that he had 'dis-inherited my poor Soul' (183) in a way prefigured by Esau selling his birthright. The temptation arrives just after Bunyan's acquisition of 'blessed evidence from heaven touching my interest in [God's] love through Christ' (132). The text he sets against this dire temptation is God's declaration in Leviticus 25: 23: '*For the land shall not be sold for ever, for the Land is mine*' (134). The context of this quotation concerns the redemption of the land of any Jewish brother who has 'waxen poor' and sold to wealthier neighbours. He and his kin should be given the opportunity to redeem their property, and if they cannot it will eventually revert to their ownership in the year of the Jubilee (which, Christopher Hill points out, Bunyan took to signify the day of judgement).[21] In material reality there was no possibility of such redemption of the land Bunyan's family had lost; yet since, ultimately, God owned all land, the humiliation of that dispossession would be erased, providing Bunyan retained the 'evidence' for his 'interest' in his fatherly love, providing, that is, he was one of the elect (antitype of the Jews). It is clear from the commercial-legal language running through this most nerve-exposing passage in Bunyan's record how desperate for him was the assuaging of feelings of dispossession. One can only guess at the meaning for him of the phrase 'Sell Christ', but it seems to me likely that the 'temptation' resembled vertigo—a horrified fascination with the ultimate act of self-destruction. The imprecision of the exchange ('*Sell Christ for this, or sell Christ for that; sell him, sell him* (135)) and the bald terms of consent ('*Let him go if he will!*' (139)) suggest that there was no envisaged gain, merely a displaced fixation on the act of his forefathers the horror of which compelled his imagination. He cannot escape the conviction (inarticulate to his

into deeper poverty. He further notes that 'Sociological and psychological historians have not got very far in explaining why there was so much despair in the late sixteenth and early seventeenth centuries' (*A Turbulent, Seditious, and Factious People*, pp. 20, 68).

[21] *A Turbulent, Seditious, and Factious People*, p. 71. I am indebted in this paragraph both to Hill's discussion, 'The Lost Inheritance', 68–74, and to Jack Lindsay's *John Bunyan: Maker of Myths* (1937), chs. 8 and 9.

conscious mind, but the more potent and bewildering for that) that he is doomed to complicity in their sin; and he succumbs to the inevitability.

But this episode, whose centrality to the narrative earns it pride of place, is by no means the only evidence in Bunyan's autobiography of the social basis of his vulnerability to a reprobate identity. As with Norwood my focus will now be on the recorded evolution of Bunyan's sense of himself (filtered as of course it is through a far from disinterested adult memory). It appears, indeed, from the words Bunyan chooses to open his narration that early memories bring with them acute feelings concerning the family's decline:[22]

1. In this my relation of the merciful workings of God upon my Soul, it will not be amiss, if in the first place, I do, in a few words, give you a hint of my pedegree, and manner of bringing up; that thereby the goodness and bounty of God towards me, may be the more advanced and magnified before the sons of men.

2. For my descent then, it was, as is well known by many, of a low and inconsiderable generation; my fathers house being of that rank that is meanest, and most despised of all the families in the Land.

The third paragraph begins:

3. But yet notwithstanding the meanness and inconsiderableness of my Parents, it pleased God to put it into their heart, to put me to School,

A residual agitation may be detected in the verbal redundancy: 'low', 'inconsiderable', 'meanest', 'most despised', 'meanness', 'inconsiderableness'. Roger Sharrock observes that Bunyan was less poor than he made out. The Bunyans' tinkering 'was not that of disreputable vagabonds' (p. xii).[23] Bunyan qualified his own claim that he and his wife married without so much as a dish or spoon between them. This was, he meant, by way of 'household-stuff' (p. xvi and 15). Yet the exaggeration is more revealing than factual accuracy could have been of the importance to Bunyan of

[22] Jack Lindsay's stimulating biographical study, *John Bunyan: Maker of Myths* (1937), pp. 2–4 *et passim*, argues for the importance of Bunyan's class sensitivity.

[23] Sharrock here follows Brown (*Bunyan*, pp. 33–4); Christopher Hill paints a different picture of the tinker as a byword for 'lower-class non-respectability and immorality' (*A Turbulent, Seditious, and Factious People*, pp. 135–8). If we equivocate and say tinkering was an ambivalent calling it is nevertheless clear how John Bunyan, with his antecedents, would be likely to feel about this ambivalence.

the *feeling* of poverty. In cooler retrospect he is able to describe the past rather more distinctly from the feeling of the past.[24] Concluding his address to the reader of *A Few Sighs from Hell* (a work which, published in 1658, was written when Bunyan was avowedly 'smarting') he is similarly self-betraying: 'I am thine, if thou be not ashamed to own me, because of my low and contemptible descent in the world.' That sentence was also revised—'I am thine to serve in the Lord Jesus' (III.674 and n.)—in a second edition when, no doubt, a more detached author saw that the defiant edge bared his own vulnerability to the social assumptions his treatise tiraded against.

Michael Walzer sees 'status anxiety' behind the fierce religiosity and political perturbations of the Elizabethan puritan ministry.[25] Patrick Collinson disagrees with this view but adds: 'We speak, of course, as Michael Walzer does, of mainstream Calvinism and not of the more radical religious tendencies which doubtless articulated the "unsettledness" of the less privileged.'[26] What Bunyan gives us is not just an objective definition of his poverty but an account of how he felt about his status (or 'condition' or 'state', words which can slip between material and spiritual senses).[27] He suffered from what sociologists call relative deprivation, relative mainly, it appears, as in Norwood's case, to family history and educated self-awareness. Most interesting in the opening of *Grace Abounding* is not the poverty itself but Bunyan's inability to detach that from the ideological value-judgements with which language imbues it. To convey the way in which he regarded himself an objective detail might have to be sharpened. But chiefly the words he used ('low', 'meanest', etc.) put across a moral attitude which permeated the social hierarchy and which he evidently internalized. And he appears to have internalized it to the extent of picturing God as the source of

---

[24] It is hard to accept Sharrock's suggestion that the stress on his poverty is 'an expression of proper Christian humility about worldly matters' (p. xii). One wonders how far up the social scale such a strange notion of propriety would apply.

[25] *The Revolution of the Saints: A Study in the Origins of Radical Politics* (1966), 115, 124.

[26] Patrick Collinson, *The Religion of Protestants: The Church in English Society 1559–1625* (Oxford, 1982), 181.

[27] See, for example, 15, 39, 41, 102, 104. For the various meanings of 'place' in *The Pilgrim's Progress* see James Turner's excellent essay 'Bunyan's Sense of Place' in V. Newey, ed., *'The Pilgrim's Progress': Critical and Historical Views* (Liverpool, 1980), 91–110.

these value-judgements, the mainstay of the ideology which later caused his 'mistrusting my condition to be naught' (39). He imagines, for example, God's sneering aside to the angels in response to his anguished supplications: 'This poor simple Wretch doth hanker after me, as if I had nothing to do with my mercy, but to bestow it on such as he . . . it is not for such as thee to have favour with the Highest' (109). The adjectives 'poor' and 'simple' (and 'Highest', implicitly opposed to lowest) should be allowed their actual social denotation of the uneducated poverty to which his sense of persecution relates.

We can also note in Bunyan's self-introduction the careful way in which he credits his rudimentary education to God while meanness is squarely placed on his parents. This seems doubly unfair since while meanness was a given of their existence sending their son to school was a laudable exercise of a narrow freedom. The spread of education, largely motivated by Reformation zeal, was mainly limited by the inability of poor people to pay fees or buy books.[28] But Bunyan's teleological view of experience strips humanity of any good and blames it for any evil: education is seen as a good, the first good to contribute to his salvation, meanness as an evil.[29] Computing as well as possible the extent of the education supplied by elementary and grammar schools in the latter half of the seventeenth century, Kenneth Charlton concludes:

we are still referring to a relative minority of the population. If such schooling had been a necessary prerequisite for achieving a 'priesthood of all believers', for achieving the kind of religious education implicit in that aspiration, then failure would have been inevitable, for the majority of the population and the majority of any congregation would have been unable to read.[30]

If Bunyan received the prerequisite education it was barely so and 'to my shame,' he confesses, 'I did soon loose that little I learned' (3). So he was, in a sense, by virtue of his minimal education, on the bottom rung of the saveable. (Baxter explicitly

---

[28] Wrightson, *English Society*, pp. 186–91.

[29] 'Confesse,' said Calvin (quoting Augustine), 'that what so ever good thou haste, is of him: what soever evell, it is of thy selfe' (*Inst.* 2. 2. 27).

[30] Kenneth Charlton, 'The Educational Background' in C. A. Patrides and R. B. Waddington, edd., *The Age of Milton: Backgrounds to Seventeenth-Century Literature* (Manchester, 1980), 125–6.

numbered tinkers among the illiterate who were inveterate
enemies of 'knowledge and religion'.[31] Bunyan the writer shares
with the literate who are reading *Grace Abounding* awareness of the
dramatic import of the youth's abortive literacy. But it is not
surprising from the tinker boy's point of view, to which the text
gives some access, that he quickly dropped his literacy skills,
strongly resented other people reading (10), and took to physical
recreation: since he could not use it his education could have
succeeded only in alerting him to his deprivation and implicating
him in self-denigration by furnishing him with the perspective of
the advantaged.

Bunyan's adolescent piety, when he fetishized the Church of
England clergy and its trappings in a way that Erich Fromm
would describe as 'masochistic strivings',[32] confirms this suggestion: 'yea I thought for the love I did bear unto them . . . I could
have layn down at their feet, and have been trampled upon by
them' (17). Later in life Bunyan was to flush out the social
contempt in which people of his class were typically held by the
Anglican priesthood. In 1672 Bedfordshire cleric Edward Fowler
—soon to be elevated to the episcopal bench—responded to
Bunyan's attack on his *Design of Christianity* (1671) with *Dirt Wipt
Off*, which he opened by questioning whether a man of discretion
should '*not disdain to defile his fingers with so very dirty a Creature as is
the person I have to do with in the following sheets*'.[33] Bunyan's own
polemic, it is true to say, had been fairly robust; but Fowler's
suggestion that Bunyan was something he had picked up on his
shoe is another order of insult, venomed with class feeling. A year
later Bunyan's stung retort to prosperous fellow church-member
William Kiffin 'stigmatising me for a person of THAT rank, that
need not be heeded or attended unto'—'What need you . . . thus
trample my person . . . so disdainfully under your feet?' (ii. 617)—
suggests the accumulated sensitivity to his own socially given
'person' which these glimpses of the Fowlers and Kiffins amply
warrant. By the time he wrote *Grace Abounding*, in 1666, Bunyan's
response to social trampling had altered. In youth, unprovided

---

[31] Hill, *A Turbulent, Seditious, and Factious People*, p. 138.

[32] *The Fear of Freedom* (1942; paperback 1960), 132.

[33] Edward Fowler, Bishop of Gloucester, *Dirt Wipt Off: Or a Manifest Discovery of the
Gross Ignorance, Erroneousness, and Most Unchristian and Wicked Spirit of One John Bunyan*
(1672), sig. A2ʳ. Bunyan's treatise was *A Defence of the Doctrine of Justification, by Faith
in Jesus Christ* (1672), in Offor, ii, 278–334.

with a strategy for relativizing the dominant ideology, he internalized the worthlessness assigned to him and, for a time, duly ascribed magnificence to those who arrogated it. Recollection—'I could have layn down at their feet, and have been trampled upon by them'—is charged with lasting resentment at the same time as it documents his seemingly voluntary prostration.

Attempts to shut out the perspective acquired from school and church failed, however, to allay self-dissatisfaction. Ignorance is a frequent lacerating self-criticism. He was 'an ignorant Sot' (48) who was 'tossed betwixt the Devil and my own ignorance' (52).[34] Bunyan's relapse into traditional village pastimes and abandonment of his literacy skills cannot be regarded as a piece of casual laxity or an unimportant choice; its significance was structured for him by developments in seventeenth-century society. 'By 1680,' says Keith Wrightson, illiteracy 'was a special characteristic of the poor.' Progressively through the seventeenth century, 'The poor had become not simply poor, but to a significant degree culturally different.'[35] Bunyan seems to have been tormentingly marginal to both cultures. (This helps us to understand why Ignorance, in allegory, is treated so brutally.)

Bunyan's sensitivity to his lack of education and educational opportunity was no personality-wrinkle. We saw the extremity of Norwood's distress when he was forced to quit school. Anna Trapnel conveys such sensitivity more obliquely when she escapes from fixation on her unworthiness to a transporting conviction of unmerited grace:

the more free grace is apprehended, the more self-righteousness is reprehended, the creature can never learn the lesson of humiliation and self-denial, till it hath been in the School of free grace, that is, the free School where the best learning is to be had, the poor and fatherless here find mercy; and here the Governor of this Free-school receiveth every poor Orphane, he refuseth none that comes, though they have not one friend to make suit for them; nay, such are soon entertained that trust wholly to this great Governors mercy, they have the best learning, here is no respect of persons, but the poor begger that lyeth in the street, that knows not where to have a piece of bread, hath nothing but a clothing of tatters, to outward view a very miserable creature, such a one is more respected that a rich *Dives* . . . oh what manner of love is this! that makes no difference between fools and learned ones, preferring ideots

---

[34] See also, for example, 29, 36, 41.   [35] *English Society*, pp. 220–1.

before the wisdom of the world, making the ignorant and erring Spirit to have the greatest understanding?[36]

The rhapsodically applied metaphor implies, in the depth of its gratitude to the fee-waiving governor, the previous sense of insurmountable disadvantage with which Norwood and Bunyan similarly contended. It was only by finding a new avenue of education, in the separatist community, that Bunyan was finally enabled to overcome disadvantage; and even then dismissiveness had to be combated with asseverations such as pastor John Burton's on Bunyan's behalf in 1656 that he had 'taken . . . heavenly degrees' from 'the heavenly university, the church of Christ' (ii.141).

Shame seems to have been the link between Bunyan's poverty and his sense of sin. Losing literacy was a source of shame. Not much further into the narrative Bunyan reports a shaming incident when he was rebuked for his violent swearing by a shopkeeper's wife in front of whose window he was 'playing the Mad-man'; 'At this reproof I was silenced, and put to secret shame . . . wherefore, while I stood there, and hanging down my head, I wished with all my heart that I might be a little childe again, that my Father might learn me to speak without this wicked way of swearing' (26–7). Bunyan gives as the reason for his swearing, the most prominently recalled form of his rebelliousness: 'I knew not how to speak unless I put an Oath before, and another behind, to make my words have authority' (28). This explanation repays consideration.

Bunyan's shame seems to have been rooted in language. He could not, in a vogue phrase, 'inscribe his subjectivity in discourse' without self-incrimination. Adopting the language of another class implicated him in its values, which included a degrading or nullifying estimate of his own social identity. An education which taught him to regard himself as low without offering the credible possibility of improvement in status was therefore plausibly replaced by his attempt to acquire authority by defying the hierarchy, God being the ultimate butt. But the self-assertive authority he sought from swearing and cursing (and general village hooliganism, the actuality of which there is no evident reason to question) merely attests his anger at the awareness that power and authority lay elsewhere. To patronize

[36] *Legacy for the Saints*, pp. 15–16.

Bunyan for quaint notions of a sinful youth would be anachronistic. Swearing was criminal behaviour against which laws were enforced.[37]

Rebellion crumpled, however, with touching pathos and Bunyan instantly traced his predicament back to social provenance, wishing his entry into language could be effected over again to free him somehow from self-condemnation. It is a wish which may have derived in part from an awareness of his family's past. As Wrightson and Levine observe, while yeomen were thought worthy to be included among those who governed the nation 'artificers and labourers had no voice'.[38] The secret and ashamed self ('put to secret shame') was conceived, as for Norwood, in the interstices between masochistic conformism and brittle rebellion, both seemingly impracticable: a consciousness remained aloof to both and provided the hinge for reprobation. This is later glumly articulated: 'I saw I had a heart that would sin, and lay under a Law that would condemn' (79). The choice was, in Donne's phrase, to 'kicke rebelliously'[39] or submit, but submission entailed despair since it involved acknowledging himself to be worthless and rejected.

For a year or so after the swearing incident he maintained an 'outward Reformation', much pleased that he was 'talked of as one that was truly Godly' (30, 32) but conscious in his own mind that he was a 'Hypocrite', that his unhappy sense of himself was not resolved by becoming a 'brisk talker' (37).[40] He had borrowed a language which improved his public image rather than investing himself in it as a subject. The distinction is clarified by his encounter with the poor Bedford women whose

---

[37] See A. H. A. Hamilton, *Quarter Sessions from Queen Elizabeth to Queen Anne* (1878), 190; also Keith Wrightson and David Levine, *Poverty and Piety in an English Village: Terling, 1525–1700* (New York, 1979), 180.

[38] *Poverty and Piety*, pp. 103–6.   [39] *Sermons*, ix. 407.

[40] Christopher Hill, convinced that Bunyan could not have passed two and a half years in the parliamentary army without being saturated by radical ideas, associates this facile fluency with Ranter tendencies (*A Turbulent, Seditious, and Factious People*, p. 58). But Bunyan seems perfectly clear about the nature of the temptation Ranters presented to him, and his rejection of it (*Grace Abounding*, 44–5); had he been more receptive to their ideas this would, suitably condemned, have been grist to the mill of documenting his wicked pre-conversion self. Parroting pious language was a socially subtler and more insidious temptation. Since Bunyan won the admiration of his neighbours at this time for an apparent transformation into 'a very godly man' whose life and manners were famously altered (32), it is hard to see why Hill detects Ranter influence here.

'talk and discourse' (40) puzzled and haunted him. What seized on his mind was their talk of 'a new birth' (37) which seemed to be confirmed by the impression they conveyed of having 'found a new world' (38), of which he soon had a dream. This dream is described in terms strongly suggestive of birth trauma. 'Shivering and shrinking in the cold,' he eventually finds a gap in the encompassing wall through which he tries to pass:

> but the passage being very straight, and narrow, I made many offers to get in, but all in vain, even untill I was well nigh quite beat out by striving to get in: at last, with great striving, me thought I at first did get in my head, and after that, by a side-ling striving, my shoulders, and my whole body; then I was exceeding glad, and went and sat down in the midst of them, and so was comforted with the light and heat of their Sun.

Bunyan himself interpreted the wall as 'the Word that did make separation between the Christians and the world' (53–5). The novel discourse of the Bedford separatists demarcated a zone of potential freedom from the dominant ideology. For them the shame of poverty, or their 'miserable state by nature' (37), had been surmounted by the achievement of fluency and assurance in a discourse—the Word—which freed them from an ideology convicting them of innate baseness. The dream fulfilled the wish to be 'a little childe again': reborn, in the crucial sense to him, to a new acquisition of language.

At the House Beautiful, in *Progress*, Christian is told that the Lord of the Hill 'had made many Pilgrims Princes, though by nature they were Beggars born'.[41] Bunyan runs two senses of nature together: in the Pauline sense of 'natural man', unable to fulfil the law of God to the letter and therefore subject to condemnation (a sense strengthened by Calvin who saw mankind in its natural state as utterly destitute of virtue), and in the literal sense of social baseness by natural birth. The close meshing of shame at low birth and the sense of inherited sin was what Bunyan, like Christian, was desperate to escape. Neither a choir-boy nor devil-may-care persona could dispel the consciousness of degradation once stimulated. The rest of the narrative retraces

---

[41] John Bunyan, *The Pilgrim's Progress*, ed. J. B. Wharey; 2nd edn. rev. Roger Sharrock (Oxford, 1960), 53. Further references, embodied in the text, will be to this edition.

and literally enacts Bunyan's attempts to inscribe himself as a subject in the redemptive discourse, or, in his terms, apply the promises of God to himself particularly. This seems at first as impossible as touching the sun with his finger (79). 'I could not believe,' he says typically, 'that Christ had love for me' (78). He needed to banish the conditioned assumption that religious ideology must endorse the *status quo* and discriminate against him. The new talk and discourse could fulfil the wish to be 'learned to speak' again as a reborn child. But first it heightened anxiety about language ('I could not now tell how to speak my words, for fear I should mis-place them' (82)).

If we pass over the main body of the narrative to Bunyan's 'Account' of his call to the ministry and 'Relation' of his imprisonment, where he surfaces again in a social context, we find that speaking with authority remained of great importance. At his trial at the Bedford quarter sessions in January 1661 Bunyan's defence was described as 'pedlers French' by Sir John Kelynge who said, Bunyan records, 'that I ought not to preach. And asked me where I had my authority?' (p. 117). Unlike earlier defiance of the law—in particular the law against swearing—this encounter reinforces the authority Bunyan has acquired from a discourse originating from God's Word, which countermanded the authority of the establishment that tried him. The judiciary are the ones who are reduced to expletives since the authority Bunyan adduces is one they must, on shared protestant principles, acknowledge. It is an important narrative climax for Bunyan because it tests the supervention of the new on the old (intimidating) ideology. As Vanity Fair shows too, physical persecution was the best antidote to psychic. The opportunity it supplied for typological identification with Paul and Christ was deeply reassuring (p. 124). So too were the opportunities for successful rebuttal of charges targeted on his areas of sensitivity: his status as tinker and lack of education (pp. 108–18). This episode enabled him to define himself against the *status quo* as an elect. Its notables were *'Adversaries of God's Truth'* (p. 129). By opposing 'God's Truth' they gave it substance.

The other main form of assistance came from his calling as preacher. Bunyan did, following Paul's injunction, remain in his tinker's calling but it was only when his unsettled mind was accommodated by his activities as an itinerant preacher that he could feel at peace:[42] 'But yet,' he admits, 'I could not be content unless I was found in the exercise of my Gift' (269). The typically passive construction suggests how his subjectivity was constructed by language. Sometimes he would go 'full of guilt and terrour even to the Pulpit-Door, and there it hath been taken off, and I have been at liberty in my mind until I have done my work, and then immediately, even before I could get down the Pulpit-Stairs, have been as bad as I was before' (277). The position of preacher was one from which he could articulate; it freed his mind by making him an unquestionable vehicle of the puritan discourse— even if he was discarded like a 'lifeless, though sounding *Cymbal*' after use (297–9). He was, he says, 'wrapt up in the glory of this excellent work' (286). 'A heart', said Martin Luther (in a slightly disconcerting revelation of the authoritarian temperament), 'shall leap and dissolve in joy when it goes to work to what has been ordered.'[43] Bunyan had, like Richard Norwood, lacked a role which could absorb his consciousness, and the ideology he had imbibed seemed to discriminate against him. He continued to feel strongly that it was God who allocated the secular calling: 'I went not out of my place and state in which God by his providence had put me; but have abode with God in the calling wherein I was called,' said Wise on behalf of the elect in *The Life and Death of Mr. Badman* (p. 227).[44] The new language and increasing integration into the Baptist community accompanied by the call to preach gradually gave the favouring ideology greater credibility. But the reprobate psychic reflexes were still easily touched off (Christian in Doubting Castle entirely loses the confidence he possessed at Vanity Fair). And on the possession of assurance of salvation, salvation itself depended. Like verbal skirmishes with secular authority and like preaching, writing the autobiography, and the allegory, consolidated the reality of the

---

[42] Jack Lindsay makes the interesting equation between Christian's burden in *Progress* and the tinker's wallet Bunyan would have carried on his back 'which marked him out as a despised toiler' (*John Bunyan*, p. 186). That Bunyan continued tinkering (while Christian sheds his burden) does not invalidate the suggestion. Once his demeaning work was supplemented by the call to the ministry it changed its significance for him and therefore the burden no longer existed as a badge of shame. It is noteworthy that it is this burden that sinks Christian more deeply in the Slough of Despond. Guilt, shame, and social decline are emblematically united.

[43] Quoted by Oscar Pfister in *Christianity and Fear: A Study in History and in the Psychology and Hygiene of Religion*, trans. W. H. Johnston (1948), 364.

[44] See Introduction, n. 12.

counter-culture, which had its basis otherwise in unstable human feeling and intangible spiritual experience.

The struggle with language was a struggle to modify perceptual habits, and success could only be partial. As a prelude to rehabilitating social self-awareness in its theological culture it may be well to quote a comment early in Bunyan's narration which firmly reminds us of their interpenetration in his mind:

> Yea, such prevalency had the lusts and fruits of the flesh . . . that had not a miracle of precious grace prevented, I had not onely perished by the stroke of eternal Justice, but had also laid my self open, even to the stroke of those Laws, which bring some to disgrace and open shame before the face of the world. (9)

Bunyan's rhetorical ordering strangely brings out liability to prosecution and worldly disgrace as a greater evil than perishing by the stroke of eternal justice. Theologically (and chronologically) the proposition is absurd and probably not too much weight should be placed on it, but it does, as a present-time reflection, seem to betray how deeply the ideology buttressing existing secular powers had etched itself into his psyche. (The episode with Giant Despair will confirm the point.)

The feeling of being inescapably on the wrong side of a socio-theological divide is one Bunyan, again in retrospect, confidently invests in fellow villagers. After recording the visitation he experienced while playing cat he uncharacteristically halts the narration to insert a parenthesized paragraph of comment on the matter. He had at this time despairingly resigned himself to damnation, thinking that since salvation was out of the question he might as well 'fill my belly with [sin's] delicates' (24). This 'temptation of the Devil', he observes,

> is more usual amongst poor creatures then many are aware of, even to over-run their spirits with a scurvie and seared frame of heart . . . which frame, he stilly and slyly supplyeth with such despair, that though not much guilt attendeth the Soul, yet they continually have a secret conclusion within them, that there is no hopes for them. (25)

The observation draws together the central ideas of the reprobate frame and the social-theological ambivalence of the persecutory imagination as a communal, and not peculiarly Bunyanesque, experience.

Keith Thomas remarks that the puritan ministry had only themselves to blame if they made salvation so difficult to attain that poor people turned to the devil.[45] It seems clear that Bunyan is, in the example just cited, speaking of the poor—who occupied their spare time with village games and loafing—as well as the pitiable. When Bunyan met his discarded friend Harry in a lane and asked him, with real concern at his 'swearing and mad way': *'what will become of you if you die in this condition?* He answered me in a great chafe, *What would the Devil do for company if it were not for such as I am?'* (43). Bunyan adds no comment. Richard Norwood had a similar experience when he had burnt his finger and responded in dismal earnest to his host Mr Blank's jesting question as to how he would cope with hell. He triggers instant rage especially when he points out how 'very few . . . even of those that live within the Church' will be saved (p. 69). Blank proclaims angrily that if one man in the world was to be saved he 'would certainly believe that he was that man'. Lodowick Muggleton, who along with the prophet James Reeve travelled around issuing sentences of damnation to locals in alehouses, seems to have underestimated the sensitivity of victims. When one staggered recipient sought confirmation (*'Wilt thou say I am damn'd to eternity?'*) and Muggleton coolly replied, 'yea, said I, *thou art,*' a friend cried out, as violence broke out: *'For God's sake,* Lodowick, *let us be gon, else we shall be killed.'*[46]

The milieu Muggleton and others depict (alehouses were typically the resort of the poor and attracted regular complaints from the better sort[47]) supports the probable accuracy of Bunyan's view that a nagging anxiety and suppressed sense of rejection was a widely felt ripple effect of the installation of Calvinism in parish life. Christopher Hill is doubtful whether the very poor, before or after the revolution, were regular church-goers, but whether they were or not it is plausible that many of

---

[45] *Religion and the Decline of Magic* (1971), 474, 520. Gloom on a statistical basis alone would, as we have seen from estimates made by such popular writers as Dent, have been fully warranted. Bunyan thinks the existing group of Bedford separatists might be 'all that God would save in those parts' (66).

[46] *The Acts of the Witnesses* (1699), 50.

[47] Keith Wrightson, 'Aspects of Social Differentiation', p. 38. See also Peter Clark, 'The Alehouse and the Alternative Society', in D. Pennington and K. V. Thomas, edd., *Puritans and Revolutionaries: Essays in Seventeenth-Century History presented to Christopher Hill* (Oxford, 1978).

them felt their exclusion. 'The poor in all places', declared
Arthur Hildersam, a leading Calvinist, 'are for the most part the
most void of grace, and not so miserable in their corporal as in
their spiritual state.'[48] The two 'states' were presumptively
linked. It was understandable if people kept their distance, but
this does not mean they were always able to banish the
discriminatory creed from their minds. Richard Coppin, who
turned Ranter, was conscious of the effort ignorance required: he
spent his youth, he recalls, 'always fearing God as an angry God;
and so kept at a distance from God, by being ignorant of God'.[49]
There was a nasty corollary to the mass education to which
protestantism supplied the impetus. Ignorance entailed damnation.

Bunyan's turning to pastime, a form of self-distraction which
relegated but did not extirpate awareness that all the time his
soul was 'damning' (85), merely exposed him to the violent
irruption of the persecutory imagination (rather as Norwood had
experienced it) in the game of cat and later, for example, during
bell-ringing. *OED* does not record Bunyan's intransitive use of
the word 'damn' (being damned). The syntactic and semantic
extension serves to convey the Calvinist idea of damnation as a
relentless process which unrolled along the temporal axis of an
individual life whether or not it was present to consciousness. It
was an attitude to time quite opposed, as Leah Marcus points
out, to that of the medieval church whose liturgical drama
'removes its participants from everyday life and draws them into
its own special timeless realm'.[50] Archbishop Laud, of course,
saw advantages in both religious ritual and game-playing: their
repetitive nature created an illusion of stasis, tending to absorb
the individual into a communal identity and dissolve awareness
of social divisions. In turning to sport Bunyan was, in one sense,
practising on himself the stratagem Laud would have had
practised on him when, in 1633, he got Charles to re-issue James
I's *Book of Sports*. This licensing of games after service on Sunday
combined with the restoration of church ceremonial in a last-
ditch attempt to shore up an already-fractured, and in any case

---

[48] Quoted by Christopher Hill in *Society and Puritanism in Pre-Revolutionary England*
(1964), 473 ff., 285.   [49] *Truths Testimony* (1655), 9.
[50] *Childhood and Cultural Despair: A Theme and Variations in Seventeenth-Century
Literature* (Pittsburgh, 1978), 77–8.

idealized, social cohesion. Herrick best conveys the seductive illusion of togetherness in an order from the forces of reaction obedience to which was jollification itself: 'Come, we'll abroad; and let's obey | The proclamation made for May.'[51]

But Bunyan's acquired self-awareness did not permit relapse into such peasant innocence and the recollection crystallizes his confident generalization. The lower orders could not enjoy the psychic security which derived from the characteristic inclusiveness of the medieval church. The reprobate paradigm tended to seep into the brain though they did their best to form a protective carapace against it. Once the 'frame' had fastened on the spirit further experience 'supplied' it with confirmatory evidence, fortifying the 'secret' despair of salvation which was almost eclipsed from consciousness. This, at any rate, was the communal imagination by which Bunyan himself was victimized, situated as he was in the no man's land between the ineducable poor and his redeemable betters. 'So long as they live in ignorance,' wrote Perkins of the poor, they live 'either of custome, or example, or necessitie, as beasts doe, and not of faith: because they know not God's will touching things to be done or left undone.'[52] Harry, 'to whom', Bunyan admits, 'my heart before was knit more than to any other' (43) has to be discarded as callously as Ignorance as a self he could easily have been. He is treated as a staging post, measuring Bunyan's necessary self-distancing from an ordinary village existence which would actively damn him. It was the nasty doctrine of reprobation—itself a persuasive homologue for social polarization— that nagged at the mind in private making a shared communal identity impossible and driving the individual to save his own soul. The impetus to individualism was this negative one, not a positive attraction to the idea of election. Christian wants to escape from the City of Destruction before he knows where to go.

There is no antecedent moment at which Bunyan's experience can be examined divested of the culture-bound thought imbuing his perception. At the age of 9 or 10, Bunyan remembers, he despaired of heaven and suffered night and day from terrified thoughts of the day of judgement (5–7). Charles Doe, Bunyan's

---

[51] *Herrick's Poetical Works*, ed. L. C. Martin (Oxford, 1956), 67.
[52] Quoted by Keith Wrightson in *English Society*, p. 205.

contemporary and first biographer, tells us that Thomas Bunyan was 'of the national religion'[53] so we may assume that this was the upshot in his son's mind of the moderate doctrine axiomatically associated with Anglican village parsons of whatever era.[54] Actually, even Christopher Hall, successor to John Kellie (the incumbent of Bunyan's early years), appears, though beneficed at Elstow under Laud in 1639 and so necessarily an Episcopalian, to have had 'godly' traits, for he survived the Interregnum, prudently christening his son Oliver.[55] We know from Bunyan that he preached against Sunday sports (20). The glimpses Bunyan gives us of these two clerics conform well enough to general expectation. 'By the 1630s,' says Keith Wrightson, 'the English church had witnessed the emergence of a resident, graduate clergy . . . Many parishes now contained a resident intellectual for the first time in their history . . . Whether puritans or not, many were concerned to improve the standards of religious knowledge and moral conduct of their flocks . . . The pastoral capability of the church had thus been greatly enhanced and the penetration of the Reformation deepened.'[56]

Margaret Bottrall declares that the reason why *Grace Abounding* is so painful to read is that Bunyan's sufferings were 'so disproportionate to any rational cause'.[57] It is difficult to define rationality, however, other than in terms of the beliefs about the world consensual in a particular culture, and in such terms

---

[53] *The Struggler,* in *The Works of John Bunyan,* iii. 765.

[54] Roger Sharrock notes: 'It may be that there was a pathological side to the nervous intensity of these fears' (p. xliii). Again there is a strange assimilation of Bunyan to our own culture and a determined mollification of seventeenth-century protestantism. How much fear would be healthily proportionate to the prospect of everlasting torment? Bunyan did not invent the object of fear.

[55] Brown, *Bunyan,* pp. 49, 57.

[56] *English Society,* p. 209. Certainly conditions varied between regions and social groups. Underdown argues, for example, that in some parts of the West country the common people maintained their festive culture unimpressed and unperturbed by ruling puritan dogma (*Revel, Riot, and Rebellion, passim*). Bunyan's testimony seems, though, to fit a common pattern. Wrightson finds in the village of Terling that resident gentry families exhibited Calvinist piety from the 1580s, yeomen from around 1605 ('Aspects of Social Differentiation', p. 42). In such communities creeping Calvinism was not easy to ignore. It clearly was not the Bedford separatists who disseminated the doctrines that gave rise to Bunyan's early anxiety attacks. The approving term 'the godly' was familiar to 'our Neighbours' in Elstow (*Grace Abounding,* 31–2).

[57] Margaret Bottrall, *Every Man a Phoenix* (1958), 105.

Bunyan's responses, both to cat-playing and bell-ringing, were utterly rational. Nor were they idiosyncratic. Christopher Hall's sermon would not have been delivered in the placatory or remote tones often adopted by modern parsons (who, consciously or unknowingly, negotiate terms with a dominant culture to which they are marginal), but would have drawn full-throatedly on the anthologies of dire sabbatarian judgements which were popularly read and no doubt much more popularly circulated. He had the backing of a communally imagined God who would not have blasted the roof off York Minster without meaning it. As did *The Life and Death of Mr. Badman*, such anthologies combined (in our terms) entirely believable anecdotes with fantastic incidents of divine or demonic intervention: not as a form of trickery (mingling truth with lies in order to make the lies convincing) but because no significant conceptual distinction between them was recognized. An *exemplum* Hall might have used is this one, from Henry Burton:

In Moorfields near London, sundry youths playing at Catt on the Lords day, two of them fell out, and the one hitting the other under the eare with his catt, he therewith fell downe for dead in the place, the other was sent to prison: but the dead for the time, by God's mercy recovering, the prisoner was released; which may be a warning both to them, and all other youth, to take heed how they so profane the Lords day.[58]

But to judge from the effect on the young Bunyan it is likely that he also included some of the kind that involved more direct divine action. Whether he did so or not we can see even from the more pedestrian example how the persecutory imagination must have developed.

When he had been under the influence of a puritan friend for about a year Bunyan reports an incident which modern readers easily take as clinching evidence of insanity. Bells, as Jonson's Ananias exclaims, were profane to puritans. Consequently Bunyan, who enjoyed bell-ringing as a hobby, felt compelled to renounce it. Yet he ventured resistance to the extent of going to the steeple-house to listen. The punitive authority he had internalized proved too powerful for him:

---

[58] Henry Burton, *A Divine Tragedie Lately Acted, Or a Collection of Sundry Memorable Examples of God's Judgements upon Sabbath-Breakers, and other like Libertines, in their Unlawfull Sports* (1636), 23.

quickly after, I began to think, How, if one of the Bells should fall: then I chose to stand under a main Beam that lay over thwart the Steeple from side to side, thinking there I might stand sure: But then I should think again, Should the Bell fall with a swing, it might first hit the Wall, and then rebounding upon me, might kill me for all this Beam. (33)

So the thought processes go on until, fearing that the steeple itself will fall on his head, he is driven away from his carefully chosen position in the doorway. To assess Bunyan's rationality (and integrity) here one need only ask whether people really believed the judgemental stories that were in circulation. The answer must be that they did if they really believed in the God who was supposed to perpetrate such acts. It was certainly a small step from believing that God would damn the majority of the species to eternal punishment to believing that he executed summary judgement to exemplify this destructive capacity on earth. God's persistent interventionism was moreover the logical correlate of the Calvinist belief in total human passivity in relations with him. In view of the apparent reality of the Calvinist God in the communal imagination there is no obvious reason for impugning the culture-bound rationality of Bunyan in responding as he did. George Fox, founder of the Quaker movement, complained on one occasion that he had been mugged by a gang of church spires: 'As I was walking with several friends, I lifted up my head, and saw three steeple-house spires, and they struck at my life.'[59] Bunyan merely expresses the rational feeling of providential persecution with unique clarity.

His apprehensions may have been in response to the tale of Thomas Perkin who in Chichester in the winter of 1635 was profaning the sabbath with his ringing when 'the rope tooke him up, and flinging him about 8. foot high, he fell downe on his head, and was taken up dead'. Indeed the fears were kept within moderate bounds if one considers the fate of some Hertfordshire boys, one of whom committed the compound felony of tolling the bell at Chidlington in order to summon his friends to a game of football:

some being come into the Church the redevoze of their meeting, suddenly it thundering was seene a blacke ball come tumbling downe a hill neere by: which tooke its course directly into the Church, there it

---

[59] Quoted by William James in *The Varieties of Religious Experience* (1902), 7.

flew into the bell free and first slew him, that tolled the bell, then it flustered about the Church and hurted divers of them, and at last bursting; left a filthy stinke like to that of brimstone, and so left a terror to all such spend thrifts of precious time.[60]

The thunderbolt behaves with far more 'extraordinary' and 'particular' providence in homing in on its targets—meting out damage proportionate to crimes—than Bunyan's rebounding bell and collapsing steeple which would only need to be nudged into convenient compliance with physical laws.

This then was the imaginative ambience in which Bunyan lived. The Calvinist God was a communal construct from which the individual could not easily escape. Whether one takes the view of historians who hold that a majority of the English people subscribed to religious orthodoxy or that of Christopher Hill that sectarian heterodoxy was rife, the persecutory imagination was, more or less, a constant for both groups.[61] Bunyan clearly resembles the earlier Norwood except that the idea of persecution apparently acquired plausibility without the assistance of parental severity. The feeling of helpless circumvention is similar: 'Now should I find my minde to flee from God, as from the face of a dreadful Judge; yet this was my torment, I could not escape his hand' (173). The differences between Norwood and Bunyan are less significant than they may seem. Norwood's family was a notch or two up the social scale from Bunyan's and he lived in a period in which Calvinism was an unquestionable ruling ideology. Paradoxically, however, while Calvinists lost control of the Church in the 1630s this is the time when the engine of religious reform by a preaching ministry had progressively penetrated humble community life with (predominantly)

---

[60] Henry Burton, *A Divine Tragedie*, pp. 18, 27.

[61] Hill criticizes Patrick Collinson's assumption that there was (up to 1625 anyway—and in his review he looks forward to Bunyan's contemporaries) a 'religious majority'. Hill points out that Collinson quotes 'one seventeenth-century preacher who thought only one in twenty of the population was "Christian indeed" ' (Patrick Collinson, *The Religion of Protestants*, p. 191, rev. Christopher Hill, *TLS* (18 March 1983), 257). This is surely a rather generous estimate in contemporary terms of those who would be saved—as opposed to those who wanted to be and could in a broader sense be called religious. Scepticism has in turn, moreover, been directed at the extent of heterodoxy suggested by historians who have concentrated on the writings of a vociferous few. John Morrill judges that 'at no point in the . . . period 1643–1654 did more than 5 per cent attend religious assemblies other than those associated with their parish churches' ('The Church in England 1642–9', in John Morrill, ed., *Reactions to the English Civil War 1642–1649* (1982), 90).

Calvinist ideas. And, of course, the Interregnum saw their restoration to the status of orthodoxy. So Norwood and Bunyan each confronted the Calvinist God at his most powerful in his own social milieu. Bunyan was, it is true, aware of the fragmentation of Calvinist belief: he had dealings with Quakers and Ranters and must have been exposed to other ideas during his years in the New Model army. In spite of this, however, he seems to have been no freer than Norwood to choose his own values.

Indeed the writings of Ranters, Quakers, and other groups almost invariably attest the experience of Calvinist despair. They confirm the extent of persecution as much as they indicate a means of escape. It was language primarily, the Ranters realized, that oppressed them. Their exhilarated emancipation took the form of inverting and abusing the language of Calvinism in order to scramble its concepts. It was an admirable exercise in bravura. In a letter to his friend Thomas Webbe and his family on 3 April 1650 Joseph Salmon lovingly wrote:

Eternal plagues consume you all, rot, sink and damn your bodies and souls into devouring fire, where none but those that walk uprightly can enter. Sirs, I wish you damnable well, because I dearly love you; the Lord grant we may know the worth of hell, that we may forever scorn heaven.[62]

The energy comes from the wildness of the defiance required if they were to buck the authoritarian ideology from their imaginations.

Bunyan, says Sharrock, 'dissociates himself from the excesses of the Ranters' (p. xv). Again one cannot help jibbing at the phrasing. Nothing could be characterized as excessive in comparison with the Calvinist orthodoxy, and the genteel restraint which seems to be ascribed to Bunyan does not correspond to his memory. What he says is that God 'did not suffer' him to join the Ranters although the temptation (of divinely sanctioned libertinism) was 'suitable to [his] flesh'. Bunyan's passive phrasing, obedient as ever to Calvinist dictates, is not merely a pious formula or a stylistic tic but the casing of a mode of experience. God 'kept [him] in the fear of his name' (45):

---

[62] Reprinted in *A Collection of Ranter Writings from the Seventeenth Century*, ed. Nigel Smith (1983), 201.

he could not escape the expectation of punishment which paralysed any move to embrace such freedom. It was not possible for him to choose what kind of God to believe in. Indeed, as his later mention of Ranters makes plain, it was not just the attractions of libertinism which commended Ranter (and atheist) tenets to him but also the despair induced by his existing beliefs: '*If you must perish*', the tempter put it to him, '*never torment yourself so much beforehand, drive the thoughts of damning out of your mind, by possessing your mind with some such conclusions that* Atheists *and* Ranters *use to help themselves withal*' (161). It was too late for Bunyan (in the throes of his despair at selling Christ) to sequester himself, as he had tried to do in adolescence, from a belief system which had burned into him so deeply. In one of his latest treatises Bunyan remained convinced that 'despair is the cause, that there are so many that would fain be Atheists in the world. For, because, they have entertained a conceit that God will never be merciful to them, therefore they labour to persuade themselves that there is no God at all, as if their misbelief would kill God, or cause him to cease to be' (i. 92). Of course recognition of the motive invalidated the strategy.

Bunyan noticed that it was the 'strict in Religion' who were 'swept away by these Ranters' (45). Jane Turner offered an intelligent explanation of what she called 'the greatest mystery of iniquity', namely the appeal of antinomian ideas, especially around 1650, to 'the most eminent Saints . . . as to personal grace and qualifications, and as to a strict conversation'. It was that, 'having been a long time in darkness and ignorance, being but newly brought from under the Bishops and Presbyterian yokes, they were generally weak in Judgement, though (it may be) strong in affection, and so the more easily deceived; like children ready to catch up anything that hath a glorious appearance, not weighing and considering whether it be really so.'[63] Though carrying the inevitable bias of a Baptist against the Ranters, this account interestingly associates the ability to break out of a dour Calvinism with the breakdown of monarchical and ecclesiastical authority. No doubt it surprises us less than it did Turner and Bunyan that it was the most repressed individuals whose behaviour took the most extravagant forms. Yet Turner is surely

<hr>

[63] *Choice Experiences*, pp. 149–51.

right about the mechanism of this uninhibited release of the affections. A heady sense of freedom resulted which outran both the actual changes in the structure of society and the residue in the psyche of long conditioning in an authoritarian climate. That is not to denigrate the Ranters, or to devalue their contribution to a radical tradition. But it was not merely timorous piety that held Bunyan back; while he was tempted, there was a level at which, 'weighing and considering whether it [was] really so', he could not persuade himself of the sustainability in his culture of such kicking over the traces.

Often the apparently successful ideological escapees confirm the inescapability of the Calvinist God. Lodowick Muggleton, who suffered from reprobate despair, comments on the splintering of religious belief after the Civil War and his own profound relief when friends informed him that death meant extinction. It was not long, however, before his 'old Fears of Hell rose up in me, as it did formerly, when a *Puritan*'. Persecuted by his culturally conditioned imagination he did not know 'which way to help myself out of Gods hands'. Because he moved on to a new religion he is able to give his responses in a less loaded way than the reviewing Norwood or Bunyan. His mind was stung to revolt and despair by the injustice and cruelty of the Calvinist God, rejecting the dishonest analogy with a potter and his clay: it merely compared God and man to the craftsman's moral advantage, '*for Man made Vessels of Honour or Dishonour, of dead senseless Clay*, that is neither capable of Honour nor Dishonour, nor capable of Pain, nor of Misery'. Above all he was obsessed by the concept of God's 'prerogative Will' and 'prerogative Power' which set him 'above the Law'. It pre-empted criticism (he need not give 'any reason why') and resistance ('who shall hinder him').[64]

While the candour is refreshing and makes explicit the subtextual murmurings in the Calvinist autobiographies it would be wrong to suppose that Muggleton left such imaginings behind. When, captivated by the charisma of his visionary cousin John Reeve, he did acquire new convictions, the scarring of his mind was all too evident. His fantasy of aggrandizement attests the virtual impossibility of escaping the mind-shaping effects of

[64] *Acts of the Witnesses*, pp. 17, 19, 25–32.

Calvinism. What seemed to him 'marvelous' about Reeve was that 'it was never heard this many Ages, that a poor Man should have that Power to Bless and Curse Men and Women to Eternity.' Terror at God's prerogative power was overcome by arrogating it ('Prophets' such as Reeve and, before long, himself 'have a prerogative Power, as God')[65] and with it the persecutory providence or maleficent magic in which they exulted.

Muggleton's fantasy, inverting his powerlessness, was desperately thin. While the Ranters, Muggletonians, and others may have taken an important imaginative step towards the overthrow of the Calvinist God and the idea of hell[66] their own minds seem often to be trapped in reaction to them. Wise, in *Mr. Badman*, wonders 'if there be such a thing as an atheist in the world' (p. 219). In the imaginative ambience the autobiographical literature constructs this does not seem an absurd speculation. G. E. Aylmer, an eminent historian who has looked for evidence of 'Unbelief in Seventeenth-Century England', professes himself unable to discover evidence, at any rate, of ' "grass-roots" unbelief, going beyond mere heterodoxy, eccentricity, or blasphemous scoffing'.[67] But what the heterodox sectarians seem to have contributed to Bunyan's environment, which makes religious experience probably more complicated than it was for Norwood, is almost the corollary of Wise's remark: certainty that there was a God seems to have been nearly as difficult to maintain as confidence that there was not. So while religious anxiety can be seen to gnaw at the minds of Bunyan's non-puritan contemporaries, and to have some shaping influence on the new views of many of the enthusiasts, there is also a significant contrary influence on Bunyan. His mind could not entirely deny admittance to the doubts circulating around it. This observation will seem to weaken the claim for the potency of the persecutory imagination. Curiously, though, it strengthens it, as Bunyan himself seems to have been aware.

Bunyan had atheistic doubts of (in our terms) a rational kind.

---

[65] *Acts of the Witness*, 42, 145.

[66] Christopher Hill judges that D. P. Walker, in *The Decline of Hell*, 'emphasizes insufficiently the contribution of intellectual radicals to this emergence of a more palatable morality' (*The World Turned Upside Down: Radical Ideas during the English Revolution* (Harmondsworth, 1975), 178).

[67] 'Unbelief in Seventeenth-Century England', in Pennington and Thomas, edd., *Puritans and Revolutionaries*, p. 31.

Could it be, he wondered, for example, 'that we onely, who live but in a corner of the Earth' should have the truth: 'Everyone doth think his own Religion rightest, both *Jews*, and *Moors*, and *Pagans*; and how if all our Faith, and Christ, and Scriptures, should be but a think-so too?' (97). Such thoughts are, however, indistinguishable in his mind from blasphemy and are naturally perceived as demonic temptations to which he has succumbed. The ironic conclusion he comes to is that 'God had in very wrath to my Soul given me up unto them' (99). He was unable to refute the arguments 'against the very *being* of God' (96), and yet his imaginary picture of God retained its potency so that (even at the time, he credibly claims) he considered his atheism a divine punishment. As for Donne ('Those are my best dayes, when I shake with feare'[68]) or James Fraser whose 'Fear of God did prove a God, and my Belief of a Deity',[69] terror, the sense of persecution, was generally the strongest religious emotion, whether it prevailed over 'flattering speaches' or intellectual unbelief. In this way the hypocrisy-rejection syndrome came into play for Bunyan. If he could disbelieve the existence of God all his claimed elect experience of him was invalidated—which meant that he was rejected. He was damned if he did believe and damned if he didn't: 'So that whether I did think that God was, or again did think there were no such thing; no love, nor peace, nor gracious disposition could I feel within me' (101).

This episode was not isolated: such doubts were recurrent. Reflecting on his agonies over mentally consenting to sell Christ Bunyan considers that it was a punishment for atheism. When his wife was screaming in labour he had, by praying for a cessation of her pain, tested whether there was a God who could perceive the thoughts of the heart. God obliged, but bore a grudge against him for a year and a half before finding the opportunity to punish the insolence. When he consented to 'Let Christ go if he will' Bunyan was reminded that God had shown that he 'knew my secret thoughts' (240–2). Two and a half years of punitive despair ensued. But the most telling admission of all is that in 'The Conclusion'. Not only do 'Inclinings to unbelief' head the list of abominations he finds in his heart 'to this day', but he unequivocally affirms in the first sentence:

[68] *The Divine Poems*, p. 16.   [69] *Memoirs of the Life* (Edinburgh, 1738), 121.

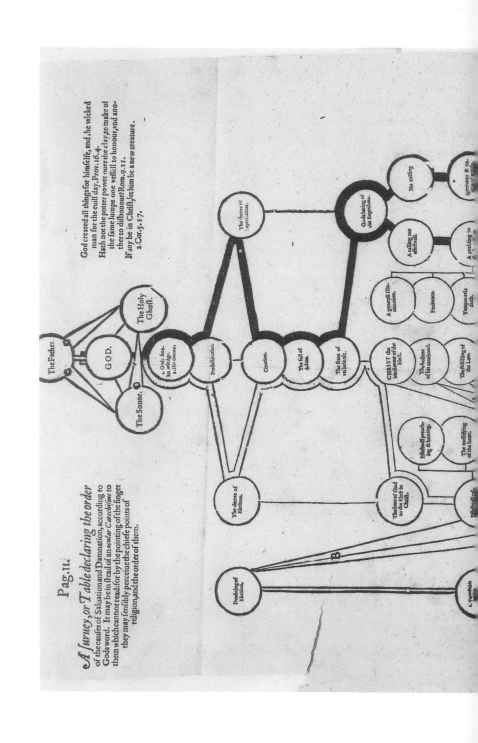

Pag. 174.

A survey, or Table declaring the order of the causes of Saluation and Damnation, according to Gods word. It may be in stead of an *ocular Catechisme* to them which cannot read: for by the pointing of the finger they may sensibly perceiue the chiefe points of religion, and the order of them.

God created all things for himselfe, and the wicked man for the euill day. Prov. 16.4.
Hath not the potter power ouer the clay, to make of the same lumpe one vessell to honour, and another to dishonour? Rom. 9.21.
If any be in Christ, let him be a new creature. 2.Cor.5.17.

A roote are Eefaie.

Goodnes in finne.

Pulnes of finne.

Duration.

Death eternall in hell.

Relapse.

Zeale.

The decris of finne.

The hardening of the heart.

An euill heart.

An vnbeleeuing heart.

Apostasie.

Deniall.

Bondage vnder the graue.

Refurrection.

Ascension.

Sitting at the right hand of God.

Intercession.

The temporarie death.

The laft Iudgement.

The declaration of Gods iustice.

New obedience.

Ramification of finne.

Imputation of righteousnesse.

Mortification.

Vivification.

Repentance.

The declaration of Gods iustice and mercie.

Gods glorie.

Doubting of iuftification.

Conscience of infidelitie.

Effectuall

Sanctification.

Glorification.

Life eternall.

Enemies of life eternall.

To the Reader.

The white line sheweth the order of the causes of saluation from the first to the last.

The blacke line sheweth the order of the causes of damnation.

The lines A, A, A, shew, how faith doth apprehend Christ, and all his benefits, and applieth them to the person of euery beleeuer, in his iustification and sanctification.

The lines B, B, B, describing, likewise shew the temtation of the godly, and their remedies.

The wide spaces C. C. C. shew the communication of the Godhead from the Father to the Sonne, and from them both to the holy Ghost.

O the altitude of the riches, both of the wisdome and knowledge of God: how vnsearchable are his iudgements, and his waies past finding out? Rom. 11.33. I count all things but dung, that I may winne Christ. Philip. 3.9.

Ignatius saying, My loue is crucified.

Perkins's 'Table'

Of all the Temptations that ever I met with in my life, to question the being of God, and the truth of his Gospel, is the worst, and worst to be born; when this temptation comes, it takes away my girdle from me, and removeth the foundations from under me. (p. 102)

This is a disclosure of enormous importance. It suggests the link between the reprobate frame, in which it seemed impossible that God was favourable to him, and the evaporation of confidence in religious experience. Bunyan's pastor, John Gifford, had pressed the congregation 'to cry mightily to God, that he would convince us of the reality' of religious truths: they must come 'with evidence from Heaven' (117). It is the imperative to feel 'the reality of the truth of his Gospel', which Bunyan does feel 'at times' (109), which both impels him to give his experience of it concrete, written form and, by forcing such claims to certitude, increases its precariousness, its vulnerability to radical questioning. Contemporary religious scepticism and the discourse of an oppressive ideology joined forces to infiltrate Bunyan's mind and expose him to the wrath of the God of his own imagination.

Bunyan absorbed the full imaginative force of the persecutory ideology—to such an extreme degree that he achieved from it a conviction of the impotence of all mankind, a credible superior awareness which, when it prevailed in his imagination, constituted his assurance of salvation. It was an assurance which seems superior to, for example, Muggleton's stridency. We may compare the composed dignity with which Bunyan responded in the court-room to the stock claim that he was possessed by the spirit of the devil (p. 117) with Muggleton's sharp-witted but somewhat shrill declaration when a Lord Mayor made the same suggestion to John Reeve: 'Sir, you have sinned against the Holy Ghost, and will be Damn'd.' Bunyan's biblical knowledge clearly rattled his opponents whereas Muggleton reports an interruption by the Recorder ('Mr. *Reeve*, Mr. *Reeve, You have spoke enough; let* Aaron *speak*')[70] which indicates the easy sarcasm with which he could be treated.

It is perhaps disappointing that Bunyan did not translate his fervour for a religion in which the poor could be redeemed into a radical politics. Yet it may be argued that his imagination

---

[70] Acts of the Witnesses, pp. 71, 77.

responds more fully to the predicament of the lower orders than that of more radical contemporaries exactly because his estimation of the insuperable power of his worldly antagonists was, at that historical juncture, accurate. Cromwell himself, it should be remembered, was determined to preserve 'the ranks and orders of men, whereby England hath been known for hundreds of years: a nobleman, a gentleman, a yeoman' (nothing lower than this got on the map).[71] He had, as Conrad Russell observes in his review of Hill's *The Experience of Defeat*, 'never believed in a world in which Saints took over power from gentlemen'.[72] For Bunyan defeat, so far as his social status went, was a foregone conclusion. The paradoxes of Christianity offered a transvaluation, so that low seemed high and high low—but the social indicators of spiritual exclusion remained hard to resist.

The conceptual frames kept effacing each other: the reprobate, which endorsed the *status quo* and discriminated against him, and the elect, which elevated him above it by virtue of his submission to an authority higher than the great ones of the world, an authority to whom they neglected proper obeisance. Faithful defends himself, tortuously but carefully, on this basis at Vanity Fair: 'he had only set himself against that which had set it self against him that is higher than the highest' (p. 93). He could have been reading Hobbes, for it is, ironically, his conservative logic that is reproduced: 'And whosoever thinking Soveraign Power too great, will seek to make it lesse; must subject himselfe, to the Power, that can limit it; that is to say, to a greater.'[73] Accordingly, Christian says to Apollyon: 'But I have let my self to another, even to the King of Princes, and how can I with fairness go back with thee?' (p. 57). To the extent that persecution became that by identifiable '*Adversaries of God's Truth*', Bunyan's 'humanistic religious experience' as one 'among minorities striving for freedom and independence' developed; but the internalized ideological persecution was always liable to reactivation. He could find himself bereft of belief in God which not only left him exposed to the condemnation and ridicule of the

---

[71] *The Writings and Speeches of Oliver Cromwell*, ed. W. C. Abbott (Harvard, 1937–47), iii. 435.

[72] Conrad Russell, review of Christopher Hill, *The Experience of Defeat: Milton and Some Contemporaries* (1984), *LRB* (4–17 Oct. 1984), 20.

[73] *Leviathan*, ed. C. B. Macpherson (Harmondsworth, 1968), 260.

ruling powers but led to the swift reinstatement of a hostile deity in his imagination. The idea that he could be 'free and responsible for his own fate' was furthermore always shudderingly rejected. His concept of total divine circumvention, whether by dramatic intervention, ordinary event, or manipulation of mental states, must be grasped in its full extremism if the imagination which informs *The Pilgrim's Progress* is to be understood. Above all the blinking doubleness of self-perception, of perception of the identity God had secreted in the soul, and the consequent ambivalence of the providence which discovered it supplies the narrative dynamic of the allegory, as it squeezed Bunyan's mind forward paragraph by paragraph in its scrupulous interrogation of his own experience.

4

The Pilgrim's Progress:
Allegory and the Persecutory Imagination

A recent essay on 'The Theology of *The Pilgrim's Progress*' asserts that 'neither election nor reprobation touches Christian's own experience. Bunyan is determined in *The Pilgrim's Progress* to present the experience of a Christian, and this emphasis precludes the serious treatment of doctrines that relate to the mind of God rather than the mind of Christian.'[1] To which one can only reply that the mind of Christian contains little besides the doctrines of election and reprobation, which constitute the simple apparatus through which both his experience and that of others is processed. As Gervase Babington said, 'Election is a thing revealed by steps.'[2] Christian devotes most of his energy to sizing up the meaning, in the light of the decrees of election and reprobation, of each step in his journey. In fact even events of the narrative, such as the Slough of Despond and Doubting Castle, express an interpretative activity motivated by fears of reprobation. Leading puritan Richard Greenham suggests, too, the way in which attention is focused less on the journey itself than on indications of the final destination: 'There be some notable

---

[1] Gordon Campbell in V. Newey, ed., *The Pilgrim's Progress: Critical and Historical Views* (Liverpool, 1980), 257. Campbell pursues a similar argument in 'Fishing in Other Men's Waters: Bunyan and the Theologians' in N. H. Keeble, ed., *John Bunyan: Conventicle and Parnassus* (Oxford, 1988). He sees Bunyan's eagerness to 'exhort his congregation and his readers to repent of their sins' as indicative of 'a discrepancy . . . between the [predestinarian] theological position he had inherited from his Bedford congregation and his private practical beliefs' (p. 149). But evangelical zeal—exhorting people to repent—was regarded as entirely compatible with predestinarian belief by most of Bunyan's co-religionists: 'we ought', said Calvin, 'to be so affectioned that we would al men to be saved' (*Inst.* 3. 23. 14). It was up to God whether such divinely inspired zeal was allowed to be the instrument of conversion. A notable exception to the usual critical aversion to the influence of predestinarian dogma is the chapter 'Bunyan's *Pilgrim's Progress*: The Doctrine of Predestination and the Shaping of the Novel' in Wolfgang Iser, *The Implied Reader: Patterns of Communication in Prose Fiction from Bunyan to Beckett* (1974).

[2] Gervase Babington, *A Profitable Exposition of the Lords Prayer, by Way of Questions and Answers for More Plainnesse* in *The Workes* (1615), 116.

markes to know whether our journey be to heaven or to hell.'[3]
Even Badman, who does not know he is on a spiritual journey,
takes 'steps' which are glossed by the godly commentators whose
awareness of a controlling reprobate teleology imposes the
ideology which should have been internalized in his conscience.
Glued to Christian's mental retina is, again, Bunyan's *Mapp*, a
grid through which the providential text of the world and the self
is organized and read.

The Pilgrim's Progress is, explicitly, a book of signs, a variation
(for which Bunyan felt some pressure to apologize) on the books
of signs which mesmerized the autobiographers and a development from the rudimentary fictions in the genre offered by
Perkins's and Dent's dialogues.[4] It is also a variation on the
autobiography—being a fictional spiritual biography seen largely
from the subject's point of view. The object of writing *Grace
Abounding* seemed to be to produce a version of the life which
tipped (a term Bunyan used himself (175)) towards an elect
reading in spite of the subtext of anxiety and loss of belief which
made the stabilizing activity necessary. Other readers could then
seek to detect similar developments by reviewing their own
experience. The exchange of such readings of experience seems to
have been the central activity in puritan culture. Experience,
'either a begetter, or an effect of knowledge', according to Jane
Turner's definition,[5] turned into, or was constituted by, post-
experiential narrative—whether undertaken in private or orally
exchanged or bridging the two with the simultaneously self-
communing and communicating written word. Outsiders also
supplied readable narratives, though they did not know it: 'His
debauched life', says Wise of Badman, 'was read and known of
all men; but his repentance was read and known of no man; for,
as I said, he had none' (pp. 283–4).

The Pilgrim's Progress manages to roll into one the book of signs,
the life of the individual Christian, and the community, hostile
and friendly, in which it was situated. This meant that readers
could fully invest themselves in the text, trying by peering into a

---

[3] *The Workes* (1599), 36.

[4] *A Dialogue of the State of a Christian Man* in *The Works* (Cambridge, 1605), 455; *The
Plaine Mans Path-Way to Heaven* (1601): Dent's subtitle runs *Wherein Every Man may
Clearly See, whether he shall be Saved or Damned.*

[5] *Choice Experiences of the Kind Dealings of God, before, in, and after Conversion* (1653),
198.

series of true and false mirrors to determine their identity. The
verses attached to the elect side of Bunyan's *Mapp* read:

> *When thou dost read this side then look*
> *Into thy Heart, as in a Book*
> *And see if thou canst read the same*
> *In thee from God by Christ his name*
> *If not, then fear the other side*
> *Which not to life but death doth guide*

Fifteen years later he concludes his Apology for *The Pilgrim's
Progress*:

> *Would'st read thy self, and read thou know'st not what*
> *And yet know whether thou art blest or not,*
> *By reading the same lines? O then come hither,*
> *And lay my Book, thy Head and Heart together.*

(p. 7)

One notes again the automatic inclusion of the corollary ('If
not . . .', 'or not') which haunted the puritan mind, at least since
Perkins's 'whether he be the child of God, or no'.[6] The book
expresses a dual teleology throughout and sets up a tense rapport
with the reader. The same is true of *Mr. Badman*: the declared
purpose is 'that thou mayest, as in a glass, behold with thine own
eyes the steps that take hold of hell; and also discern, while thou
art reading of Mr. Badman's death, whether thou thyself art
treading in his path thereto . . . whether thou art one of his
lineage or no' (p. 139). Bunyan anthropomorphizes the book,
which raids households and makes arrests (p. 140). Equally the
book was likely to meet with rough treatment: Badman's
fraternity, Bunyan expects, will 'rend, burn, or throw it away in
contempt' (p. 142). Bunyan himself not only expected to be
struck in his psyche by verses from his Bible but was incited to
physical violence towards it: 'for about a fortnight before, I was
looking on this very place, and then I thought it could not come
near my Soul with comfort, and threw down my Book in a pet.'[7]

In his quaint 'Authors Way of Sending forth his Second Part of
the Pilgrim' the book is identified with its central figure,
Christiana, who is instructed to call at doors announcing herself.
The timorous book pipes up with various objections:

[6] *Works*, p. 502.   [7] *Grace Abounding*, 223, 204.

What shall I do, when I at such a door,
For *Pilgrims* ask, and they shall rage the more?

(p. 169)

—again an unsurprising reaction to the question on which the book impaled the psyche. Bunyan's ambulating book nerving herself up on the doorstep is a natural development from the conception of Christiana as a reader of Christian's narrative who, like any other reader, invests herself in the text, laying together book, head, and heart: she follows his way. Real readers are then invited to identify themselves in her text, and so it goes on, people transforming themselves into texts and texts taking on anthropomorphic vitality. Both book and person insert themselves into a discourse—the (puritan) Word—of which they become vehicles. Allegory could push the assimilative process beyond the scope of spiritual autobiography, bringing together body and soul by anchoring the spiritual record to a material ambience, so that a fuller sense of the book as a literally encapsulated life was possible.

The allegory, then, united several functions of cultural transmission and reinforcement. It also acted as a solvent for physical-psychical-spiritual distinctions which meant little to puritans. As has been partly shown these distinctions did not much signify in the puritan imagination for the simple reason that the providential agency of God (or the devil) was equally evident and equally the object of interest in all three realms. To the book of conscience could be added the book of creatures, the book of providence, and the Bible; and all derived significance for the puritan from the inferable intention of the divine author who had or had not included them in the book of life. All events were supernatural in the sense that they were caused by God (sometimes through the devil's agency), whether they were mental events or events in the external world. There is no qualitative difference in the nature of imprisonment in Vanity Fair and in Doubting Castle, no formal encouragement to distinguish between the two in terms of a physical-psychical opposition. We are in a sense aware that one represents a physical and the other a psychic persecution but the mode of presentation denies significance to the distinction, insisting instead on the assessment to be made of the divine purpose behind both incidents.

Physical, psychic, and metaphysical events are blended, through allegory, in a textual continuum. The sudden materialization of a hand proferring 'leaves of the Tree of Life, the which *Christian* took' (p. 60) occurs without fuss in a narrative embodying belief in a habitually interventionist God whose synecdochic hand protruded from the clouds in familiar emblem books—usually to perform some internal operation on the heart.[8] James Fraser unexceptionally records feeling 'some physical sensible Touch of God's Hand on the Will, determining me and bowing me to assent, taking away the Resistance'.[9] Christian's recuperation after his fight with Apollyon is real, whether conceived of as physical or psychological, and he naturally attributes it to a, for him, real (divine) cause. 'God asserts his possession of omnipotence,' said Calvin, 'and claims our acknowledgement of this attribute; not such as is imagined by sophists, vain, idle and almost asleep, but vigilant, efficacious, operative, and engaged in continual action.'[10] The allegory makes the hand of providence material just as it makes physical and psychic imprisonment material: all have equivalent reality-status.

The Life and Death of Mr. Badman also conveys the felt insignificance of conceptual distinctions between inner, outer, and supernatural—and, moreover, between active and passive. When Badman 'ran away' from the puritan master to whom he was apprenticed Wise quickly deprecates the idea that he has acted autonomously, turning Badman into the recipient of a divine judgement: 'for a wicked man to be by the providence of God turned out of a good man's doors, into a wicked man's house to dwell, is a sign of the anger of God . . . This was, therefore, another judgment that did come upon this young Badman' (p. 192). Other 'judgments' include acts of self-destruction (the gory suicide of the despairer John Cox (pp. 293–4)), natural disasters (Dorothy Mately 'sinking into the ground' in a minor landslide (p. 169)), and supernatural events (the man from

[8] See, for instance, David Cramer, *Emblemata Sacra. Hoc est Decades Quinque Emblematum ex Sacra Scriptura* (Frankfurt, 1624). This was an influential protestant emblem book. See also Barbara K. Lewalski, *Protestant Poetics and the Seventeenth-Century Religious Lyric* (Princeton, 1979), 195 ff.

[9] *Memoirs of the Life* (Edinburgh, 1738), 132.

[10] Quoted by Charles Trinkaus in 'Renaissance Problems in Calvin's Theology', *SIR* 1 (1954), 59–80, p. 68.

Salisbury who drank the devil's health and promptly disappeared through a window on which witnesses found blood stains (p. 268)).

Bunyan, it should be clear by now, believed such reported incidents to have taken place. It is very hard to get back to what actually happened on any of these occasions; what actually happened was instantly woven into the providential text, details no doubt being shaped by the reading grid. But we do have reason to believe that nothing as crude as arbitrary invention was responsible. Dorothy Mately eked out a living by sifting for lead ore. Accused of thieving twopence from a lad's trousers (Bunyan is more precise about the circumstances of the crime than his known sources, no doubt wishing to make God's point more emphatic), she 'violently denied it, wishing that the ground might swallow her up if she had them'. Ashover parish burial register records the sequel: '1660. Dorothy Matly, supposed wife of John Flint, of this parish, foreswore herself; whereupon the ground open, and she sanke over hed March 1st; and being found dead ['with the boy's single two pence', says Bunyan, 'in her pocket'] she was buried March 2nd.'[11]

With equal solemnity, it appears, Bunyan once encouraged a woman to press charges of witchcraft on the basis of claims Judge Windham dismissed, at Cambridge Assizes in 1659, as 'a meer dream, and a phantasie'. The luckless Margaret Pryor was, she complained, plucked from the connubial bed, transformed into a bay mare, mounted by two Quakers, and ridden four miles to a banquet at Maddenly House where she was reined to a door-latch. From this position she noted consumption of lamb, mutton, and rabbit; she was able to identify the revellers who, Bunyan apparently recorded for his informant, 'as they sate at the table did shine so bright as if they had been Angels'. Outraged Quaker James Blackley detected mendacity in the claim that 'they had Lamb at that time of the year, in *November*', denied that a mare could make such observations, and found a clinching contradiction in Bunyan's record of a bay 'horse' (not

[11] *Life and Death of Mr. Badman*, p. 169; H. E. Rollins, ed., *The Pack of Autolycus: Or Strange and Terrible News of Ghosts, Apparitions, Monstrous Births, Showers of Wheat, Judgments of God, and Other Prodigious and Fearful Happenings as Told in Broadside Ballads of the Years 1624–1693* (Cambridge Mass., 1927; reissued 1969), 62–7; J. C. Cox, *The Parish Registers of England* (1910), 133.

mare). Of more evidential force perhaps was the victim's failure to exhibit sore feet or bruising after her equestrian outing; she had, however, dirtied her smock: 'what,' Blackley reasonably exclaims, 'can a horse be ridden in a womans smock?'[12]

W. Y. Tindall discusses this incident in a rather puzzled appendix. But there is no puzzle (except perhaps in Bunyan's logistical inattentiveness); to Bunyan the woman's tale documented an entirely plausible demonic feat. Tindall, who himself points out that several of the judgements contained in *Mr. Badman* derive from anthologies such as Jessey's and Clarke's, says that 'each of Bunyan's stories contains the customary details, so essential to the suspension of disbelief, of name, place, and date.'[13] But Bunyan is not an eighteenth-century novelist playing tricks with truth and fiction. Wise insists, after recounting two reported incidents from Samuel Clarke's *A Mirrour or Looking-Glasse* (1646) (by the same respected author as the frequently repeated eulogistic comments on Perkins), that 'they are as true as notable'. Bunyan believed his spokesman to be telling the truth (at least we have no reason to doubt this). He does not try to convince us that Mr Badman is a real person. The comparatively level-headed Richard Baxter believed such tales as that New England antinomian Mrs Hutchinson 'brought forth about 30 mishapen Births or Lumps at once,' that another, Mrs Dyer, 'did . . . bring forth a Monster, which had the Parts of almost all sorts of living Creatures,' and so on, ingenuously documenting his source: 'as you may see in a little Book of Mr. Tho. Welds'.[14] Where factual claims—especially in print—coincided with general presuppositions even the best-educated puritans were credulous. Judgements such as those compiled by Beard, Reynolds, Burton, Clarke, Jessey, and others were just dramatic examples of the activity of providence everywhere, controlling the evolution of elect and reprobate destinies.

Although the imagination informing both *Progress* and *Badman* is the same—and has suffered no attentuation since *Grace Abounding*—*Progress* has the advantage of not relying on discursive

---

[12] James Blackley, *A Lying Wonder Discovered, and the Strange Newes from Cambridge Proved False . . . Also this Contains an Answer to John Bunions Paper touching the Said Imagined Witchcraft* (1659), 2–7.

[13] *John Bunyan, Mechanick Preacher* (New York, 1934), 221, 199.

[14] *Reliquiae Baxterianae*, ed. M. Sylvester (1696), 74–5.

commentary to convey it. *Mr. Badman* is, in our terms, more realistic but it is into the allegory that Bunyan's mind more easily funnels his culture and its imaginative habits. Like a dream it contains a proportion of realistic material but it also questions the boundaries of our reality, merging mind and matter and revealing them to be interpenetrating. Christiana, for example, has a dream, within Bunyan's dream, in which she peruses 'a broad Parchment . . . in which were recorded the sum of her ways', the book of her life to date, and becomes aware of the reality of her black prospects.[15] This self-appraisal could have taken place easily enough when awake but the dream enforces the reader's sense of God's agency: it is his providence that inserts awareness of sin into the brain. Then, we are told, 'she thought she saw two very ill favoured ones standing by her Bed-side, and saying, *'What shall we do with this Woman?'* (p. 178). We may ask, though it is probably not a question we do ask when reading, whether these devils are meant to be real. She merely thinks she sees them in a dream (which is within a dream). Bunyan seemingly downplays the reality of devils. Yet he himself thought he not only saw the devil but felt him tug his clothes when he was praying.[16] Hannah Allen believed she heard two 'Devils in the likeness of Men, singing for joy that they had overcome me',[17] and such fantasies of persecution had, we know, ample backing from theology. Bunyan's apparent hedging of the demonic visitation is not, we may be sure, supposed to make us sceptical about devils but aware, rather, that what is thought to happen in a dream is as real and effective an aspect of divine providence as any other. It is not whether the devils are *really there* that matters but what it is that God does with them, figmental or real.

Even episodes which seem to rely on straight metaphor, such as the River of Death, turn out on inspection to bear a far from simple relationship to what, with empiricist naïvety, we might call the real world. First of all, it should be realized that the powerful River of Death episode, where the depth changes according to the wader's state of mind, is lifted direct from the discourse of Bunyan's culture. Here is Martin Luther, whose

---

[15] The verses heading Bunyan's reprobate chart begin: 'These Lines are blak.'
[16] *Grace Abounding*, 107.
[17] *Satan's Methods and Malice Baffled* (1683), 22.

commentary on Galatians, Bunyan felt, 'had been written out of my heart':[18]

> If we believe, the waters below us depart and . . . harm us not but flee from us . . . And those above us stand up high as though they would overwhelm us: these are the horrors and apparitions of the other world, which at the hour of death terrify us. If, however, we pay no heed to them and pass on with a firm faith, we shall enter into eternal life dry shod and unharmed.[19]

Even closer to Bunyan's fiction is John Abernethy's advice:

> Looke not downe to death, but looke over it, holde not thy eie downeward to the streame of ugly terrors, while thou art going through deaths deepest river, but set thy foote sure on ground, and cast thy eye upon the bancke on the other side and fixe thy sight on that mount Sion and celestiall Jerusalem.[20]

Bunyan's version, then, too well known to quote (see pp. 156–8), is an assimilated gobbet of shared discourse—and perception. For the River of Death, like most of *The Pilgrim's Progress*, is scarcely metaphorical to Bunyan if the idea of metaphor is taken to presume the existence of another, more natural, mode of understanding. The treatment of death makes this point particularly clearly since any understanding of the experience (as opposed to external observation) is necessarily metaphorical: no one could claim to be producing a transcript. Even the fear of death must be metaphorically expressed—as Donne's is when he personifies death—since there is no direct knowledge of the object of fear. Bunyan easily accedes to the conceptualization his culture seems to have favoured. The blurring of the metaphorical and the actual—the refusal of the distinction—helps to account for the strange power of the persecutory imagination which finds its ideal literary vehicle in allegory.

The river's variable depth, moreover, is certainly not beyond the bounds of the puritans' imagination—their 'thought-imbued perception' (to call on Mary Warnock's definition of imagination)[21] of the real world. Richard Baxter reported amongst God's

---

[18] *Grace Abounding*, 129.
[19] Quoted by Gordon Rupp, *The Righteousness of God: Luther Studies* (1953), 354–5.
[20] *A Christian and Heavenly Treatise containing Physicke for the Soule* (1615), 368.
[21] Mary Warnock, *Imagination* (1976), 196.

'strange Judgments', personally verified, 'the drying up of the River *Derwent* in Darbyshire, upon no known Cause in Winter'.[22] A world in which God might choose to employ steeples as projectiles was as shiftingly unpredictable as the states of mind, or frames, colouring its perception. And since it was God who manipulated both (world and mind) there was, in Bunyan's vision, no ontological reason for drawing a clear distinction between them. Things are kept quiet for Mr Fearing in the Valley of the Shadow of Death and the River of Death is low (he is 'not much above wet-shod' (p. 253), recalling Luther) because his internal fears are quite enough for him: God controls both inner and outer. He hesitates for over a month at the Slough of Despond yet he also contrives to carry a Slough in his mind (p. 249). The logical modern mind, once arrested, might conclude from this that the Slough Christian fell into really was a bog, or represented external impediments. But again, in reading the allegory, the disjunction between metaphor and actuality blurs: the mind is not tempted to find inconsistency. Rather, experience of the physical world merges with its perception. The Lockian severance of perceiving self and external world, we realize, did not commend itself to the puritan imagination. The bog expresses the recalcitrance of the physical world when the mind is paralysed by a sense of failure or, in puritan terms, self-despair. We can recognize the experience as more or less transcribed from nightmare when the body is immobilized in the act of escape and the mind is impotent to direct it. It is of course the sense of being persecuted—by his own mental state—that gets Christian into this lather ('*Fear* followed me so hard, that I fled the next way, and fell in' (p. 15)). In *Grace Abounding* Bunyan could find no more literal way of expressing the feeling that he could not act in the physical world without sinning and exposing himself to punishment than that he stood 'on a miry bog, that shook if I did but stir' (82). The admonition delivered by the fate of Dorothy Mately and others whom the ground swallowed up made it not just an apt description but a reasonable forecast. But that God could do this was no more of a threat (statistically overwhelmingly less) than that he could deliver him into despair of salvation. The significance of both

---

[22] *Reliquiae*, p. 433.

was that they were trap-doors into hell.[23] Water (and bog) levels inside the mind and outside (such as when Bunyan nearly drowned as a child[24]) are manipulated by the same authority, and allegory could erase the distinction between them, providing the natural vehicle of puritan perception.

We can see, then, why it was that Bunyan '*Fell suddenly into an Allegory*' (p. 1). It is a product of the puritan culture both in the sense that it consolidates traditions of cultural transmission and in the sense that the allegorical mode is congruent with the puritan mode of perception. But there is another implication in Bunyan's falling suddenly into an allegory which is pointed up if we remember that the allegory is also a dream. As such it is a piece of wish fulfilment. 'Language,' writes Freud in 'Creative Writers and Day-Dreaming', 'in its unrivalled wisdom, long ago decided the question of the essential nature of dreams by giving the name of "daydreams" to the airy creations of fantasy.'[25] Medieval dream visions, like *The Parliament of Fowls*, are essentially wish-fulfilling even though many unpleasant things can happen in them: the dream finds a fantasy resolution. *The Pilgrim's Progress*, moreover, is more than just formally a dream. Describing his creative process Bunyan disavows conscious intention:

> *When at the first I took my Pen in hand,*
> *Thus for to write; I did not understand*
> *That I at all should make a little Book*
> *In such a mode.*
>
> (p. 1)

The fast-multiplying allegorical ideas came to him unbidden while he was working on a treatise—and even when he proceeded to organize and develop these he had only to draw latent material out of his mind: '*Still as I pull'd, it came*' (p. 2). The importunate allegorical sparks testify to a powerful imaginative need which they offered to satisfy. As with *Grace Abounding* an assumption of primarily didactic intent should not be allowed to supervene on Bunyan's own, unpuritanical claim: '*I did it mine own self to gratifie*' (p. 1). Bunyan discloses, therefore, both that the allegory's

---

[23] George Swinnock, in *Heaven and Hell Epitomized* (1663), 32, uses the metaphor of the trap-door into hell.   [24] *Grace Abounding*, 12.

[25] *Complete Psychological Works*, trans. J. Strachey *et al.* (1953–74), ix. 148.

production was self-gratifying and, to update his words, that its ingredients were largely thrown up from his unconscious. The flux of expressions and images current in puritan culture (such as those to do with death) had seeped into his mind where they had apparently coalesced with unconscious images and feelings. These latent images and feelings were often the repressed sediment, it seems, of painful social experience. Bunyan's writerly excitement brought them leaping to the surface insisting on articulation in spite of rebuke by the conscious mind for their irrelevance. That the ideas took shape so readily, and so much to the surprise of their author, suggests that the dream-work had already been done.

While his conscious mind was busying itself with making dogma convincing by discursive means, his unconscious was building bridges between the theology and the social and psychological experience to which it evidently answered. It is ironic that it should be Bunyan's own announcement that refutes intentionalist critiques such as that of Stanley Fish: Bunyan's 'intention', he declares, 'is nothing less than the disqualification of his work as a vehicle of the insight it pretends to convey'.[26] While the work does, automatically, fall in with puritan methods of cultural transmission, which are didactic, and while the commentary (by narrator, obedient character, or judgemental event) inescapably endorses the viewpoint of the Calvinist God, Fish, by concentrating on the text's wrist-slapping lessons, overlooks why and how the allegory came into being. By exposing the metaphorical forms in which the puritan culture is incarnated with Manichaean zeal he restores something resembling the treatise Bunyan's off-duty self felt comparatively free not to write. What the allegorical sparks throw up, however, is the experience of living under the regime of a Calvinist God—the social basis and psychological consequences of oppression by that figment. Drawing attention to the involuntariness of the creative process is not intended to support the Coleridgian mystification that 'the Bunyan of Parnassus had the better of the Bunyan of the Conventicle', or, in more modern terms, that 'Bunyan's imagination transcends his theological convictions';[27]

---

[26] Stanley E. Fish, 'Progress in *The Pilgrim's Progress*' in *Self-Consuming Artifacts: The Experience of Seventeenth-Century Literature* (1972), 225.

[27] Gordon Campbell, 'Fishing in Other Men's Waters', p. 150.

rather it is meant to suggest that the imagination was welded to the convictions prior to conscious thought and that separating them in order to privilege either a didactic or an imaginatively transcendent meaning introduces interpretative distortion.

On the one hand, then, the allegory accommodates the puritan experience more fully and therefore communicates it more effectively than any other form.[28] The allegory's perceptual modes are not learned, as Fish supposes, so as to replace rationalist assumptions. The providential reading of the world and self was already in place as the natural way of seeing. On the other hand the allegory is also a dream which seeks to transform the negative components of the vision it expresses so as to produce a desired outcome. 'The motive forces of phantasies', says Freud, 'are unsatisfied wishes, and every single phantasy is the fulfilment of a wish, a correction of unsatisfying reality.'[29] Like *Grace Abounding* it is written against despair, the narrative itself being the means by which an elect teleology is made to triumph over a reprobate. But this is by no means easily accomplished and the dynamism of the narrative and of Christian's career (which U. Milo Kaufmann sees as undermined by the subjection of his actions to predestination[30]) derives from the contrast between these teleologies of acceptance and rejection, protective and persecutory providence—and from the ambivalence of the dream resolution itself.

We explored the difficulty in *Grace Abounding* of establishing command of the protean substance of Bunyan's own recollected experience, of subduing it persuasively to the redemptive discourse. *The Pilgrim's Progress* must do more than combat

---

[28] In a word: drama cannot easily naturalize the supernatural or give substance to subjective perception of the world; the content of epic is much more constrained by its conventions and the experience of the individual must be subordinated to grander concerns. Of course the novel later provided a better match for a somewhat secularized 'puritanism'.

[29] *Complete Psychological Works*, ix. 146.

[30] U. Milo Kaufmann, *'The Pilgrim's Progress' and Traditions in Puritan Meditation* (1966), 116–17. Campbell's and Kaufmann's views (respectively, that predestination does not impinge on the narrative and that its imposition eliminates dynamism) are opposed but rest on a common assumption: that the form the influence of predestination must take, if it is present, is to make one outcome seem certain. This assumption ignores the kind of experience Thomas Goodwin describes where two opposed readings of experience unhappily cohabit in the same mind. This mode of looking at the world and the self depends on predestinarian doctrine in a way that makes for extreme tension and therefore dynamism towards resolution.

doubts of personal salvation; it must combat the presumption of the dominant ideology that the dissenting counter-culture is based on illusions and delusions. This will seem paradoxical. At first I argued that the allegory expressed a vision of the world so obsessed with the executive power of God that distinctions between physical, psychic, and metaphysical were nearly obliterated and now, turning to the idea of dream, I am suggesting that *Progress* wish-fulfillingly opposes the official ideology which is characterized by the denial of the dissenter's vision. There is a twofold answer to this apparent inconsistency, towards which analysis of *Grace Abounding* has pointed. The first is that Bunyan's scepticism about his beliefs did not diminish, in fact it paradoxically increased, their imaginative hold on him. The second is that Bunyan's texts reveal a natural propensity to believe that supernatural power aligned itself with the powers it had installed in the world, that the hierarchy that declared him inferior would be transferred to, not inverted by, the eternal hereafter.

Richard Baxter wrote in his *Reliquiae*: 'But yet it is my daily Prayer, That God would increase my Faith, and give my Soul a clear sight of the Evidences of his Truth, and of himself, and of the invisible World.' The present-tense confession of uncertainty is far more relaxed than Bunyan's nervous reference to the 'abominations' in his heart. Baxter, a grand old man of nonconformity, had by his declining years acquired the confidence to be truthful: 'whatever men may pretend,' he avers, 'the subjective Certainty cannot go beyond the objective Evidence.'[31] Of course Baxter's assured line-drawing between subjective and objective is a curious *fin de siècle* amalgam of faith and empiricism. Consideration of what is assigned to the category of objective truth (the behaviour of the River Derwent, or Mrs Hutchinson's biological accomplishments) points not to 'enlightenment' but to the partial substitution of one cultural frame of reference for another. None the less Bunyan was, we saw, exposed to the same incipient discursive shift while simultaneously being forced into the position of pretending to such certainty. If objective evidence of the invisible world was felt to be wanting it obviously followed that subjective certainty of his own salvation (itself prerequisite to salvation) was also wanting.

<hr/>

[31] *Reliquiae*, pp. 23, 128.

Bunyan's allegory satisfies the wish, the intense need, that the invisible world become a reality as incontrovertible as the visible. This need was entangled both with the threat of despair of salvation and with the alternative to such certainty which was not so much that the material world was all there was but that the ideology imbuing it, which nullified the poor dissenter, was back in force.

The brief appearance of Atheist shows how nicely the allegory meets Bunyan's need. He informs the pilgrims that they 'are like to have nothing but your travel for your paines'. Christian responds: '*Why man? Do you think we shall not be received?*' At which Atheist exclaims: 'Received! There is no such place as you Dream of, in all this World.' The ideas of rejection and the unreality of the dreamt-of celestial realm occur, as usual, together. Atheist goes on to say that he has been looking for the Celestial City without success for twenty years (p. 135). The allegory effortlessly makes him look foolish, however, for the Celestial City lies in a topographical continuum with the City of Destruction. The difficulty of obeying Evangelist's instruction to 'believe stedfastly concerning things that are invisible' (pp. 86–7) is diminished within a dream, in which the favouring spiritual world materializes.

The element of wish-fulfilment can be shown in more unquestionable ways, since the satisfaction of the wish can involve departures from official dogma which allegory presumably disguised from Bunyan. Christian's family is, in Part Two, for example, allegorically translatable into the Christian community, the invisible church, which drew its members, the elect, from whatever quarter the whimsical Spirit blew in. An entire family might be enlisted (the comfortable view was sometimes expressed that the boon of Christian parentage could be a providential intimation of divine favour[32]) but this was very far from being guaranteed. It is easy to see why puritan parents had the impulse to put their children on side with God by conferring on them promising allegorical names. Bunyan's allegory disguises its wishfulness, conveniently conflating the Christian family with the literal family in such a way as to satisfy both doctrinal and

---

[32] See Perkins, *Works*, p. 459, and *Mr. Badman* where Wise conversely sees it as 'a very great judgment of God upon children, to be the offspring of base and ungodly men' (p. 213).

emotional needs. This is evident throughout Part Two but it comes out directly in a conversation in which Great-Heart tells Gaius that the boys take after their father and Gaius proceeds to trace their genealogy back to the Apostles (pp. 259–60). We witness in Part Two the mollifying of doctrine by such means to consort with Bunyan's more comfortable position as pastor and parent. Far from being passive victims of Giant Despair, for example, the Christians seek him out and kill him (pp. 281–2). The episode is nonsense allegorically since despair as a state of mind lives on to menace future Christians. But we can see the imaginative needs it meets: personal victory over his direst enemy is triumphantly attested, oppression by the landed classes is avenged, and his own children are protected from the terrors he underwent.

In Part One the allegory more desperately combats the allied threat to personal salvation and to the imaginative validity of the dissenting culture. There is a need, for example, to congeal the reality of the elusive but mandatory assurance of salvation in the form of Christian's roll. Arthur Dent's *Plaine Mans Path-Way* provides Bunyan's allegorical suggestion for this when his Theologus sets the ignorant Asunetus right. 'I will never beleeve that any man', he had said, 'can certainly knowe in this worlde whether he shall be saved, or damned: but all men must hope well, and be of good beliefe.' 'We see worldly men', comes the didactic retort,

will bee loath to hold their Lands and Leases uncertainely, having nothing to shew for them. They will not stand to the curtesie of their Land-lords, nor rest upon their good willes . . . Shall we hold the state of our immortall inheritance by hope, hope well, and have no writings, no evidences, no seale, no witnesses, nor any thing to shew for it. Alas this is a weake Tenure, a broken Title, a simple hold indeed.[33]

God, as Dent's analogy unwittingly indicates, resembled in the collective imagination a landlord whose good will could not be relied on. How could a poor man come by the spiritual equivalent of a written lease and persuade himself that it had not just equal but greater reality? And how could he be persuaded that the spiritual landholders would typically be not the untrustworthy grandees on whom God himself seemed to be

---

[33] *Plaine Mans Path-Way*, pp. 263–5.

modelled but the lower orders, even the expropriated such as
Bunyan himself? It is no wonder that, as a new convert, Bunyan
had relaxed his grip—'*Let him go if he will!*'—on his evidence of
God's guarantee to restore his lost land.

The allegory addresses the task of projecting instead of the
feared spiritual extrapolation an inversion of empirical reality.
While Dent's Theologus had to battle somewhat vituperatively
against his sceptic, Asunetus, Bunyan's Atheist is pitiably
unenlightened not to perceive the evident contours of his world,
as is Ignorance not to obtain the concretely real certificate which
Dent had to conjure out of analogical rhetoric. But in spite of the
dream's success in vanquishing scepticism and despair by
reifying the invisible world the reprobate frame and the social
experience to which it adheres gain admittance in potent form.
We form a strong impression in the early stages of *Progress* of the
massive opposition facing Christian both in his own mind and in
the external world. Parallels with *Grace Abounding* are strong—
except that the social dimension of persecution is more explicit.

People become religious, runs one sociological hypothesis,
'because in some way they [feel] deprived and [are] unable to
perceive the real causes of their condition, or, if perceiving these,
[are] unable by rational action to affect them. Religion then
[becomes] an agency of compensation.'[34] This is at once truistic
(they must feel deprived, if only of religion) and presumptuous
(what authorizes the definition of rationality?). Nevertheless the
observation points to an interplay between religion and 'real
causes' which the allegory, unlike the self-referential discursive
language of a religious sect, uncovers.[35] It is in Christian's
dealings with authority, which fuse secular and religious
oppression and constitute most of the narrative climaxes, that the
'real causes' show up most clearly. Christian's experience is
dominated by this authoritarian-masochistic pattern evident in
Grace Abounding. Self-vilification, internalized punishment, and

---

[34] Bryan R. Wilson, 'Becoming a Sectarian: Motivation and Commitment', *Studies
in Church History*, 15 (1978), 500. (Wilson himself rejects this view.)

[35] See James Turner, 'Bunyan's Sense of Place', in V. Newey, ed., *'The Pilgrim's
Progress': Critical and Historical Views* (Liverpool, 1980). Turner impressively analyses
the pilgrims' exclusion from property and the allegory's consequent spatial
metaphorics. I have, in seeking to get behind theological language, emphasized
authority rather than property and narrative rather than metaphor, yet some of the
following discussion endorses Turner's views.

the need to submit himself to a greater power are recurrent features. But the allegory makes us imaginatively aware of the social circumstances which induce these traits. Like Bunyan Christian is isolated by self-awareness from his environment ('he would . . . walk solitarily in the Fields' (p. 9)) and is negatively impelled on his journey in search of *'some way of escape'* (pp. 8–9). His apocalyptic imagination extends to the whole society (the City of Destruction) the imminent destruction by which Bunyan felt personally threatened. Stay in 'the place . . . where I was born', he warns Obstinate and Pliable shortly before he falls into the Slough, and 'You will sink lower than the Grave' (p. 11). The burden which sinks Christian more deeply into the Slough where he is left to 'tumble . . . alone' is the guilty consciousness of his degradation. The Slough represents a wallowing in masochism, the cause of which, as the allegory expresses, is both inside Christian's mind and pressing on him irresistibly from the outside.

The combination of dirt and drowning (self-denigration and helplessness to resist) begins a chain of imagery in the allegory which is picked up from *Grace Abounding* where Bunyan uses the word 'sink' as an automatic metaphor for despair and likens himself to horses that 'flounce' to get out of the mire (250) or a child who 'scrable[s] and spraul[s]' to escape drowning in the mill-pit (198). Their own unaided action, expressed in the demeaning active verbs which the puritan employed on principle, is futile. Again, this was shared discourse. Robert Bolton describes the hypocrite unsupported by grace in the same terms: 'And yet all these goodly hopes and earnest ejaculations, growing onely from a *forme* and not from the *power of godliness*, are but . . . as so many catchings and scrablings of a Man over-head in water.'[36] John Sym anticipates the Slough in both image and meaning: 'So long as men, in distresse of conscience for their sinne, looke not out off, or beyond themselves, for ease and comfort, they cannot but sinke under their owne burden.'[37] But Bunyan's imagery in the three-dimensional allegory connects such figurative language to the idea of social degradation.

Filth, as well as floundering, bothered Bunyan; and he seemed

[36] *Instructions for a Right Comforting Afflicted Consciences* (1631), 238.
[37] *Lifes Preservative against Self-Killing* (1637), 219.

to connect it with his origins. He retorted to William Kiffin's slighting remarks about his social status ('trampl[ing] my person') that this was 'To bespatter a man, that his doctrine might be disregarded' (ii. 618). There seems to be a painful shame which draws him into a degree of collusion with this social mudslinging. Bunyan described himself as having sprung 'out of the dunghill';[38] and in *Progress* Christian is gratified to learn that the Prince 'had made many Pilgrims Princes though . . . their original had been the Dunghil' (p. 53). Christiana witnesses the completion of the inversion of status in a dream in which she sees 'a House now given him to dwell in, to which, the best Palaces on Earth, if compared, seems to me to be but as a Dunghil' (p. 182). There is no hint of a spiritual translation of this vision. 'I seek an *Inheritance*', Christian had said (p. 11): reparation in the allegorical medium can blamelessly be made material; but it suggests too a material basis for the aspiration it meets. The dunghill is biblical in origin: not only does God lift the beggar or needy from the dunghill (1 Sam. 2: 8; Ps. 113: 7), he can also punish people by making their houses dunghills (Ezra 6: 11: 'let his house be made a dunghill for this'; likewise in Dan. 2: 5 and 3: 29). The word's biblical associations capture Bunyan's religious ambivalence: by bringing his degraded status to consciousness he cannot help assuming divine hostility (his 'father's house', far from having many mansions, has been reduced to a dunghill). His struggle is to apprehend a transformation of this inimical providence into one favourable towards him.

The first thing we learn about Christian is that he is '*cloathed with Raggs*' (p. 8). No explanation (beyond a scriptural annotation) is offered for this, either at the literal or allegorical level. Rags belong as it happens to the iconography of melancholy and despair (as we see in Spenser's Despair[39]), but this is unlikely to have affected Bunyan. The rags are the objective correlative for the feeling of social shame (which *Grace Abounding* expressed by exaggerating poverty). Like the burden, they are discarded at the Cross when Christian is attired more beseemingly. The biblical text legitimating the idea ('All our righteousnesses', says Isaiah 64: 6, 'are as filthy rags') is situated in a socially neutral context.

---

[38] Quoted by Monica Furlong, *Puritan's Progress: A Study of John Bunyan* (1975), 158.
[39] *The Faerie Queene*, I. i. 36.

In a typical paradox Bunyan turns the soiled rags to spiritual advantage since they assist the perception of universal human unrighteousness which, it is implied, robes and furred gowns conceal. By withholding allegorical translation of Christian's rags the idea, rooted in his experience, that literal poverty supplied the incitement to spiritual betterment is allowed independent force.

If we refer back to the young Bunyan's encounter with the 'three or four poor women' (37) (poverty is the one constant predicate of this reiterated subject), we find them glancing at the same text: they 'did contemn, slight, and abhor their own righteousness, as filthy, and insufficient to do them any good' (37). This was where Bunyan first glimpsed the redemptive possibilities of a self-mortification to which he was already prone. While 'these poor people' (41, 53, 77) were in a 'miserable state by nature' (37), he was a 'poor Wretch'—not only, like them, one of the poor but wretched and pitiable because 'ignorant' (the words combine at 36 and 50) of the sunny side of fulsomely abhorring one's filthy rags. Bunyan exploits the scriptural simile again in *A Few Sighs from Hell* in what may be seen as an aggressive reaction to his self-contempt. He uses the parable of Dives and Lazarus to sanction a revenge fantasy directed at those who 'bear . . . sway while they are in the world' who see 'the poor saints, even the Lazaruses or the ragged ones that belong to Jesus, to be in a better condition than themselves'. This time he glories in the double sense of 'condition': 'O! who do you think was in the best condition?' (iii. 685)

The cluster of ideas discussed here was again current in Bunyan's culture. Anna Trapnel anticipates him for example: 'although the evil one may hang his rags on Gods Priests, they shall not abide, because they are of a royall descent, they are the Kings children, rags are the clothing of such that sit on dunghils, and filthy garments for such that tumble in the mire; but Saints clothing is whiter then snow in Salmon . . . and this spirituall part of a Saint, nothing can defile.'[40] The family romance of lost royal origins is present of course in Christian's quest for the 'inheritance' held for him by the King in the Celestial City. The thrill of discovering election seems, for Bunyan, to be related to this fantasy. It was not enough to be miserably poor. God could

[40] *A Legacy for the Saints* (1654), 46.

not be 'wrought on by misery of the creature, as a procuring
cause' because election must be 'of his own princely mind'
(i. 644). Trapnel, appositely for a Calvinist, makes it clear that
the elect discover, in sloughing the rags, an original but disguised
identity. The filthy rags of social circumstance cannot defile the
identity God has secreted in the soul. One might compare the
reverse situation in Middleton's Beatrice-Joanna, whose original
identity (she is a changeling) is belied by the beatific and divinely
graced nature promised by her name, looks, and social circumstances, by which she is herself seduced.[41] Trapnel lacks the
dimension of vindictive satisfaction. Middleton's acerbity allows
room for little else. For Bunyan revenge on the oppressor seems
to be emotionally correlated with the aggrandizement of the
oppressed.

   Inversion of status, then, is the transformation the dream
effects. Confrontations with authority demonstrate, on the other
hand, the extent of the text's problems in entertaining a world
turned upside down. First Christian is offered an accommodation
with the establishment by Mr Worldly-Wiseman. Bolton again
anticipates this temptation to be rid of the burden of sin, giving a
cue for Bunyan's ironic treatment: 'yet it is our good hap,
sometimes to meet with some mercifull men, who will help us to
Heaven without so much adoe, and upon easier Termes, etc.'[42]
And again what Bunyan principally adds is the social animus in
Wiseman's characterization. Following his advice leads to an
irruption of the persecutory imagination in the form of Mount
Sinai which threatens to fall on him. Whatever patronizing
pretence of concern the ruling class extends to him he is still
condemned under its law and its metaphysical counterpart.
While Mount Sinai represents divine law it is Legality, 'a
gentleman', who resides there and administers it (p. 20). This
conflation helps to explain Bunyan's readiness to make a similar
connection in *Grace Abounding*. Bunyan's contemporaries were
unable to rid themselves of 'reverent devotion to the law' in spite
of their 'hatred and contempt for lawyers'.[43] Gentlemen and the

[41] See John Stachniewski, 'Calvinist Psychology in the Tragedies of Middleton', in
R. V. Holdsworth, ed., *Three Jacobean Revenge Tragedies: A Casebook* (1990).

[42] *Instructions*, p. 179.

[43] Conrad Russell, review of Christopher Hill's *The Experience of Defeat* (1984), LRB
(4–17 Oct. 1984), 20.

law always went together. Even the Calvinist disciplinary
system, set up in the 1640s, was dominated by gentlemen in co-
operation 'with the well-to-do yeomen and farmers in their
villages'.[44] And regulations and statutes aimed primarily at the
poor had multiplied in the Elizabethan and early Stuart period.[45]
The law was formidable to Bunyan for what it legitimated was
his exclusion.

Behind the treacherous reasonableness of Worldly-Wiseman
lay the violence of Apollyon. The compounding of secular and
spiritual oppression in the poor Christian's imagination, which
Apollyon and Giant Despair embody, is well suggested in
impersonal terms by Richard Baxter who, while on the side of
dissent, seems comparatively liberated from the persecutory
imagination of his lower-class co-religionists:

It is too common a sort of oppression for the rich in all places to
domineer too insolently over the poor, and force them to follow their
wills and to serve their interest, be it right or wrong . . . Especially
unmerciful landlords are the common and sore oppressors of the
countrymen. If a few men can but get money enough to purchase all the
land in a county, they think they may do with their own as they list, and
set such hard bargains of it to their tenants, that they are all but as their
servants . . . An oppressor is an Anti-Christ and an Anti-God . . . not
only the agent of the Devil, but his image.[46]

What is striking about this passage is the way in which it tallies,
from the point of view of the poor, with the Calvinist vision of
human powerlessness to resist the will of the devil if God grants
him power. The breakdown of the feudal model of reciprocal
obligations between lord and vassal is still condemned and
resented, long gone though it was. No doubt the model was
always more myth than reality. But what had apparently
obtained very widely was village solidarity, sometimes maintained
against seigneurial pressure.[47] The new gentry, status-conscious
presences in most villages, made the most of their advantages in
the way Baxter describes. From the inflationary, over-populated,
late sixteenth century, poor people had begun to constitute a

[44] Christopher Hill, *Society and Puritanism in Pre-Revolutionary England* (1964), 236.
[45] Keith Wrightson, 'Aspects of Social Differentiation in Rural England 1580–
1680', *Journal of Peasant Studies*, 5 (1977–8), 39.
[46] Quoted by R. H. Tawney, *Religion and the Rise of Capitalism* (1922), 224.
[47] Wrightson, 'Aspects of Social Differentiation', p. 34.

class; 'a substantial proportion of the population', says Wrightson, 'was living in constant danger of destitution, many of them full time wage labourers. In both town and country a permanent proletariat had emerged, collectively designated the poor.'[48]

Christian asserts his right—since exploitation of labour has replaced a village ethos of mutual support—to sell his labour to the best market, to migrate;[49] yet in doing so he exposes himself to the violence of Apollyon:

I was born indeed in your Dominions, but your service was hard, and your wages such as a man could not live on, *for the wages of Sin is death*; therefore when I was come to years, I did as other considerate persons do, look out, if perhaps I might mend my self. (p. 57)

Faithful reports a parallel encounter with Adam the First who offered him employment and wages, but Faithful's burning apprehension that 'he would sell me for a Slave' (p. 70) drove him to resist. These statements gloss Christian's vague anticipation of sinking lower should he remain in 'the place where I was born'. He apprehends the social trend to which he is subjected. Though he worked unreflectingly for Apollyon 'in my none-age' (p. 57), realization of deprivation and abuse has made him a 'considerate person' who, like Bunyan, finds his 'inconsiderable' status insufferable. Yet Apollyon's assault nearly matches that threatened by Mount Sinai.

Apollyon's persecution evidently springs in large part from doubts in Christian's own mind. The human lineaments of Worldly-Wiseman are replaced by the grotesque form of nightmare assailants; yet in the allegory Apollyon is no less real. His imaginative reality can be better understood if we think of the violence that actually did irrupt when authority was challenged. When, for example, a tithingman retained his hat in Sir Samuel Sandys's presence, and spoke disrespectfully to him, servants were dispatched to beat him up.[50] The Quaker Thomas Ellwood supplies a fuller example in his autobiography when he plucked up courage to extend to his father the equalitarian treatment ('with respect both to *Language* and *Gesture*'—retaining

[48] *English Society 1580–1680* (1982), 141.
[49] David Underdown speaks of the 'constant migration by people in search of work or land' in this period (*Revel, Riot, and Rebellion* (1985), 18).
[50] *Revel, Riot, and Rebellion*, p. 22.

his hat and employing the familiar 'thou' form) demanded by his faith. Recurrent scenes of murderous violence followed. '*Sirrah, If ever I hear you say* Thou *or* Thee *to me again, I'll strike your Teeth down your Throat*' was a rare verbal substitute for action. The attacks were patriarchal reflexes of a not generally brutal man—he deeply regretted his inability to contain himself. The assaults of Apollyon and Adam the First express a violence always implicit in the contemporary patriarchal ethos which ruled most potently in the minds of those subordinated to it. Ellwood had 'considered . . . the Extent of *Paternal Power*: which I found was not wholly *Arbitrary* and *Unlimited* but had Bounds set unto it'.[51] He was from boyhood a singularly resilient character and he espoused a faith which unambiguously authorized this challenge to authority. The violence he encountered physically is internalized in the more typical mind of Christian.

While Christian's acquired '*frame of the heart*' (p. 18) obliges him to defy the discourses of medical pathology (which his own family has obediently imbibed (p. 9)) and civility (with which Mr Worldly-Wiseman tries to invalidate his anguish (p. 19)), this defiance also provokes the violent authoritarian mental reflex. He has to negotiate between two versions of the authoritarian ethos, both of which, as an individual, he is incapable of resisting. Perseverance in defiance of the *status quo* offers his only chance of rescue by the potentially greater power of God—if he can generate confidence that both powers are not conspiring against him. (The idea of freedom, of not serving any master, does not, of course, fall within the pilgrims' imaginative compass.) Vanity Fair reveals both the readiness of the authorities to inflict the final punishment (Bunyan was threatened with hanging on his first conviction[52]) and the liberation of the mind from masochism when such confidence can be generated. In this episode emphasis falls squarely on spiritual or conscious ideological migration: the issue of worldliness versus unworldliness can be decided in its own explicit terms. The relieved conscious mind takes command. As in Bunyan's 'Relation', persecution of the faith confirms the distinction between the two sources of authority. In this instance of vilification—the inhabitants 'besmeared them with dirt' (p. 91)—the mud does not stick because

---

[51] *History of the Life*, pp. 57, 49–50.
[52] *Grace Abounding*, p. 118.

it is not masochistically internalized. In *Grace Abounding*, too, inner assurance is derived from being 'bespattered' by false accusation since, Bunyan says, 'it belongs to my Christian profession to be vilified' (311, 312). Anna Trapnel, who made a similar move to Bunyan's from psychic persecution to exultant pride under physical persecution, declared: 'Saints clothing [i.e. Jesus Christ] is the purest white, no dirt throwed upon it can soil it.'[53] The Bible sustains the pilgrims by judging their judges (p. 95); it was 'the traditional protestant counter-authority to the authority of the hierarchy'.[54] But the reinforcement of faith in Vanity Fair by no means eliminates the reprobate frame from Christian's psyche.

The climactic confrontation of the narrative, the incident with Giant Despair, intensifies the authoritarian intimidation to which the pilgrims' sensitivity, like Bunyan's, is extreme. The literal crime for which Christian and Hopeful are gaoled by Giant Despair is trespass. One is bound to ask therefore why the text connects Christian's gravest spiritual peril with such a seemingly trivial literal idea. 'You have this night,' says Giant Despair darkly, 'trespassed on me' (p. 113). It is a revealing conflation for while on the literal level trespass is a specific crime against property it is also a near biblical synonym for sin; to be exact the Greek word for trespass in the New Testament means, aptly for Bunyan's allegory, 'falling aside'.[55] Every New Testament use of 'trespass' attaches it to the idea of forgiveness, most famously in the Sermon on the Mount: 'For if ye forgive men their trespasses, your heavenly Father will also forgive you: but if ye forgive not men their trespasses, neither will your Father forgive your trespasses' (Matt. 6: 14–15). The laws of trespass were unforgiving, as were the landowners who brought the prosecutions and the judiciary, dominated by them, which implemented sentences (justifiably simplified in the allegory into a single oppressor). The biblical resonance of the word 'trespass' together with the literal sense indicates how the would-be ideological escapee could be held captive. The ethic of forgiveness is not adopted by the hierarchical system which dispossesses and then oppresses him, not least by controlling the definition of

[53] *Legacy for the Saints*, p. 15.
[54] Christopher Hill, *Society and Puritanism*, p. 159.
[55] Robert Young, *Analytical Concordance to the Holy Bible*, 8th edn. (1939).

words like 'trespass'. And having indeed fallen foul of the law the
offender has to acknowledge the justice of his punishment. 'So
they were forced to go,' says Bunyan with irresistibly simple
logic, 'because he was stronger than they. They also had but little
to say, for they knew themselves in a fault' (pp. 113–14). In
Pauline terms, transgressing the law was inevitable, dire
punishment was logical and just, and only the grace (free gift) of
forgiveness could prevent it. Nothing could compel this grace
and the evidence, extrapolated from the Giant's treatment, seems
to announce its denial.

The Giant's behaviour is clearly to be contrasted with the
pilgrims' hospitable reception elsewhere (notably at the Palace
Beautiful). 'The tradition', says Christopher Hill, 'that big
property-owners should dispense hospitality and relieve the poor
goes back a very long way.'[56] By the late sixteenth century, Peter
Clark similarly observes, specifically of landowners' treatment of
migrants (which is of course what the pilgrims are), 'traditional
hospitality was in decline.'[57] Paternalistic benevolence appears
to have persisted in pockets of the country; but in general,
regardless of the circumstances driving people to wander in
search of work or subsistence, vagrants were to the propertied, in
Underdown's words, 'by definition idle and dishonest'.[58] Violence
to the ideal of hospitality, then, characteristic of Bunyan's age,
produces resentment in the text. The alert biblicist might note
that the Giant's refusal to forgive trespasses promised a long-
range revenge on the oppressive gentry, eventually exacted in
Part Two, but this is a narrative interpolation, not a consolation
which falls within the compass of Christian's experience. (Indeed,
as Bunyan firmly deprecated revenge as being 'of the flesh' (ii.
739), even this eventual exaction of revenge has to be veiled—by
its moral-allegorical presentation—from consciousness.)

The overriding impression of the episode is of the pilgrims'
passivity and lugubrious resignation not just to the landowner's
power but to the justice of their arrest. At his prison interview
with Paul Cobb, the Clerk of the Peace, Bunyan had said:

[56] *Society and Puritanism*, p. 259.

[57] Peter Clark, 'The Alehouse and the Alternative Society,' in D. Pennington and
K. V. Thomas, edd., *Puritans and Revolutionaries: Essays in Seventeenth-Century History
presented to Christopher Hill* (Oxford, 1978), 55.

[58] *Revel, Riot, and Rebellion*, p. 35; see also Paul Slack, 'Vagrants and Vagrancy in
England, 1598–1664', *Economic History Review*, 2nd Ser., 37 (1974), 364–6.

I did look upon myself as bound in conscience to walk according to all righteous laws, and that whether there was a King or no; and if I did any thing that was contrary, I did hold it my duty to bear patiently the penalty of the law, that was provided against such offenders.[59]

His intimated feelings have been converted, not by any diminution in awed respect for the law but by his allegiance to a greater law-giver, into a form of assurance.[60] But illegal behaviour which did not carry a clear divine sanction tended, in Bunyan's mind, to align punitive authority with a punitive deity. As he warned his readers at the conclusion of his treatise, *Seasonable Counsel* in 1684: 'Fear God, honour the king, and do that duty to both which is required of you by the Word and law of Christ, and then, to say no more, you shall not suffer by the power for evil-doing' (ii. 741). The episode with Giant Despair, whose size indexes the big landowner's might in the perspective of the propertyless, demonstrates the force of internalized ideology when confidence in the rectitude of his actions deserted the poor Christian.

This small offence hair-triggers the lurking feeling that God is on the side of the high-ups. Christian's journey sought, like Richard Norwood's, to put distance between himself and the existing social structure in order to escape from the idea that it reflected a divine economy which rejected him. Biblical metaphor (which drenches the allegory) was already ominous in what it suggested of the landless: 'It is to be noted,' said Calvin, 'that where mention is made of the land, it is a visible signe of the secret severing [election] wherin the adoption is conteined' (*Inst.* 3. 21. 5). And the literalism with which this could be felt derived from the political reality of rural life: social status and power, as Wrightson observes, 'was based primarily upon the possession of land'.[61] The trespass laws both remind Christian of his landless-ness ('I seek an *Inheritance*,' he said as he set off (p. 11)) and put him in the wrong so that, so far from receding to give room to the

---

[59] *Grace Abounding*, p. 124.

[60] Bunyan's church, it is worth observing, far from granting its members antinomian immunity from the laws of the land, added their own punishments to those of the courts—as Oliver Dicks found when convicted for appropriating a stray sheep to replace one he had lost: 'he was by general consent withdrawne from' ('The Minutes of the First Independent Church (now Bunyan Meeting) at Bedford 1656–1766', ed. H. G. Tibbutt, *Publications of the Bedfordshire Historical Record Society*, 55 (1956), 25).

[61] Wrightson, 'Aspects of Social Differentiation', p. 35.

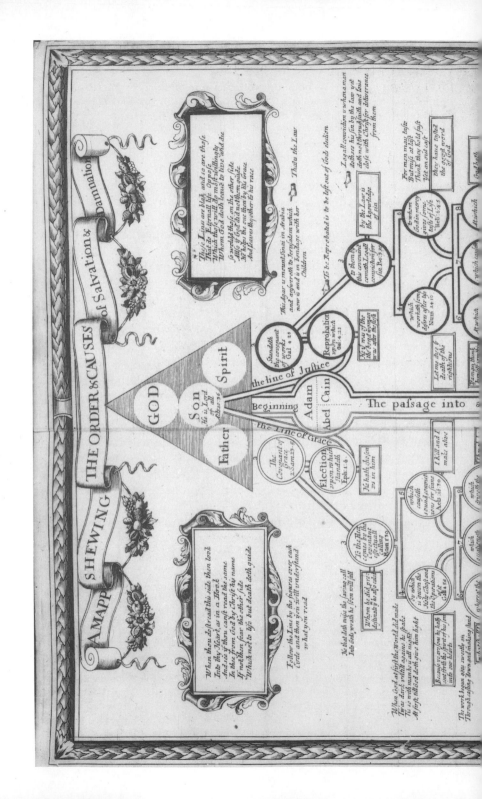

Bunyan's 'Mapp'

By John Bunyan, Author of the Pilgrims Progress

development of an alternative ethos, the *status quo* imposes itself
on the mind as the sole and insuperable reality to which spiritual
laws conform. The jealous assertion of property rights ('Insistence
on status,' Underdown judges, 'was accompanied by insistence
on property rights as land came increasingly to be viewed as a
source of profit rather than responsibility'[62]) acts to intensify the
misery. In *The Crying Sin of England, of Not Caring for the Poor*
(1653) clergyman John Moore wagged his finger at cruel
landlords (especially the beneficiaries of the laws of enclosure
who, as Giant Despair may have done, fenced round land to
which there had formerly been common rights): 'although thou
are a *civill Owner*, yet thou art a *spirituall Usurper*.'[63] Even here,
though, the rhetorical form of the accusation implies a presupposition that, in the proper way of things, civil and spiritual
rights were coextensive. This presupposition, sharpened in its
invidiousness by the observable pattern of social change,
impressed itself on the powerless people the pilgrims represent.
Christian feels himself to be under the condemnation of the Law
as well as the law.

The association of Doubting Castle with Giant Despair
confirms the link between scepticism and despair: that they are
in a state of doubt about the reality of the invisible world exposes
the pilgrims to the beatings of despair. When that world
evaporates they are left prey to the existing powers. The paradox
of the name Doubting Castle also helps the point. That the most
insubstantial of feelings is expressed by the most solid of objects
conveys the way in which the massy constraints of the ruling
ideology press on the pilgrims in proportion to their own lack of
belief in the invisible world. The Castle reverses the wish-
fulfilling process of the allegory as a whole. The Giant conveys, in
line with Calvinist teaching, the impotence of the will when
gripped by a mental state which seems to arise autonomously
and imperiously from within but which is also counterparted in
the real world. Bunyan re-expresses the kind of unconscious
despair which he described, in *Grace Abounding*, as infiltrating the
mind and making him susceptible to judgemental terrors when,
preceding the Giant's irruption into consciousness, we are told:

[62] *Revel, Riot, and Rebellion*, p. 22.
[63] Quoted by Joyce Oldham Appleby in *Economic Thought and Ideology in Seventeenth-Century England* (Princeton, 1978), 62.

'it was in his grounds they now were sleeping' (p. 113). They
have the dormant feeling of being in the wrong. Giant Despair
who 'falls to rateing of them as if they were dogs' (p. 114) is the
superego before which the frail ego cowers, a derivation from the
patriarchal order while that order remains as a physical fact. He
is a physical-mental compound as his name indicates. Again the
experience is prepared for in *Grace Abounding*, where Bunyan says,
'this kind of despair did so possess my Soul' (24), or, 'despair,
would hold me as Captive' (106), but the social correlate of this
helpless victimization by an ideologically infiltrated imagination
is now fleshed out.

Like a child, from whose felt helplessness and diminutiveness
the adult world of giants is projected, Bunyan's Christian, as
Calvinist man, glumly submits to a power he is bound to
recognize. He is, in the terms of the Baxter quotation, a victim of
demonic power but, still worse than this, his plight seems to be
one in which God colludes. Bunyan spoke to his flock in the
preface of *Grace Abounding* of the feeling that 'God *fights against
you*' (p. 3) and we have seen how both he and other autobiographers entertained a God-Devil concept when they felt
persecuted. The violence Giant Despair metes out, which
narrative teleology attributes (as in the autobiographies) to
demonic power, had, in experience, far more to do with a picture
of God since the devil only had power at God's behest. Bunyan
describes a similar experience in *Acceptable Sacrifice*: 'He reckoneth
at night, when he goes to bed, that like as a lion, so God will tear
him to pieces before the morning light' (i. 699): a fear justified in
Christian and Hopeful's case by Giant Despair's early morning
clubbings and skeletal exhibits ('and when I thought fit, I tore
them in pieces' (p. 117)). The pilgrims' confusion or sense of the
conspiracy of their oppressors is encouraged by an anticipation of
their incarceration in Interpreter's House where Christian was
shown the caged 'man of despair'.[64] He recriminates himself in

---

[64] George Offor identifies this living exemplum as John Child, a one-time fellow-
preacher with Bunyan who conformed after 1660, unable to withstand persecution
(iii. 72–3). As the church minutes attest Child had an edgy relationship with the
church from 1656 to 1659 ('The Minutes of the First Independent Church', pp. 22–
34). He fell into despair and committed suicide in 1684. Bunyan apparently visited
him in his terrors. Roger Sharrock (p. 318 n.) and N. H. Keeble (ed., *The Pilgrim's
Progress* (Oxford, 1984), 268 n.) repeat the identification. But Child maintained his
adversarial stance towards Bunyan until at least 1676 when he issued a challenge to

much the way Bunyan himself did in *Grace Abounding* ('I have done despite to the Spirit of Grace: Therefore I have shut my self out of all the Promises') and God assumes the role of Giant Despair: 'there now remains to me nothing but threatnings, dreadful threatnings, fearful threatnings of certain Judgement and firy Indignation, which shall devour me as an Adversary.' God, he says, has 'denied me repentance' and has 'shut me up in this Iron Cage: nor can all the men in the World let me out' (p. 35).

Clearly the experience in Doubting Castle comes over, experientially, as the same, though as far more powerful since seen from the inside. If the pilgrims knew God was not an enemy, despair could not hold them. The reprobate frame has usurped the mind. The idea of being locked into a state of mind is a

public disputation with him (*A Moderate Message to Quakers, Seekers, Socinians . . . Three Questions Offered to be Disputed with John Bunyan before any Public Audience*); whereas Sharrock (pp. xxix–xxxv) and Keeble (p. 264 n.) agree that Bunyan wrote most of Part One (published in 1678) before his release from prison in 1672. There is, however, more conclusive evidence of misidentification. Sharrock cites Offor's authority for his conjecture, *A Relation of the Life and Death of John Child*, published in 1710, and overlooks contemporaneous versions, including *The Mischief of Persecution Exemplified: By a True Narrative of the Life and Deplorable End of Mr. John Child* (1688), which is explicit about the date of Child's publicized despair. In 1682 Child published an attack on nonconformists entitled *The Second Argument for a More Firm Union amongst Protestants*, after which 'he signified to some of his intimate Acquaintances, that his mind was perplext, for what he had therein done; but yet bare the trouble so, as not to make any great shew of it in his general Behaviour, until the beginning of July 1684, when he could no longer bear or conceal the horrors of his mind' (p. 9). It was after this date that he made a spectacle of himself to sundry visitors, including one J. B. (pp. 26–7), probably Bunyan. Child did not dare return to the dissenting fold for fear that his property would be confiscated (p. 20). After the Conventicle Act of 1670 propertied nonconformists were in a particularly miserable position, as fines levied on impecunious co-religionists were passed on to them; and if the accumulated fines could not be paid property was seized and sold (see Gerald Cragg, *Puritanism in the Period of the Great Persecution 1660–1688* (Cambridge, 1957), 17). It was an effective way of stripping nonconformists of potentially powerful support. Child's inability to face destitution apparently reinforced his conviction that he was unable to repent, and he killed himself in despair of his salvation in October 1684. The erroneous identification of John Child as the Man of Despair is not revealed for pedantic reasons but in order to indicate that Bunyan was not as short of cautionary examples as it implies. There is no indication, in this typical portrait, of any cause for the man's despair as specific as Child's apostasy and shrinking from persecution. It may be that, in line with the noted general tendency to slight the significance of despair in puritan experience, these editors were over-eager to associate the Man of Despair with a single widely bruited case. The text's uncompromising condemnation and extreme punishment give rise to a need to pin on him a more deserving guilt than it supplies.

natural way of expressing this; unsurprisingly it had cropped up
in puritan discourse before. Thomas Goodwin says of despairers:

through much poring upon, and considering onely what might make
against them, they have had the bolts of their hearts so far shot into
despaire, and fixed in desperate sorrow, and the true wards of sound
evidences so far wrung and wrested by false keyes, that when the
skilfullest and strongest comforters have come with true keyes to shoot
back the bolt, they would not turne about, nay could scarce get
entrance.[65]

Bunyan's own, unnecessarily implausible, treatment of the key
allegorizes, in the very arbitrariness of its discovery, the Calvinist
psychology. As William James remarks: 'In the extreme of
melancholy the self that consciously *is* can do absolutely
nothing.'[66] Bunyan's, like Goodwin's, prisoners attest this. 'The
law', said Luther in his *Commentary* on Galatians, one of three
books mentioned in *Grace Abounding* which must have become
items of permanent furniture in Bunyan's mind, 'is a prison
civilly and spiritually.' And this 'shutting up must endure but
until faith come, and when faith cometh this spiritual prison
must have its end'.[67] Moralizing about the pilgrims therefore
does not do justice to the quintessentially protestant experience
of the impotence of the will whose imaginative truth the allegory
dramatizes.

Roger Sharrock artificially separates theology from experience
in his comment on this incident:

Bunyan makes his theological point, though with some detriment to the
effect of the adventure story: Christian had no need to despair of his
salvation; Scripture showed that the promise of God's covenant with
him prevented his repentance from being rejected.[68]

But the power of the so-called adventure story comes from the
way in which it elides, in the medium of dream, into the story of
the harried psyche. This is enforced here by the ambiguous
expression of Christian's discovery of the key 'in my bosom'
(p. 118). God's covenant with Christian is, from a human

[65] *A Childe of Light Walking in Darknes* (1636), 187.

[66] *The Varieties of Religious Experience* (1902), 244.

[67] Martin Luther, *A Commentary on St. Paul's Epistle to the Galatians*, trans. E. Middleton, ed. J. P. Fallowes (1940), 210.

[68] Roger Sharrock, ed., *The Pilgrim's Progress* (Harmondsworth, 1965), 376 n.

viewpoint, constantly open to re-examination which the repeated destruction of spectral selves keeps urging. The key which unlocks a mental state seems real only when it is found. Like his sealed roll or the steps in the Slough of Despond, it may, from God's or the narrator's point of view, have been there all the time but access to it is blocked until God gives his arbitrary, inexplicable grace—and then, in another exclusive frame, he knows it was there all the time; he always was chosen. There is an ironic reference back to this when Ignorance is asked for his admission certificate at the Celestial Gate and 'fumbled in his bosom for one, and found none' (p. 163). The embarrassment of the feigned search, the habit-formed cover-up in circumstances of total exposure, and, paradoxically, the forlorn hope of discovering 'one' (whatever it is the official seems to require) about his person is all caught in the word 'fumbled'. At the same time it is a psychological fumbling 'in his bosom' for something very like what Christian is lucky enough to find. The dream motif of nakedness or exposure strengthens the physical-mental interplay. The incident is the counterpart of Christian's discovery, living out the fears which are lifted from him.

The experience of despair, then, is one of absolute envelopment while the opposite state of mind (which Christian and Hopeful are able to discuss) is an entirely theoretical possibility. Escape from the mind-blanketing mood occurs as if directed by an external power. Stanley Fish rightly points out that remembering the key of promise is not a consequence of Hopeful's arguments but the moral he gathers is that 'memory is an exercise of the will rather than the end of a process'.[69] This seems to me to go not far enough in attributing action to God. It is God who exerts pressure on the will. 'There is no perswasion will do,' an earlier marginal note had said, 'if God openeth not the eyes' (p. 39). Accordingly, when Christian breaks out of despair, it is 'as one half amazed' (p. 118): he is startled to find his mind repossessed of the elect apparatus of understanding: '*What a fool*,' he blurts out, '*am I, thus to lie in a stinking Dungeon, when I may as well walk at liberty? I have a Key in my bosom, called Promise, that will, (I am perswaded) open any Lock in Doubting Castle*' (p. 118). It is hard to know what can be meant by calling this an act of will. The

---

[69] Fish, *Self-Consuming Artifacts*, pp. 256–7.

usual Renaissance psychological triad was memory, understanding, and will, will being exercised ideally at the end of a
process of ratiocination which memory informed. Bunyan's
Calvinist rejection of this process (which gave mankind psychological autonomy) is in favour of revelation or seizure of the will
of the kind Christian expresses. It is an act of God. Norwood too
was suddenly struck by his 'foolishness . . . in suffering myself to
be holden in the snares and delusions of Satan . . . Upon this,' he
finds, 'the bands of Satan became presently as flax that is burnt
with fire' (p. 97). It is to God though that he attributes liberating
enlightenment.

But just as the pilgrims do not will themselves out of despair it
should not be forgotten that they did not will themselves into it
either; they were taken by force. Christian therefore was not
really a fool 'to lie in a stinking dungeon'; the idea that he was
free to leave is psychologically absurd (though Sharrock and Fish
seem to suggest this). On the other hand we can well see why
Christian feels, now that the mind-controlling frame has switched,
that he has been a fool: the two states of mind, with their full
theological panoply, are inaccessible to each other. The naïve
expression of release conveys the sense of wakening from a
nightmare or moving from one dream-logic to another in which
the previous rules compelling obedience now seem silly.

Fish arraigns the pilgrims for forgetfulness: 'in their eagerness
to condemn themselves', he says, Christian and Hopeful

forget about the merciful inclinations of a higher tribunal and the
redemption promised to them as the beneficiaries of Christ's sacrifice;
and, paradoxically, this forgetfulness has its roots in the harshness of the
judgement they make on those who fail to remember Lot's wife.[70]

What Fish himself seems to forget—as the seventeenth-century
puritan could not—is that God really did turn Lot's wife into a
pillar of salt, merely for looking back: 'for we read not', says
Hopeful, 'that she stept one foot out of the way' (p. 109). The
physical presence of the pillar of salt expresses the aliveness of
the Bible's episodes maintained by the typological conviction
that contemporary lives corresponded to the human models of
election and reprobation to be found there. The pilgrims are

[70] Ibid. 254.

reminded too of the 'severest Judgments' which observably befall miscreants. Allegory is suspended here: what is discussed is too real to be veiled. Those who err after seeing the example of Lot's wife resemble 'them that pick Pockets in the presence of the Judge'. They are 'sinners *before the Lord*, that is, in his eyesight' (pp. 109–10). The dream eschews the identification of this supervising providence ('the Lord') as the King of the Celestial Country, who must retain his distant fairy-tale character. He is the object of the dream-quest, the mythical king to whom the wronged subject brings grievances (though, more logically, he should be held responsible for them). The Lord's conduct, on the other hand, trains the pilgrims' minds on the Sword of Damocles hanging over them. It seems less than fair, therefore, to ascribe harshness of judgement to them. It is, moreover, chiefly themselves they warn: 'she may be to us both Caution and Example; Caution that we should shun her sin, or a sign of what judgment will overtake such as shall not be prevented by this caution' (p. 109) (and typically the passive phrasing—'such as shall not be prevented'—denies them the freedom to act on the warning). Memory does not help them to think of 'the merciful inclinations of a higher tribunal' if it is their recent experience which is to be remembered. The strange notion of their 'eagerness to condemn themselves' scarcely needs to be adduced.

Another incident whose conditioning effect on the pilgrims should be considered is the fate of Vain-confidence. We know nothing of Vain-confidence that differentiates him from Christian: he too is walking in By-Path Meadow under the impression that it leads to the Celestial Gate. Not only does he materialize to express the sinful state of the deviant pilgrims, he is also an independent person, as a marginal gloss (*'see what it is too suddenly to fall in with strangers'*) indicates. What they very nearly fall in with him is a deep pit 'which was on purpose there made by the Prince of those grounds, to catch *vain-glorious* fools withall'. He 'was dashed in pieces with his fall'. As an ectoplasmic extension of Christian himself, Vain-confidence expresses not just his sin but the destiny that instantly shapes itself to his imagination out of the mould of reprobate experience. As an actual reprobate he is a terrifyingly immediate reminder of the unmerciful inclinations which (on the statistical evidence of *Progress* itself) generally prevailed with the higher tribunal. At the moment when

Christian draws closest to Vain-confidence psychologically he therefore has to distance himself most emphatically. We find here the strange combination of empathy and callousness which puritan theology engendered (and which was evident in *Grace Abounding* when Bunyan turned his old friend Harry into an object-lesson). The pilgrims call to Vain-confidence and hear his groaning—at which Hopeful says, 'Where are we now?' (p. 112).

This is the typical process of self-reference which made it necessary for them to moralize about Lot's wife. It comes naturally to Bunyan to present people as projections of unwanted parts of Christian himself. Puritans sought a stable identity in the toing and froing of the mind between others and self motivated by the unitary ego-ideal of the elect Christian. This was the reading process in which they had to engage. On the one hand seeing themselves in others produced the fracturing of the ideal image but on the other it offered the opportunity to displace this unwanted heterogeneity of experience on to those people who reflected it back, and so dispose of it. In spite of the psychological interest of Bunyan's varied characters it is a nearly solipsistic world-view that the allegory expresses. Other people were allowed to have a separate existence but so far as the individual Christian was concerned they and the things that happened to them had been arranged by providence to assist in deciphering one's own place in the scheme of things. This is done by processes of incorporation and expulsion—Faithful and Hopeful having the same ambiguous status (as real people and phantom selves) as Vain-confidence and Ignorance. Psychological interest in others was paradoxically impelled by the need for self-understanding.

At the same time as being forced into the severity for which Fish faults them the pilgrims are unable to shake off the fear that they could be treated similarly—and the reason for this is not their judgemental disposition but the witnessed evidence of God's peremptory judgement on those with whom they share affinities. Fish blames them for not employing memory. Memory itself is inevitable: the question is what is to be remembered. Despair necessitates extrapolation; it is narrative in character, taking a view of the future which has its basis in the curve experience seems to have plotted from the past to the present. Christian and Hopeful in this sense have their memories to blame for their plight. Memory can constitute identity as either elect or reprobate. They do 'Remember Lot's wife' and Vain-confidence, and these memories are presumably fortified by other reprobate incidents they have witnessed. Interpreter had enjoined them to remember the man of despair: 'Let this mans misery be remembred by thee, and be an everlasting caution to thee' (p. 35). And Apollyon had been able to jog Christian's memory of a train of interpretably reprobate experiences (p. 58). So a reprobate teleology supplies the pilgrims with plentiful memories to imprison them in despair. The shadow-narrative always threatens the imagination, and in Doubting Castle it assumes control.

The influence of the reprobate threat on the narrative is evident, too, after the pilgrims' escape from Doubting Castle. They are handed a perspective glass by the shepherds on the Delectable Mountains to see if they can make out the Celestial City. Here is Fish's comment on the narrative logic:

The 'last thing that the Shepherds had shewed them' was the 'by-way to Hell' and this specter is enough to shake their confidence in the fact of their salvation, that is, in the efficacy of the promise. (This, as Bunyan tells us in the margin, is the '*fruit of slavish fear*'.) Even at this late date Christian's faith is not firm enough ('they could not look *steddily*') to enable him to keep 'that light' *continually* in his eyes.[71]

But the context given here is rather selective. Bunyan's marginal comment ('*The fruit of slavish fear*' (p. 123)) looks like an attempt to retract the sympathy the passage evokes for the pilgrims: a brief review shows why it is needed.

The pilgrims' hosts have taken them for a pleasant stroll in the hills, welcome recuperation after their recent confinement, torture, and near death. Agreeing to 'shew these Pilgrims some wonders' (p. 120), the shepherds proceed, without consulting their guests, to subject them to a series of harrowing sights. They display, of all things, the victims of Giant Despair blindly stumbling over tombs just as the wicked Giant himself had exhibited the skeletons of suicides. Christian and Hopeful are so shocked that they burst into tears. They are then treated to the cries of the damned and are informed that this by-way to Hell is

---

[71] Fish, *Self-Consuming Artifacts*, 247.

for hypocrites, 'namely, such as sell their Birthright with *Esau*: such as sell their Master with *Judas*' (p. 122). We learn here that Bunyan—years after writing *Grace Abounding*—does not regard his own feared typological identification with these biblical reprobates as neurotic folly. Some of the Judas and Esau anti-types had, the pilgrims learn, '*a shew of Pilgrimage as we have now*' (p. 122). Bunyan's hypocrites do not know they are hypocritical. Calvin had considered how far the reprobate 'goe . . . forwarde with the children of God' (*Inst.* 2. 7. 9) and Perkins had urged his readers to 'go beyond all reprobates'.[72] The terror of the inauthenticity of elect experience is what impels the pilgrims forward. It is to secure this effect, presumably, that the euphemistic 'wonders' were put on show. The emphasis is on the arbitrariness of election and the possibility of being deceived.

It is after this that their 'skill' at perceiving bright futures for themselves through the glass is tested. Only by detaching ourselves entirely from the illusion the narrative cultivates that the characters represent people undergoing a sequence of experiences can it seem sensible to blame the pilgrims for failing to look steadily at the Celestial Gate. No consideration is given by Fish to why these refugees should be subjected to such horrors (representing in Bunyan's culture no 'specter' but thoroughly real destinies). The familiar system of mind control, playing on fears of hypocrisy and rejection, is being practised—on the contemporary reader as well as the characters. In Part Two, it is interesting to note, Bunyan finds an excuse for not terrorizing the family group in the same way: 'The Reason was, for that these had *Great-heart* to be their Guide, who was one that was well acquainted with things, and so could give them their Cautions more seasonably' (p. 288). We never in fact see him do anything comparable. Bunyan's compassionate pastoral role has moved to the fore in his imagination. Confidence in the refashioned world of the dissenting community makes the oppressive world the one more likely to disappear. A fiend looms up in the Valley and immediately vanishes 'to all their sights' (p. 241); robbers are announced but do not appear (p. 258). Meeting oppressors can make them, instead of the pilgrim's faith, melt into air. Part Two as a whole is an expression of pride in the achievement of

---

[72] *Works*, p. 431.

Christian, a path-breaking dissenter whose fugitive energy has succeeded in opening a psycho-social space for the next generation to inhabit. His offspring tread, with collective assurance, in his pioneering steps (p. 259).

We should conclude with the conclusion of the narrative of Part One to see how the exorcism of despair is finally accomplished—and at what cost. Right to the last Christian is battling against despair of salvation. ' 'Tis you, 'tis you they wait for' (p. 157), he plangently cries to Hopeful as he sinks (once more) in the River. But moments later he is admitted into the Celestial City. The dreamer's eye then turns to Ignorance and the narrative ends with the ugly scene of his ejection.

The damnation of Ignorance, all the more unpalatable because the character's amiable ordinariness has been familiarized to us, demands an explanation in some way adequate to the shock it delivers. Vincent Newey says it 'is neither something relished nor something regretted. It is a fact to which Bunyan responds with both sympathy and acceptance.'[73] While it is a fact to Bunyan that people like Ignorance will be damned it is a culture-bound fact which can lead us to ask what role it plays in the communal imagination to which the work of art provides access. The event's positioning urges consideration of its relationship to the structure it completes and of the imaginative needs it satisfies. Explanation belongs to the different but related levels with which the chapter as a whole has tried to keep in touch. First there is the function of cultural transmission in which the work participates. Then there are the effects of dogma in the individual imagination. These are located in a social milieu which is dominated by antagonistic powers. Finally there is the attempted dream resolution.

To the extent, then, that Bunyan is superimposing actual lives on a book of signs Ignorance rounds off the 'or not' of the paradigm to which the narrative conforms. Ignorance was the main target of the proselytizing efforts of puritans and this Ignorance's insouciance right up to death dramatizes a commonplace of puritan polemic. W. Y. Tindall congratulates Bunyan for eschewing the crudely horrific deaths of the books of judgements when he came to deal with Badman's demise: 'Bunyan

---

[73] 'Bunyan and the Confines of the Mind', *The Pilgrim's Progress: Critical and Historical Essays*, p. 44.

ingeniously discovered the peaceful death of a sinner to be not a
fault of justice but the evidence of a celestial severity beyond that
of common judgements and a paradox for the consolation of the
hopeful.'[74] But it was not his discovery and it should be a relief
not to have to debit him with such a variant on the abominable
fancy. 'The common opinion', says Robert Bolton, endorsing
Perkins, 'is, that if a man die quietly, and goe away like a
lambe . . . then he goes straight to heaven . . . But the truth is
otherwise: For indeede a man may die like a lambe, and yet goe
to Hell: and one dying in exceeding torments, and strange
behaviours of the body, may goe to heaven.'[75] It is 'the ignorant
people', said Richard Greenham, 'will still commend such
fearfull deaths, saying, he departed as meekly as a lambe'.[76]
Asked how Badman took his death, therefore, Wise replies
firmly: 'As quietly as a lamb.' The question was a set-up,
Attentive explains: 'For there is such an opinion as this among
the ignorant, that if a man dies, as they call it, like a lamb . . .
they conclude . . . that such a one is gone to heaven' (p. 291). In
depicting Ignorance personified ferried over the River of Death
by Vain-hope and Christian's troubled passage Bunyan is
transmitting the wisdom of his culture.

No hypocrites cross the River in Part Two however. And
Arthur Dent's Asunetus, the prototype for Ignorance, is allowed
to repent:[77] an exemplary outcome of the didactic process
directed through him at the ignorant reader. It may be clearer
why Part One is driven to this down-beat conclusion if we
compare another dislocated fictional ending: that of *Jane Eyre*.
There the self-martyring personality of Jane is left stranded from
the resolution. The imagination is unable to accept that so
central a constituent of the identity built up for her by the
narrative (and by the culture that feeds it) should evaporate: the
text seems compelled to divert the energy elsewhere. So the
curious last paragraph comes to rest on St John Rivers who fulfils
Jane's need for martyrdom and, by leaving the last impression,
robs the reader of the illogical happiness to which the heroine,
conventionally, has attained. Ignorance fulfils a similar function,
the function, one might say, of the Gadarene swine. The only

[74] *Mechanick Preacher*, p. 200.   [75] *Instructions*, p. 230.
[76] *Workes*, p. 144. See also John Sheffield, *A Good Conscience the Strongest Hold* (1650),
p. 250.   [77] *Plaine Mans Path-Way*, pp. 407 ff.

figures in Part Two to be haunted by reprobate fears in their
dying moments are the peripheral (and mildly patronized)
Despondency and his daughter. Despondency describes their
fears as '*Ghosts*, the which we entertained when we first began to
be Pilgrims, and could never shake them off after'. Their will—or
anti-will—he says, 'is, that our *Disponds*, and slavish Fears, be by
no man ever received, from the day of our Departure, for ever;
For I know that after my Death they will offer themselves to
others' (p. 308). The difference from Part One is that little
imaginative pressure is exerted by the narrative itself to relieve
the Christians of the persecutory alternative; Christian's imagination on the other hand has been inhabited throughout by the
reprobate paradigm.

Christian has been haunted by a ghosting reprobate destiny
both in the form of his own 'desponds' and of the protean
doppelgänger who has materialized his feared shadow-self. Vain-
confidence was an example. A fleeting incident in the Valley of
the Shadow of Death clarifies the process: 'one of the wicked ones
got behind him, and stept up softly to him, and whisperingly
suggested many grievous blasphemies to him, which he verily
thought had proceeded from his own mind' (p. 63). This is a
simple dramatization of *Grace Abounding*. Bunyan thought himself
possessed of the devil when 'some most horrible blasphemous
thought or other would bolt out of my heart against [God]' (101).
It is a rudimentary example of the way in which the alternative
self was disavowed. It bears a relationship, of course, to the later
doppelgänger. Stevenson's Mr Hyde, it may be remembered,
scrawls blasphemies in Dr Jekyll's treasured devotional books.[78]
Closer to Christian, as a victim of Calvinism, is Robert
Wringhim, in *Confessions of a Justified Sinner*, who is preoccupied
with the destiny his actions obey. It turns out, reversing the usual
process of the autobiography, that his assumption of election is
subsumed to a reprobate teleology—which had been embodied
in his demonic double.[79] Because Christian interrogates his
destiny throughout with the binary apparatus of understanding,
other characters (apart from social or religious superiors) are

---

[78] *Dr. Jekyll and Mr. Hyde and Other Tales*, Everyman (1925), 40, 61.

[79] James Hogg, *The Private Memoirs and Confessions of a Justified Sinner*, ed. J. Carey
(Oxford, 1969). It is no accident that the *doppelgänger* is generally found in the
literature of the most protestant countries: Germany, Scotland, and America.

always doubles, establishing identity or polarity. The reprobate frame controls Christian's perceptions in his dying moments; yet he cannot take this *doppelgänger* into the Celestial City with him. Even in Part Two there is a sensed need to bequeath the reprobate ghosts; something should be done with them. Then, though, the generous hope that the ghosts may dissolve away is affordable. Like the martyrdom of Jane Eyre, the persecution of Christian must provide itself with a whipping boy.

Ignorance is not, imaginatively, an accidental choice. Q. D. Leavis applauds his damnation because it gives her the opportunity to recruit Bunyan 'on the side of the highbrow'. Apart from the anachronism of the claim, she is guilty of an icier cruelty than Bunyan, especially since she notices that his characterization is not 'black and white' but 'really subtle'. Should we not be less disturbed by the damnation of a black character or an abstraction? Like Tindall she prefers a sophisticated argument for the infliction of crude punishment. When she says Bunyan has 'no cheap system of rewards and punishments'[80] it is the system of assessment, not the judgement it leads to, in whose refinement she is interested. But the text is too embroiled with its culture to be making judgements as magisterial as hers; the damnation of Ignorance is needed rather than wanted.

Ignorance is a young man who can be taken to represent Christian before he apprehended the City's ruin—the simpleton or 'ignorant sot' he, and Bunyan, might have remained. While Ignorance is described as 'a very brisk Lad' (p. 123), Bunyan was, in his churchy phase, 'a brisk talker also my self in the matters of Religion', though 'ignorant of Jesus Christ' (37, 36). Ignorance, who obeys Anglican imperatives ('I Pray, Fast, pay Tithes, and give Alms' (pp. 123–4),[81] lacks a continuous sense of

---

[80] *Fiction and the Reading Public* (1965), 100, 98.

[81] This view of Ignorance as a dutiful but duped Anglican identifiable with the young Bunyan is supported by typical puritan autobiographers' characterizations of their own benighted worship. Baptist Jane Turner, for example, 'took it for granted that that was religion which was then in force from King and Bishops . . . and I thought the more I abounded in fasting, book prayer, and observation of daies and times . . . the better it was . . . Then being acquainted with some who were then called Puritans . . .', the scales fell. With some encouragement from her new friends she judged herself to be 'very ignorant' and 'began to be more frequent in reading the Scriptures, and hearing Sermons' (*Choice Experiences*, pp. 11–12, 13). Ignorance's emphasis on being 'a good Liver' who, for example, gives alms (pp. 123–4) suggests that he accepted the version of Christianity advanced by Edward Fowler and

himself—unlike Faithful and Hopeful who both supply a précis narrative of their spiritual experience, Christian, whose sense of himself is coterminous with the narrative as a whole, and Christiana who is identical with the text of Part Two. Failure to apprehend the forces controlling his destiny—or read himself— means that his soul is damning, and the allegory grants the opportunity to demonstrate how destiny catches up with him. His apparent ability to ignore the persecutory imagination makes him the natural victim of Christian's displaced pain. 'A true saying it is,' Perkins had said, 'that the right way to goe unto heaven, is to saile by hell.'[82] Ignorance has evaded the rites of passage which guaranteed the reality of the separatists' new world and so must suffer if Christian's suffering is not to be invalidated. He is both another possible self and a vindication of the differentiation the narrative itself has accomplished for Christian. The moment Christian ceases to feel persecuted Ignorance begins—and if Christian's reprobate ghost is to be relinquished for ever the punishment of its recipient must, to balance the psychological equation, be eternal too.

Ignorance was an ally of the established authorities who stifled his self-consciousness (pp. 150–1) and, when pressed, tried to nullify the counter-culture: Christian's religion, he says huffily, is 'the fruit of distracted braines' (p. 148). His exposure therefore completes the expulsion of scepticism to which the allegory as a whole is addressed. Gordon Campbell argues that the roll Christian hands in and Ignorance lacks at the Celestial Gate 'does not merely serve as an allegorical representation of some doctrinal truth' because 'one clearly does not submit one's assurance at the Heavenly Gate. And poor Ignorance, who brims with confidence, is not given a false roll to represent false assurance.'[83] He quotes later verses by Bunyan where a certificate ('To show thou seest thyself most desolate; | Writ by the master with repentance seal'd') admits the holder into the

denounced by Bunyan as a religion of works (ii. 278–334). Fowler, who disturbed Bunyan with his influence in Bedfordshire, advocated 'an obedient temper of mind' and strongly commended alms-giving as being meritorious in itself (ii. 324, 329). The two 'brisk' young men lacked the biblical knowledge that might awaken them to religious experience independent of the manipulative control of their social and educational betters.

[82] *Works*, p. 457.
[83] 'The Theology of *The Pilgrim's Progress*', p. 260.

church. But assurance of salvation ('this Roll was the assurance
of his life' (p. 44), we are told) was alike the condition of entering
Bunyan's church (which required spoken testimonies[84]) and of
entering heaven. Although human judgement of authenticity was
seen as fallible (the visible church was not coextensive with the
invisible) the requisite assurance was in principle the same.
Submission at the Heavenly Gate figures, moreover, since
Christian's assurance of faith is 'the evidence of things not seen'
(Heb. 11: 1), so once the things not seen become visible retention
of the roll would clearly spoil its allegorical meaning. Tenacious
certainty, and the evidence supporting it, is no longer required
and can be cashed in. You do not keep a winning raffle ticket
when you have collected your prize although it was your
evidence and assurance. For the elect, assurance was a seemingly
objective validation of this kind in which belief had to be
mustered.

It is therefore very much to the purpose that Ignorance has not
a false certificate but none at all because this allegorizes how he
misses the point that 'it is one thing indeed to have these [the
elect experiences], and another thing only to think so' (p. 145). A
difference could be stressed between the painful accumulation of
evidences which were prone, owing to the impairment of the
believer's faculties, to be clouded (the condition ascribed by
onlookers to the dying Halyburton[85]) and a sanguine cast of
mind sufficient to itself. This difference is what the narrative
itself stood for; and Ignorance may help to shore up the sense the
elect should have of the objective existence of their assurance
since they can judge this breezy subjectivist by communal
criteria to be an uncertified claimant. In part theology made this
a compulsion: numbers had to be made up and polarization
achieved. In *The Righteous Man's Evidences for Heaven: Or a Treatise
Shewing how every one while he Lives here May Know what Shall Become
of him after his Departure out of this Life* (1619) Timothy Rogers
asked readers to ponder 'what multitudes daily (departing this
world) throng in at the infernall gates of hell, for want of the
assurance of their salvation'.[86] But reified assurance was a
political imperative too. It was the real condition of dissenters'

---

[84] The practice is evident in 'The Minutes of the First Independent Church', p. 23.

[85] *Memoirs of the Life*, 2nd edn. (Edinburgh, 1715), 171.

[86] *The Righteous Man's Evidences for Heaven* (1619), sig. A4ᵛ.

perseverance since equipped with anything less they would succumb to their brow-beating betters who told Bunyan he was 'medling with that for which I could shew no warrant' and that he was the ignorant one.[87]

This brings one back to Dent's point about not trusting landowners. Ignorance, like Talkative (or Dent's Antilegon who sneers at those who 'know their seates in Heaven'[88]) does not appreciate the need for substantiation—for a certificate of any kind. In Calvin's words, the reprobate 'do never conceive but a confused feeling of grace, so that they rather take holde of the shadowe than of the sounde bodie [substance]' (*Inst*. 3. 2. 11). To lay claim to your spiritual land (to return, as Bunyan did in a late treatise, to Leviticus 25) evidence of ownership was required (i. 188). Trusting to the good will of the establishment and an incorporative divinity was the surest route to destruction. That Ignorance is, in Q. D. Leavis's words, 'decent, honest, and God-fearing' makes the point with all possible force.[89]

After Christian's admittance to the City the dreamer himself—and the reader—is left ambiguously disconsolate: 'And after that, they shut up the Gates: which when I had seen, I wished my self among them' (p. 162). Even the deprivation of bell-ringing is made good there. The wistfulness is reminiscent of Bunyan's response to his earlier dream in *Grace Abounding*, after which he was left for days 'in a forlorn and sad condition' (56). The dream protagonist has fulfilled what he has not. The shutting of the gates in the dreamer's and reader's face is followed by the undoing of Ignorance so that the ambiguity as to whether the longing to be among them is the anticipation of the elect or the gnawing sense of exclusion of the reprobate is reinforced. And the closing words—'So I awoke, and behold it was a Dream' (p. 163)—re-evoke the related ambivalence of the reality-status of what has been depicted.

Here is Baxter again, coolly ranking his beliefs in descending order of conviction:

My certainty that I am a Man, is before my certainty that there is a God. My certainty that there is a God, is greater than my certainty that

[87] *Grace Abounding*, pp. 108, 111.
[88] *Plaine Mans Path-Way*, p. 302.
[89] *Fiction and the Reading Public*, p. 99.

he requireth love and holiness of his Creature: My certainty of *this* is greater than my certainty of the Life of Reward and Punishment hereafter: My certainty of that, is greater than my certainty of the endless duration of it . . . So that as you see by what Gradations my Understanding doth proceed, so also that my Certainty differeth as the Evidences differ.[90]

Bunyan could not tolerate such degrees of certainty because they exposed him to the retaliatory providence. His dream answers the need to reify the invisible world which sustained the dissenting counter-culture, as his autobiography had objectified his own assurance of salvation. But the status of the allegory is teasingly ambiguous, as the debate in the prefatory verses suggests. In one sense it is 'feigned' while in another it has just the 'solidness' his critic also faulted it for lacking (pp. 3–4). Bunyan becomes increasingly tetchy with the critic whose judgement he first politely solicited (he becomes a 'Carper' who had best look to his own life (p. 5)), for he plainly felt that his work bridged dogma and experience in a gratifying way. In spite of discouraging reading for diversion ('playing with the out-side of my Dream' (p. 164)), he needed the physicality of the metaphors Fish thinks he wholly disowns. Progress was needed to demonstrate the reality of estrangement from the familiar community in which Christians actually remained (*'as if* they had found a new world, *as if* they were people that dwelt alone, and were not to be reckoned among their Neighbours' (my italics)[91]). Nevertheless such statements in the text as 'Heaven is but as a Fable to some, and . . . things here are counted the only things substantial' (p. 200) spotlight the problem of the reality-claims made within a dream or a fable. The fable fulfils the wish that the invisible world materialize but it does so by super-imposing a dream-world on reality which cannot help drawing attention to its illusoriness—or feigning. As in the autobiography, theology and social oppression demand of the Christian absolute assurance of salvation, but the further the imagination is driven to substantiate this certainty the more it exposes itself to an immanent critique. Bunyan fell into the allegory because it was congruent with puritan modes of perception and fulfilled

---

[90] *Reliquiae*, p. 128.
[91] *Grace Abounding*, 38.

multiple functions of cultural transmission, but above all because the dream gave substance to and therefore substantiated the higher reality which assured him of a protective providence. Its status, though, remains that of a dream—at once solid and feigned—and its energies are, to the end, addressed to the exorcism of the persecutory fears it has dramatized.

Part II

5

Robert Burton and Religious Despair in Calvinist England

SINCE Nicholas Tyacke's seminal article 'Puritanism, Arminianism and Counter-Revolution' most historians seem agreed that Calvinism was the doctrinal orthodoxy of the English Church in the reigns of Elizabeth and James. Dissidents, says Tyacke, had to lead 'a more-or-less clandestine existence'.[1] Public opponents of Calvinism in both universities attracted notoriety.[2] It was prohibited to publish views which supported the Dutch theologian Arminius who in the first decade of the century launched a protestant attack on Calvin's teaching on predestination and

[1] 'Puritanism, Arminianism and Counter-Revolution', in C. Russell, ed., *The Origins of the English Civil War* (1973), 130. Unless otherwise noted historical information in this opening is derived from Tyacke. References to his article will be given only for quotations. See also Tyacke's full development of his argument in *Anti-Calvinists: The Rise of English Arminianism c. 1590–1640* (Oxford, 1987). An attempt has been made to rehabilitate the idea that the Church of England as a whole maintained, throughout most of James's reign, a studied ambiguity on predestinarian dogma (Peter White, 'Calvinism and the English Church 1570–1635', *P&P* 101 (1983), 34–54). White denies that there was any 'rise in Arminianism': this was a puritan scare provoked by the international situation in 1625 (Arminians rejected predestination altogether, whereas figures such as Laud saw themselves as adhering to the Thirty-nine Articles which could be taken to obscure the Calvinist idea of reprobation while retaining the long-established doctrine of the predestination of the elect). White's attempt to dilute the Calvinism of the Jacobean church has, however, been substantially rebutted on the grounds that the identification of individuals who demurred or reserved their position does not impugn the argument for Calvinist dominance: 'The basic point, therefore, concerns Calvinist hegemony. But hegemony is not monopoly. Despite Calvinist predominance, there were anti-Calvinists in the Elizabethan and Jacobean church. Indeed one can easily accept the claims of men like Humphrey Leech and Benjamin Carier that their open expression of dissent represented but the tip of an iceberg of discontent and unease. The existence of such people and their silence represent powerful evidence of the extent to which Calvinism had established itself in control of the crucial cultural media of the day and was thus able to suppress overt criticism' (P. G. Lake, 'Calvinism and the English Church 1570–1635', *P&P* 114 (1987), 32–76, p. 34 *et passim*; see also N. Tyacke, 'Debate: The Rise of Arminianism Reconsidered', *P&P* 115 (1987), 201–16, and Peter White, 'A Rejoinder', *ibid.* 217–29). For evidence of Calvinism's domination of the cultural media, see Dewey D. Wallace's survey of printed books: *Puritans and Predestination: Grace in English Protestant Theology* (Chapel Hill, 1982), 29–111.

[2] See H. C. Porter, *Reformation and Reaction in Tudor Cambridge* (Cambridge, 1958), and C. M. Dent, *Protestant Reformers in Elizabethan Oxford* (Oxford, 1983).

maintained that God's grace was freely given to all who chose to have faith. In 1618 the Synod of Dort, whose proceedings were dedicated to James I, formally condemned Arminius and reaffirmed Calvinist dogmas. What episcopal dissent there appears to have been—Lancelot Andrewes's pre-eminently— was circumspect. Even Archbishop Bancroft, 'a Jacobean anomaly',[3] was obliged—though he disliked Calvinist pre-destination—to allow publication in 1608 of an official Calvinist commentary on the Thirty-nine Articles. And in 1609 he declined to support Humphrey Leech, an Oxford Arminian who was consequently driven to Rome. According to C. M. Dent 'even the Archbishop now appeared . . . to favour Calvin's opinions'.[4]

To give credal specificity to the collective extremism the Calvinist consensus promoted, it is worth quoting the revised Lambeth Articles authorized by Archbishop Whitgift in 1595:

I: God from eternity has predestined some men to life, and reprobated some to death.

II: The moving or efficient cause of predestination to life is not the foreseeing of faith, or of perseverance, or of good works, or of anything innate in the person of the predestined, but only of the will of the good pleasure of God.

III: There is a determined and certain number of predestined, which cannot be increased or diminished.

IV: Those not predestined to salvation are inevitably condemned on account of their sins.

V: A true, lively and justifying faith, and the sanctifying Spirit of God, is not lost nor does it pass away either totally or finally in the elect.

VI: The truly faithful man—that is, one endowed with justifying faith—is sure by full assurance of faith of the remission of sins and his eternal salvation through Christ.

VII: Saving grace is not granted, is not made common, is not ceded to all men, by which they might be saved, if they wish.

VIII: No man can come to Christ unless it be granted to him, and unless the Father draws him: and all men are not drawn by the Father to come to the Son.

IX: It is not in the will or the power of each and every man to be saved.[5]

---

[3] Tyacke, 'Puritanism, Arminianism and Counter-Revolution', p. 126.

[4] *Protestant Reformers*, p. 236.

[5] Quoted in translation by Porter, *Reformation and Reaction*, p. 371.

The Laudian party's ascendancy in the late 1620s was sudden and provocative. Arminian at least in rejecting double predestination, it adopted the ploy of stigmatizing all dogmatic Calvinists as puritans. The term had formerly been applied to sectaries and nonconformists who were pressing for an instantaneous transformation from an episcopalian to a presbyterian system of church government. In James's reign, Tyacke argues, 'contemporaries would have found any suggestion that Calvinists were Puritans completely incomprehensible'.[6] Most leading English churchmen had been content to be episcopalian Calvinists. Sebastian Benefield, for example, Lady Margaret professor at Oxford (and disciple of Perkins), became a famous antagonist of Arminianism; yet he regarded ecclesiological matters such as surplices and communion wafers, let alone presbyterian church government, as 'things indifferent'. Like Perkins who considered himself (and appears to have been considered) 'in the mainstream of the Church of England, which he often defended'[7] his overriding concern was for an effective preaching ministry. The Laudians extended application of the smear-word 'puritan' in an attempt to make the orthodox look like subversives and deflect attention from the radicalism of their own reforms. The campaign has probably foxed historians and literary historians more than it fooled contemporaries.

The correction of perspective is quite a shock to literary critics nurtured on the Eliotic myth that Lancelot Andrewes speaks for the Church of England in his era. There is of course no simple relationship between the teachings of the church and Elizabethan and Jacobean literature. Yet once Calvinism has been uncoupled from puritanism, so regaining in our eyes its historical centrality in the life of the nation, literary critics are faced with a new task. Interpretation guided in the past by unhistorical prejudices, by the assumed existence of a benevolent religion known usually as 'moderate Anglicanism', must be reappraised. Firmly established as the hegemonic contemporary belief-system Calvinism pervaded the language available to writers. So, as in Part I, I mean to show through close analysis how the persecutory discourse of Calvinism infiltrates texts and plays a shaping role in the creative process.

---

[6] 'Puritanism, Arminianism and Counter-Revolution', p. 120.
[7] R. T. Kendall, *Calvin and English Calvinism to 1649* (Oxford, 1979), 54.

But two new complications arise. Not only is there critical
disagreement over the theology present in the texts discussed;
they do in fact bear various relationships to the Calvinist-puritan
culture. Criss-crossing discourses enter into shifting relations
with each other—as Robert Burton's *Anatomy of Melancholy*, often
ingenuously, reveals.

Lawrence Babb says of Burton: 'His opinions on Church
government and on ceremonial worship seem to align him with
the Laudian conservatives. Yet doctrinally he stands with the
moderate Calvinist Puritans. His infrequent references to Calvin
are all deferential.'[8] In the light of the history available to him
Babb makes here a reasonable observation (except that it treats
Burton's mind as a stable object transparently accessible through
his writing). In fact, however, the position he describes is not
that of an individual with an interestingly split allegiance but the
orthodox Church of England stance of an episcopalian Calvinist.
Burton's opinions on church government did not, in 1621,
possess the political significance they would have had in the lead-
up to the Civil War. And while Babb regards Burton as
positively choosing to believe Calvinist dogma we can now see it
as a given of his milieu. Practically living in the Bodleian
Library, he was well placed to benefit from the undeviatingly
Calvinist doctoral theses lodged there between 1580 and 1620.
Tyacke gives this selection, providing an idea of the theological
climate in which Burton worked: 'No one who is elect can perish'
(1582); 'God of his own volition will repudiate some people'
(1596); 'According to the eternal predestination of God some are
ordained to life and others to death' (1597); 'Man's spiritual will
is not itself capable of achieving true good' (1602); 'The saints
cannot fall from grace' (1608); 'Is grace sufficient for salvation
granted to all men? No' (1612); 'Does man's will only play a
passive role in his initial conversion? Yes' (1618); 'Is faith and
the righteousness of faith the exclusive property of the elect? Yes'
(1619); and 'Has original sin utterly extinguished free will in
Adam and his posterity? Yes' (1622).[9] The titles themselves are

---

[8] Lawrence Babb, *Sanity in Bedlam: A Study of Robert Burton's 'Anatomy of Melancholy'*
(New Haven, 1959), 90.

[9] Quoted in translation in 'Puritanism, Arminianism and Counter-Revolution',
p. 120.

careful not to risk an interval for scholarly doubt before correct answers are supplied.

To Burton, then, Calvinist beliefs were merely orthodox Christianity. But although his theology appears to agree with that of, say, Perkins and trifling matters such as surplices and communion wafers would not have come between them they were on different sides of a cultural divide. While Perkins would have heartily endorsed Burton's nationalistic pride in 'the Gospel truly preached, church discipline established'[10] their emphases differed. Perkins cultivated a tense rapport with the populace in pulpit, print, and parish life aimed at the establishment of household religion. Retrospectively he is labelled a puritan because of the continuity of this culture. Indeed it appears that the most zealous Calvinists (because of their zeal rather than their Calvinism) did in the Jacobean period attract the term. Norwood recalled the consternation surrounding him as a child in Stony Stratford at the accession of James owing to rumours 'that he would be more severe against Puritans (as pious Christians were there called) than against Papists' (p. 13). Martin Marprelate's Papist complained that 'It was never merry world since there were so many Puritans and such running to sermons as there is now.' And George Wither remarked in 1622 that

> *many a man,*
> *Fearing to be entitled Puritan*
> *Simply neglects the means of his salvation.*[11]

There is evidence too of more narrowly relevant features which hostile contemporaries identified as puritan. Richard Corbett, who manifested Arminian sympathies in Oxford at an early date (1613) and progressed, under Buckingham's patronage, from the Deanery at Christ Church (1620) to a bishopric at Oxford (1628) and thence to Norwich (1632), lampooned puritans in his posthumously published *Poetica Stromata* (1648) in terms which

---

[10] Robert Burton, *The Anatomy of Melancholy*, ed. Holbrook Jackson (1932), i. 87. Further references, embodied in the text, will be to this edition unless otherwise indicated.

[11] Quoted by Hill in *Society and Puritanism in Pre-Revolutionary England* (1964), 14–15, 18.

note the centrality of despair and reprobation to the making of a puritan:

> I have bin in dispaire
> Five times a yeare,
> And cur'd by reading Greenham . . .
>
> I observ'd in Perkins Tables
> The black Lines of Damnation:
> Those crooked veines
> Soe stuck in my braines,
> That I fear'd my Reprobation.

The poem appears to have been written before 1621.[12] It reinforces the impression that the cultural identity of puritans derived in part from the intensity with which, under the leadership of the likes of Greenham and Perkins, they contemplated the negative side of Calvinism. If this cultural criterion of puritanism is applied to Burton a wedge inserts itself between his religion and Perkins's. Burton was more interested in the maintenance of order in society, and religious zeal repelled and amused him. His vast and eclectic reading, antiquarian interests, and sceptical and conservative temperament do not suggest a writer who would be attracted to the intellectually closed Calvinist system of theology. His distaste for its cultural and social implications coexist unhappily with his inability to reject it.

As the only writer to discuss religious despair at length from a position distinctly outside the puritan movement Burton directs a valuable sidelight on to its place in puritan culture. But the *Anatomy* also demonstrates the difficulty contemporaries found in resisting the Calvinist diagnosis of human experience. My analysis begins by considering the humanist implications of Burton's section on 'Religious Melancholy' (iii. 311–432). Two discourses, the medical-humanist and the theological, contend for explanatory supremacy in the same area of experience. Whatever Burton's fixed sympathies may have been (the whole enterprise of the *Anatomy* expresses a humanist orientation) the actual writing reveals an interplay between different vocabularies and therefore value-systems over which his only control is

---

[12] 'The Distracted Puritane', *Poems*, ed. J. A. W. Bennett and H. R. Trevor-Roper (Oxford, 1955), 58, ll. 47–9, 50–4; pp. 133, 141.

exercised through a constantly shifting tone of facetiousness, half-irony, and disavowal. Particularly when he reluctantly writes about the 'Cure of Despair' the authority of Calvinist-puritan discourse asserts itself in spite of the satirical restiveness. He is forced into the role of spiritual counsellor and has to accommodate what he says both to audience expectation and orthodox modes of expression, over which Calvinist-puritan divines seem to have held a monopoly. It is when he arrives explicitly at the touchstone of predestination that the nature of the contradictions and perplexities thrust on him by Calvinist orthodoxy emerges most fully. While undercover satirical resistance to the Calvinist ideas the text overtly and perhaps consciously supports seems to spring from humane as well as sceptical impulse, there is an underlying allegiance to the idea of a stable conservative polity which harmonizes at a temperamental political level the intellectual contradictions.

The last part of the *Anatomy*, on 'Religious Melancholy', gave the erudite anecdotalist delicious scope to quarry inexhaustible sources of bizarre belief and conduct, and the survey culminated logically with the most prominent examples of extreme religious behaviour in his own society, the victims of religious despair. Dealing with the subject of religious despair put him, however, in a strange position. He was himself a divine who had at least a theoretical pastoral duty to the people whose foibles he meant to dissect and with whose misery he set out to make merry. He appears, in fact, to have been just the sort of neglectful pluralist parson—'lead[ing] a monastic life in a college' (i. 417)—whom puritans were eager to eject from their livings [13] Weighing up the claims on his authorial efforts of 'humanity and divinity', he archly qualifies his choice: 'Not that I prefer it to divinity'— which has the precarious half-irony characteristic of the *Anatomy*, especially when followed by the observation that 'whole teams of oxen cannot draw' the existing provision of religious books. (As librarian of Christ Church, presiding over the influx of reformed literature from wills and inventories which took place at the beginning of the seventeenth century, he doubtless speaks with feeling.[14]) Yet an awareness of the pressure towards a religious viewpoint and its uneasy relationship with humanist or medical

[13] See Dent, *Protestant Reformers*, p. 162; *Anatomy*, ed. Jackson, p. vi.

[14] *Protestant Reformers*, pp. 95, 97, 99.

leanings is also registered: the *Anatomy* may be felt to be 'over-medical' or 'savour too much of humanity' (i. 35, 38). Clearly this medical-humanist penchant along with the satiricism he combined with it was going to present problems when he dealt directly with religious subject matter.

'I have no pattern to follow as in some of the rest, no man to imitate,' says Burton at the beginning of his section on 'Religious Melancholy' (iii. 311). The claim is slightly misleading. When he writes of religious despair not only does he lift whole paragraphs from earlier writers he even follows another writer's arrangement of his material.[15] Nor can he easily be granted the originality of gathering disparate subject matter under one head. Timothy Bright's *Treatise of Melancholy*, Burton's most obvious forerunner, also combines medical and religious subjects and investigates the relationship between melancholy, fanaticism, and religion. Where originality does lie is in Burton's peculiar slant on his material, a slant implicit in his novel title, 'Religious Melancholy'.[16]

Running together religion and melancholy courts the view that being religious can make you ill since the dominant meaning of melancholy belonged to medical pathology. Timothy Bright had been more sensitive to this theological embarrassment. Written by a physician who subsequently became a divine (so reversing the order of Burton's interests who was 'by my profession a divine, and by mine inclination a physician' (i. 37)), the *Treatise* devotes proportionally more of its pages to the prescription of medical cures for melancholy than does the *Anatomy*. Yet the emphasis of its argument is on the danger of overrating these and failing to see their inapplicability to spiritual disease. Succumbing to this, warns Bright, would lead one 'to judge basely the soule'. The reasons are twofold: one is the implication (in accordance with Galenic materialism) that bodily disorders can affect the state of the soul, so causing its decay; the other is the confounding of the distinction, 'betwixt natural melancholie and that heavie hande of God upon the afflicted conscience,

---

[15] Jerome W. Hogan, 'Robert Burton's Borrowings from John Abernathy's *A Christian and Heavenly Treatise*', *Neophilologus*, 60 (1976), 140–4, points out some of the correspondences.

[16] Timothy Bright, *A Treatise of Melancholy*, ed. Hardin Craig (1586; facsimile New York, 1940).

tormented with remorse of sinne, and feare of his judgement'.[17]
Burton, however, is non-committal when he comments on the
influence of the body on the soul in the first part of the *Anatomy*
(i. 374). And although he appears to distinguish between
melancholy and the afflicted conscience (citing Bright and
Perkins as authorities), he radically departs from them on the
other side of a semi-colon with the assertion that 'melancholy
alone again may be sometimes a sufficient cause of this terror of
conscience' (iii. 396). Bright and Perkins were arguing for a
qualitative distinction between the two conditions. 'Many are of
opinion', writes Perkins, 'that this sorrow for sinne is nothing els
but a melancholike passion' but 'sorrow for sinne is not cured by
any physicke . . . sorrow for sinne ariseth of the anger of God,
that woundeth and pierceth the conscience . . . And yet howsoever they are differing, it must be acknowledged that they may
both concurre together: so that the same man which is troubled
with melancholie, may feele also the anger of God for sinne.'[18]
Perkins's point is that melancholy cannot be a sufficient cause of
terror of conscience. While others, therefore, were insisting on
the segregation of religion and melancholy, Burton was content
to let them blur into one another.[19]

It begins to emerge that medical and spiritual discourses are in
ideological opposition, an opposition which was to develop in
future decades. John F. Sena writes that 'Although French
physicians such as André du Laurens [one of Burton's sources]
and Jean Riolan, writing in the late sixteenth and early
seventeenth centuries, attributed the conduct of the extreme
protestant sects to melancholic vapours, the first English works
which described enthusiasm solely as a physical and mental
abnormality caused chiefly by melancholy appeared in the mid-
seventeenth century.'[20] He is thinking of Meric Casaubon and
Henry More[21] but to some extent Burton can be seen as the
author of an earlier work which employs (as far as its author

---

[17] Ibid. fol. iii[r,v].   [18] *The Works* (Cambridge, 1605), 435.

[19] Robert Bolton (*Instructions for a Right Comforting Afflicted Consciences* (1631), 207)
gives further evidence of the emphasis placed on this point by authors known to
Burton.

[20] 'Melancholic Madness and the Puritans', *Harvard Theological Review*, 66 (1973),
297.

[21] Meric Casaubon, *A Treatise concerning Enthusiasme* (1655); More, *Enthusiasmus
Triumphatus* (1656).

dares) the same strategy for discrediting and disarming extreme puritan experience.[22]

The historian Michael MacDonald writes in *Mystical Bedlam*:

> Alarmed by the threat he perceived to ecclesiastical and civil harmony posed by the Puritans, Burton declared they suffered from a mental disease, which he named 'religious melancholy', and that they spread this malady to the populace through their fiery preaching. He argued that the deluded imaginations of the Puritan ministry prompted their resistance to the rituals and authorities of the established church.[23]

MacDonald does not clarify his use of the term 'puritans' but he seems to equate them with Burton's 'mad giddy company of precisians' (iii. 370). This slightly simplifies Burton's position since it makes him appear only to be attacking those outside the ranks of the orthodox. Certainly Burton's specific censure is directed at the safely attackable sectaries such as the Anabaptists and Familists; these are all 'quite mad' (iii. 370–1). But he was generally out of sympathy with religious fervour, which he readily ascribed to hypocrisy: 'others out of hypocrisy frequent sermons, knock their breasts, turn up their eyes, pretend zeal, desire reformation' (i. 55). The most influential puritan preachers—those who seem to have been most effective in producing religious intensity or melancholy, especially in the most aggravated form of despair—were people like Perkins, Greenham, and Bolton, whom Burton treats with ostensible respect and on whose work he draws—especially in his belated subsection on the 'Cure of Despair'.

Distaste surfaces in the way in which Burton relays the ideas of these respectable puritans. As a conservative he found himself embarrassed. In spite of its intended social conservatism Calvinism, by promoting religious activism in the country and giving primacy to individual conscience, not only provided a seed-bed for the disruptive 'precisians' but threatened to build a base of popular power. On the other hand dissent from Calvinist

---

[22] Luther complained that those few of his contemporaries who suffered acute religious anxiety attributed it on the advice of doctors 'to the complexion, or to melancholy, or the influence of the heavenly planets, or they find some natural cause' (Gordon Rupp, *The Righteousness of God: Luther Studies* (1953), 114–15).

[23] Michael MacDonald, *Mystical Bedlam: Madness, Anxiety, and Healing in Seventeenth-Century England* (Cambridge, 1981), 223–4.

theology would make him a radical. What he therefore does is to use the medical discourse to invalidate intense religiosity as far as possible without falling foul of the theology which induced it. Fanatics are ridiculed, serious-minded casualties of Calvinist rigours are more gently patronized as 'devout and precise' (iii. 400) and 'religiously given' (iii. 398), and puritan divines are specifically praised but unspecifically and timidly criticized for harshness.

Puritans were well aware of the ideological opposition of the medically minded. 'Religion ... and religious courses, and conformities', asserts Bolton, one of the divines Burton relies on in his 'Cure of Despair', 'doe not make melancholike men mad; as the great *Bedlams* of this world would beare us in hand.'[24] The rivalry of the explanatory ideologies is clearly located in practical social experience by such writers as Arthur Dent, whose *Antilegon* dismisses the guilt the pious Theologus succeeds in inducing in the religiously ignorant Asunetus as 'a melancholicke humour'.[25] Bolton, too, evidently aware of the need to join a popular debate, impersonates his opponents: '*You see now, what becomes of so much reading the scriptures* . . . Her so much reading the scriptures, and such poring upon precise bookes . . . hath made her starke mad: *The Puritane is now besides herself, etc.*'[26] Burton himself almost echoes this slur (iii. 398, 419).

Burton's rulings on sanity have an airy arbitrariness. The 'memorable example of Francis Spira' is cited: 'he felt (as he said) the pains of hell in his soul; in all other things he discoursed aright, but in this most mad' (iii. 407). Nathaniel Bacon's version reports that certain friends 'laid all the blame upon his Melancholicke constitution' but that the verdict of the Paduan doctors was that 'all their skill effected nothing'. Burton, who speaks of the 'excellent physicians', also notes their failure to prevent his self-starvation, but in order to stress the extremity of Spira's disease, not, as Bacon, the irrelevance of their efforts. When in fact Spira was charged by his nephew with 'hypocrisy and dissimulation, or frenzie' he replied: '*I would it were frenzie, either fained or true.*'[27] Burton does not explain the basis for his

---

[24] *Instructions*, p. 199.   [25] *The Plaine Mans Path-Way to Heaven* (1601), 408.
[26] *Instructions*, pp. 199–200.
[27] Bacon, *A Relation of the Fearefull Estate of Francis Spira, in the Yeare 1548* (1638), 47, 52, 151–2.

diagnosis but it does implicitly discredit the best-known case of reprobate despair, which Calvin had regarded as an exemplary judgement.[28] Burton was not, however, the only churchman to extend medical diagnosis into apparently religious states. Richard Hooker intimates (but does not pursue) the same view that despair can be 'but a melancholy passion, proceeding only from that dejection of mind, the cause whereof is the body, and by bodily means can be taken away'.[29] Hooker was of course the most plausible church author to support the assimilation of Reformed theology with minimum institutional or political change. This view is therefore in line with his conservatism: it took authority away from the individual conscience.

We also find evidence of the hostility of the medical profession to puritan experience. Burton's contemporary, Richard Napier, left copious records of his medical practice as a would-be psychiatrist and showed himself 'very unsympathetic to people whose religious dilemmas were occasioned by "Puritanical" consciences'.[30] Sena's above-quoted comparison of the dates at which extreme religious *Angst* was medically diagnosed in France and England tells us nothing of course about respective receptivity to rational thought. The idea of melancholic vapours had no more rational basis than that of divine agency. It was, in France, open season on protestant sects and the greater strength of medical discourse there indicates its function in both countries as an ideological weapon. This was to be bitterly clear to the likes of John Bunyan and George Fox, surrounded by Worldly-Wisemen who insultingly tried to nullify their most urgent experience with it.[31] While Richard Napier despised puritanical consciences he practised exorcism and distributed amulets and rings engraved with astral symbols to his patients to cure their maladies.[32] So the contest between the explanatory discourses cannot be characterized as science versus superstition. Most of the medical cures were more overtly superstitious. Surgery, trepanning the skull for example (an operation of which Burton

---

[28] See ch. 1 n. 44.

[29] Richard Hooker, *Works*, ed. J. Keble (Oxford, 1836), iii. 589.

[30] MacDonald, *Mystical Bedlam*, p. 31.

[31] Fox was advised to take up smoking to soothe his troubled mind (*A Journal or Historical Account of his Life, Travels, Sufferings, etc.* (1694), 38).

[32] MacDonald, *Mystical Bedlam*, pp. 220–2, 31.

approved[33]), could be lethal as well as futile. Contemporary pre-psychiatric practice was almost confined to physical treatment of mental disease.[34]

Religious despair, then, was a prominent cultural phenomenon in the eyes of the antiquarian don which demanded inclusion in his *omnium gatherum* of human eccentricity. But in writing analytically about despair he was entering a field of contemporary discourse where orthodox views had been established and were being daily reinforced. Burton has abstracted his discussion from the customary religious context and made the subject part of a new pattern of religious pathology but although he is by inclination a physician he remains a professional divine and does not want to collide with orthodox theology. His dominant writing attitudes, of course, are sardonic amusement at the follies of mankind and, according to his lights, a patronizing humaneness. Those attitudes posed a difficulty when it came to writing about despair—especially its cure. While he could, with licensed avuncular flippancy, solve the problem of pining lovers ('let them go together, and enjoy one another' (iii. 228)) he could only hope to cure religious despair by joining the solemn 'physicians of the soul' and framing his advice in the puritan language which victims would find meaningful. There are hints, furthermore, in the earlier subsections that Burton sees that these same physicians of the soul have contributed to the pathological condition they set about curing. In the first edition, therefore, he ducks the uncongenial task of cure and concludes cursorily by referring 'such as are any way troubled in mind' to Perkins, Greenham, Hayward, Bright, and Hemingius who 'are copious in the subject. Consult with them and such others.'[35]

The single page on the cure of despair in the first edition must have looked unbalanced and heartless to anybody who took seriously the psychiatric pretensions of the *Anatomy*, especially after the cool announcement, under 'Prognostics', that 'Most part, these kind of persons make away themselves' (iii. 408). Burton himself had said in the preface that 'there is no remedy'

[33] Berger Evans and George J. Mohr, *The Psychiatry of Robert Burton* (New York, 1944), 82.

[34] Richard Hunter and Ida MacAlpine, *Three Hundred Years of Psychiatry 1535–1860* (1963), 55.

[35] Robert Burton, *The Anatomy of Melancholy* (Oxford, 1621), 783.

(i. 97) for melancholy and had ridiculed the idea of curing 'so universal a malady' (i. 121). When the second edition appeared with a 'Cure' subsection longer than the other subsections put together, the expansion is therefore quite credibly attributed to the influence of his brother and a friend, James Whitehall.[36] That he had been jogged about his responsibilities as a divine seems to me a sufficient explanation but several critics find a more earnestly pious motive: 'Burton the preacher, the divine, wanted some opportunity to stress the importance of faith in God as the final and best solution to man's problems, and here was a way he could do that';[37] 'in this section we find Burton the divine speaking; and he speaks not of theoretical theology and meta-physics; he speaks of practical comfort for the distressed soul.'[38] J. B. Bamborough thinks Burton himself may have 'experienced the tortures of religious despair' and affirms that he 'did address himself seriously to the task of rectifying the fault'.[39]

But why, it must be asked, was Burton so careless—if religious uplift was this important to him—as to omit such significant material from the original work? What we find on inspection of this 'Cure' subsection is that Burton is quite unable to stick to his task as counsellor; after six pages his tone begins to wobble. He is, after all, drawing on the work of a cheerless company of authors. Perkins's solitary suggestion for his readers' recreation was to look at a rainbow (as often as they could find one) and think about God's promise not to drown the world again. It was laughter, not despair, that signalled madness to him.[40] A fellow spirit, Michael Wigglesworth, affirmed pithily: 'when creatures smile god is undervalew'd.'[41] Bamborough supports his argument for Burton's new-found sobriety with the suggestion that Burton chose to resite the 'Author's Conclusion' in the 'Satyricall Preface' so as to end gravely.[42] While this seems plausible the revision can, I think, be better explained by the guidance these

---

[36] *The Anatomy of Melancholy*, 2nd edn. rev. (Oxford, 1624), 544.
[37] Robert G. Hallwachs, 'Additions and Revisions in the Second Edition of Burton's *Anatomy of Melancholy*', unpublished Ph.D. thesis, University of Princeton, 1942, p. 36.
[38] Dennis Donovan, 'Robert Burton's *The Anatomy of Melancholy*', unpublished Ph.D. thesis, University of Princeton, 1965, p. xxxiv.
[39] J. B. Bamborough, 'Burton and Hemingius', *RES* 34 (1983), 441–5, p. 445.
[40] Perkins, *Works*, p. 647.
[41] *The Diary of Michael Wigglesworth 1653–1657*, ed. E. S. Morgan (New York, 1965), 7.   [42] 'Burton and Hemingius', p. 442.

belated thoughts offer the reader at the outset on how to assess the work's overall tone—even in the 'Cure of Despair'; it may well be that only after writing did Burton fully realize that the whole *Anatomy* was a 'confused lumpe' like a bear whelp which had not been licked into shape, that it was 'writ with as small deliberation, as I doe ordinarily speake', that it was 'Comicall, Satyricall, as the present subject required, or as at the time I was affected' (1st edition, p. 787), and, perhaps most important, that 'our style bewrayes us' (1st edition, p. 785). All this elaborates the simultaneously self-masking and self-disclosing play with his satirical persona in 'Democritus to the Reader', and belongs with it to stress his un-solemnity throughout. Hardin Craig criticizes Burton for hiding behind his authorities[43]—which is true—but his techniques of doing this are also his means of self-revelation. Authorities are stalking horses he keeps swapping and sniping from behind; they free him from the constraints of logical consistency. These undercutting satirical habits are not suddenly shed in the expanded 'Cure'.

'I will', says Burton, 'for the benefit and ease of such as are afflicted, at the request of some friends, recollect out of their voluminous treatises some few comfortable speeches' (iii. 409). How then does Burton measure up as a spiritual counsellor and to what extent is his style self-betraying? The writers on whom he draws in the 'Cure' subsection (Robert Bolton is added in the little-changed fourth edition (1632, p. 705)) are doctrinally unanimous, and, for all, the sole purpose is didactic. We come with Burton from a quite new angle—the angle of the outsider— at 'a whole literature', which, as Haller says, 'appeared on the bookstalls for the purpose of teaching the people how to dissect and physic their souls'.[44] Timothy Bright differs from the others by writing a medical treatise; yet he addresses an imaginary patient, M., as a representative of readers who suffer from melancholy mixed with actual religious guilt. The doctor–patient relationship was regularly favoured as an analogy. Abernethy, for example, sustains the analogy of physical and spiritual discourse throughout his *Physicke for the Soule*. They all have therapeutic pretensions (*Instructions for a Right Comforting Afflicted*

---

[43] Hardin Craig, *The Enchanted Glass* (Oxford, 1950), 244.

[44] *The Rise of Puritanism* (New York, 1938), 92. Haller's first chapter is entitled 'Physicians of the Soul'.

Consciences; *The Sanctuarie of a Troubled Soule*, etc.[45])—though, as we have seen, many readers seem to have come away with the conviction of having diagnosed in themselves something far worse than an inoperable cancer. Like Bright, others, such as Perkins, liked to construct a dialogue to defeat the impersonality of print and move closer to private conference with mesmerized readers. An interview might be staged between a minister and a representative of the troubled in conscience; or, an experienced Christian would lecture a worried and attentive novice, as in *A Dialogue of the State of a Christian Man*.[46] Such methods obviously encouraged interplay between what was read and what was acted out in the family or the community, so disseminating puritan culture and increasing the pressure on individuals to seek out their own place in the theological scheme.

When Burton writes on despair, he absorbs not only a good deal of the terminology of these authors but their sense of an audience too. Yet he appears unable to control the flux of his own sympathies and maintain the pastoral didacticism of his sources. His admission that he 'writ with as small deliberation as I doe ordinarily speake' (i. 31) guides us in how to read the despair section: its inconsistencies make sense if we think of different levels of conversation regulated by the changing identity of his imagined interlocutor and sudden accesses of uncensored thoughts. Disturbances of the bond Burton appears to cultivate with his spiritual patients in the 'Cure' subsection point up his lack of sympathy with the theology he ostensibly shares with the spiritual physicians and their victims.

At times Burton is clearly addressing the stereotyped religious despairer who is consistently the object of his source-writers' concern. 'Yea, but, thou repliest, I am a notorious sinner' (iii. 411). He keeps this up fairly consistently for the opening pages of the 'Cure', quoting reassuring authorities and biblical texts and retaining contact with the imagined sufferer through second person address. This slips slightly when he starts sprinkling around the familiar Calvinist phrases with which they torment themselves and the sense of distance is reflected in a switch to the third person. He has offered the guarantees that

---

[45] Bolton, *Instructions*; Sir John Hayward, *The Sanctuarie of a Troubled Soule* (1616).
[46] *Works*, p. 455.

follow on repentance but then seems to remember that anxiety centres for the serious Calvinist on the withholding of repentance: ' 'Tis true indeed, and all-sufficient this, they do confess, if they could repent; but they are obdurate, they have cauterized consciences, they are in a reprobate sense' (iii. 414), and so on. But he quickly recovers a sense of his project, using the patronizing singular 'thou' to draw himself up to the status of counselling divine, increasing the density of puritan phrases, this time to impersonate and answer the victim:

All this is true, thou repliest, but yet it concerns not thee, 'tis verified in ordinary offenders, in common sins, but thine are of an higher strain, even against the Holy Ghost Himself. . . . Thou art worse than a pagan, infidel, Jew, or Turk, for thou art an apostate and more, thou hast voluntarily blasphemed . . . thou art worse than Judas himself, or they that crucified Christ.

The puritan linguistic community is unmistakable here; an addressee of puritan habits is in Burton's mind's eye: 'thou didst never pray, come to church, hear, read, or do any divine duties with any devotion, but for formality and fashion sake.' Quite suddenly, however, this timid, over-scrupulous personality is broken up. Burton can no longer sustain the role of counselling divine which his task of gaining the afflicted reader's confidence and involvement required, and from the kind of person who questioned the sincerity and devotion with which religious duties had been performed, his interlocutor, it suddenly appears, 'never mad[e] any conscience' of murder, adultery, oppression, drunkenness, and so forth (iii. 416). Perhaps the idea of the transformation irresistibly amused Burton; his pusillanimous patient was becoming tiresome.

That the level of conversation is now changing is again signalled by the altered personal pronoun: 'blasphemous thoughts have been ever harboured in his mind, even against God Himself, the blessed Trinity; the Scripture false, rude, harsh, immethodical; heaven, hell, resurrection, mere toys and fables, incredible, impossible, absurd, vain, ill contrived' (iii. 416). This is the tone of scandalized gossip spoken behind the hand to the sane and like-minded reader—the reader, perhaps, whom he was addressing when he said of the excessively religious: 'they will take much more pains to go to hell than we shall do to heaven'

(iii. 350). But the reported speech is already merging with Burton's own voice. Burton's protective persona, combined with his tendency to run the ideas of his authorities or those ascribed to others into his own, enables him, habitually, to loose off at anything—including religion itself—as the mood 'affected' him. What he now relates as blasphemy is indistinguishable from his earlier attacks on exploitation of religion and superstition:[47] 'religion', he goes on, is 'policy and human invention, to keep men in obedience, or for profit, invented by priests and lawgivers to that purpose' (iii. 416).

Changes in personal pronouns continue to index the shifts in his sympathies. After the sentence just quoted, he slips into the first person plural: 'If there be any such supreme power, He takes no notice of our doings . . . or else He is partial, an excepter of persons, author of sin, a cruel, a destructive God, to create our souls and destinate them to eternal damnation.' The writing, since he sloughed his counselling role, has become more fluent and forceful. Vituperation and anecdotal glee on the subject of superstition and heresy gave unrestrained release to his anarchic impulses in the earlier parts of 'Religious Melancholy'. Here we see a nearly automatic return to that authorial personality. The effect of his writing is to draw the reader into the blasphemous suggestions, especially in the emotive appeal of the ensuing rhetorical questions: 'why doth He not govern things better, protect good men, root out wicked livers? . . . why makes He venomous creatures, rocks, sands, deserts, this earth itself the muck-hill of the world, a prison, an house of correction?' (iii. 416–17).

When this anarchic energy has spent itself, Burton abruptly disclaims responsibility by re-invoking his blasphemer: 'They cannot some of them but think evil' is his shocked comment. He describes the expressions sampled above as 'not fit to be uttered' although he himself not only uttered them but expanded them for his 1628 edition.[48] He does concede, however (it is tantamount to a confession), 'that no man living is free from such thoughts in part'. The devil, being a spirit, can 'mingle himself with our spirits' and 'suggest such devilish thoughts into our hearts'

[47] See, for example, iii. 329, 331, 335, 340. He does not here except religious views of his own from attack.

[48] *The Anatomy of Melancholy*, 3rd edn. rev. (Oxford, 1628), 636–7.

(iii. 417). As he says in the Preface: 'I have overshot myself' (i. 122). He resumes the hortatory role but his credibility for the patient has already been forfeited.

Perkins also considers objections to Calvinism, but they are firmly controlled within a didactic framework. 'God might be thought cruell, if that he had ordained the greatest part of the world to destruction' is the dispassionately stated 'Object X' followed by a longish paragraph of 'Ans.', beginning with firm confidence: 'God could well enough have decreed, that even all men should utterly have been rejected, and yet he should have beene never a whit either cruell or unjust.'[49] Burton's own doctrinal instability is exposed in his failure to reproduce this kind of pattern; the blasphemer is given too eloquent a voice, and no argument is offered in rebuttal. It may have been with some self-knowledge that Burton originally avoided proposing a cure for despair. In his Preface he confesses to a lack of tonal control: ' 'tis a most difficult thing to keep an even tone, a perpetual tenor, and not sometimes to lash out' (i. 123).

Despite Burton's recommendation of the treatises of Perkins and the rest and his attempt merely to 'recollect' their phraseology and emulate their style, we can detect his ambivalent attitude towards them. This emerges even in passages of almost direct quotation. Half of the subsection 'Prognostics of Despair' is taken from Abernethy, yet it is instructive to look at Burton's modifications—to the following comment by Abernethy on suicide of the insane for example: 'if they have given testimony beefore of their regeneration, in regard they doe this not so much of the minde, as of the body; we must make the best construction of it.'[50] Burton alters this to: 'if he have given testimony before of his regeneration, in regard he doth this not so much out of his will as *ex vi morbi*, we must make the best construction of it, as Turks do, that think all fools and madmen go directly to heaven' (iii. 408). Burton's addition to this last sentence of a plundered paragraph is inescapably facetious. In Abernethy's theological

[49] *Works*, p. 122.

[50] *A Christian and Heavenly Treatise containing Physicke for the Soule* (1615), 404. J. W. Hogan (see n. 15 above) concludes this debt too early, at the word 'regeneration', obscuring the pointedness of Burton's inserts. See also John Stachniewski, 'Robert Burton's Use of John Abernethy's *A Christian and Heavenly Treatise*', *Neophilologus*, 62 (1978), 634–6.

outlook (Burton's, too, one might have thought from earlier remarks on Turks[51]), that a religious opinion was held by Turks would argue against its veracity. And while Abernethy's concluding phrase is sagely reticent on a questionable issue, Burton's 'go directly to heaven' is the opposite, immediately casting doubt on its reliability.

In another borrowing Abernethy writes reassuringly, 'None can gather the perswasion of their reprobation from themselves, for all men are liers, we cannot have this perswasion from the divell for hee is a lier from the beginning. *Gods spirit* maketh no perswasion in this point.'[52] Burton's version runs: 'this persuasion cannot come from the devil, and much less can it be grounded from thyself: men are liars, and why shouldest thou distrust?' (iii. 420). Again Burton's mistransmission is instructive. Abernethy's remark that all men are liars might itself seem unconsoling since lies are generally motivated by self-interest. But it is underpinned by the ensuing doctrine that it is not the devil either but only the Holy Spirit who can validate a spiritual conviction, and that the Holy Spirit does not imprint on the mind the assurance of reprobation. By omitting this doctrinal logic Burton clumsily puts his finger on the sore spot: just because belief in election was to their own advantage, disbelief often seemed to people less likely to be self-delusion. In addition, Burton's rhetorical machinery oddly brings out the devil as less deceitful than the self. William Perkins has phrasing almost identical to Abernethy's;[53] the linguistic community of puritans was tightly knit and, as we see in *The Pilgrim's Progress* where interlopers like Talkative are minutely interrogated, sensitivity to verbal deviation was extreme.

Elsewhere, Burton shows himself directly influenced by what he has read in Abernethy. Writing of life's miseries he comments: ' 'Tis no new thing this, God's best servants and dearest children have been so visited and tried. Christ in the garden cried out, "My God, my God, why hast Thou forsaken me?" ' (iii. 426). The astonishing inaccuracy of this biblical reference is prompted, it seems, by a vague recollection of Abernethy's assurance that

---

[51] Burton comments on the Turks' cynical use of religion in persuading men that if they die in battle they will 'go directly to heaven' (iii. 330). He also pours scorn on the Koran (iii. 332).

[52] *Treatise*, p. 141.   [53] *Works*, p. 459.

'The most deere to God have beene thus handled as Christ in the garden, and on the *Crosse*.'[54] For such confusion of Gethsemane and Calvary (which stands from the second edition onwards) Burton would be held in contempt by any self-respecting religious despairer, poring tirelessly over his or her Bible.

One detects, in these deviations from Abernethy, tendencies to be jocose or casual, or simply unversed in theology. Direct borrowings confirm, then, that Burton differs, at least temperamentally, from his predecessors. But in addition to his inability to maintain the counselling style and framework, and doubtless in part causing it, are theoretical differences of viewpoint. These, like his inclinations towards blasphemy, are to a degree clouded by an evasive style. Only once, for example, does his uneasiness with puritan methods bring him close to singling out a particular book, but then, in what looks like a failure of nerve, he names Robert Parsons's *Christian Directorie*:[55] 'I have heard some complain of Parsons' Resolution, and other books of like nature (good otherwise), they are too tragical' (iii. 400). This is a work by a Catholic which insists on the universality of God's offer of grace. Three pages later Burton says himself: 'I see no reason at all why a papist at any time should despair' (iii. 403). 'Our indiscreet pastors' are said, however, to 'come not far behind' the Papists in the spreading of terror by speaking 'so much of election, predestination, reprobation *ab aeterno* . . . by what signs and tokens they shall discern and try themselves, whether they be God's true children elect' (iii. 399–400). Again, he does not question the theology, it is the energy with which it is disseminated at which he apparently jibs. A hint of Burton's ulterior view of greater protestant culpability is given, significantly, in the last sentence of the 'Causes of Despair' subsection after adducing, with apparent scorn, the priestcraft employed to ease the minds of Catholics: 'The causes above named must more frequently therefore take hold in others' (iii. 404).

Burton observes that it is those who adopt a puritan style of life—who are 'devout and precise', 'have tender consciences', and 'follow sermons, frequent lectures'—that are 'most apt to mistake, and fall into these miseries' (iii. 400). But this was no

---

[54] *Treatise*, p. 141.
[55] Burton is referring to the first volume of *A Christian Directorie Guiding Men to their Salvation* (1585).

challenge to his puritan authors who considered such miseries *de rigueur*, especially since he is simultaneously endorsing their authority. In the preceding section he readily echoed puritan talk of 'cauterized consciences' and of people who are 'in a reprobate sense' and 'go to hell . . . in a dream' (iii. 389). The self-aggravating despair of those who, he says, 'misconceiv[e] all they read, or hear, to their own overthrow' is actually quite logical given doctrinal premises which Burton himself seems unable to dislodge. Nevertheless, by stressing the extremism of their symptoms, he convinces himself that their problem is privately psychological rather than theological in origin: 'the more they search and read Scriptures, or divine treatises,' he goes on, 'the more they puzzle themselves, as a bird in a net, the more they are entangled and precipitated into this preposterous gulf' (iii. 419). He preferred to think of religious despair as a 'malady' (iii. 399) afflicting the 'religiously given' (iii. 398), and is prepared to blur the literal medical and metaphorical religious uses of the word.

Burton further deflects attention from the divines by placing emphasis on the folly of the victims rather than the cruelty of the system. They 'misconceive' what they read; the gulf they fall into is 'preposterous'; they 'puzzle themselves' with divine treatises. Criticism of purveyors of the offending notions is timidly implicit. No exact reference is made to William Perkins when Burton writes: 'God's eternal decree of predestination, absolute reproba-tion, and such fatal tables, they form to their own ruin, and impinge upon this rock of despair' (iii. 419). Clearly he has in mind the 'Table' prefixed to 'A Golden Chaine'. Burton's use of 'fatal' in this context draws attention both to the fatalism of the 'Table' and to the dire consequences which flow from this. In the letter which provides the strongest documentary evidence of his Arminian sympathies Laud complained in 1625 of the 'fatal opinions' contained in the Lambeth Articles.[56] Casualties, says Burton, 'doubt presently whether they be of this number of the elect or no'. Yet Perkins appears in the *Anatomy* only in the role of healer—as one of those to whom Burton refers those 'troubled in mind'. Clear condemnation of puritan methods of regulating people's lives could hardly be undertaken without alternative theological convictions. Burton appears to have lacked these. In

---

[56] See Tyacke, *Anti-Calvinists*, p. 70.

'Causes of Despair' he lists the most telling textual evidence that the Bible offers in support of Calvinism, ascribing the despairer's condition to 'misrepresentation' (iii. 398) and asserting that election, predestination, and reprobation are 'preposterously conceived' by him (iii. 399). He does not favour the reader with the correct interpretation, nor does he explain in what way the despairer should understand these doctrines.

The densest locus of Burton's self-betrayal in the 'Cure of Despair' subsection is his peroration on predestinarian dogma (iii. 419–24). This begins with his bemusement at the spiritual lemmings he is supposed to be physicking and sidelong glance at the 'fatal tables' which might encourage them and ends—in the 1638 edition[57]—with citation of the royal declaration of 1628 (Burton says 1633) prohibiting debate, especially by university divines, on the question of predestination. Soon after this he returns to the preferred terrain of medical science where he joins such progressive minds as Richard Napier in the prescription of amulets to ward off demons (iii. 429) (for the use of which Napier battled against local puritans in the treatment of at least one patient[58]). There are conflicting critical interpretations of the purposes behind this passage.

David Renaker finds in it 'an exceedingly complex statement' in favour of Arminianism followed by 'an equally complex counter-statement' supporting Calvinism, both deployed from politically self-protective motives. He adduces support for this view from Burton's elaboration for the 1628 edition of his Calvinist 'palinode' specifying adherence to the strongest (supra-lapsarian) formulation of the doctrine of predestination. His reasoning, however, is obscure, his history partly inaccurate, and his reading of Burton's text selective. 'Here we see', he concludes, referring to the 1628 revisions, 'that as it becomes more dangerous to take any stand on predestination, Burton's palinode becomes both more elaborate and more extreme. Surely this indicates strongly that it is meant as a form of protection.' Since Renaker argues that Burton must have felt himself under political threat both from Calvinists and Arminians it would seem strange for him to set about protecting himself by adopting

---

[57] *The Anatomy of Melancholy*, 5th edn. rev. (Oxford, 1638).

[58] MacDonald, *Mystical Bedlam*, pp. 30–1.

a more extreme position on either side of the debate. The argument is bemusing.

Historical exactitude depends on recognition of the suddenness with which the Arminian party, supported by the new king, captured control of the church's command structure in the late 1620s. Burton prefaces his strongly Calvinist statement: 'we teach otherwise' (iii. 423). 'This palinode', says Renaker, 'is a false statement, and Burton cannot have been unaware of its falsehood . . . he knew that the Anglican position on predestination was limited to the non-committal Article XVII.'[59] Burton is, however, quite correct in asserting, up to 1628, that 'most' Church of England clerics were supralapsarian Calvinists. This was the position of Beza to which, as Kendall shows, English Calvinists generally adhered.[60] And Dent, who accepts Tyacke's national findings on Calvinist dominance, examines the way in which 'Beza's stricter doctrine of election became one of the fundamental pillars of the Oxford reformed synthesis.'[61] In any case, Burton also adds, without prejudice, the sublapsarian alternative ('or from *Adam*'s fall as others will'), so he is in no contemporary sense being extreme. Renaker does not, moreover, notice that Burton subsequently changed 'most' to 'many' in the phrase 'as most of our Church holde' (an emendation which contradicts the claimed strategy of becoming more extreme to protect himself). Article XVII (framed in 1552) is open to a strong Calvinist interpretation. As Lawrence Babb says: 'The term *reprobation* is avoided, but the idea is clearly implied.'[62] As noted above, an official Calvinist commentary on the Thirty-nine Articles had been published in 1608. The revisions Renaker mentions occurred before King Charles's declaration in 1628 prohibiting university divines from preaching or printing 'any thing either way' on the subject of predestination.[63] It was this and the retaliatory parliamentary threat to Arminians in 1629[64]

---

[59] David Renaker, 'Robert Burton's Palinodes', *SP* 76 (1979), 162–81, pp. 164, 179–80, 178. From the experiential perspective, the three Calvinist positions Renaker distinguishes (supralapsarian, modified supralapsarian, and sublapsarian) made no difference. Since they were all crushingly predestinarian it would be distracting to discuss them.   [60] Kendall, *Calvin and English Calvinism*, pp. 55 ff.

[61] *Protestant Reformers*, pp. 231, 100.   [62] *Sanity in Bedlam*, p. 88.

[63] *Articles Agreed upon by the Archbishops and Bishops of Both Provinces, and the Whole Clergie* (1628), 4.

[64] See S. R. Gardiner, *Constitutional Documents of the Puritan Revolution* (1889), 80.

that might have supplied Burton with reasons for self-protection
had he felt at risk. A slight tilt towards the Arminian party can,
in fact, be detected from 1628. As well as changing 'most' to
'many' Burton added the word 'some' to a parenthetic description
of Arminians: '(though in another extreme some)' (iii. 421). But
this can be ascribed rather to Burton's ideological chameleonism
than to political intimidation.

Such emendation is certainly the last thing a committed
Calvinist at that time would have done. Lawrence Babb's
account of Burton's reference (in his 1638 edition) to the 1628
declaration therefore requires comment too. Burton accompanies
the citation, and terminates discussion, with a quotation from
Erasmus which ends: '*Et siquid est tyrannidis, quod tamen non cogat ad
impietatem, satius est ferre, quam seditiose reluctari*' ('It is better to
endure tyranny, so long as it does not drive us to impiety, than
seditiously to resist') (iii. 424). Babb takes this 'depreciatory
reference' to the king's declaration to be an implied protest at its
use by Oxford's Vice-Chancellor, William Smith (abetted by his
Chancellor, William Laud), to expel three ministers from the
university in 1631: 'Being a predestinarian, Burton would
naturally sympathise with the insubordinate divines.'[65] But this
is a difficult view to hold—on Babb's own evidence. Burton
registers no protest in his fourth edition in 1632.[66] It was a long
time to wait (till 1638) to score an oblique point—an over-subtle
one, surely, if one recalls that Burton dates the proclamation in
1633, two years after its relevant use.

As for the quotation from Erasmus: much more in keeping
with Burton's twinkling wiliness is the pretence of being
oppressed by a decree which actually suits him quite well. He
had himself complained about over-insistence on predestinarian
rigours; and he readily altered his comment on Arminians to trim
to the new wind. The emphasis in the Erasmus quotation is on
the propriety of submitting to any law which does not force one
into impiety. Clearly Burton did not consider that deprivation of

---

[65] *Sanity in Bedlam*, pp. 89–90.

[66] Babb argues (p. 89 and n.) that the troubles came too late for Burton to alter his
fourth revised edition (1632) and that printing of the fifth commenced before August
1634. This is still a considerable lag, and we do not know how long the fourth edition
was with the printer, or that Burton could not anyway have inserted a new sentence
or two in the closing pages if they had topical importance for him.

his freedom to controvert predestination and related issues infringed his or others' piety. A dedicated Calvinist could not take this view, any more than he could indicate the slightest sympathy for Arminianism. Babb surmises that Burton 'has revised, perhaps severely pruned, his discussion of predestination to conform with the royal injunction. He has not, however, been frightened into retraction . . . the 1638 discourse is substantially the same as the 1632 version.' Babb's confidence that Burton has a settled position ('Whatever his reasoning, Burton is a pre-destinarian')[67] gets him into more difficulty here. Since the injunction was issued in 1628 Burton might as easily have been frightened by it in revising for 1632. But more peculiar than this is the positing of a 'revised', 'pruned' discussion when the 1638 version is 'substantially the same as the 1632' and when Burton had the same knowledge of risk when he wrote the conjectural piece as when he pruned it. Needless to say, he had not availed himself of his freedom to expatiate on the subject in 1621, 1624, or 1628.[68]

Burton is, all the evidence suggests, one of those Church of England clerics who were quiescently conformist Calvinists. He conveys discomfort with the subject of predestination and welcomes the wry excuse to close off his inconclusive remarks (which had been just as inconclusive before). It is just conceivable that Burton did wish also to notify the authorities of his obedience in case he really had stumbled into a political minefield, but nobody at the time would have mistaken the quaintly voluble eccentric for a polemicist of either colour—and the hint of tyrannical legislation seems to indicate that he knew this.

It seems in the end less profitable to ask what some hypostatized 'Burton' believed (since he contradicted himself so frequently) than why the text twists this way and that at particular moments. Babb bases his view that Burton is a committed Calvinist predestinarian on a couple of clear textual endorsements but ignores their ideological context and their rote

---

[67] Babb, *Sanity in Bedlam*, pp. 90, 88.

[68] Although James had issued a similar prohibition on preaching about pre-destination and so forth in 1622, 'learned men' (amongst whom Burton obviously numbered) were exempted from the restriction (see Tyacke, *Anti-Calvinists*, pp. 102–3, and Gardiner, *Constitutional Documents*, pp. 75–6).

delivery, and subordinates their inconsistency with other parts of the text. The consequence is that he soaks up Burton's self-contradictions. 'To God's elect, the truly repentant,' he says, 'he offers the comforts of his predestinarian Christianity, and to tormented mankind in general he extends his understanding sympathy.'[69] The second attitude is incompatible with the first. Such contradictions should not be skimmed over since they are at the heart of what Burton ingenuously discloses about his society and the nature of available responses to the dominant protestant ideology. Renaker's approach is, like Babb's, intentionalist; the complex statement and counter-statement are ascribed to some subtle purpose (which Renaker fails to clarify) but the idea of the palinode which he adduces to account for contradictions is insufficiently flexible to explain the shifts and slips (sometimes just one word) which occur continually, if not continuously, in the *Anatomy*. The flux of Burton's thought and feeling can only be monitored by close analysis.

Stanley Fish, who does supply close analysis, concludes of Burton's 'Religious Melancholy' in general that 'the "properly" religious man becomes a will-o'-the-wisp; like the "sane" and "wise" man who never appears in the preface . . . he is a chimerical member of an empty category.'[70] But while this is a validly gained impression it again ascribes to Burton too stable an intention. We have every reason to suppose Burton's conscious purpose in the 'Cure of Despair' subsection, for example, to have been the 'recollection' and transmission of counsel from the properly religious authors on whom he drew, so that the properly religious man is, for the first few pages, speaking. But Burton's mind is traversed by other ways of thinking, other discourses (or, as he would say, 'dialects' (iii. 384)) and these interfere with and fragment his assumed persona.

This process, and the resulting symptoms of perplexity the writing displays, may be observed in the development of the discussion of predestination, beginning with the acknowledge-

---

[69] *Sanity in Bedlam*, p. 109. Babb is not alone in viewing Burton simply as a Calvinist; see, for example, Nicholas Tyacke, 'Science and Religion at Oxford before the Civil War', in D. Pennington and K. Thomas, edd., *Puritans and Revolutionaries: Essays in Seventeenth-Century History Presented to Christopher Hill* (Oxford, 1978), 81.

[70] *Self-Consuming Artifacts: The Experience of Seventeenth-Century Literature* (1972), 348.

ment that predestinarian theology plays an instrumental role in religious despair. Burton's first advice to the despairer is to reject the idea of being reprobate as a demonic suggestion, but he accompanies this advice with an anecdote which, we will see, advocates religious ignorance in flat opposition to the views he is supposed to be echoing and the convictions of his spiritual patient (iii. 419–20). He then turns to stressing the largesse of God's mercy and falls into what Renaker calls the 'pure Arminianism'[71] of the view that 'His grace is proposed to . . . each man in particular, and to all.' This statement certainly is Arminian; but Burton goes on:

'Tis an universal promise, 'God sent not His Son into the world to condemn the world, but that through him the world might be saved' (John 3. 17). He that acknowledgeth himself a man in the world, must likewise acknowledge he is of that number that is to be saved. (iii. 420)

The slide away from Calvinism has gone a good deal further than Arminianism here. Burton evidently realizes that what he is saying clashes with his official view and makes a stab at sorting out the muddle:

Now there cannot be contradictory wills in God; He will have all saved, and not all, how can this stand together? be secure then, believe, trust in Him, hope well, and be saved. Yea, that's the main matter, how shall I believe, or discern my security from carnal presumption? (iii. 420–1)

There is not a glimmer of logic here. He has wanted to comfort the despairer by insisting on the availability of grace but this brings him into collision with his own supposed theology. He ought to follow his professor, Sebastian Benefield, in trumping the apparent offer of salvation to all with 'God will have mercy on whom he will have mercy' (Rom. 9: 18), but he cannot resolve the contradiction without injuring his patient, so resorts instead to encouraging noises. By using the word 'secure', however, he touches off a new discursive reflex: 'security' in puritan parlance was distinguished from (proper) assurance of salvation as meaning self-generated over-confidence.[72] Burton at first uses the word positively, in the general sense familiar to him, but, seeing

---

[71] 'Robert Burton's Palinodes', p. 177.
[72] See, for example, Perkins, *Works*, 439; Thomas Adams, *The Works 1612–1629* (Edinburgh, 1862), i. 499.

the ambiguity, he catches hold of it and pretends (though it is unconnected with the question he has just raised) that it is his main logical thread. He is still, however, from a puritan point of view mishandling the language since 'security' was synonymous with 'carnal presumption' (another parroted phrase), not its antonym, and both were opposed to the term Burton should have been using and ventriloquized on the previous page ('How shall they be assured of their salvation? by what signs?')—'assurance'.

The next paragraph again skirts round imputing blame to predestinarian preaching and interestingly introduces Arminianism as having arisen in order 'to mitigate those divine aphorisms' (iii. 421). The phrase is self-consciously euphemistic but at the same time Arminians are described as 'in another extreme'. If logic was to be expected we would have to deduce from this that Burton has discovered some middle ground between a denial and an acceptance of human freedom to repent and obtain salvation. Instead of explaining himself he proceeds to cite still 'less orthodoxal' writers, including Origen who thought even the devils would be saved in the end. Like blasphemy in the earlier passage, heresy finds an exhilarated response in Burton, checked only by one unconvincingly parenthetic 'he erroneously concludes', a sprinkling of disavowing speech marks, and an occasional satiric inflection. The force of the protest remains, climaxing in a rhetorical question: 'For how can he be merciful that shall condemn any creature to eternal unspeakable punishment, for one small temporary fault, all posterity, so many myriads for one and another man's offence, *quid meruistis oves?*' (iii. 423). The question is unattributed, but it is ruthlessly suppressed in the sentence that follows: 'But these absurd paradoxes are exploded by our Church, we teach otherwise.' Then follows the breathlessly protracted sentence, studded with Latin phrases, to which David Renaker attaches importance:

That this vocation, predestination, election, reprobation, *non ex corrupta massa, praevisa fide*, as our Arminians, or *ex praevisis operibus*, as our papists, *non ex praeteritione*, but God's absolute decree *ante mundum creatum* (as many of our Church hold), was from the beginning, before the foundation of the world was laid, or *homo conditus* (or from Adam's fall, as others will, *homo lapsus objectum est reprobationis*) with *perseverantia sanctorum*, we must be certain of our salvation, we may fall, but not finally, which our Arminians will not admit.

It seems almost an angry parody of the casuistry of his theological colleagues, a rehearsal of a rote-learned orthodoxy which seems inadequate to the radically humanist question just put. No elaboration of these theological terms is offered and no counter-argument to the foregoing heresy. Perhaps the pedantry is just meant to defuse it. Certainly if there is a momentary recognition of the contradiction between his 'predestinarian Christianity' and his 'understanding sympathy' for 'tormented mankind' it rapidly disappears in the verbal swill. The discussion of predestination soon peters out with a desultoriness justified in retrospect by the pantomime of being gagged.

Burton's ideological osmosis makes the *Anatomy* a fascinating document of the thinkable in his time. Discourses normally confined to particular fraternities jostle one another in a work that declines obedience to the law of non-contradiction. But while analysis of the flux of Burton's writing indicates that he does not possess consistent intellectual convictions this is not to say that he transparently mediates the ideas he transmits. As he confesses, his style betrays him. For instance, when his protest against a rigidly predestinarian God extends into protest against eternal punishment itself Burton's humaneness is checked with typical satiricism: 'The world shall end like a comedy, and we shall meet at last in heaven, and live in bliss altogether' (iii. 423). Like most satirists he appeals to an assumed common sense. Here the ironic tone indicates that the notion of everyone being saved could only have been greeted publicly as a joke. And the less radical criticism is invalidated with the more. Common sense or intuition will, of course, tell people contradictory things so consistent appeal to what Burton takes to be normative values does not make him intellectually consistent.

But this appeal to the communal intuition of his envisaged readers is only one dynamic of his style. The other, complementary to it, centrifugal perhaps rather than centripetal, is privately anarchic. If all there is to verify a conviction is, not logic or evidence, but communal intuition and if, as Burton knew from his wide reading, communal intuition differed between communities, all truth is irrecoverably relativized. So when Burton is not comfortably serving up an idea to the ridicule of the like-minded he is suggesting, by other stylistic hints, that one idea is as likely to be true as another. Indeed the two effects can be simultaneous (the questioning of eternal punishment partly survives its send-up). The ends of subsections quite frequently intimate his Pyrrhonism. For instance, this is how he finishes up his discussion of atheism (as usual adducing another author):

He sets down at large the causes of this brutish passion (seventeen in number I take it), answers all their arguments and sophisms, which he reduceth to twenty-six heads, proving withal his own assertion: 'There is a God, such a God, the true and sole God,' by thirty-five reasons. His colophon is how to resist and repress atheism, and to that purpose he adds four especial means or ways, which whoso will may profitably peruse. (iii. 392)

This may be taken to imply (publicly) that the refutation of atheism is too self-evident to his readers to need expounding or (privately) that Burton is not much interested in resisting and repressing it. This conclusion has something in common with the bored wave of the hand with which he cut short the original 'Cure of Despair' ('Consult with them and such others' (1st edition, p. 783)) and with the allusive pedantry of his rehearsal of the Calvinist position. It seems to be suggested here that all you can do with arguments is count them.

Like Swift, who thought scepticism about religion should be concealed where it could not be overcome,[73] he believed in conformity to the national church more as an institution and an instrument of social control than as the custodian of faith. That his Calvinism is merely coated on to a deeper commitment to the retention of a stable hierarchical polity—that 'the Gospel truly preached' was secondary to 'church discipline established' (i. 87) has been betrayed in many ways but it is sharply focused by his, perhaps accidental, use of notorious Catholic advocacy of blind trust in the church.

Burton's suggested response to the fear of reprobation is to do as the proverbial collier did:

For when the devil tempted him with the weakness of his faith, and told him he could not be saved, as being ignorant in the principles of religion, and urged him moreover to know what he believed, what he thought of such and such points and mysteries: the collier told him he believed as the Church did; 'But what' (said the devil again) 'doth the

---

[73] 'Thoughts on Religion', *Satires and Personal Writings*, ed. W. A. Eddy (Oxford, 1932), 418.

Church believe?' 'As I do' (said the collier); 'And what's that thou believest?' 'As the Church doth,' etc.; when the devil could get no other answer, he left him. (iii. 419–20)

OED's (undated) definition of the collier's faith ('unenquiring or unreasoning assent to the prevalent religious trends') is one suitable to Burton's own faith, which he here commends to others. It signals, however, how out of genuine sympathy he is with Calvinism. The early English Calvinists, such as John Hooper and William Whitaker, frequently inveighed against Catholic identification of saving faith with faith in the Church. Hooper treats the collier's faith as a familiar proverb:

Qui ergo populum Dei ad carbonarios, vel ad quoscunque alios quibuscunque titulis et nomine inscriptos, et non ad verbum Dei relegant, impostores sunt, Deique et hominum hostes.

He goes on to characterize Catholic teaching:

Deinde certitudinem fidei nostrae ab ignaro, indocto, atque imperito carbonario petendam esse docent, qui quid sit fides plane ignorat.[74]

It suited Calvinists to take up the idea of the collier's faith and, in the most effective proselytizing traditions, recast existing lore to carry their ideology: the collier connected uneducated social baseness (and a reputation for cheating) with an emblematically demonic blackness.[75] The point they were seeking to enforce was that ignorance of the faith evidenced reprobation not holy simplicity. As we know from Bunyan there was a socially discriminatory aspect to this. Puritans tended to consider that those whose tenure was on the lowest rungs of society were lost.[76] They seemed ineducable. When Ulpian Fulwell, a Calvinist

---

[74] John Hooper, *Later Writings*, ed. C. Newinson (1852), 543. 'Those therefore who refer the people of God to colliers—or to anybody else, under whatever name or title—rather than to the Word of God are imposters and enemies of God and men.' 'And then they teach that we should aspire, with respect to assurance of our faith, to the example of the ignorant, untaught, and unpractised collier, who obviously does not know what faith is.' (My translation.)

[75] 'As the sayinge is,' wrote John Bale in his *Apology of J. B. agaynste a Ranke Papyst* (1552), 'lyke wyl to lyke, as the devyl fyndeth out the colyer' (p. 93). Samuel Butler (in 1663) confirms the link with sootiness in *Hudibras*: 'He could transforme himself in Colour As like the devil as is a Collier' (1. 2. 350). Example cited in *OED*, 'collier' sb. 3.

[76] Richard Baxter, in his mellower days, regretted his undervaluation of 'the Life of the poor Labouring Man' (*Reliquiae Baxterianae*, ed. M. Sylvester (1696), 134).

clergyman, wrote an interlude in 1568 called *Like Will to Like, Quoth the Devil to the Collier*, which follows the careers of six reprobates, social inferiority seems to be their unforgivable sin. Tom Collier's reprobate prospects are signalled early by his possession of a West Country burr, and the 'shamefulness' of the reprobates in general is put down to their lack of schooling in 'virtue and learning'.[77] Reprobation is interpreted by the play as environmental determinism. Dent's *Plaine Mans Path-Way*, which predates the *Anatomy* by twenty years, like *Progress* discouraged the ingenuous belief (voiced by Asunetus) 'that God is a good man, he is mercifull'. Theologus concludes: 'So then it is cleare, that ignorance is not the mother of devotion, as the Papists do avouch: but it is the mother of errour, death, and destruction, as the scripture affirmeth.'[78] Finally, confirming the currency of the protestant view when Burton so surprisingly adopts the Catholic attitude, Francis Rous in 1622 described popery as 'generally a Religion very neere fitted for brute beasts, for it teacheth them to be saved in ignorance, and by beleeving as the Church beleeves. Which is upon the matter of beleeving that which they know not, and by not knowing what they beleeve.'[79] The part of the Devil, in Burton's anecdote, was played by puritans, or serious Calvinists, and a Calvinist despairer who followed Burton's advice would only confirm his or her own reprobation.

It was not just Burton's humaneness that made him side-step a zealous engagement with Calvinist teachings. Related to that attitude—as we may see in the patronizing solicitude of Mr Worldly-Wiseman—was distaste for their vulgar appeal. The vulgarity was literal: he speaks of the 'preposterous zeal' of 'Great precisians of mean conditions and very illiterate' (iii. 372), effortlessly assuming that the mean conditions make the zeal preposterous. What he advises for despairers, as far as his gestural orthodoxy permits, is just what, as Bunyan found, they could not achieve: a return to mindlessness. He counsels avoidance of solitariness (an imperative phase, for Bunyan, of spiritual development) but also of 'such companies' where he will be encouraged to read tracts (iii. 409, 432), favours 'honest game and pleasure' such as cock-fighting and bear-baiting, and

---

[77] In *Four Tudor Interludes*, ed. J. A. B. Somerset (1974), 157, ll. 1014–15.

[78] *Plaine Mans Path-Way*, pp. 30, 358.

[79] Francis Rous, *The Diseases of the Time Attended by their Remedies* (1622), 189–90.

commends what remains of the rituals of the church (iii. 370, 495–6 n.). According to an almost lone biographical detail Burton derived habitual amusement, on venturing a few yards from his cloister, from eavesdropping on the colourful language of the bargees at Folly Bridge.[80] He was clearly well insulated from taking proletarian experience seriously—though one cannot easily prefer the kind of serious interest in the common people taken by the puritan divines.

On the matter of ignorance, as on others, Burton contradicts himself. In the collier passage 'ignorance in the principles of religion' is a demonic charge. But not long before he had been chastising 'ignorant persons, that neglect and contemn the means of their salvation' (iii. 390). Then he had been concerned not with the threatened radicalism of puritanism but the wild conduct of those unbridled by fear of the hereafter. Snatches of puritan phrasing work well in that context to rebuke his culprits. We can see that Burton's writing is actuated not by a coherent intellectual position but by congeries of unargued-for prejudices. His conservatism depends upon his scepticism about the remediability of the bizarre human nature he documents. Momentary discharges of anger or anarchic impulse are swiftly neutralized both by their extremism (which tends to topple them into irony) and by the relentless undercutting implication of the *Anatomy* as a whole that wherever you look human nature presents the same spectacle of comically dismaying extremism. Any social or religious change will merely give fresh scope to humanity's destructive lunacy, especially if it encourages the belief amongst the lower orders that they are the possessors of brains.

Looking at the *Anatomy* from the angle not of authorial individuality but of cultural history, specifically the competition between alien discourses to shape an understanding of experience, helps us to see both the contradictions in Burton and the way in which the work interacts with the world that produced it. The *Anatomy* resembles Bunyan's works and, as we shall see, Donne's 'Holy Sonnets' in being a response to ideological pressures experienced in the form of an acute self-consciousness ('I write of melancholy,' says Burton, 'by being busy to avoid melancholy'

---

[80] See *Anatomy*, ed. Jackson, p. v.

(i. 20)). But while they tried to mend a sense of inner fracture, in part produced, in part rationalized by Calvinism, he wrote to keep emotional pressures at bay, locating disharmony in the world at large. The work's elaborate structure counteracts the actually chaotic and formless nature of the universal malaise he explores. When, like Thomas Goodwin, Burton invoked 'these double or turning pictures' (i. 115), rather than search for integration he resigned himself to the inconstancy and ambivalence of human experience, including his own (i. 120). The *Anatomy* is dedicated to superficiality. George Williamson observes of the treatment of scientific controversies: 'Although Burton verifies the impetus which the new astronomy lent to the idea of mutability and decay, he does not sound its emotional depths; that office fell chiefly to the preachers and poets.'[81] The breadth of his erudition (and no doubt donnish ensconcement) similarly rescued him from too personal an engagement with protestant psychology. As in the *Anatomy* and society as a whole, formal order in religion was a substitute for inner coherence. In spite of this comparative detachment the *Anatomy* registers the authority in Burton's society of the Calvinist system of indoctrination, documenting its effects, regurgitating its language, and deferring to its leading exponents. It demonstrates the imbrication of puritan culture with the Church of England establishment in the early decades of the seventeenth century, and the difficulty of resisting the Calvinist hegemony.

[81] George Williamson, 'Mutability, Decay, and Seventeenth-Century Melancholy', *ELH* 2 (1935), 121–50, p. 126.

6

John Donne: The Despair of the 'Holy Sonnets'

I F Burton provides a case study in a Church of England cleric who did his best to shrug off Calvinism (attesting in the attempt its authority in his society), Donne is probably the best example of a victim of the Calvinist persecutory imagination whose critics have resolutely evaded this fact on his behalf.[1] My purpose in this chapter, therefore, is to establish a strong Calvinist involvement in the 'Holy Sonnets' and their related expression of a dominant mood of despair. This necessitates tangling with previous criticism, especially since it is the commonly held view that the sonnets constitute a sequence which charts a progression towards peace of mind. Dissatisfaction with these interpretations and the critical assumptions informing them leads to a view of the poems as discrete *cris de coeur*. After identifying a typical process of the subversion of ostensible argument in Donne's poetry I investigate the Calvinist pressure on his imagination which forces the poems to disclose emotions of fear, resentment, and despair. Finally I gather in the Calvinist ideas which pervade the sonnets and suggest reasons for Donne's responsiveness to a theological system many consider alien to him.

Helen Gardner's interpretation of the 'Holy Sonnets' has, as I shall note, already met with some criticism. It does nevertheless remain dominant: partly, no doubt, because of the difficulty of disentangling it from an edition of the *Divine Poems* which has much to recommend it, but as much because alternative readings have generally adopted her assumption that the poems compose a sequence (or sequences) through which a movement towards

---

[1] But see adumbrations of a Calvinist reading in Paul R. Sellin, 'The Hidden God: Reformation Awe in Renaissance English Literature' in R. Kinsman, ed., *The Darker Vision of the Renaissance: Beyond the Fields of Reason* (Berkeley, 1974). John Carey, *John Donne: Life, Mind, and Art* (1981), 52–7; Alan Sinfield, *Literature in Protestant England 1560–1660* (Beckenham, 1983), 9–11. This chapter is itself a developed version of my article of the same title in *ELH*, 48 (1981), 677–705.

spiritual assurance can be charted. And such readings, repudiating Grierson's view that 'Each sonnet is a separate meditation or ejaculation,'[2] have seemed no more plausible than Gardner's.

Suspicion of Gardner's argument should begin with the flimsiness of the textual evidence on which her argument for Ignatian influence on the structure of the 'Holy Sonnets' depends. This can, since the appearance of her revised edition, be indicated very simply. We are told in this edition that the discovery that the Westmoreland MS is in the hand of Donne's close friend, Rowland Woodward, 'enhances the already high authority of the Westmoreland manuscript' (p. 148).[3] We were, moreover, informed previously that this manuscript 'was plainly copied with great care from two excellent sources'.[4] Since, however, Gardner's ordering of the 'Holy Sonnets' is not that of the Westmoreland manuscript, she is forced to contend either that Woodward's scrupulosity did not extend to copying the poems out in the order in which he received them or that Donne presented them to him in a form which disrupted their unity. Gardner reasonably opts for the latter (p. xlii n. 2). But of course this clearly suggests that Donne saw no important connection between the poems in the sequential sets for which she argues: he took no pains to maintain one. Other points could be made, such as the failure of any manuscript or edition prior to hers to mark the groups off from one another; but the evidence from the Westmoreland MS is certainly the most telling.

Dissatisfaction with the critical argument—that the structure and content of the poems are influenced by Donne's inbred familiarity with St Ignatius Loyola's *Spiritual Exercises*—is immediately stirred by the qualifications and modifications which bulk very large in Gardner's argument. She first presents a seemingly rigid method of arousing devotion: 'A meditation on the Ignatian pattern, employing the "three powers of the soul", consists of a brief preparatory prayer, two "preludes", a varying number of points, and a colloquy.'[5] But the ensuing description of the application of this method makes it appear so slipshod that

[2] *The Poems of John Donne*, ed. H. J. C. Grierson (Oxford, 1912), ii. 231.

[3] See ch. 2 n. 75.

[4] *John Donne: The Divine Poems*, ed. Helen Gardner (Oxford, 1952), p. lxxx.

[5] Helen Gardner's account of the influence of the Ignatian meditation on Donne occupies pp. l–lv. My discussion of her views makes close reference to these pages.

the purpose of mental discipline would seem to be defeated.[6] Even in the first six sonnets, which form her clearest meditational sequence, fragments of the method operate at random. The *preparatory prayer* naturally occupies the first. The following three 'show very clearly the two preludes of a meditation, which correspond neatly to the two parts of a sonnet' (although the sestet of the second is later admitted to be 'hardly a petition'). And apart from something 'like a "point" drawn out from a meditation on hell' (a 'meditation proper', we are told, usually had three to five points) and a 'petition' (synonymous with a second *prelude*) which follows instead of preceding it in the fifth, this is the extent of the meditation's application. The sixth 'in manner and temper is quite undevotional'. There is, then, no *colloquy*, in this set of six, only a third or a fifth of one *meditation* (which is followed by its *prelude*), and a number of *preludes* and a *preparatory prayer* for 'meditation[s] proper' which never arrive. And the concluding sonnet is altogether unconnected with the method. It is puzzling, after this, to be faced with the statement that it is 'not in the structure of the sonnets' that the meditational influence is felt in the next series of six. Instead the influence is here supposed to be evident in 'such things as the vivid sense of the actualities of the Passion in "Spit in my face",' etc. Imaginary participation in the Passion is, to expand Gardner's 'such things', an example of the Catholic method in meditation of applying oneself to the subject. But Barbara Lewalski convincingly argues that 'Spit in my face' enacts rejection of the Catholic mode of identification with Christ and its replacement by the antithetical protestant meditation technique (Donne applies the subject to himself).[7] Gardner then declares the subsequent group of four poems to be 'less obviously medita-

---

[6] That the point of the meditational exercise lay in its total performance is confirmed by Anthony Low, who endorses Helen Gardner's argument for Ignatian influence on the 'Holy Sonnets': 'The goal of a meditative exercise, it was generally agreed, is in its last stages: emotions, acts of the will, determinations of amendment, colloquies with God. Without this kind of outcome the exercise would be meaningless' (*Love's Architecture: Devotional Modes in Seventeenth-Century English Poetry* (New York, 1978), 39).

[7] *Protestant Poetics and the Seventeenth-Century Religious Lyric* (Princeton, 1979), 270–1. This and *Donne's Anniversaries and the Poetry of Praise* (Princeton, 1973) by the same author fully explore protestant techniques of meditation. See also John N. Wall Jr., who notes that Donne differs from contemporary Catholic poets and favours protestant methods ('Donne's Wit of Redemption: The Drama of Prayer in the "Holy Sonnets" ', *SP* 73 (1976), 189–203, pp. 191–2).

tions'. The three presumably later sonnets were always allowed to be 'separate ejaculations' (p. xii).

It is difficult to see how Donne could, in presenting his relationship to God, have avoided intermittent use of the techniques and subject matter Ignatius prescribes. The *compositio loci* (first *prelude*), in which situations as well as places are vividly conjured up, is a regular feature of the short dramatic lyric. Petition to God, examination of specified religious situations, and outpouring of devotion were fundamentals of protestant spiritual life (it is a myth that protestants did not at this time possess their own literature of devotion). And the structural employment of memory, reason, and will (the 'three powers of the soul') pertains as much to Donne's secular poetry, as Stanley Archer has shown, as to the religious.[8] As for subjects such as sin, death, judgement, even the atonement in its soteriological aspect, these exert an attractive force over anyone who doubts salvation, as the spiritual autobiographies amply attest.

Helen Gardner's introduction of the Ignatian meditation to discussion of the 'Holy Sonnets' is, above all, redundant. Employed systematically in the poems, it could be accepted as Donne's 'way of thinking' (p. liv). Fragmented as it is, it presents little that is distinctive. It is, in view of this, unsurprising that embarrassing clashes can be detected between the accounts of Helen Gardner and Louis Martz of precisely how the Jesuit influence is transmitted in the poetry.[9] Their independent arrival at similar conclusions supplies not, as Helen Gardner supposes (p. liv), corroboration so much as mutual refutation.

Other critics of the 'Holy Sonnets' tend to take Gardner as their point of departure but are influenced by her to the extent of arguing for sequence. Don M. Ricks begins by remarking that 'Gardner's discussion of the relationship between the formal meditation and the sequence involves so many qualifications that it is rather easy to suspect Ignatius does not explain Donne's

---

[8] Stanley Archer, 'Meditation and the Structure of Donne's "Holy Sonnets" ', *ELH* 28 (1961), 137–47.

[9] See Archer, ibid. 137–9. Stanley Archer also questions Helen Gardner's biographical evidence. The *Spiritual Exercises* were, Father Gerard's autobiography suggests, not even taught to boys who were candidates for the priesthood (pp. 145–6). If Donne read the *Exercises* after going to university, their mental discipline would not have become second nature to him; thus Helen Gardner's somewhat odd argument that this explains the liberties he is able to take with the model loses its basis.

structure at all.' But Ricks himself argues, as improbably, for sequence in the Westmoreland order. Awkward joins appear in the argument:

So religious love, not fear, contols the thematic tone of the third group.

   The prayer-like climax in *Batter my heart, three person'd God* brilliantly recapitulates both the negative and positive sections of the sequence.

The phrase 'thematic tone' has the defensive vagueness of Helen Gardner's 'way of thinking'. And Ricks employs an old ruse to explain why 'Batter my heart' steps out of line—ascribing to the brilliance of the poet the ingenuity to which his own theory drives him. The account of the last three poems is even thinner. Having extolled 'Batter my heart', he proceeds: 'Such a satisfying conclusion suggests we should read any following sonnets as an anti-climactic epilogue.'[10] He ventures no suggestion, however, as to the function of an epilogue containing poems as disparate— and emotionally taut—as that on the death of the poet's wife, that on the state of the church, and that on his own spiritual instability.

   Ricks concludes with an attempt to offer 'Oh to vex me' as a summary (or, in view of 'Batter my heart', a second summary) of the rest:

The whole sonnet sequence . . . represents the fruits of one of the poet's 'best dayes.' He began fearfully; therefore he courted God. That exercise reassured him of the possibility of redemption, but also of the need continuously to make himself worthy of it. Being human, however, he is inconstant; and he must recognise that there will be many 'bad days' after.

This is riddled with misreadings and illogicalities. Here are the lines on which he is commenting:

> I durst not view heaven yesterday; and to day
> In prayers, and flattering speaches I court God:
> To morrow'I quake with true feare of his rod.
> So my devout fitts come and go away
> Like a fantastique Ague: save that here
> Those are my best dayes, when I shake with feare.
>
> (p. 16)[11]

[10] Don M. Ricks, 'The Westmoreland Manuscript and the Order of the "Holy Sonnets" ', *SP* 63 (1966), 187–95, pp. 188, 192, 193.

[11] To avoid the impression of sequence I am referring to the poems by page number and by their first half-line.

Taking Donne's yesterday, today, and tomorrow in literal relation to the act of writing, he appears to think that yesterday's fear produced today's poetic attempt to ingratiate himself with God. This reassures him, but he reminds himself that tomorrow he may be in the dumps again. But it is today, the day of flattery, which is the bad day (not Donne's term), not tomorrow, the day of fear. 'Those are my best dayes,' says Donne, 'when I shake with feare.' Ricks at first attaches 'best dayes' to yesterday and then lets it slip to today where it opposes tomorrow's bad days, although tomorrow, when he quakes with fear of God's rod, is, exactly, one of his 'best dayes'. If Donne uses yesterday, today, and tomorrow to indicate more than a fluctuating pattern of experience, it is his present state of mind which is alarming for its insincerity. There are other errors in the passage. Nowhere in the sonnets does Donne think it lies in his power to 'make himself worthy' of redemption. And one cannot, from the poem, assume any causal relation between Donne's fear and flattery (though there may be one), rather they are indications of his inconstancy. There was no reassurance to be had, moreover, from shared humanity, nor does Donne suggest this. Inconstancy is a symptom of his spiritual condition which he worries over frequently, in 'A Litanie (p. 21 no. xv) for example, and throughout the *Devotions*. Ricks's analysis permits him the vulgarizing and inaccurate (but reassuring) conclusion that 'the poet is chuckling over his fallibility, not trembling in fear of his sins.'[12]

Ricks's argument may not seem to justify so much attention, yet it is, I think, worth mentioning for three reasons. First, it exemplifies well how much strain critics are prepared to put on the interpretation of individual poems to make them perform their role in the postulated sequence. Second, Ricks's sequence is the Westmoreland order, and this is the order which seems to me most defensible (although again it is probable that Donne himself, indifferently, supplied also the order of manuscript groups I and II). And third, the pattern Ricks follows resembles that of other critics. Douglas Peterson, for instance, begins with an attack on Helen Gardner: 'her classification of the four groupings according to theme is arbitrary. It violates the essential unity of the *Holy Sonnets* as a group, misconstruing

[12] 'The Westmoreland Manuscript', p. 195.

Donne's intentions and distorting, in several instances, the meaning of individual poems.' And a fear/love movement structures the sequence for him (as it does for Ricks), this time in the service of the 'Anglican doctrine of contrition'. The last four sonnets of the 1635 edition and the three Westmoreland sonnets are explained as having the theme of 'contrite' sorrow. This again is a strange view of a poem occasioned by bereavement and another concerned with the church. And the theme of 'Oh to vex me' cannot be called attrite let alone contrite: fear of divine punishment (unattended by sorrow for sin) did not qualify. In fact Peterson handles 'Oh to vex me' more sensitively in his specific analysis,[13] but his argument for irony in this poem nevertheless undermines the supposed progression over the sequence from fear to love to contrite sorrow.

Even when sequential development is not urged, critics have been disposed to believe that the poems were written in an assured frame of mind. Louis Martz, who argues that the Ignatian meditation is performed in individual poems, exemplifies Donne's technique from 'Thou hast made me' where the speaker is said to summon feelings of terror as a salutary exercise; the feelings are then firmly repelled, in the sestet, by confidence in God's grace.[14] We shall see later, however, that the firmness of Donne's confidence in this poem is highly suspect. John N. Wall Jr., with self-evident arbitrariness, concludes of 'Oh to vex me' that 'the mood at the end of this sonnet is one of peace with life lived in this way.'[15] And Barbara Lewalski, who hedges her bets on the issue of sequence, prejudges the question of the degree of Donne's assurance by assimilating the experiences in the sonnets to those of biblical heroes, especially St Paul. But 'Paul's experience of the predicament of the Christian'[16] was, after his lightning conversion, hardly one of diffidence in God's mercy. A rabid persecutor of Christians, he certainly suffered from no pre-conversion *Angst*.

Helen Gardner's example, then, of editing out the disturbance in the 'Holy Sonnets' is followed in various ways diverting readers from the doctrinal pressures which bear down on the

---

[13] Douglas L. Peterson, 'John Donne's "Holy Sonnets" and the Anglican Doctrine of Contrition', *SP* 56 (1959), 504–18, pp. 504–5, 506, 517.

[14] *The Poetry of Meditation: A Study in English Religious Literature of the Seventeenth Century* (New Haven, 1962), 132.   [15] 'Donne's Wit of Redemption', p. 203.

[16] *Protestant Poetics*, pp. 253–82, esp. p. 254.

writing. When agitation cannot be ignored Gardner deprecates it as gratuitous gusto in the performance of prescribed exercises. 'There is', she asserts, 'a note of exaggeration in them' (p. xxx). She remarks that it is the special danger of 'the meditation's deliberate stimulation of emotion . . . that, in stimulating feeling, it may falsify it, and overdramatize the spiritual life' (p. xxxi). Assuming that 'the spiritual life' is constant throughout history and that the purpose of the poems is to conform to its proprieties, of which she is a custodian, she disqualifies parts of them as spiritually and poetically inauthentic. Yet, while accusing Donne of over-dramatization and therefore presumably impugning the poems as a true record of his state of feeling, Gardner concedes that 'the mere fact that his mind turned to' meditation on sin and judgement 'suggests some sickness in the soul'. But if Donne was spiritually sick, he would not need to stimulate the feeling Gardner finds offensive. In view of the excesses she detects it is odd that she should argue that, although Donne wrote the poems because of some spiritual malaise, the poems are not expressive of that malaise. She interposes the Ignatian exercises between the sickness and the poems. And such exercises have both a vigilantly policed piety and securely predetermined outcome. Their endings, as for example Martz's reading of 'Thou hast made me' clearly shows, will be taken pre-emptively as successful expulsions of feelings which were, after all, conjured up deliberately rather than attempts to come to terms with an oppressive and unchosen theological discourse which obtruded itself on Donne's daily consciousness.

The idea of performing a meditation posits a poet in full conscious control of his poetry and the meanings it releases. The same implication is conveyed by arguments that Donne is following theological models from an earlier age. St Ignatius Loyola is himself systematizing an ancient exercise.[17] Barbara Lewalski takes the poems' origins as far back as first-century Palestine. And Patrick Grant insists that the sonnets 'belong firmly within a definable and distinctly medieval Augustinian spiritual tradition'.[18] Reformed theology did, of course, owe

---

[17] The antiquity of the meditation is the first thing to which Helen Gardner draws attention (p. 1).

[18] Patrick Grant, 'Augustinian Spirituality and the "Holy Sonnets" of John Donne', *ELH* 38 (1971), 542–61, p. 561.

much to Augustine and beyond him to Pauline concepts and terminology, but Donne belonged to a theologically dominated culture of his own. His vital ideological exposure was to Pauline and Augustinian teaching as it was interpreted, modified, and translated into experience in his own time. Donne regarded Augustine and Calvin jointly as the greatest Bible exegetes,[19] and Calvin, the more immediate figure, is independently influential in his poetry. The idea of Donne as a cultural throwback insinuates a view of his poetry as erudite, richly traditional, but not, as it really is, bristling, like the love poems, with an acute contemporary sensitivity. It is easy to share the bemusement of the historians, Charles and Katherine George, who remark:

> It is somewhat odd that so much attention has been lavished on putting the poetry of Milton in the context of 'puritanism' and so little on understanding Donne as a Protestant poet and preacher, in the context, that is, of contemporary English religiosity . . . In fact, the level of Protestant religious intensity in Donne's thought is far above anything to be found in the 'puritan' Milton.[20]

Arguments for sequence, the presupposition of an optimistic outcome, and the intellectual and emotional detachment of the poems from the period in which they were written operate similarly to emphasize craftsmanship and to discourage the idea that they record the wriggling movements of a mind pinned by the contemporary phrases with which it is compelled to understand itself. When Douglas Bush speaks of 'the personal involvement that gives such urgency to the best religious poems',[21] he speaks for the commonest response of readers: recognition that they are the site of desperate struggle. The sense of personal urgency is an effect, as in the spiritual autobiography, of a theology which forced oscillation between contradictory self-definitions. Donne is of course exercising some form of control. No verbal effusion in an excited state of mind confines itself to fourteen five-footed lines and a regular rhyme scheme. The formal order is evidently the correlate of a desire to subdue conflict. The poems consequently embody the strain between an

[19] John Donne, *Biathanatos*, facsimile (New York, 1930), 98.

[20] *The Protestant Mind of the English Reformation (1570–1640)* (Princeton, 1961), 69–70 n.

[21] Douglas Bush, *English Literature in the Earlier Seventeenth Century (1600–1660)* 2nd edn. (Oxford, 1962), 319.

agitated state of mind and its attempted counteraction. The writing (as Donne explains in another context) sets out to discipline the feeling that gave rise to it:

> Then as th'earths inward narrow crooked lanes
> Do purge sea waters fretfull salt away,
>   I thought, if I could draw my paines,
> Through Rimes vexation, I should them allay.
> Griefe brought to numbers cannot be so fierce,
> For, he tames it, that fetters it in verse.[22]

The sediment of salt—the salt of his tears, of aggravated feeling—is deposited on the craggy lines themselves. The writing is an attempt to rid himself of pain.

If it is assumed that Donne wrote poems about spiritual conflict from a pious and assured position, the 'Holy Sonnets' will not trouble other assumptions about the kind of God he believed in or about the responses this God evoked. That the writing wrestles with the oppressiveness of the collectively imagined deity and accompanying values can be, and with amazing success has been, rendered invisible. Arguments for sequence have helped to achieve this since the impact and meaning of individual poems in a sequence which plots a thematic development is controlled and restricted by the overall artistic design to which they contribute. A sonnet occupying a position in this sequence sacrifices the emotional complexity which thrives on the brevity of the dramatic lyric to a unifying idea and attitude over which the artist exercises purposeful control. Few critics of the 'Holy Sonnets' would wish to dissent from the view of William Halewood (another critic who sees the poems as Augustinian meditations) that they were written 'within a secure framework of belief' and 'that they were written according to a formula that could produce only "poetry of exclusion"—to recur again to Richards's term for poetry which commits itself to the suppression of emotional ambiguities'.[23] If, however, the poems are read as independent articulations in which the discipline of a tight verse form is brought to bear on an often disturbed psychic

---

[22] 'The Triple Foole', *John Donne: The Elegies and the Songs and Sonnets*, ed. Helen Gardner (Oxford, 1965), 52 ll. 6–11. Further references to this edition will be embodied in the text.

[23] *The Poetry of Grace: Reformation Themes and Structures in English Seventeenth-Century Poetry* (1970), 83, 82.

state, emotional ambiguities will, on the contrary, constitute their vital meaning.

Donne did write religious poetry, around or a year or two before the probable time of composition of the 'Holy Sonnets', which fits the description 'poetry of exclusion' much better. Both 'La Corona', with its reassuring circularity, and 'A Litanie', containing a calm inventory of temptations and petitions in a format traditional to the church, are reverently muted sequences which allude to but shelter from sources of disquiet. R. C. Bald, who sees the years 1607 to 1610 as 'probably the most disturbed and anxious years' of Donne's life says of 'La Corona' and 'A Litanie': 'there is a ritual element that gives them a certain restraint and formalism which are much less strongly marked in the "Holy Sonnets".'[24] This suggests that in so far as Donne was following traditional religious prescriptions as to the form and content of his poetry he was inhibiting the expression of his real spiritual preoccupations. No such inhibitions need be read into the 'Holy Sonnets'.

Donne was acutely aware of the limitations imposed on him by theological propriety. In all the *Songs and Sonnets* there is not one formal sonnet; yet in the 'Holy Sonnets' he imposes this discipline on himself. It represents the frame to which, by spiritual contortions, he is to fit his thoughts and feelings. He fails. The thoughts and feelings escape. The poems, 'Since she whome I lovd' (p. 14), occasioned by the loss of his wife two years after he entered the ministry, and the earlier 'Batter my heart' (p. 11), a more general expression of spiritual crisis, illustrate this process. 'Since she whome I lovd' represents a failed attempt by Donne to wrench his mind into acceptance of the loss of his wife as an act of love on God's part. The ambiguity of the second line—'and to hers, my good is dead'—contains both his natural emotional response and the response he wishes to inculcate in himself: she is now dead to the good of their relationship, and it is for their good that she has died.[25] He then speaks of the gentle love of God to which his wife introduced him

---

[24] R. C. Bald, *John Donne: A Life*, completed and edited by W. Milgate (Oxford, 1970), 235, 233. Even in these poems, however, there are several references to the troubles they generally exclude.

[25] Helen Gardner first recorded this ambiguity (*The Divine Poems* (1952), 79).

('so streames do shew the head'), his pleasure in this, and a holy yearning for further communion.

This serene discovery of God is of a piece with the Catholic Neoplatonism of, for example, *The Spiritual Combat*:

When the beauty of mankind impresses you, you should immediately distinguish what is apparent to the eye from what is seen only by the mind. You must remember that all corporal beauty flows from an invisible principle, the uncreated beauty of God. You must discern in this an almost imperceptible drop issuing from an endless source, an immense ocean from which numberless perfections continually flow.[26]

In the sestet, however, this Neoplatonism in which God is ineffable, to be yearned for, and to be understood partly through the finest human qualities, is replaced by a stiffly protestant conception of God as jealously intrusive in Donne's life. Instead of a source of benignity to which he applies, God has become a character whose love has plans of its own:

> But why should I begg more love, when as thou
> Dost wooe my soule, for hers offring all thine.

He has become the pursuer, demanding attention by exercising his power to remove distractions, regardless of the fact that, as Donne sees it, his wife actually drew him to God. But because of this fact there is a suppressed plaintiveness in the final lines, a feeling that the poet is excusing and praising behaviour which really he finds inexcusable.

The God of the octave and the God of the sestet are different from one another, or, if the same, then exhibiting greatly differing aspects of one Deity. The first is passively sublime, responsive if found, and discoverable through a woman. The second is also loving but in an active, ruthless, and jealous way, so that the woman becomes identified with the temptations of the world, flesh, and devil rather than an aid to worship. This is the anthropomorphized protestant God who will not tolerate sharing human devotion with saints and angels, let alone women. 'Let us therefore', said Calvin, 'forsake that Platonicall philosophie, to seeke the way to God by Angels, and to honour them' (*Inst.* 1. 14. 12). The poem ends, not so much with a realization that his

---

[26] Lorenzo Scupoli (attributed), *The Spiritual Combat*, trans. rev. William Lester and Robert Mohan (Westminster, Md., 1947), 67.

wife died for his own good as with a tentative suggestion of the monstrousness of God's love. Of course he cannot resist God's overwhelming advances but he does imply, through his own account of his wife's function, that his jealousy is groundless. In 'A Litanie', it might be noted, Donne asks to be delivered from thinking 'that thou'art covetous | To them whom thou lov'st' (p. 21 no. xv). He had misgivings about the character God revealed in his actions.

It is interesting to notice the shift Helen Gardner is put to in her interpretation of the ending of this poem. Here are the last four lines:

> And dost not only feare least I allow
> My love to saints and Angels, things divine,
> But in thy tender jealosy dost doubt
> Least the World, fleshe, yea Devill putt thee out.

Helen Gardner paraphrases:

God has not only removed his 'saint and Angel', fearing that he might love her too much; but has also guarded him against temptation by continual disappointments and mortifications. (p. 79)

Why she should wantonly change the number of 'saints and Angels' and equate the phrase with Donne's wife rather than understand its literal denotation of the objects of his aberrant youthful devotion might ordinarily baffle speculation. Even George Herbert, *habitué* of Little Gidding, wrote a poem, 'To All Angels and Saints', on why he could not write a poem to angels and saints. Again the protestant God's jealous love is the reason. Herbert bows to him:

> But now, alas, I dare not; for our King,
> Whom we do all joyntly adore and praise,
> Bids no such thing.[27]

The ending of 'Since she whome I lovd' is difficult, however, because it shockingly depicts God viewing a situation, Donne's relationship with his wife, through the distortions of a base passion, jealousy. It must have been this (doubtless compounded by an Anglo-Catholic reluctance to picture God as disapproving

---

[27] George Herbert, *The Works*, ed. F. E. Hutchinson (Oxford, 1941), 77–8, ll. 16–18.

of devotion to saints and angels) which disturbed Helen Gardner into her untenable interpretation. Barbara Lewalski, who follows her in misinterpreting 'saints and Angels' to include Donne's wife, finds the ending 'less unified and effective than is usual with Donne',[28] and implicitly prefers this state of affairs—where the 'not only . . . But' construction has no logical force—to a unified and effective poem which verges on blasphemy.

The protestant God was, as we have seen, heavily interventionist in the world and in human lives, being transformed from a transcendent sublimity into a humanoid giant manipulating physical objects, circumstances, and events to express his variable attitude towards individuals. The passivity the Calvinist God conferred on mankind was correlated by a vigorous divine providence all the more closely scrutinized in order to decipher the 'particular' message it delivered. It was not enough, thought Donne himself, to believe in 'a great and incomprehensible power, that sits . . . *in luce inaccessibili*, in light that we cannot comprehend. A God that enjoyes his owne eternity . . . but . . . communicates nothing to us' (*Sermons*, iii. 87).[29] When the grief-stricken father of a drowned boy came to Richard Greenham wanting to know what sin he could have committed the assumption of his question was wholly accepted. Greenham catalogued the possibilities: God might be correcting his over-great sense of security, or his immoderate love of his son, or his unthankfulness for his son's spiritual development, or his failure to pray enough for him, or perhaps God wanted him to have more time to devote to him.[30] To the English protestant, then, especially to puritans, the death of a spouse was attributed directly to God's hand in a sense which was scarcely thought of as metaphorical. Diarists and autobiographers regularly record coming to terms with this punitive stroke. Thomas Shepard's reaction would have been the correct one for Donne: 'this made me resolve to delight no more in creatures, but in the Lord.'[31] Robert Blair expresses a reaction closer to Donne's:

But when I came to the highway my sorrows were renewed, and the bitterness of my mind increased upon this ground, that I had made an

---

[28] *Protestant Poetics*, p. 273.
[29] See ch. 2 n. 76.   [30] *The Workes* (1599), 45.
[31] Quoted by Lawrence Stone in *The Family, Sex and Marriage in England 1500–1800* (New York, 1977), 215.

idol of a gracious companion, and had so provoked the Lord, in removing her to himself, to smite me so grievously.[32]

Like Donne he attributes his bereavement to God's righteous jealousy but the bitterness differs by being directed solely at himself. God's treatment of Donne is similar but the genuine submissiveness of his posture is more questionable.

In the case of both Blair and Donne the sensed need for punishment again represents Erich Fromm's 'masochistic strivings'. To make surrender to God possible it was necessary to obliterate the claims of self and undergo what puritan divines called 'humiliation'. The will had to be crushed before it would be, or while it was being, taken over by God. The poem 'Batter my heart', amplifying the plea of 'Good | friday, 1613. Riding Westward' ('O thinke mee worth thine anger, punish mee' (p. 31, 1. 39)), instantiates the masochistic strivings whereby Donne tried to subject the whole of himself to God. It attempts to enact, through its solicitation of divine aggression and rape, the conversion process described by William Perkins: 'he that will beleeve in Christ must be *annihilated*, that is he must be bruised and battered to a flat nothing.'[33]

The experience Donne invites resembles that described in the paradigmatic conversion narrative of St Augustine. On the threshold of conversion he felt God 'redoubling the lashes of fear and shame, lest I should again give way'. With this assistance he bullied his will into singleness of purpose:

For, not to go only, but to go in thither was nothing else but to will to go, but to will resolutely and thoroughly; not to turn and toss, this way and that, a maimed and half-divided will, struggling, with one part sinking as another rose.[34]

Donne's problem, though, lies in his fundamental inability to forfeit, as Augustine wills to do, his independent identity. As a result, his only hope—to use a phrase both sanctioned by 'Batter my heart' and often adopted to characterize Calvin's conception of conversion—is for divine rape.[35] The doctrine of the irresist-

[32] *The Life of Mr. Robert Blair containing his Autobiography from 1593 to 1636*, ed. Thomas McCric (1848), 97.   [33] *The Works* (Cambridge, 1605), 501.

[34] St Augustine, *Confessions*, trans. E. B. Pusey (1838), 168, 165.

[35] Ironically Thomas Carew applied the idea to Donne, who, he said, had 'Committed holy Rapes upon our Will' ('An Elegie upon the death of the Deane of Pauls, Dr. John Donne', *The Poems*, ed. R. Dunlap (Oxford, 1970)), 72, 1. 17.

ibility of grace is, significantly for Donne, a key point on which Calvin departed from Augustine.[36] Calvinist conversion involved God's simultaneous and irresistible seizure of all the faculties, and it is this that Donne invites:

> Take mee to you, imprison mee, for I
> Except you'enthrall mee, never shall be free,
> Nor ever chast, except you ravish mee.

Crashaw's 'To the Noblest and the best of Ladyes, the Countess of Denbigh' points up the contrasting Catholic attitude to conversion:

> This Fort of your fair selfe, if't be not won,
> He is repulst indeed; But you'are undone.[37]

There is no doubt here of the ardour of the assailant or suitor, and the lady has it in her power to capitulate or resist.[38] The prudential reason which should defend Donne's interests by admitting God is, in Calvin's terms, captive to a depraved will and 'proves weake or untrue'. Donne's is a second-order desire for God: he wants to want. But in fact his psyche, 'like an usurpt towne', is in the grip of a more powerful resistant force: the depraved will allies itself to the devil. The 'demonic' attitude in him which rebels against his own interests was the natural response to the God of his imagination. Attributing it to an external inhibiting agent made it more comprehensible. For Crashaw, whose God offers mercy to all, this complication does not arise: there is no important role for the devil in transactions between mankind and God. The Calvinist conception of conversion is the only one that can make sense to Donne. If God chooses to save him he must employ irresistible force to do it.

Barbara Lewalski remarks on the 'paradoxical reversal of Christ's customary relationships with the soul—as liberator . . . and as Bridegroom'.[39] The paradox, as ever in Donne's best poetry, is not mere ingenuity but contains complexity of feeling:

---

[36] See F. Wendel, *Calvin: The Origins and Development of his Religious Thought*, trans. P. Mairet (1963), 280.

[37] Richard Crashaw, *Poetical Works*, ed. L. C. Martin (Oxford, 1957), 238, ll. 67–8.

[38] Donne continued to hold the view that Catholics made repentance too easy (*Sermons*, i. 203) and in *Biathanatos* he had previously pointed out, following Calvin, that Judas had fulfilled their criteria (*Biathanatos*, pp. 207–8).

[39] *Protestant Poetics*, p. 272.

the ideas of imprisonment, enslavement, and rape are deeply affronting. While embracing God's action he intimates the loss of integrity which would be involved in the gain (evidently not yet secured) of salvation. The paradoxical expressions convey a genuinely ambivalent attitude towards God.

Wilbur Sanders's comment that the 'violence of sentiment' in the sonnets 'springs from the attempt to bend a stubborn temper to something which is seen, from a position *outside* the stubbornness, as a good' seems particularly relevant to 'Batter my heart'.[40] It is a shame, though, that he presents it as a criticism; as though the poems ought to have been wholehearted in their devotion to the 'good' or openly hostile (or not written at all). But their fascination lies in their inability to simplify in this way. The 'stubborn temper' is not the isolated attribute of an individual but exists in relation to, may even be seen as the product of, a 'good' whose definition the individual does not control. Donne's 'stubborn temper' gives psychological reality to the unregenerate will held to be common to all mankind. The relationship between a culturally imposed 'good' which brutalizes self-esteem, the 'stubborn temper' which consequently resists it, and the helpless 'position *outside* the stubbornness' which draws melancholy inferences is the subject matter of the poems. They are not factitious attempts at a devotion the poet does not feel (a speculative intentionalism which reduces their meaning); they exhibit a consciousness inhabiting particular ideological conditions of which the compulsion to strain after repellent attitudes is a fascinating component. Just as the energies of 'Batter my heart' seek to burst out of the constricting sonnet form so Donne is unable to reduce himself to the size and shape of God's demands.

One sees from these two sonnets that while the form and subject of the poem imply the strait-jacketing of theological propriety, other thoughts and emotions prove irrespressible: suspicion, resentment, refusal to subject himself entirely to the divine will. And the range of God's characterization is extended to include jealousy, a distorted perspective on events, and a capacity to violate the apparent autonomy of his creatures. This process, of depositing feelings in the poems which belie the ostensible argument, or of actually saying something which contradicts what he appears to intend to say, is important in

[40] Wilbur Sanders, *John Donne's Poetry* (Cambridge, 1971), 124.

Donne's secular poetry, too, in extending the range of the poem's feeling. ('The Triple Foole', quoted above, goes on to explain that the poem, instead of removing, reactivates his grief.) 'The Calme' simplifies the technique in its concluding argument:

> How little more alas
> Is man now, then before he was? he was
> Nothing; for us, wee are for nothing fit;
> Chance, or our selves still disproportion it.
> Wee have no will, no power, no sense; I lye,
> I should not then thus feele this miserie.

In this case the inadequacy of the argument to the emotional situation which provoked it is made explicit. But a passage from 'Metempsychosis' suggests the way in which arguments can explode themselves. Speaking of heretics, he says:

> their reasons, like those toyes
> Of glassie bubbles, which the gamesome boyes
> Stretch to so nice a thinnes through a quill
> That they themselves breake, doe themselves spill:
> Arguing is heretiques game, and Exercise
> As wrastlers, perfects them; . . .[41]

Arguing itself, not just the reasoning of heretics, is a strenuous sport—as the difficulty of enunciating the last two lines, with a mouthful of consonantal gravel, testifies. It is practised in search of personal advantage but is in fact worthless as an instrument for arriving at objective truth. Donne's poems frequently dramatize this view, blowing up conceits or arguments so far that they burst, giving way under their own pressure.

Donne tried to use his agility of mind as a means of exercising control over his flighty emotional states—and the poetry merely extends this habit. 'Therefore sometimes', he wrote in a letter from Mitcham attributed by Gosse to the spring of 1608,

when I find myself transported with jollity and love of company, I hang leads at my heels; and reduce to my thoughts my fortunes, my years, the duties of a man, of a friend, of a husband, of a father, and all the incumbencies of a family; when sadness dejects me, either I counter-mine it with another sadness, or I kindle squibs about me again, and fly into sportfulness and company: and I find ever after all, that I am like

---

[41] *John Donne: The Satires, Epigrams, and Verse Letters*, ed. W. Milgate (Oxford, 1967), p. 59, ll. 51–6; p. 31, ll. 114–19.

an exorcist, which had long laboured about one, which at last appears to have the mother, that I still mistake my disease.[42]

The poems are responses to, attempts to rid himself of, extreme emotions, but the process of exorcism is self-defeating or self-betraying: either by landing him, as this letter suggests, at another, equally unhealthy extreme (perhaps best exemplified by 'Oh to vex me contraryes meete in one') or, more common and interesting in the poems, by confirming the strength of the mental state in defiance of which the argumentative process was set to work. In the 'Holy Sonnets' the manipulation of mood is particularly unavailing since he is confronting what he sees as the ultimate reality of his position. Self-bamboozlement is worse than useless. The poem's meaning lives in the tension between the argument and the emotion and this tension tends to make us aware that the despairing sonnets are not, as they may at first appear, balanced by the confident ones.

'Death be not proud' (p. 9), for example, is illuminated by awareness of this characteristic tension. Highly rhetorical and declamatory—

> Death be not proud, though some have called thee
> Mighty and dreadfull, for, thou art not soe—

its tone is one of bravura rather than assurance. It blatantly travesties the character of death and the blatancy discloses an underlying hysteria. Donne first creates the illusion of death as a person: he is proud, he thinks, he tries to kill people. By pretending that death is a person Donne can believe, or appear to believe, that he dominates it. Like the dying Tamburlaine (whose words are no longer oracles), he calls death a 'slave'. But death is far more obviously a beneficiary of 'Fate, chance, kings, and desperate men' than a slave to them. And the very idea of personifying death—as unlike a living, vulnerable, and unpredictable human being as heterogeneous ideas can be—highlights the disparity between the bravuristic view and the actuality. Elsewhere in the poem there is lame logic:

> From rest and sleepe, which but thy pictures bee,
> Much pleasure, then from thee, much more must flow, . . .

---

[42] Edmund Gosse, *The Life and Letters of John Donne* (1899), i. 183–4.

The strength of the 'must' draws attention to the statement's weakness. Donne presents an analogy as an argument, but analogies do not constitute arguments: they merely illustrate them. And even in terms of the analogy, this is not, as Hamlet found, the only imaginable resemblance between sleep and death.

Towards the end of the poem Donne's insecurity emerges more palpably. The question 'why swell'st thou then?' supposes that death is in fact, at this moment in the poem, assuming large proportions in Donne's own mind. And the poem ends with a theatrical gesture: 'Death thou shalt die.' But if the flourish is more than a hollow paradox, it points to the awe in which Donne still holds his subject. Had death been effectively diminished, the verb 'die' would not have seemed a strong one with which to conclude.[43] Martin Luther pointed out the unsatisfactoriness of this trope: 'So death [that of Christ] killed death, but the killing death is life itself. But it is called the death of death, by a vehement indignation of spirit against death.'[44] Donne displays the vehement indignation of spirit but shows little imaginative awareness of the life which for the assured Christian triumphs over death or, more exactly, had already triumphed. Pierre de la Primaudaye also observed that 'our death dieth, and is not able in any sort to hurt us, if we behold with the eies of faith the death of Jesus Christ' but this reassurance had limited application for the obvious reason that death is 'happy to the elect, and unhappy to the reprobate'.[45] In the 'Resurrection' sonnet of 'La Corona' (p. 4) Donne speaks of 'Death, whom thy death slue' and goes on:

> nor shall to mee
> Feare of first or last death, bring miserie,
> If in thy little booke my name thou'enroule.

Although Helen Gardner finds this sonnet 'joyful' (p. 63) the removal of Donne's fears depends on his soul—at present 'stony hard, and yet too fleshly'—being moistened with a drop of

---

[43] I owe this observation to John Carey. See his *John Donne: Life, Mind, and Art*, p. 199.

[44] *A Commentary on St. Paul's Epistle to the Galatians*, trans. E. Middleton, ed. J. P. Fallowes (1940), 83.

[45] Pierre de la Primaudaye, *The French Academie*, trans. T. B[owes] (1589), 757, 750.

Christ's blood. There is, too, the wheedling qualification expressing anxiety about his election.[46] Fear of death should diminish in proportion to the individual's belief in his appropriation of Christ's victory. The conclusion of 'Death be not proud', however, confirms the fear which is the basis of the poem. It is no surprise that shortly afterwards Donne recanted, apologizing to death for his attempt to 'diminish' its menace.[47]

Another apparently confident poem, 'This is my playes last scene' (p. 7), collapses itself because it employs, as Peterson points out, 'a deliberately fallacious argument which dates back at least to the medieval "Debate of the Body and Soul" '.[48] The poem, as often, comes to a climax at the close of the octave, with characteristic terror of God:

> But my'ever-waking part shall see that face,
> Whose feare already shakes my every joynt.

The attempted resolution of this fear lies in the idea that just as his soul and body will separate at death to return to their source—heaven and earth respectively—so also his sins will plummet to hell rather than remain with him until the day of judgement to involve him in their fate. Peterson notices, however, that Donne rejects this argument in 'At the round earths imagin'd corners' by pointing out that 'it is the whole man—not the soul alone—that will be judged on Doomsday.' Moreover, in 'Thou hast made me' (p. 12) the same thought, that sin 't'wards hell doth weigh' him, is not afforded the same relief. Similarly, Donne's invocation of the Lutheran doctrine of imputed righteousness—'Impute me righteous'—is unavailing

---

[46] Helen Gardner prefers 'little booke' to Westmoreland's 'life-booke', though she is, once she has arbitrarily asserted that 'It is plainly not the "Book of Life" ' (p. 63), at a loss to explain either. Only the tense seems to me puzzling. Donne uses the future tense in a similar way in 'As due by many titles' ('thou lov'st mankind well, yet wilt not chuse me' (p. 6)). From his human point of view, of course, disclosure of election is a wished-for future event. Calvin commented on a similar biblical use of the future tense ('As though God did beginne to write in the booke of life, them whom he reckeneth in the numbre of his'): 'the holy ghoste frameth his talke,' he explains, 'to the smale measure of our sense' (*Inst.* 3. 24. 8).

[47] 'Elegy on Mistress Boulstred', *The Epithalamions, Anniversaries, and Epicedes of John Donne*, ed. W. Milgate (Oxford, 1978), 59–61. The first two lines read: 'Death I recant, and say, unsaid by mee | What ere hath slip'd, that might diminish thee.' The dominant metaphor for death in this poem is of a huge beast or bird of prey; people are helpless victims awaiting their turn to be devoured.

[48] Peterson, 'John Donne's "Holy Sonnets" ', p. 509.

since the benefit of Christ's death involved in the doctrine (whereby God's gaze is met by Christ's sinlessness in place of the Christian's sin) was appropriated at conversion and therefore took effect, necessarily, within life. He abuses the doctrine, too, by denuding it of its Christological significance, linking it instead to a mechanical process for shedding sin. Again the self-conscious casuistry is a subtle and effective method of establishing the dominant emotion—this time intense, even physical, terror of God's judgement.

Once we are fully alert to these strategies, the assurance towards which the poems gesture visibly shrivels. Peterson appears to be less alert when his own unified sequence is threatened. Commenting on 'If faithfull soules' (p. 14) he says: "The penitent is in a state of grace: "valiantly I hels wide mouth o'rstride" "[49]—a strange daredevil stance which has little to do with assurance of salvation and much in common with the precarious assertiveness of 'Death be not proud'. The line recalls grim puritan adjurations such as Sir John Hayward's: 'Looke downe into hell, I say, over which now thou hangest, by the slender-twyned threede of this life.'[50] Even in poems which, like this one, manifest a degree of composure Donne's condition is expressed in negative ways. His conception of the state of grace as not going to hell would not have been seen as a sign of spiritual health.

'What if this present' (p. 10) asks in similar vein, 'And can that tongue adjudge thee unto hell . . . ?'; and concludes, I would submit, ambiguously:

> No, no; but as in my idolatrie
> I said to all my profane mistresses,
> Beauty, of pitty, foulnesse onely is
> A signe of rigour: so I say to thee,
> To wicked spirits are horrid shapes assign'd,
> This beauteous forme assures a pitious minde.

The poem's underpinning conceit plays against the Petrarchan notion of the beloved's picture carried at the lover's heart. Donne is practising therapy on himself by presenting his soul with the

---

[49] Ibid. 514.
[50] *The Sanctuarie of a Troubled Soul* (1616), 119.

picture of Christ in place of that of a woman ('Marke in my heart, O Soule, where thou dost dwell, | The picture of Christ crucified'). This is what makes sense (in terms of the poem's unity) of what might seem the incongruous vanity of recalling his love prattle in the sestet. But while picking up this thread may help the poem to justify itself artistically it does not strengthen the case for the poet's spiritual serenity. Donne, who is consistently sceptical about the Petrarchan tradition and its associated Platonic ascent from the physical to the spiritual, literalizes the idea of the 'Picture in my heart' with a vengeance in 'The Dampe' where his *post mortem* is imagined to disclose the identity of his murderess (p. 49). The terms, moreover, of the reassurance he offers himself prompt consideration of the context of such flattery, which would occur, almost certainly, on the point of rejection by his mistresses. That the argument expresses flattery rather than conviction is shown by his Problem 8, which asked, 'Why are the fayrest falsest?'; and, for example, 'Goe, and catche a falling starre' ('No where | Lives a woman true, and faire' (p. 29)). The love poems by no means unequivocally suggest that the beauteous form of his mistress did in fact bespeak a piteous mind. Analogously, Donne knows perfectly well that Christ does adjudge countless millions to hell ('Depart from me, ye cursed, into everlasting fire' (Matt. 25: 41)). Donne's wording seems to imply the wickedness of this action. But this, together with the deceptive analogy, can only provoke disturbing thoughts on his standing with Christ.

'If poysonous mineralls' (p. 8) begins with protest against God and pivots towards penitence, but with deep ambivalence:

> If poysonous mineralls, and if that tree,
> Whose fruit threw death on else immortall us,
> If lecherous goats, if serpents envious
> Cannot be damn'd; Alas; why should I bee?

Like the despairing Faustus and the spiritual autobiographers Donne repines at his innate liability to damnation, unshared by other naturally malignant creatures.[51] He repeats his envy in another sonnet with the sigh, 'You have not sinn'd, nor need be

---

[51] Bald points out this and numerous other close parallels between the 'Holy Sonnets' and *Grace Abounding, Life*, p. 234 n.

timorous' (p. 10). Giles Firmin protests later in the century against the Calvinist theology which produced such cravenness:

He envies the happiness of the beasts that are filled, and play in their pastures. We have heard of him, who when he saw a Toad, stood weeping, because God had made him a *Man*, so excellent a Creature and not a Toad, so abominable; the goodness of God then, it seems, as he apprehended it, made him weep: but this man he meets a Toad, and he weeps also; but why? because he is a *man*, who thinks his estate infinitely worse than the condition of a Toad, and if it were possible to obtain it, would change states with the Toad, that hath no guilt of sin, fears no wrath of God, is not under power of lusts or creatures; God is no enemy to it, which is his miserable estate.[52]

The burden of being human under a God of Calvinist character seems to Donne too heavy. His resentment in this poem indicates that he resists such utter abjectness, which was at a staggering extremity from the humanist aggrandizement of man coexisting with it in another region of his mind. Nevertheless God remains as an irresistible imagined fact. Donne expresses his protest until it mounts to a blasphemous climax. Although emotional, it has not been illogical. But the final strength of such a God is his irrefragability.

Expression of the hardships of the human predicament becomes cruelly self-defeating. God's unreasonableness is of no force as an argument against him, for the only decisive arguments are those from power. For Calvin, God's justice was subsumed to his power: 'For how should he commit any unjustice, which is judge of the world?' (*Inst.* 3. 23. 4), he asks.[53] His justice is vindicated by his power to judge. And Calvin's warning against protest is prudential, not moral: 'What good doth it you therfore with mad searchyng to plunge your selves into the bottomlesse depth, which reason it self teacheth you that it shalbe to your destruction?' (*Inst.* 3. 23. 5). Recognition of this fact of power, of there being no court of appeal beyond an omnipotent God, was tragically made in contemporary literature. In John Marston's *Antonio's Revenge*, for example, Antonio bitterly exclaims:

[52] *The Real Christian, Or a Treatise of Effectual Calling* (1670), 71–2.
[53] Calvin echoes Abraham's question in Genesis 18: 25 but distorts its meaning. There it was an emotional plea for justice; here it is a defence of anything God does as just, specifically decreeing reprobation (with which Abraham had no concern).

> Ay, Heaven, thou may'st; thou mayst Omnipotence.
> What vermin bred of putrefacted slime
> Shall dare expostulate with thy decrees?
>
> (4. 4. 1–3)

Pointing out God's unreasonableness from a human viewpoint constituted for Donne, in his later prose and sermons, the sin of 'murmuring'. The octave of the poem, the protesting part, must therefore be read as an exemplification of Donne's sinfulness, while the sestet consists in repentance for this. There is no attempt to reply to the question:

> And mercy being easie, 'and glorious
> To God, in his sterne wrath, why threatens hee?

So that, unless the cringing exclamation which ensues is brought on by a sudden sense of presumption, the two parts of the poem have no connection with one another.

Like the ending of 'Since she whome I lovd', the fulcrum of this poem disturbs Barbara Lewalski and Helen Gardner. Barbara Lewalski's comment on Donne's protest against God's preference for retribution—'It is a specious argument, as he recognizes in his outcry'—has no textual warrant.[54] Donne only recognizes that he should not advance any argument against God, not that he sees that this argument is unfounded, nor even that it must, objectively, be false. And her remark, presumably intended again to protect Donne's piety, that he 'admits readily that his sins deserve damnation' is seriously misleading since this is pointedly what he does not admit in the poem. He asks why he should be damned but nowhere volunteers an answer for God. Indeed his phrasing in the opening question presents him as an indignantly passive victim even of sin and its punishment by death ('that tree, | Whose fruit threw death on else immortall us'). And to God's mercy he opposes, not the usual (but prejudicial) word 'justice', but 'wrath'. Milton's Satan, who knows himself to be trapped in language which automatically sides with God, speaks of his compulsion to do 'What e'er his wrath, which he calls justice, bids'.[55] In the penitent sestet Donne beseeches God to forget his sins but does not say that they merit damnation.

---

[54] *Protestant Poetics*, p. 269.

[55] *The Poems of John Milton*, ed. J. Carey and A. Fowler (1968), 2. 733. Further references to poems by Milton will be to this edition and embodied in the text.

Gardner, almost by contrast, complains about 'the strained note of such lines as these: "But who am I, that dare dispute with thee? ..." ' (p. xxx). But to a spiritual comprehension like Donne's, thinking such thoughts might provoke God to immediate punitive action and, under such circumstances, excessive grovelling was impossible (though one can agree that such representation of a process in the poet's consciousness—thought-crime followed by penitence—hardly befits a controlled meditation). Donne is in fact echoing St Paul's strained question in Romans 9: 20 ('Nay but, O man, who art thou that repliest against God?'). The context is the notorious passage concerned with predestination which proceeds to the analogy with the potter and his clay. Sebastian Benefield typifies contemporary use of this passage. People who (like Donne) question the decree of reprobation are 'busie and too curious demanders', for 'this point of doctrine, is to be beleeved by faith, not to be examined by reason'. It is easy to see therefore why Donne feels trapped by his very nature into damnation—by 'reason, borne in mee'. It is the reason he has employed in the octave that distinguishes him from the undamnable beasts and exposes him to dire punishment. He cannot avail himself of Benefield's advice in the sestet because he has pre-empted it by asking, reasonably, why he should have been lumbered with the faculty in the first place. Short of a lobotomy, his reason predestines him. Yet he is grimly aware of such warnings as Benefield's to 'them that shall so plead against God' that 'the same God, with his scepter of yron shall crush and breake [them] in peeces like potters vessels'.[56]

So Donne's penitent cry obeys Calvin's dictum that the thought '*O homo, tu quis es?*' should silence such protest.[57] But it may be questioned how far Donne is able to inform such a phrase with Calvin's spirit of abject humility. Henry More, the Cambridge Platonist, suffered in youth from religious despair which he ascribed directly to Calvin's doctrine of double predestination.[58] His manhood coincided, however, with an era in which the rigours of Calvinism were more open to criticism. In

---

[56] Sebastian Benefield, *Eight Sermons Publikely Preached in the University of Oxford . . . in the Yeare 1595* (Oxford, 1614), 7, 8.

[57] *Concerning the Eternal Predestination of God*, trans. and ed. J. K. S. Reid (1961), 19.

[58] Henry More, *Opera Omnia*, ed. John Cockshut (1679), pp. v–vi.

Psychathanasia, still smarting under the memory of his recent terror, he asks:

> Why be not damned souls devoyd of sense,
> If nothing can from wickednesse reclaime;

and again: 'Why will not God save | All mankind?'[59] The lines, especially the last quoted where the line division supplies a Donnian pause in conversational syntax (comparable to the bemused 'and glorious | To God'), are perhaps indebted to this poem. But they do not have its strain. More writes rhetorically of an intellectual conflict which has already been resolved. Donne has only emotions of protest which cannot be formulated into a satisfactory theoretical attitude; instead they have to be repressed.

But prudential orthodoxy is not, I think, the poem's final word. The theological rationality is undermined by the inclusion of a sly irony—a furtive gesture of rebellion perhaps—in pleading for his sin's consignment to oblivion. He prays God to 'make a heavenly Lethean flood, | And drowne in it my sinnes blacke memorie'. God's capacity for voluntary amnesia is frequently appealed to in the Bible,[60] and in fact, though titivated by classical allusion, the lines seem to draw again on a specific biblical context: 'he retaineth not his anger for ever, because he delighteth in mercy. He will turn again, he will have compassion upon us; he will subdue our iniquities; and thou wilt cast all their sins into the depths of the sea' (Mic. 7: 18–19). The snag here, on Donne's side rather than God's, is that he has memorialized his sin in the octave of the poem as certainly as his consequent repentance. It would appear that he was reluctant to deny his perception of God's predilection for sternness (it does not seem to him that the Calvinist God he contends with 'delighteth in mercy') while presenting an extravagant show of submission.

We see in the poems analysed here that the sensibility of Donne's religious poetry is deepened and complicated by the interplay of reason, unreason, and emotion; also, that subversion of the piety the poems gesture towards, far from liberating him,

---

[59] Henry More, *The Complete Poems*, ed. A. B. Grosart (Edinburgh, 1878), 86.

[60] Such appeals are to be found, for example, in Psalm 79: 8 and Isaiah 64: 9. God undertakes to forget sins in Jeremiah 31: 34 and Isaiah 43: 25.

betrays his fear, resentment, protest, and, subsuming them all, despair. The source of the despair can moreover be located in precise Calvinist doctrines. The rationale of Calvinist theology was that it boosted God's sovereignty at the expense of human autonomy: humanity was made quite powerless, powerless to contribute to its salvation in any way, powerless even to reject salvation should God have decided to bestow his grace. And Donne's extreme passivity is a strikingly consistent feature of the sonnets. Even as a suppliant he must wait for God to empower him to repent: 'here on this lowly ground, | Teach mee how to repent' (p. 8); 'That I might in this holy discontent | Mourne with some fruit' (p. 13). When, in one poem, he does lay claim to 'true griefe' he credits this to God who 'put it in my breast' ('If faithfull soules', p. 14). The sestet of 'Oh my blacke Soule' (p. 7) begins:

> Yet grace, if thou repent, thou canst not lacke;
> But who shall give thee that grace to beginne?

The sonnet's turning tide is stemmed by the 'But' of the tenth line so that the poem's structure enforces the implication that the necessary grace may be withheld. Donne is alluding to the doctrine of prevenient grace, the doctrine that God must dispose people to repentance before they can enact it. In asking, 'But who shall give thee that grace to beginne?' Donne implicitly endorses the Calvinist elaboration that, because God has determined not to save the majority of mankind, such grace is likely to be denied. Richard Hooker cleverly removes the emphasis from God's selectivity when he touches on such questions: 'It is not,' he says, 'in every, no, not in any man's own mere ability, freedom, and power, to be saved, no man's salvation being possible without grace.'[61] And Catholics insisted that God readily offered the grace to repent.[62]

Another poem, in its first line, poses the question, 'Thou hast made me, And shall thy worke decay?' (p. 12). It is by no means an idle one assuming a negative reply. Donne, in his sermons, both recognized and admired God's ability to forsake his

---

[61] *Works*, ed. J. Keble (Oxford, 1836), ii. 752.
[62] See Robert Parsons, *A Christian Directorie Guiding Men to their Salvation* (1585), i. 806.

creatures; and he insisted as a preacher that acceptance of the possibility of this happening to oneself was essential to a Christian response to God (see, for example, *Sermons*, viii. 279, 290). The poem goes on to express Donne's despair and his feeling that sin is weighing him down towards hell. It is from this sonnet that Martz exemplifies Donne's meditational technique: 'we watch the speaker,' he says, 'in the octave of the poem, deliberately arouse sensations of "despaire" and "terrour" at the thoughts of sin and death and hell, and then, in the sestet, firmly repel them by confidence in God's grace.'[63] The inarticulate vagueness of 'Such terror' (Despaire behind, and death before doth cast | Such terrour'), where the line-ending enacts Donne's helpless groping for a phrase adequate to his feeling (the phrase itself gesticulating at it), does not suggest the deliberate generation of sensations. More importantly, the sestet, which according to Martz repels the despair, can do no more than qualify it with a contingency.

The sestet is connected to the octave by a sustained conceit:

> and my feebled flesh doth waste
> By sinne in it, which it t'wards hell doth weigh;
> Onely thou art above, and when towards thee
> By thy leave I can looke, I rise againe:
> But our old subtle foe so tempteth me,
> That not one houre I can my selfe sustaine;
> Thy Grace may wing me to prevent his art
> And thou like Adamant draw mine iron heart.

The spatial metaphor is elaborated and belongs, it appears, to a circulating figurative discourse which occupied the protestant imagination. The commonest trope here is that of looking up to God, which signalled repentance and drew mercy. But as in 'Oh my blacke Soule' the ability to repent, or look up, depends on God's permission. The 'By thy leave' obstructs the incipient optimism of the sestet, in the same tenth-line position. Without God's permission to repent Donne continues to sink towards hell under the weight of his sins, unable to remain buoyant by his own efforts. As Helen Gardner observes (p. 75) what he is tempted to by the devil is despair, so, as for Bunyan, sinking in despair and sinking to hell is a continuous process.

---

[63] Martz, *Poetry of Meditation*, p. 132.

'Repentance', said Robert Burton, 'is a . . . spiritual wing to erear us . . . an attractive loadstone to draw God's mercy and graces unto us' (iii. 413).[64] This looks on the bright side of the Calvinist teaching on the irresistibility of grace to which Donne's identical emblem-type metaphors less sanguinely allude. Repentance itself (sometimes referred to as the grace of repentance) is a divine rescue operation. On God's wing, as for Herbert in 'Easter Wings', heavenward flight is guaranteed. Repentance is fused with salvation as a single process (or as links in the golden chain of elect experiences). Yet Donne's verb 'may' is consistent with the other examples of his sense of being at God's whimsical mercy. It is in God's power to supply such grace and it is possible that he will choose to do so, but Donne can muster no confident anticipation of it; his conception of God evidently did not permit this. Should God bestow his adamantine grace, Donne will be drawn however hard (iron) his heart is. Knowing that the process had such mechanical certainty and lay outside his control made awareness of not being drawn all the more crushing. Helen Gardner's observation that 'Donne comments on the dangers of the doctrine of the "irresistibility of grace" in a sermon' (p. 75) is diversionary since it would have been more apposite to have pointed out that these lines depend on his subscription to it. What he later thought is another matter (actually, while objecting to the phrase as jargon, he substituted the barely different 'infallibility'[65]). Donne is adhering strictly to Calvin—in preference, as we noted in discussing 'Batter my heart', to Augustine. Calvin considered that the idea of successful resistance implied both an infringement of God's sovereignty and an overestimation of the effectiveness of the human will.

That Donne is utilizing a common fund of protestant discourse can be confirmed by Massinger's use of the same complete conceit (except for the magnet) to express utter despair. 'Look upward | I dare not,' says the riotously self-accusing Grimaldi:

> No, I must downeward, downeward: though repentance
> Could borrow all the glorious wings of grace,

---

[64] Compare also Thomas May, *The Heir*, Robert Dodsley, ed., *A Selection of Old English Plays*, 4th edn. rev. and ed. W. C. Hazlitt (1874–6), xi. 515: 'There was no other loadstone could attract | His iron heart.'

[65] William Halewood remarks on this, *Poetry of Grace*, pp. 61–2.

> My mountainous waight of sins, would cracke their pinions.
> And sincke them to hell with me.[66]

Donne's sestet uses the conceit less melodramatically to express acute anxiety about his spiritual prospects. He plainly did not feel magnetized (who can blame him?) by the God in whom he believed. The conclusion contradicts Martz with respect both to the religious tradition to which the content belongs and to the state of mind to which it testifies. It is certainly true that the Jesuits, especially Fray Luis of Granada, gave powerful expression to fear of God, but the deliberateness of its arousal was matched by the efficacy of its banishment. Donne's poem reveals that his fear pre-dates and post-dates the poem, that it lodges in the poet's psyche.

'As due by many titles' (p. 6) registers Calvinist influence in its reversal of the usually attempted move from fear to hope. It begins by enumerating God's rights over Donne and recalling the lengths God has gone to for him. Indeed the form of the opening ('As due by many titles I resigne | My selfe to thee'), with its reluctant pause—its regretful sigh—before delivering this precious object, 'My selfe', suggests that it is Donne who has to conquer his own resistance. But the poem ends by entertaining the doubt that God will not trouble himself over his individual soul, despite his love for mankind:

> Why doth the devill then usurpe in mee?
> Why doth he steale, nay ravish that's thy right?
> Except thou rise and for thine owne worke fight,
> Oh I shall soone despaire, when I doe see
> That thou lov'st mankind well, yet wilt not chuse me,
> And Satan hates mee, yet is loth to lose mee.

The lines are haunted by the fear that God will disdain to intervene in Donne's behalf. God could exert himself to beat off the devil, but whether he does so will depend on his free, unobligated choice. So again the doctrinal basis of the poem is decidedly Lutheran and Calvinist. Martin Luther compared the human will to a horse:

---

[66] *The Renegado* (3. 2. 63–4, 69–72), *The Plays and Poems of Philip Massinger*, ed. Philip Edwards and Colin Gibson (Oxford, 1976), vol. ii. The play was licensed for performance in 1624 so it is unlikely that it was influenced by Donne's poem (still in manuscript).

When God sits upon it, then it desires to go and does go where God wills
. . . When Satan sits upon it, it desires to go and does go where Satan
wills, and it has no choice as to which rider it will carry, nor can it seek
him, but the riders themselves dispute its possession.[67]

This poem, it will be noticed, does not presume to beg God for
help; merely it represents to him reasons why he might choose to
'rise and for thine owne worke fight'. Helen Gardner and
Douglas Peterson ameliorate this conditional defeatism by
paraphrasing respectively that Donne 'laments the power of the
devil upon him and asks for grace' (p. li) and that he 'seek[s]
the grace that is essential to contrite sorrow'.[68] Donne evidently
feels, however, that the reasons he has supplied for God's intervention are not conclusive, the ending gloomily predicting
despair.

Calvinist influence is reinforced in the poem where Donne
complains to God 'That thou lov'st mankind well, yet wilt not
chuse me'. William Perkins ridiculed the syllogism: '*Christ died for
all men*: Thou art a man: Therefore Christ died for thee.'[69] And
although in his ministry Donne attacked the Calvinist qualification of 'all', in such contexts, to mean 'all sorts' (see *Sermons*,
v. 53; viii. 125; iv. 81), the Calvinist interpretation finds
unequivocal acceptance in this sonnet; loving mankind does not
signify loving John Donne (those whom God did not choose he
necessarily hated for their sin). Such doctrine is Hooker's
implicit target when he writes of the devil's attack on simple faith
in 'the naked promise of God': he corrupts the mind 'with many
imaginations of repugnancy and contrariety between the promise
of God and those things which sense or experience or some other
fore-conceived persuasion hath imprinted'.[70] Catholics, moreover, were aggressively explicit on this point: 'What is ther in this
general and universal promises,' asks Robert Parsons, 'whereof
anie man in the world should have pretence, to make any least
doubt or question?'[71] It was only through the exercise of free will
that the Catholic could forfeit salvation.

[67] Quoted by Gerhard Ebeling, *Luther: An Introduction to his Thought*, trans.
R. A. Wilson (1970), 222. Calvin, who used the same metaphor, gave imaginative
reality to the consequences for the reprobate (*Inst.* 2. 4. 1).

[68] Peterson, 'John Donne's "Holy Sonnets" ', p. 508.

[69] *Works*, p. 122.

[70] *Works*, iii. 593.

[71] Parsons, *Christian Directorie*, i. 551.

This ending is consistent with the curiously self-defeating conclusion to 'At the round earths imagin'd corners' (p. 8):

> Teach mee how to repent; for that's as good
> As if thou'hadst seal'd my pardon, with thy blood.

Of course for the Christian, and most emphatically for the protestant, there was no route to salvation alternative to Christ's atoning death. The allusion seems to be to the Calvinist doctrine of limited atonement, according to which Christ died only for the elect. This is the case even if Donne's expression is inaccurate; he may mean that if he is empowered to repent that will provide evidence that Christ died for him—so, conversely, if he is not so empowered, Christ did not die for him. That the octave of 'As due by many titles' suggests that Christ's blood has bought him is an inconsistency which may be explained, like the changing picture of God in 'Since she whome I lovd', by that sonnet's pivot effect. The poem enacts realization of the greater inner conviction commanded in Donne by the Calvinist view. Hence the 'Why . . . then' of the ninth line: the logic of Christ's redemption of all mankind would appear to be that everyone was free to accept or reject this—a freedom Donne does not feel.[72] Once again we can see that Donne presents himself as a victim of Calvinist tenets which he appears to have found irresistible.

In line with Calvinist theology, then, Donne sees God as 1. beyond the scrutiny of human reason and morals; 2. arbitrarily selective in the bestowal of the grace necessary to repentance and thus to salvation; 3. irresistible by those he chooses; 4. loving all kinds of person but not all individuals. Human faculties are, moreover, totally depraved:[73] conversion is through divine rape or not at all. If it is asked where Donne speaks of double predestination, of an eternal decree of reprobation, it may be replied that while this was commonly the focus of anxiety, the other Calvinist doctrines logically intertwined with it constituted an adequate recipe for despair. He points to it (in 'If poysonous

---

[72] In more theological terms Donne may be seen to oscillate in these two poems between the positions of Beza and Calvin (see discussion in ch. 1, 'Theological Basis'). The inconsistency suggests, as I indicated before, that this distinction was not perceived as significant.

[73] Donne supported the doctrine of total depravity even in his sermons. For man to suppose there was anything undepraved about him was, he thought, to multiply sins against God: there was no rectitude in the human will (*Sermons*, x. 135).

mineralls' for example) while refraining from explicit mention.
He did, it is true, later attack the doctrine of reprobation from
eternity but it was a limited form of dissent which did little to
affect the imaginative picture of God. He rejected the idea that
God could 'make us to damne us' but nevertheless believed that
everyone was born part of the *massa damnata*, that there was a
'separation of vessels of honour and dishonour in Election and
Reprobation' which, he said, 'was in Christ Jesus', and,
crucially, that it was only 'by the working of Gods Spirit' that the
elect acquired 'a desire, and after a modest assurance' of
salvation (*Sermons*, ii. 34, 170, 323). Reprobation remained,
therefore, but followed the Fall and it was predestined so far as
individuals were concerned because they could not will their
salvation. A gauge of his continuing extremism (in our terms) is
his ability to declare, in a late sermon, that it was possible to be
damned in the womb, 'though we be *never borne*' (x. 232).[74]

The most significant theological influence on the 'Holy
Sonnets', then, is not Jesuit or Catholic, not Anglo-Catholic or
even Hookerian-Anglican but Calvinist. Why, though, should
Donne, a Catholic by upbringing and finally a preacher to the
court of Charles I, write Calvinist poetry? The answer of
historians presents itself again: Calvinism held sway in the
Church of England to which he turned and was especially
powerful in the period at which most of the sonnets are now
thought to have been written. Helen Gardner argues for the years
1609–10 as the probable date of composition for the 'Holy
Sonnets', excluding the Westmoreland additions (pp. xlii l). The
evidence for 'Death be not proud' belonging to this period is
almost incontrovertible and some of the other evidence is strong.
Acceptance of this dating means that Donne wrote the poems
long before the ascendancy of Laud—before, that is, those who
promoted Calvinist dogma were, by the expedient of identifying
them with supposedly disreputable 'puritans', polarized to an
ideological extremity, and before this manoeuvre enabled a
critique of Calvinism, in some circles, to be confidently developed.
To quote a different authority for this point, W. K. Jordan
observes that Laud's policies 'admitted no place for the

---

[74] The extremism here is specifically Calvinist. Calvin's 'Confessio Fidei Gallicana'
of 1559 proclaims the damnation 'even of little children in the mother's womb'
(P. Schaff, *The Creeds of the Evangelical Protestant Churches* (1877), 366).

toleration . . . of men who had a decade before been regarded as most truly representative of the Church of England'.[75] Donne's mind, like Burton's, soaked up the prevailing orthodoxy (though it was penetrated much more deeply).

It would be possible, however, to overstate this point. When the Lambeth Articles, which formulated the main points of Calvinism at its most uncompromising, were approved by the Archbishops of Canterbury and York in 1595, some circumspect criticism was voiced. Lancelot Andrewes, who wrote a 'Judgment of the Lambeth Articles' purportedly in support of them, objected to the idea that God condemned the reprobate to sin.[76] He approaches the Arminian position in maintaining instead that God would bestow grace on everyone were it not for the hardening of the will. And when Richard Hooker gave his version of the Articles he discreetly omitted the sixth, which required of the elect 'full assurance of faith', and reworded Article VIII in such a way as to leave open the possibility that God seeks to draw all people to Christ.[77] Thomas Fuller can nevertheless be trusted when he affirms of the Lambeth Articles that 'Their testimony is an infallible evidence what was the general doctrine of England in that age about the forenamed controversies.'[78] Laud's was the first authoritative voice to reject them out of hand.[79]

Donne could, then, like Hooker and Andrewes, have quietly dissented from the most harsh and morally repugnant elements of Calvinist dogma. He was not, moreover, a clergyman so he need not, like Burton, have been cagily sceptical or reluctantly conformist. Hooker, Andrewes, and others were able to steer around Calvinist doctrinal emphases in their ecclesiastical careers. That Donne does not do so in his private poetry indicates more, then, than political duress. His poetic use of Calvinist ideas (often at turning points or climaxes) bespeaks an emotional conviction of their truth.

This, I think, must be the basis for explaining what looks most bizarre of all: not that Calvinist doctrines are registered but that

[75] W. K. Jordan, *The Development of Religious Toleration in England. From the Accession of James I to the Convention of the Long Parliament (1603–1640)* (1936), 129–30.

[76] Lancelot Andrewes, *Minor Works*, ed. J. Bliss (1846).

[77] *Works*, ii. 752–3.

[78] *The Church History of Britain*, ed. J. S. Brewer (Oxford, 1845), v. 221.

[79] William Laud, *The Works*, ed. W. Scott and J. Bliss (Oxford, 1847–60), i. 130–1.

the tails of so many of the poems seem to sting their author with them. Donne prided himself on his honesty, an honesty which particularly showed itself in sceptical testing of the lines he tried to sell himself. He makes two surprisingly unguarded references to it ('my muses white sincerity', and 'my mindes white truth' (pp. 2, 14)) in the divine poems. Candour seems to be the one thing he unequivocally feels he has earned the right to claim for himself. Extreme candour is probably never psychologically simple, and certainly is not in Donne; but one or two observations may help towards understanding. First, I have indicated in my analysis Donne's resistance to the total reconstruction of his identity ('make me new', not 'seeke to mend' (p. 11)) which would be required before he could persuasively assume the posture of the humble Christian. To some extent the Calvinist doctrines which seemed to exclude him and provoked suspicion and resentment were a way of keeping at arm's length a God he did not, finally, want any nearer. It is then a plausible extension of this argument to suggest that some of his resistance was unconscious (after all Donne himself was sufficiently mystified by it to attribute it to the devil), and insinuated its way into poems in the form of doctrinal misstatements. Thirdly, Calvinism itself provides a motive for the combination of exacting honesty about one's spiritual state and insistence on that sincerity which was relevant to others (Richard Kilby, for example) and may very well apply to Donne. Such ruthless honesty provided the only hope for future salvation. Donne preferred to face up to his present recalcitrance and sense of rejection rather than consign himself to the irredeemable class of hypocrites (witness, for example, 'Oh to vex me'). He understood the futility of aping a piety he did not feel, though his poems track his attempts to approach God and probe the resistance on both sides. It is this honesty with himself that tacitly pleads for him with God. But all these notes rest on the premiss that Donne was, when he wrote the 'Holy Sonnets', emotionally persuaded of the truth of the negative side of Calvinism. My analysis of the textual evidence should have shown this to be so; but a further layer of explanation ties together the dominant religious ideology of Donne's society with the position he occupied in it.

Donne had an imaginative comprehension of what it was in

Calvinism that spoke to the condition of so many in this transitional period of social and economic history and especially, of course, to his own predicament. As R. C. Bald said, the years 1607–10 were probably the most troubled in Donne's life. L. C. Knights observes that his letters 'in the period between his marriage and his ordination show how mere poverty can distort the outlook and depress the spirit. There is no need to-day to emphasize the miseries of unemployment.'[80] Donne himself makes the connection between his circumstances and his spiritual state when he says in 'A Litanie' that 'want, sent but to tame,' can 'worke despaire a breach to enter in' (p. 23 no. xxi): the affliction is interpretable as evidence of implacable divine hostility rather than discipline. In Donne's authoritarian society the feeling of rejection aggravated and made sense of the miseries in the cruellest manner. Everything that happened was 'sent' for a purpose. One cannot speak of 'mere poverty' when ideological extrapolation was itself an inherent part of the experience.[81] It has been pointed out that one group which was particularly susceptible to Calvinism during the Reformation comprised gentlemen who felt socially or economically excluded from their proper rank.[82] John Donne's failure to find a suitable niche in society was, in his late thirties, at its most emphatic. Calvinism's peculiar appeal seems to have resided in its ability to corroborate theologically the feeling or knowledge in post-medieval society that individual success or failure in (and beyond) life were both likely to be extreme and lay outside one's own control.

For Donne divine patronage proved as elusive and had to be waited on as helplessly as secular. As late as 1621 he wrote suing for advancement to the Duke of Buckingham: 'to tell your Lordship that I ly in a corner, as a clodd of clay, attendinge what kinde of vessell yt shall please you to make of Your Lordship's

[80] 'Seventeenth-Century Melancholy', *The Criterion*, 13 (1933–4), 108.

[81] John Carey observes that there is 'no theme to which [Donne] returns more often in his sermons' than the need for an occupation (p. 60). Donne dated his conversion from his ordination (Bald, *Life*, p. 492) and although an analysis of his later writing could show that he never shook off anxiety about his salvation it is clear that he had previously been unable to overcome the conviction that a calling was a pre-condition.

[82] See D. W. Howe, 'The Decline of Calvinism: An Approach to its Study', *Comparative Studies in Society and History*, 14 (1972), 319.

humblest and thankfullest and devotedst servant'.[83] He alludes, more directly than in 'If poysonous mineralls', to the Pauline idea, much leant on by Calvinists, of the vessels of honour (election) and dishonour (reprobation) and the right of the potter to dispose of his clay as he willed. No Calvinist doctrine was absolutely novel in the history of the church. What was new were the historical circumstances which proved hospitable to it. Donne shared in these. He was a man of supreme ability, fully developed by his education, whose fortunes were determined not by this ability but by the caprice of those who could elect to patronize him. By the mid-life period in which the 'Holy Sonnets' were written it was painfully clear that self-recommendation and personal effort were unavailing: the favour of the great was distributed arbitrarily and the economic structure ensured that only the minority could be lucky. It is not strange that Donne accepted as cosmic reality the orthodox ideology of his day when that ideology seemed such an accurate projection from his own experience of life. He felt his dependence on God to resemble his dependence on secular patronage with its attendant frustration, humiliation, and despair.

[83] Quoted by Bald, *Life*, p. 372; David Aers and Gunther Kress remark on the similarity of the language in which Donne addresses God and his would-be patrons. Their analysis of some of Donne's verse letters reveals the troubled sense of self which resulted from his position as an alienated intellectual unable to detach himself from the social structures which excluded him (David Aers, Bob Hodge, and Gunther Kress, *Literature, Language and Society in England 1580–1680* (Dublin, 1981), 68–9, 23–48).

7

Doctor Faustus and Puritan Culture: Confronting the Persecutory Imagination

Doctor Faustus is a more literal document than modern criticism has made it. It reveals rawly and authentically what it could feel like to be at the sharp end of Reformation thinking. First, since the case is not generally accepted by critics, I give reasons for seeing the theology in the play as accurately dramatized Calvinist dogma.[1] Then I explore how the play exploits in its audience the cultural divisions at once rationalized and exacerbated by this theology. This leads to an examination of the consciousness invested in Faustus himself in the cultural circumstances to which it is confined.

Calvin had a three-tiered concept of causation which the Prologue to *Doctor Faustus* appears to articulate. There is 'no absurditie', thought Calvin, 'that one selfe acte be ascribed to God, to Satan, and to man' (*Inst.* 2. 4. 2). God first determined what would happen. Then the devil would for his own malignant purposes necessarily set about effecting what God had decreed. Finally human will would concur with what had been determined twice over by these greater powers. Calvin explains:

Where it is sayde that the will of a naturall man is subject to the rule of the Devell, to be stirred by him, it is not mente thereby that man as it were striving agaynst it, and resistyng is compelled to obeye, as we compell bondeslaves against their wil, by reason of beying their lordes, to do our commaundementes: but that beyng bewitched with the deceites of Satan, it of necessitie yeldeth it selfe obedient to every

---

[1] See also Wilbur Sanders, *The Dramatist and the Received Idea: Studies in the Plays of Marlowe and Shakespeare* (Cambridge, 1968), chs. 11, 12; P. R. Sellin, 'The Hidden God: Reformation Awe in Renaissance Literature', in R. Kinsman, ed., *The Darker Vision of the Renaissance: Beyond the Fields of Reason* (Berkeley, 1974), 177–86; R. G. Hunter, *Shakespeare and the Mystery of God's Judgments* (Athens, Ga., 1976), chs. 2, 3; A. Sinfield, *Literature in Protestant England 1560–1660* (Beckenham, 1983), 116–20. All have contributed valuably to a Calvinist reading of the play, though I should say I disagree with Hunter (pp. 43 ff.) and Sinfield (p. 119) that it will also support a 'semi-Pelagian' or 'Arminian' interpretation. At points in the first section there will inevitably be some overlap with these critics.

leadyng of him. For whome the Lord vouchesaveth not to rule with his spirite, them by just judgement he sendeth away to be moved of Satan. (*Inst.* 2. 4. 1)

It is this idea of the convergence of wills on the same event, combined with the inevitability of human succumbing to demonic mesmerism, which is often missed in casual discussion of Calvinism, as if Calvinist theology could only be expressed by a crude display of *force majeure*.

So it is that the apparent contradiction in Marlowe's Prologue between the idea of God conspiring Faustus's overthrow and Faustus preferring magic to heaven would, to a Calvinist, make perfect sense (whatever the logical strain apparent to us). The three phases of causation are rehearsed in their correct order:

> And melting heavens conspirde his overthrow.
> For falling to a divelish exercise . . .
> He surffets upon cursed Negromancy . . .
> Which he preferres before his chiefest blisse.[2]

It may appear gratuitous for God to conspire the fall of an Icarus, which seems to occur by natural process, but, as the 'For' of the next line shows, this line announces a shift to a different level of explanation.[3] These closing lines supply the causal logic behind the process the Prologue has been reviewing. God first conspires by means of predestinarian decrees which are to be executed through providence in which, in the case of the reprobate, the devil plays an active manipulative part. Lastly there is the concurrence of the human will, chiming in with an antecedent necessity. While Faustus's choice is thus doubly determined he is still held responsible, as the word 'preferres' suggests, for the evil he perpetrates. Bewitched though he inevitably is, he none the less yields to the devil's leading.

---

[2] Except where specified I have used the A-Text of the parallel-text edition by W. W. Greg, *Marlowe's Doctor Faustus 1604, 1616* (Oxford, 1950). Most scholars have now, it seems, rejected Greg's argument for the higher authority of the B-Text (see Constance Brown Kuriyana, 'Dr Greg and *Doctor Faustus*: The Supposed Originality of the 1616 Text', *ELR* 5 (1975), 171–97). But since the case has not been established that Marlowe had no hand in the B-Text readings and since they can, anyway, be of interest, I have sometimes drawn on them, but nowhere, I believe, to make a point contradicted by evidence in A.

[3] Nicholas Brooke suspects that this use of 'conspire' is 'simply conventional' but does not explain what he means or cite supporting evidence ('The Moral Tragedy of *Doctor Faustus*', *Cambridge Journal*, 5 (1952), 662–88).

Knowing from the Prologue what is to become of him we then discover Faustus going through the motions of choice. Tossing aside alternative pursuits he turns demonstratively to the books of magic already on his desk by which he is entranced (1. 79 ff.). 'Tis Magicke, Magicke', he exults a few lines later, 'that hath ravisht mee' (1. 143)—the word deftly suggesting spellbound assent. He then appears to conjure up a devil; but according to 'B' the devils are already on stage, and in both versions, on being asked, 'Did not my conjuring speeches raise thee?', Mephostophilis replies:

> That was the cause, but yet per accident,
> For when we heare one racke the name of God,
> Abjure the scriptures, and his Saviour Christ,
> Wee flye, in hope to get his glorious soule.
>
>   (3. 290–4)

Faustus's will is a causal wheel within wheels. Robert Burton saw that magicians were duped (or themselves bewitched) in this way: 'Not that there is any power at all in those spells, charms, characters, and barbarous words; but that the devil doth use such means to delude them' (*Anatomy*, i. 205). It was, then, a familiar 'devilish exercise'. As Faustus accusingly reflects:

> O thou bewitching fiend, 'twas thy temptation,
> Hath rob'd me of eternall happinesse.
>
>   (B. 5. 2. 1986–7)

Far from denying the charge Mephostophilis antedates his manipulative role:

>   when thou took'st the booke,
> To view the Scriptures, then I turn'd the leaves
> And led thine eye.
>
>   (B. 5. 2. 1990–2)

Alan Sinfield, who sees the Calvinist implication of these lines, allows the possibility that Mephostophilis is lying.[4] Mephostophilis risked considerable frankness, however, in pointing out that Faustus's wand-waving was ineffectual; and no one supposes he is lying when he explains to Faustus what hell is like. He

---

[4] *Literature in Protestant England*, pp. 116, 119.

appears unable, even, to lie about who made the world. On this occasion no purpose would be served by deception: even the Good Angel has given up on Faustus. Faustus's famous selective quotation, the valediction to divinity which enables him to turn to magic (original, incidentally, to the play) is, therefore, also part of the devilish exercise. By combining Mephostophilis's confession with the juxtaposition of these texts Marlowe dramatizes what Luther called 'the Devil's syllogism'.[5] Luther was solicitous, however, about those who appeared to psyche themselves out of salvation by succumbing to the devil's pseudo-logic. For Calvin, content in the *Institution* to spectate on the reprobate snaring themselves, the two texts ('The reward of sinne is death' and 'If we say that we have no sinne, | We deceive our selves, and theres no truth in us' (1. 70, 72–3)) enforce a binding logic on the reprobate: their inevitable sin entails damnation by a 'just' God. Marlowe's literalization conveys not the Lutheran emphasis ('This is how the devil wants you to think') but the Calvinist ('This is how the devil, carrying out divine fiat, takes possession of your faculties and lays claim to your soul').

What, though, of the Good Angel and the Old Man who appear to some to countervail the delusive Calvinism of the evil agents?[6] While Calvinists denied that the reprobate were free to repent they did not deny that they had terrified impulses to do so. The elect should, moreover, exhort them to this so that their resistance could confirm their rightful condemnation: 'whome soever we finde,' said Calvin, 'we shall travaile to make him partaker of peace' although 'it shalbe the worke of God to make it profitable to them whome he hath foreknowen and predestinate.' As for the reprobate, when they 'do not obey the word of God opened unto them, that shalbe wel imputed to the malice and perversenesse of their heart, so that this be therwithal added that

---

[5] See S. Snyder, 'The Left Hand of God: Despair in Medieval and Renaissance Tradition', *SIR* 12 (1965), 18–59, pp. 30–1.

[6] Pauline Honderich, in an article entitled 'John Calvin and *Doctor Faustus*' (*MLR* 68 (1973), 1–13) argues that it is the devils who are Calvinists and that Faustus is guilty of 'an individual error' (p. 10) in accepting their theology rather than the 'moderate Anglican conception of human destiny' (p. 13). It is a common view, which I hope I have rebutted. Taking this line, it should further be remarked, forces the play to point the dotty moral that God consigns Faustus to everlasting torment for the 'error' of failing to realize how merciful he is.

thei are therfore geven into this perversnesse' in order that they
should 'set forth his glorie with their damnation' (*Inst.* 3. 23. 14;
3. 24. 14).[7] Victims, moreover, could take the same view of the
good offices they received. A Mr Collins, for example, believed
he was 'one of those whom the means of grace was only for their
hardening against the day of wrath'.[8] It was only in the late
seventeenth century that a species of Calvinism developed in
England in which preaching to the unconvertible was deprecated—so the forces of good in *Doctor Faustus* behave as good
Calvinists.[9]

The Good Angel and the Old Man should be viewed in their
relation to the morality tradition because they are ironized
conventions. The point of the external tempters and counsellors,
whether or not they personified abstractions, was, in the
traditional morality, to represent alternatives the hero could
choose the victor. Marlowe inverts the morality role of the
endowed with the decisive power of free will.'[10] While the Good
and Bad Angels in *Doctor Faustus* possess an external reality
(Calvin insisted that angels were more than divine excitations of
the mind (*Inst.* 1. 14. 19)), Marlowe encourages the belief that
they are simultaneously forces which do combat inside Faustus's
mind: 'Hell strives with grace for conquest in my breast'
(13. 1331). As in Donne's sonnets, the site of struggle does not
choose the victor. Marlowe inverts the morality role of the
hero's confederates (such as the good and bad angels in *The Castle
of Perseverance*): instead of objectifying the hero's freedom to
choose between possibilities external to him (or 'giv[ing] voice to
the concept of free will'[11]), they invade his mind and take over his
will. The Good Angel represents hopeful impulses in Faustus; the
Bad Angel represents the knowledge based on the idea of
reprobation which crushes them ('Faustus, repent yet, God wil
pitty thee . . . I but Faustus never shal repent' (5. 641, 646)).

---

[7] See Sellin, 'The Hidden God', p. 181; Sinfield, *Literature in Protestant England*, p. 118.

[8] 'The Relation of Mr. Collins' in *The Diary of Michael Wigglesworth 1653–1657*, ed.
E. S. Morgan (New York, 1965), 108.

[9] See Peter Toon, *The Emergence of Hyper-Calvinism in English Nonconformity 1689–1765*
(1967), 151 *et passim*.

[10] Robert Potter, *The English Morality Play: Origins, History, and Influence of a
Dramatic Tradition* (1975), 41.

[11] Martha Tuck Rozett, *The Doctrine of Election and the Emergence of Elizabethan
Tragedy* (Princeton, 1984), 218.

Faustus, like Mr Collins, draws the doleful inference ('My hearts so hardened I cannot repent' (646)). As with Bunyan, such representation of mental processes—the counterparting of internal and external spiritual agents—is less mechanically allegorized than might be assumed. Many of Sir Richard Napier's patients who despaired of salvation were convinced, for example, that their good angel had been vanquished.[12]

Robert Potter takes the Old Man to be 'a perfectly rendered example of the morality agent of repentance'.[13] The structural position he occupies suggests that he is a relic of the morality. Confession in *Everyman*, Mercy in *Mankind*, Good Hope in *Magnyficence*, even Repentance in *Piers Plowman*, all stand in for the Catholic priest who has the apostolic authority to dispense divine mercy: 'the least priest in the world,' says Confession, '. . . beareth the keys [of the blessed sacraments], and thereof hath the cure | For man's redemption.'[14] *Faustus*'s Old Man is, however, what we are told he is: an old man. The painracked lines he speaks after Faustus's departure, for which there is no comparable humanizing detail in the morality treatment of its priest-figures, ought to deter the impulse to abstract allegory from him.[15] Far from the allegorical miracle-worker of which the audience might have an atavistic expectation, he appears as emphatically enfeebled, lacking the authority to overrule Faustus's own conscience. Transplanted from his medieval habitat he points up Faustus's isolation from assistance and the painful consequences of Luther's promotion of the priesthood of all believers. The troubled individual cannot appeal to an authority higher than his own conscience, or consciousness of his spiritual state.

[12] Michael MacDonald, *Mystical Bedlam: Madness, Anxiety, and Healing in Seventeenth-Century England* (Cambridge, 1981), 144.

[13] *English Morality Play*, p. 126.

[14] *Everyman and Medieval Miracle Plays*, ed. A. C. Cawley (1977), ll. 715–18. Further line references to morality plays, embodied in the text, are to these editions: *Mankind* and *Nice Wanton* in *English Moral Interludes*, ed. Glynne Wickham (1976); *Like Will to Like* in *Four Tudor Interludes*, ed. J. A. B. Somerset (1974); Nathaniel Woodes, *The Conflict of Conscience*, facsimile, ed. J. H. Davis and F. P. Wilson (1952).

[15] Martha Tuck Rozett's recent emollient treatment of Elizabethan puritanism—which she says, quite wrongly, preached that 'repentance is everywhere and at all times possible'—leads her to the arbitrary assertion that 'The Old Man is not of the same order of reality as the other human characters in the play; rather he is an allegorical embodiment of divine love and mercy' (*The Doctrine of Election*, pp. 209, 234).

Paul Kocher believes that the Old Man's lines about an angel he says he sees hovering over Faustus's head, offering to pour grace from a vial into his soul (13. 1320–2), 'sum up the theological meaning of the play. Coming from a character whose Christian faith even Mephostophilis admires, they make untenable any theory that Faustus' fall is predetermined in a Calvinistic sense.'[16] As an elect, however, the Old Man can only extrapolate from his own experience of God's mercy. There is no stage direction to indicate this angel's presence (although the Good and Bad Angels do, of course, appear on other occasions and Mephostophilis is at this moment on hand to oblige the suicidal Faustus with a dagger). The vial of grace is, moreover, self-evidently figurative (grace is not a liquid). The Old Man speaks of his own vision: as an elect he could count on troops of angels as agents of grace on all sides (*Inst.* 1. 14. 7). Looked at from a complementary angle, the irony of the Old Man pointing to the 'angel' over Faustus's head is that his problem is precisely his inability to 'look up'. Were he able to do so the entourage of the elect would leap into existence for him. He is denied the ability to repent. As he explains to the Scholars, one of whom exhorts him to 'looke up to heaven' (14. 1400): 'I would lift up my hands, but see, they hold them, they hold | them' (1419–20). For him it is the devils whose imaginative reality is overpowering. They actively inhibit any move towards repentance: a function attributed to them by Calvinists alone.

Bearing many features of a medieval morality *Doctor Faustus* draws the contemporary audience into its experience by playing on inherited expectations. In this way the play's theology becomes dramatically significant: not merely a set of abstract dogmas (which might as well have derived from some other theological system) but an active cultural force which reaches beyond the play's own world. *Doctor Faustus* grows out of and addresses itself to a living culture in which Calvinist theology is embedded. The pristine morality play, which Potter sees as 'the acting out of a complex psychological experiment aimed at catching the conscience of the audience and evoking the repentance they advocate,'[17] had already undergone deformation

---

[16] Paul Kocher, *Christopher Marlowe: A Study of his Thought, Learning and Character* (New York, 1946), 108.

[17] *English Morality Play*, p. 36.

(as a Catholic might say) by the time Marlowe wrote *Faustus*. Both the social attitudes and the psychology expressed through the old structure had changed.

The rhythm of the medieval morality, cathartic enactment of delinquency, shared penitence, and renewed docility towards an authority which can be only childishly resented, is benignly inclusive. Mankind typifies the attitude in addressing the audience:

> I hope unto His bliss ye be all predestinate:
> Every man, for his degree, shall be participate.
>
> (*Mankind*, ll. 188–9)

Conflicting concepts—the divergence of humanity implied by predestination and the inclusion of all at the allotted level in the great chain of being—are run together, the second mysteriously subsuming the first. It is Mankind, Everyman, who is eventually saved.

The memory is just one layer, however, of the audience awareness *Doctor Faustus* addresses. Medieval tolerance of saturnalian escapades had been sharply rejected by such plays as *Nice Wanton* (1560) in which trivial offences snowball and Calvinist theology accompanies a stiff penal code in punishing a perceived threat to social order. Mankind, fed up with work, threw down his spade. *Nice Wanton*'s ominously named adolescents Dalilah and Ismael seem equally innocuous when they play truant. Yet in pious brother Barnabas's rebuke—they are 'losing [their] time and learning' which would bring them 'knowledge of God' and an 'honest living' (ll. 45–7)—the puritan accent begins to be heard. Religious education, profitable use of time, and patient application to work are anxiously insisted on throughout the rest of the century in an attempt to curb the effects of economic change and social mobility. Top of Henry Arthington's list of sins of the poor is 'their misspending of former times in idlenesse, when they might have wrought' and he also blames them for 'their seldome repairing to their parish Churches, to heare theire duties better'.[18] Dalilah had merely

---

[18] Quoted by Helen C. White in *Social Criticism in Popular Religious Literature of the Sixteenth Century* (New York, 1944), 250.

been curious to know 'What "pastime" meaneth' (l. 74): she finds out, brutally, when she dies from venereal disease. Ismael is unluckier still since while his sister manages to repent he is hanged in Iniquity's company and shares his destination. Parents are berated through the suicidal mother Xantippe for lack of discipline in the home, to which—perennial conservative reflex response to intractable social problems—crime is attributed. Plays such as clergyman Fulwell's *Like Will to Like Quoth the Devil to the Collier* (1568), ramming home the same message ('If my parents had brought me up in virtue and learning | I should not have had this shameful end' (ll. 1014–15)), menace audiences with their preponderant reprobates. In its attempt to tighten its moral grip the church became culturally divisive: some submitted to the 'godly' discipline, others did not or could not. The stress now fell on exclusion, which the idea of reprobation both threatened and rationalized.

The more psychological-theological concomitant of this Calvinist deformation of the morality tradition (*Faustus*, we will see, inherits both) is revealed by (again cleric) Nathaniel Woodes's *The Conflict of Conscience* (1581). A dramatization in morality style of the apostasy and despair of Francis Spira, it exerts the typical Calvinist sermonic discipline by addressing contradictory selves. The prologue asks the audience to identify with Spira, changing his name to Philologus lest anyone think 'That all by SPERA spoken were, our selves we should not finde,' yet at the same time appeals, as though in a revenge play, to its 'patience'—to be rewarded by Philologus's confession that he would have been 'Farre happier, if that unborne and lyfelesse he had bene'. Ideal spectators or readers should manage this balancing act, profiting from the frisson of alarm at the raw immediacy of Philologus's despair (which but for the grace of God would be their own) and toning up their distancing piety with vengeful sentiment on behalf of the injured deity. Woodes's play is in fact an anti-morality: allegorical confederates do not dramatize the protagonist's moral freedom; Philologus's 'pleasures manyfolde' (l. 1722) are judiciously excised; the audience cannot share in contrition and forgiveness. It is the reprobate who casts himself in the role of morality hero, licensing betrayal of the faith on the expectation of repentance and forgiveness raised by the genre. He imagines that, like Peter whose betrayal of Christ saved his life, 'Even so shall I in tract of time, with bitter teares complaine' (l. 1884). Woodes means us to see, though, that Peter did not calculate this outcome: Philologus earlier lectured himself on the sin of 'presumption' (ll. 1558–9). Slow learners clinging to facile optimism about a forgiving deity are nastily implicated when 'presumptuous' generic expectation is disappointed.

Philologus—as Spira did—becomes a type against whom the audience measures itself. And since emphasis falls on the obduracy of his reprobate despair rather than his merely symptomatic apostasy the less robust of Woodes's parishioners might well have found the specific message (the play was probably meant to steel audience resolve in case the Inquisition shortly had the opportunity to put it to the test) overshadowed by the general and shareable anxiety over their spiritual identity. Philologus sees his affliction as an experience of divine wrath rather than chastisement because 'My name within the Book of lyfe had never residence' (l. 2033). He had been doomed to fail— as the Prologue says, 'constrained by the flesh, to yeld to deadly sinne'—and to be denied repentance—'Then (wretch accurst) no power hath, repentance to beginne.' This could be true of anyone.

These two types of Calvinist morality forced the tradition into the service of the pulpit. Whilst the social teaching lashed the audience, in response to fears of a breakdown of law and order, into good conduct, predestinarian theology encoded the realization that people had scant control over their destinies and exploited the anxiety it induced. It was a formidable pincer movement and it held many under its discipline. Puritanism squeezed the play out of plays. An audience dieted on Calvinist sermons would know that anything spectated on was grist to the mill of self-application. The world was a theatre and the first evidence of faith, said Calvin, was to remember that everything meeting the eye was the work of God and that its purpose should be meditated upon (*Inst.* 1. 14. 20). Especially edifying were the 'Frequent examples of Gods immediate vengeance . . .: spectacles set up in the vast Theatre of this world, whereof *quocunque sub axe*, whither soever thou turnest thine eyes, thou must needes be a spectator.'[19] Plays were a subclass of such spectacles:

[19] Thomas Adams, *Mystical Bedlam* (1615), 41–2.

> And whil'st thou view'st, consider that thou art
> No bare spectator, but dost act a part.
> And as thou shalt within these Scenes engage,
> So must thou fare, when Time pulls down the stage.[20]

It is not difficult to see in the light of such austerities why protestant culture operated, as Patrick Collinson says, 'to polarize communities between those who gadded to sermons and those who gadded to dances, sports, and other pastimes'.[21] By evoking the atmosphere of a morality play *Doctor Faustus* secures the traditional spiritual engagement of the audience (if only in the form of a heavily overlaid reminiscence). By combining in the play the Calvinist distortions of the kidnapped tradition in the milieu of the public theatre (the venue epitomizing the second polarity in the quotation to which Collinson alludes) Marlowe superimposes the values of the one community on the values of the other in the minds of an audience which, by its presence, has taken its side. *Faustus* embeds the old morality conventions, as I noted in discussing the Old Man and the Angels, in ironic contexts. It stresses unfreedom to choose spiritual destiny, un-priests dispensing un-mercy to the un-repentant who are un-forgiven. Treating the seemingly momentous pact with Lucifer as a symptom rather than a cause (if the pact was legally binding or spiritually efficacious what purpose would be served by its renewal?), it lines the audience up with Faustus, generalizing his predicament by stressing despair at the expense of the *Damnable Life's* more outlandish features.[22] It stresses too—and this is where the audience is most deeply implicated—the presumption of entertainment and attaches its punitive metaphysics both to this and to the disruption of social order associated with it.

What is most important to understand about the experience *Faustus* addresses and embodies is that, while Collinson's polarized communities were a reality, there was traffic between the two. The values of both have to be seen in relation to each other: they cohabited in individual minds. This becomes apparent if, before returning to the play, we enter the worm's eye

[20] Prologue to T[homas] S[herman], *Youths Tragedy* (1671; 3rd edn. 1672).

[21] *The Religion of Protestants: The Church in English Society 1559–1625* (Oxford, 1982), 230.

[22] *The Historie of the Damnable Life and Deserved Death of Doctor John Faustus*, trans. P. F. Gent (1592).

view of an early contemporary spectator whose most private mental processes can be shared.

In 1612, when the 22-year-old Richard Norwood had obtained freedom from the master to whom he had been bound apprentice sailor and lived 'idle and unsettled' in London, he frequented the Fortune theatre in Golding Lane. He even wrote an unfinished play. Eventually—providentially as he later saw it—he fell out with the players over a seat he claimed and forsook the theatre in pique. In 1602 the Admiral's company which first performed *Doctor Faustus* moved to this new house where they revived the play (with Edward Alleyn once more in the title role). Perform-ances appear to have taken place periodically at the Fortune until the eve of its closure in 1642.[23] It is virtually certain, therefore, that Norwood was familiar with the play, either in performance or in one of the quarto editions, as well as through his association with the players who no doubt regarded it as their showpiece. He thought himself 'bewitched' by plays (a use of Calvin's term for demonic seduction easily suggestive of *Doctor Faustus*). He was 'never satiated, which was a great means to withdraw and take off my mind from anything that was serious, true, or good, and to set it upon frivolous, false, and feigned things' ('Confessions', p. 42). The tensions from which *Doctor Faustus* derives its power are adumbrated here, yet if we probe further into the conflicting cultural values which tormented Norwood's mind we will understand better how the play embroils its audience in ineluctable contradictions, and under-stand better, too, the representativeness of Faustus.

Norwood's adult mind retained the imprint of early wonder at the phenomenal world and its presumed intersection with spiritual localities. He had wanted to know, as a child, 'how far it might be from earth to heaven? Whether there might not be some means devised to go up thither? Whether the heavens did not touch the earth in some places, as at the horizon?' If he could find Eden he thought he might be able to persuade God to let him in. Such ideas about religion were not distinct for him from the curiosity stimulated by natural phenomena:

When I saw rivers they seemed to be as it were some infinite thing, the waters always running and yet remaining full. I wondered whence they

---

[23] See John Jump, ed., *Doctor Faustus* (1962), p. lix.

came, and thought, when I should be my own man, I would search from whence and whither they were, supposing to find there were many rare things. (pp. 38–9)

The childhood questions resolved themselves into a general belief that the world awaited his voyage of discovery and this partly motivated him actually to set sail.[24] He was convinced that learning offered the *summum bonum*, and travel was essential to its acquisition: he had 'a great desire to search and see the world, led by an imagination of some extraordinary and fantastic good that I thought was in the world, which would scarce have been satisfied without some experience in travel' (p. 44).

While in London in 1612 the same 'roving and unsettled mind' kept him up at night studying Cornelius Agrippa's *De Occulta Philosophia*: 'much affecting the lofty style of the author and being curiously bent to pry into those mysteries commonly called the black art' (p. 43). Agrippa's pretensions make it clear how anyone fascinated, like Norwood, by the properties of the natural world and their tie-in with the world of the spirit might seize on his work: 'Magick', he declared, 'is a faculty of wonderfull vertue, full of most high mysteries, containing the most profound Contemplation of most secret things, together with the nature, power, quality, substance, and vertues thereof, as also the knowledge of whole nature.'[25] But when Norwood turned to Book 3 on magical practices he felt cheated: it seemed 'very base in comparison of the speculative part so loftily proposed in his other books, that I could scarce believe that to be his'.

He continued to flirt with necromancy (see p. 60), as one symptom merely of his thirst for knowledge, until he confronted 'that which for many years had seemed to be as a paradox to me, namely that "The fear of the Lord is the beginning of wisdom" '. It is a confession of defeat which attests the hold over his mind of the protestant values imbuing perception of experience:

I affected wisdom, but against this saying my corrupt heart would usually rise and reason: How can the fear of the Lord be wisdom? Well it may be piety or have some near affinity with it, but how can it be wisdom or the beginning of wisdom? Those I thought to be wise men who had attained to a large measure of knowledge in philosophy, the

---

[24] Other aspects of his motivation were considered in ch. 2.

[25] Henry Cornelius Agrippa, *Three Books of Occult Philosophy*, trans. J. F. (1651), i. 2–3.

mathematics, in sundry arts and ingenious practices, to which as I conceived the fear of God did nothing confer. But now I began to understand that a man might have all these and yet be a most miserable man, and so a great fool, 'for what availeth it if a man should win the whole world and yet lose his own soul?' And those things cannot bring a man to salvation; yea, without some measure of the fear of God, and grace restraining the wickedness of man's heart, he would (as by experience I had found) be so beslaved unto sin and Satan that he should neither make use of those natural faculties which God had given him for the attaining of those knowledges, nor having attained them could ever make any good use of them or scarce have leisure to think upon them; he should not get so much freedom from his bondage and task-masters. And miserable wisdom is that which leaves the possessor of it so wholly in misery. (p. 76)

The protestant God his imagination had willy-nilly to accommodate was hostile to the likes of Agrippa (who had been 'always from my youth a curious, and undauntable searcher of wonderfull effects, and operations full of mysteries'). Attempted ascent through the medium of the natural world to God, Agrippa's *'guides [by which] the soul of man ascendeth up into the Divine nature'* [26] was, under the protestant dispensation, assigned to 'the black art'. Norwood found, it seems, that the process of quest left him with an overdeveloped ego: he was 'prone to spiritual pride, to be too well conceited of myself, and to presumption. I was proud of that measure of grace and such other gifts (of mind especially) which the Lord in mercy had vouchsafed to me' (p. 77). Punitive agents sprang fully armed from his imaginative ambience:

And indeed I found myself so weak, and so habituated and prone to despair, and Satan to have gotten such power over me by custom, that I much feared that as soon as he should perceive me about to return and to lay hold upon the promises (which I had long neglected) he would assail me with all his power and be ready to overwhelm me with utter despair.

He questioned whether he was a devil incarnate, 'and therefore did seem to wish that I had never been or that I might fly somewhere from God'. Furtive approaches to repentance met what he experienced as the violent opposition of vigilant demons: 'But notwithstanding my secrecy it seems that Satan perceived

[26] *Occult Philosophy*, sig. A3ᵛ, iii. 357.

my drift (whether by turning to some places of Scripture or otherwise, I know not) and thereupon did assault me more furiously than ever before' (p. 95).

What is evident from comparison with Norwood's record is that *Doctor Faustus* exhibits experience from the inside, showing how it is invaded and constrained by contemporary belief, rather than moralizing on it from the outside and censuring it according to canons of virtue, whether humanist or Christian. It is less the 'Faustian' fable—humanist or Christian—it is usually taken to be than an emboldening of the contours of shared, peculiarly contemporary experiences, even if they were only experiences of mental events. At the crudest level a literal-minded response to the play is attested by the widely circulated tales of an occasion when the devil joined in. The earliest report is Prynne's, in *Histrio-Mastix*, noting '*the visible apparition of the Devill on the stage at the Belsavage Play-house, in Queene* Elizabeths *dayes, (to the great amazement both of the Actors and Spectators) whiles they were there prophanely playing the History of* Faustus (the truth of which I have heard from many now alive, who well remember it,) there being some *distracted with that fearefull sight*.'[27] The contagious spasm of terror need not be seen as an outbreak of hysteria amongst half-wits in the audience (or merely as puritan propaganda) but as the breakthrough of latent fears conditioned by a shared religious nervous system which the play teases.

Far from minimizing entertainment-value, as Woodes did, Marlowe (notwithstanding the 'additions') packs the middle parts of the play with it, simultaneously dramatizing the Calvinist point of view. For it is of course the devils who provide the hero with diverting spectacles in order to distract him from the question of salvation. Typical of the tactic is the introduction of the parade of Deadly Sins just after Faustus has contemplated repentance:

Faustus, we are come from hel to shew thee some pastime: | sit downe, and thou shalt see al the seaven deadly sinnes ap- | peare in their proper shapes.
Fau: That sight will be as pleasing unto me, as paradise | was to *Adam*, the first day of his creation.
Lu: Talke not of paradise, nor creation, but marke this | shew.
(6. 730–6)

---

[27] William Prynne, *Histrio-Mastix* (1633), fo. 556.

The grotesques that follow are meant to be ridiculous. Relics, again, of a medieval outlook they pose no threat as itemized sins. It is his sitting down for the diverting pastime that expresses Faustus's jeopardy. The demonic origin of entertainment within the play, taking the form often of such theatrical spectacles, indicates that the hilarity of its middle sections, which distracts Faustus from 'deepe dispaire' (6. 654), exemplifies the dangers puritans detected. Presented with dancing devils Faustus asks— it is a trained reflex—'what meanes this shewe?' and receives Mephostophilis's reply: 'Nothing Faustus, but to delight thy minde withall, | And to shewe thee what Magicke can performe' (5. 527–9). The achievement of magic, and entertainment in general, is to distract spectators from the moral meaning and opportunity for self-application in what they perceive.

Both Faustus and his low-life parodists do for the audience what the devils do for Faustus: entertain and distract. And the demonic source of such entertainment is constantly reinforced by the connection with necromancy. The demonic entertainment the audience is given by the demonically entertained Faustus is further emphasized by the spectacles he stages for on-stage audiences. The last words of Act 4, before the gloom of Act 5 descends, are those of the Duke who says: 'His Artfull sport, drives all sad thoughts away' (B. 4. 7. 1773). He speaks for Faustus and the audience as well as himself; and yet the refusal to entertain 'sad thoughts' (sad meaning serious: *OED* 4*d*) will, the audience is about to see from Faustus's fate, condemn them.

The author of *Nice Wanton* apparently failed to notice that his medium rubbed out his message, that he was conniving at the sin of 'pastime', the root of his characters' evil, by beguiling his audience in medieval morality fashion with their misbehaviour; Woodes excised entertainment; Marlowe has Lucifer offer Faustus, and through him the audience, the 'pastime' of the Deadly Sins, punishing the audience for succumbing to the saturnalian revelry he provides; Norwood fell under the 'artful' demonic spell which 'take[s] off [his] mind from anything that was serious, true, or good'. The audience has passed time, squandered that invaluable commodity, in watching the play, distracted from its elapse as Faustus has been for twenty-four years: 'We must give accounts at the day of judgement,' said Philip Stubbes, scourge of stage-plays, of every minut and jot of time, from the day of our birth to the time of our death: for there is nothing more precious than time, which is given us to glorifie God in good works, and not to spend in luxurious exercises after our owne fantasies and delights.[28]

It has participated in what Faustus calls 'mine owne fantasie' (1. 136); Richard Norwood has vicariously fulfilled his 'great desire to search and see the world, led by an imagination of some extraordinary and fantastic good'. But Time pulls down the stage, in brutal fashion, exposing the parts the spectators have played in the privacy of their minds.

Pastime was not of course an isolated object of puritan hostility; its nexus with the failure to pursue a calling was evident in *Nice Wanton*. *Doctor Faustus* opens with a man 'malecontent with his particular calling' who does not, as 'Every man must', in Perkins's words, 'judge that particular calling, in which God hath placed him, to be the best of all callings for him'. Like Norwood, he has 'a roving and unsettled mind':

> Settle thy studies *Faustus*, and beginne
> To sound the deapth of that thou wilt professe:
> Having commencde, be a Divine in shew,
> Yet levell at the end of every Art.

> (1. 31–4)

This intention to branch out, under cover of what he has begun to profess (his calling as a divine), instantly expresses his jeopardy. Anyone moving 'without the compasse of his calling,' said Perkins, '. . . bereaves himself of the protection of the Almighty: and lies open and naked to al the punishments and plagues of God'. Perkins invites readers to 'looke what judgements befall men . . . when they are foorth of their callings, which GOD hath prescribed them to keep'. Moreover, the nature of Faustus's calling—the same, of course, as Marlowe's was to have been—unites it unavoidably (though as we have seen this was theoretically true of all particular callings) with his general calling, or profession, as a Christian. Faustus's gallop through the other professions to embrace devilry, then, dramatizes the connection between abandonment of calling and loss of salvation. Bereft of a function contributing to the common weal Faustus

---

[28] *The Anatonie of Abuses* (1583), sig. NI[r].

becomes—on an exalted level no doubt—one of Perkins's

wandering and straggling persons who have no settled place of abode, and being neither members of any civill society, nor annexed to any particular Church, have no personall calling wherein to live, and therefore cannot either glorifie their Creatour, or doe the least good unto men.

A calling functioned, it was believed, on a personal level, 'to subdue the excess of corruptions' and, in society as a whole, to maintain order.[29] Lacking any structure to give meaning to his activities Faustus does randomly follow his appetites. At the same time he has a lamentable effect on social decorum which climaxes with the subplot gatecrashing the main plot (with his connivance) in the court of the Duke of Vanholt, erasing sanctified hierarchical distinctions (B. 4. 7. 1675 ff.). Ruling-order contemporaries would have found Faustus's antics less arbitrary and innocuous than they may appear; his wish to clothe students in silk for example (1. 122–3) would be perceived as a threat to the whole social structure.[30]

In the end Faustus bewails the desertion of his calling:

Ah my sweete chamber-fellow! had I lived with | thee, then had I lived stil, but now I die eternally. (14. 1390–1)

Yet it should be remembered that in puritan parlance 'Unfaith-fulnesse in our calling' was—as it appears on Arthur Dent's forbidding list—one of the 'signes of condemnation',[31] not, therefore, the cause. And, in fact, a few lines later, Faustus pushes his regret further back: 'O would I had never seene *Wertenberge*, ne-|ver read booke' (14. 1407). This raises a vexed area of puritan culture which has a considerable bearing on the play's meaning and impact, that of education.

The puritan stress on education has been noted because it was, at a rudimentary level, preconditional to salvation. And more generally, in uneasy alliance with humanism, the Reformation supplied an impetus to learning.[32] Many of the Calvinist clergy,

---

[29] *The Works* (Cambridge 1605), 931, 910, 905, sig. 4K1ᵛ; Sibbes quoted by R. S. Michaelsen, 'Changes in the Puritan Concept of Calling or Vocation', *The New England Quarterly*, 26 (1953), 321.

[30] See D. M. Palliser, *The Age of Elizabeth: England under the Later Tudors 1547–1603* (1983), 83–4. [31] *Plaine Mans Path-Way to Heaven* (1601), 34.

[32] See R. L. Greaves, *Society and Religion in Elizabethan England* (Minneapolis, 1981), 346 ff.

from humble backgrounds, were like Faustus socially advantaged
by it. Yet at a certain point Calvinism had to lash out to protect
its ideological hold on the mind. Calvin tried to distinguish
between the understanding to be used for terrestrial and celestial
matters;[33] and in terms that anticipate *Faustus*'s Epilogue he
attributes to 'vayne curiositie, but also a gredynesse to knowe
more than is mete for them' any attempt to submit the celestial to
the investigative methods appropriate to the terrestrial (*Inst.*
1. 4. 1). Puritan endorsements were commonplace. Henrie Smith
comes closest to the Epilogue: 'the well of Gods secrets is so
deepe, that no bucket of man can sound it'; and he gives as an
example of dangerous speculation Faustus's own most insistent
question ('Some have a good deale more desire to learne where
hell is, than to knowe any way how they may escape it.')[34]
Faustus's pact with the devil and resort to magic obediently play
out a recognized consequence of the chafing intellect (again
termed 'curiositie'): a man dissatisfied with his knowledge, said
Perkins, 'aspires to search out such things as God would have
kept secret'; attempting magic is 'a way to get further knowledge
in matters secret and not reveiled, that by working wonders, he
may purchase fame in the world'.[35] Norwood reveals how provocative this guarding of God's secrets was to quite ordinary people.

The fact was that a clear distinction between the two realms
could not be maintained. Calvin himself rhapsodizes about those
who delve into the liberal arts 'to looke into ye secrets of Gods
wisdom . . . As for example: to the searching out of the movings
of the starres' (*Inst.* 1. 5. 2). And he celebrates 'the nimblenesse of
the minde of man which veweth the heavens and earth and
secretes of nature' (*Inst.* 1. 15. 2). Just when it was applauded
and when it was condemned to rifle God's secrets is never
adequately expained. 'Religion did not say, and in the nature of
the case could not say,' observes Kocher in *Science and Religion in
Elizabethan England*, 'exactly where man's capacity to know the
physical world ended,' 'where the natural stopped and the
supernatural began.'[36] Faustus's education, like Norwood's, has
stimulated a general empirical curiosity which seems to have

---

[33] See Charles Trinkaus, 'Renaissance Problems in Calvin's Theology', *SIR* 1
(1954), 73.   [34] Henrie Smith, *Sermons* (1593), 996–7.
[35] *A Discourse of Witchcraft* (1608), 11.
[36] Paul Kocher, *Science and Religion in Elizabethan England* (New York, 1953), 76, 67.

expected the terrestrial and celestial, nature and supernature, to
exist in a continuum. Faustus mixes his questions to Mephostophilis on such matters as the whereabouts of hell (5. 562) with
others about, for example, the motions and dispositions of the
'planets of the heavens' (5. 619; see also 6. 664 ff.) and,
touchingly, a request for a comprehensive herbal (5. 622–4).
When, soon after, he tours the heavens he sees them as the
habitat of the saved (6. 628–30). Along with 'royal courts' and
the like they rank amongst the 'rarest things' he has seen (7.
931–2). Norwood, too, was allured by 'sundry rarities and
excellent things to be seen': as easily as the East or West Indies
he might stumble on the Garden of Paradise. Inverting the
normal morality attached to callings, he 'thought men very
negligent that followed every man some particular business of
their own' instead of seeking out these 'rare things' (p. 39).

Ambivalence towards learning is central to the ambiguity of
Doctor Faustus's judgemental frame, its Prologue and Epilogue.
What it points to is the realization that all Faustus's 'sins' are
symptomatic of a culturally endemic destiny. This accords, of
course, with Calvinism and the causal theory the Prologue itself
advances. It does, however, make the social meaning of the idea
of reprobation more comprehensible, so that ambiguity lies in
whether or not the solicited response is the apparent one of
condemnation. From the Prologue's potted biography with its
implied causal chain—tailed off by the identification of agency—
the Calvinist idea of an unfolding reprobate destiny and a covert
appeal to self-implicating audience sympathy seem to fuse:

> To patient Judgements we appeale our plaude,
> And speake for *Faustus* in his infancie:
> Now is he borne, his parents base of stocke,
> In *Germany*, within a towne called *Rhodes*:
> Of riper yeeres to *Wertenberg* he went,
> Whereas his kinsmen chiefly brought him up,
> So soone hee profites in Divinitie,
> The fruitfull plot of Scholerisme grac't,
> That shortly he was grac't with Doctors name,
> Excelling all, whose sweete delight disputes
> In heavenly matters of *Theologie*,
> Till swolne with cunning of a selfe conceit,
> His waxen wings did mount above his reach,
> And melting heavens conspirde his overthrow.

By soliciting 'patient Judgements' Marlowe's Prologue may easily be assumed to mean, like Woodes's, that retributive expectation will at length be satisfied by the villain's overthrow. As the Pope puts it in a later scene: 'the Gods, creepe on with feete of wool, | Long ere with Iron hands they punish men' (B. 3. 1. 906–7). But if we take the first line as logically connected with the second the phrase assumes a different appearance. The plain sense of 'speak for' (since 1300) is 'To make a speech . . . on behalf of' (*OED*). Appealing for a tolerant appraisal, then, the Chorus speaks for Faustus by providing what can only be called a sociological account of his aspirations.

Geographically and socially mobile from base beginnings Faustus, like many contemporaries, finds education the instrument of self-betterment. Repetition of 'grac't' is suggestive. Harry Levin points out that in Cambridge doctors' names were entered in what was known as the Grace Book.[37] The pun conveys how Faustus was encouraged to equate social advancement and academic achievement with the workings of God's grace, while in fact the Book of Grace, or Life, in which the names of the elect are inscribed, bears no relationship to the Grace Book. Academic accolade entices Faustus on and up 'Till' he crosses the frontier, a chronological fulfilment of a logical process, of permitted activity. His 'selfe conceit' is the conception of himself developed in the apparently laudable pursuit of learning. Actively gracing 'the fruitfull plot of Scholerisme', he, like Norwood, is naturally 'prone . . . to be too well conceited of [him]self' and 'proud of that measure of grace and such other gifts (of mind especially) which the Lord in mercy had vouchsafed to [him]'. Norwood's 'skill and knowledge' were for him too 'the principal means whereby it pleased the Lord to raise me from that poor condition' (pp. 44–5). If, then, Faustus 'surffets upon cursed Negromancy', if his intellectual and moral system is deranged, it is, as the metaphor indicates, a consequence of his having been 'glutted . . . with learning's golden gifts'.

Like the Prologue the Epilogue is more equivocal than it looks:

> Cut is the branch that might have growne ful straight,
> And burned is *Apolloes* Laurel bough,

[37] Harry Levin, *The Overreacher: A Study of Christopher Marlowe* (1953), 133.

That sometime grew within this learned man:
Faustus is gone, regard his hellish fall,
Whose fiendful fortune may exhort the wise,
Onely to wonder at unlawful things,
whose deepenesse doth intise such forward wits.
To practise more than heavenly power permits.

Calvin could almost have delivered this moralization. He spoke
of the 'perversnesse' of those who 'wylfully bring darknesse upon
them, yea with vayne and froward pride do make them selves
fooles. Whereupon foloweth, that their foolishness is not excus-
able, wherof the cause is not onely vayne curiositie, but also a
gredynesse to knowe more than is mete for them, joined with a
false confidence' (*Inst.* 1. 4. 1). Almost, but not quite. The clipped
closing rhyme supported by prim alliteration alerts the audience
to the cruel glibness of the concluding couplet, the arbitrariness
of what God permits. In the opening line the agent has been
obscured but the metaphor must prompt the question whether,
since the branch is Faustus, or a part of Faustus, he can easily
have cut it himself. Recollection of biblical parables of pruning
and casting unwanted branches into the fire then identifies God
as the agent (see John 15: 6; Matt. 3: 10 and 7: 19). The
conclusion invited is that Faustus could have continued to grow,
extending the scope of human achievement, had not God
intervened to destroy him. Though a natural process, Faustus's
growth is seen by God as virulent. It is difficult to read the lines
as the Chorus appears, by its moralistic tone, to intend them: to
mean that Faustus could have continued to grow 'ful straight'
within the traditional Christian limits;[38] it is, after all, *Apollo*'s
laurel bough, emblem of knowledge in general, which is
destroyed. To achieve its entelechy it has had to grow beyond the
'fruitfull plot of Scholerisme' it once 'grac't'.
     Pointing out these cultural-deterministic suggestions is not to

---

[38] It should perhaps be said that Calvinists did not proscribe the use of conditional
clauses. They used them, though, in a teasingly ambiguous way, as the Chorus does
here. Perkins's famous treatise title, cited in my Introduction, is an example: . . . *And
if He Be in the First the Estate of Damnation, How He May in Time Come out of it* . . . From a
human point of view he may, or may not: it depends on whether he is one of the elect.
Marlowe is doing something subtler with his 'might', as I try to show, and as could be
shown by analysis, too, of the Old Man's weave of future and conditional clauses
when he exhorts Faustus to hope. It is a snake-infested benevolence to which Faustus
responds with aggravated despair (B 5. 1. 1813–33).

deny that Faustus's pursuit of knowledge is a dismal failure, depraving the faculties, as Norwood saw it, on which it relies: a process exhibited by the progressive triviality of Faustus's prankstering. The practice of magic turns out—as Norwood judged from his reading of Agrippa—to be cheap, wholly incommensurate with its promise. Chafing at the 'end' of traditional avenues of thought (Faustus uses the word five times in his first speech to indicate frustration both with their limits and purpose), he loses all sense of direction without them. Rejection of the curbs placed on him may be inevitable but, lacking a framework, a discipline, to give his life an end he finds that experience does change his mind: it is damned souls to which 'no end is limited' (14. 1488), hell which 'hath no limits, nor is circumscrib'd' (5. 567). For puritans (Norwood finally resigned himself to this) education should always have an end: either religious instruction or practical application. Detached from practice, said John Downame, the arts and sciences developed into the *summum bonum* Norwood identified in himself, producing an insatiable search for more useless knowledge.[39] The play seems to endorse that view, as it faithfully dramatizes puritan lore throughout, since Faustus's quest becomes a rudderless dilettantism held together only by his own ego.

Norwood at his humbler level experiences the restiveness knowledge brings: a learned man, he decides, cannot 'enjoy so comfortable a condition in this life as a man unlearned; and for the life to come [learning] could promise nothing' (p. 44). The vagrancy of both Norwood and Faustus connects their 'free-wheeling pursuit of knowledge with their lack of a calling. The clearest difference between 'Anglicans' and puritans concerning education, says Richard Greaves, 'was the latter's disapprobation of educational travel on the Continent'.[40] Education, as they saw it, should strengthen not militate against the vocational sense.[41] Faustus's dizzying *Wanderlust* expresses the alienated detachment from social functions to which his quest leads and which exposes him to a punitive psychic backlash similar to that experienced by Norwood.

[39] John Downame, *Second Part of Christian Warfare* (1611), 91–103.
[40] *Society and Religion in Elizabethan England*, pp. 372–3.
[41] For an example of puritan stress on the vocational sense in education see Robert Cleaver, *Godlie Forme of Government* (1598), 332.

It is not as though his spectacular activities emancipate him from the ideology which condemns him. Nor is it only his anxiety attacks that tell us this. His social ascent is pitifully modest, hampered (since in theory he could lord it over the world's potentates) by his own habit of servility and respect for hierarchy. More revealing even than his fawning on the German Emperor and the Duchess of Vanholt is his spiteful use of magic to teach a knight respect for scholars (10. 1051–130). Lawrence Stone, we recall, describes England at this time as 'a two-class society of those who were gentlemen and those who were not'.[42] Faustus cannot escape the knowledge that he is not.

The more puritan cultural attitudes had been internalized, the greater the build-up of apprehension, of sensed exclusion, even, in cutting loose. Hence Norwood's seemingly authentic discovery (corresponding to the Epilogue's distinction between 'the wise' and 'forward wits') that the fear of the Lord is the beginning of wisdom. Faustus's mind shuttles agitatedly between introspective *Angst* and frenetic distraction so that one can credit, in these cultural circumstances, Norwood's claim that taskmasters would leave no time for intellectual exploration. Yet 'forward wits' would—the principle inhered in the promotion of learning—be 'enticed' beyond existing frontiers; only the backward were 'wise' enough to be exhorted. Puritans were aware that the learning of 'wise men' tended to be a barrier to salvation.[43]

In that he too is a victim of puritan conservatism Faustus resembles the indigent vagrants the moralities harassed. In her discussion of sixteenth-century views on 'contentation' Helen White points out (*pace* Weber) that the doctrine of callings was 'viewed by the preachers at least as something very different from an instrument of individual advancement'. It was indeed 'an instrument of social stabilization of great potential importance'. William Perkins, she says, was 'trying to substitute for the . . . self-assertive spirit of his day one of quiet labour within the limits of one's appointed place in the world'. While 'heroic' in his efforts he was, however, 'throwing himself across the main line of advance of his day'. Consequently his preaching in this area was of 'very limited effectiveness'.[44] A reliable modern historian

---

[42] Lawrence Stone, *The Crisis of the Aristocracy 1558–1641* (Oxford, 1965), 49.
[43] Samuel Wright, *Divers Godly and Learned Sermons* (1612), 194.
[44] *Social Criticism*, pp. 245–54.

agrees that 'contemporaries were concerned about the extent of individual mobility, and even about a threatened dissolution of the whole social structure'. Exaggerated stress on status and deference (of which Ulysses' inflated speech on degree is probably representative) was a 'natural' response to 'an age of rapid individual mobility'.[45] The position puritans adopted on callings in this mobile, unpredictable society may not have arrested economic trends but its impact on the psyche could be far from benignly ineffectual. If a square peg did not fit into a round hole the puritan solution was to hit it very hard. Calvinism criminalized those who did not, because they could not, fit in, from the rootless poor to the rootless intellectual—who was driven into the arms of the devil. Since Faustus's destruction seems to be implicit in the educational process itself it is not surprising that he ends up wishing he had never read a book or that his last thought is to offer to burn all those he has. Marlowe's rakish associates Greene and Nashe appear to have felt similar sentiments.

The consciousness invested in Faustus himself absorbs the puritan cultural attitudes as well as the broadly defined humanist influences which conflicted with them. It is a *donnée* of the play, and not just his opinion, that he is a clever (if compulsively combative) man: he has, with his syllogisms, 'graveld the Pastors of the Germaine Church' (1. 146). Being moreover a Wittenberg theologian he cannot be thought un-aware of Luther's 'devil's syllogism' or of the sequel to his biblical quotations.[46] Equally, when he describes the books of magic as 'heavenly' (1. 80) or Mephostophilis as 'Full of obedience and humilitie' (3. 274) it is jejune to consider him merely the object of irony, not the ironist.[47] Harry Levin says that through the understanding of Mephostophilis 'we participate in the dramatic irony' of the play.[48] Dramatic irony would, however, strip Faustus of heroic status. Marlowe would be supplying a crudely intrusive moral commentary and the audience could feel superiority—specifically intellectual

---

[45] Palliser, *Age of Elizabeth*, p. 84.

[46] The usual view is that his syllogism is a 'fatal error' (Kocher, *Christopher Marlowe*, p. 106). Sellin also views it as a 'fatal misinterpretation of scripture' ('The Hidden God', p. 179).

[47] For a protracted analysis along these lines, see Douglas Cole, *Suffering and Evil in the Plays of Christopher Marlowe* (Princeton, 1962), 203–31.   [48] *The Overreacher*, p. 139.

superiority—to Faustus. Pity might remain (though hardly for a man of Aristotelian nobility) but terror would be removed by our possession of superior awareness. Self-ridiculing dramatic irony is normally kept for clowns such as Pedringano in *The Spanish Tragedy* who jests from the gallows in the mistaken belief that the boy's box contains his pardon.

Some of Faustus's ironies are plainly deliberate: his responses, for example, to the prospect of the parade of Deadly Sins on the day when he destroyed his soul: 'as pleasing unto me, as paradise | was to *Adam*, the first day of his creation' (6. 733–4) (though Lucifer does not share his boyish sense of humour); or, starkest of all, his echo of Christ's *consummatum est* (5. 515). Were dramatic irony intended as a method of supplying authorial comment it would be seriously damaged by such inconsistency.

Faustus—unlike Middleton's villain-heroes—consciously despairs. In Alan Sinfield's pithy phrase, 'Faustus is not damned because he makes a pact with the Devil, he makes a pact with the Devil because he is damned.'[49] It is not just from the first speech that this is to be inferred. The point is emphasized in the opening words, invested with meditative sobriety by their study setting, of the scene in which the transaction is to occur:

> Now Faustus must thou needes be damnd,
> And canst thou not be saved?
> what bootes it then to thinke of God or heaven?
>
> (5. 438–40)

The first two lines are interrogative premisses rather than open questions, as the conclusive form of the third indicates. Faustus rebukes his self indulgence ('Away with such vaine fancies and despaire'), reminding himself, correctly if he is a reprobate, that God does not love him (441, 447).

Despair was the usual Calvinist interpretation of the unpardonable sin against the Holy Ghost.[50] Faustus enacts it here, and the interpretation is deftly dramatized when he responds to

---

[49] *Literature in Protestant England*, p. 116.

[50] Those who argue that Faustus forfeits the opportunity to repent at some point in the play later than his first speech must find another explanation of this sin. The most influential suggestion has been W. W. Greg's 'demoniality' ('bodily intercourse with demons') ('The Damnation of Faustus', *MLR* 41 (1946), 97–107). For a convincing refutation see Nicolas Kiessling, 'Doctor Faustus and the Sin of Demoniality', *SEL* 15 (1975), 205–11.

the scholar's exhortation to 'looke up to heaven': 'But Faustus offence can nere be pardoned' (14. 1400, 1402). Perkins said despair 'cannot be forgiven . . . because after a man hath once committed this sin, it is impossible for him to repent'.[51] This was not a new idea. In the medieval (or Catholic) context to which, for example, Arieh Sachs relates it, however, since God's mercy is offered to all, it is easier to see the 'sinner' as perverse.[52] In Calvinist England the reprobate was, by despairing, carrying out a divine decree. And again, if we look to social history, we find that pacts with the devil consequent on such despair were, though the theologians' creation, no mere theologians' abstraction. Keith Thomas documents a number of cases where, convinced that they were reprobates, people turned to witchcraft or conceived themselves to sell their souls to the devil—generally for the kind of pittance the Clown in *Faustus* refuses:[53] social derelicts, they knew from puritans that God would not have them. The transaction was easily accomplished if Bunyan's experience of consenting to 'Sell Christ' is at all comparable. Autobiographer John Rogers was one such despairer who resisted the devil's blandishments but he is suggestively matter-of-fact about the experience: 'the *Devill* did often tempt me to study *Necromancy* and *Nigromancy*, and to make use of *Magick*, and to make a *league* with him.'[54]

Faustus, too, makes a virtue of necessity, When the Prologue says he 'preferres' magic to bliss, this may be both a judicial statement of fact (he puts it before—*OED* v. 3) and an ascription of preference in the modern sense (consciously favouring—*OED* v. 7). He seems aware of the antecedent necessity to which his will conforms. This agreement of Faustus's will with God's would probably make him, to the Calvinist connoisseur, a more gratifying exhibit than the derelicts who leagued themselves with the devil out of a more abject despair. 'Among all the workes of Gods eternall counsell,' drooled William Perkins, 'there is none more wonderfull then is *Desertion*: which is nothing else but an action of God forsaking his creature'; the beauty of it was that 'God never forsakes the creature against the will thereof: but in

[51] *Works*, p. 118.
[52] Arieh Sachs, 'The Religious Despair of *Doctor Faustus*', *JEGP* 63 (1964), 625–47.
[53] Keith Thomas, *Religion and the Decline of Magic* (1971), 474 ff.
[54] *Ohel or Beth-shemesh, a Tabernacle for the Sun* (1653), 428.

the very time of Desertion, it voluntarily forsaketh and refuseth grace, and chooseth to be forsaken.'[55] Faustus embraces the destiny he knows he cannot elude.

Irony is the mode he uses to express a dual perspective on experience: the simultaneous knowledge of objective reality which makes him powerless, helpless, and destined to failure and rejection—a victim of his circumstances, of the devil, and ultimately of God—and the conscious cultivation of the illusion ('mine owne fantasie' (1. 136)), for which magic is the aptest vehicle, that he is autonomous, free to shape his own destiny. While he gestures towards expansion of the frontiers of knowledge, by embracing devil-dependent magic he simultaneously confirms in all its crudity the metaphysical belief-system he wants to transcend. If the devil, then God—as contemporaries were apt to remind themselves.[56] The attraction of magic was that it was the most extravagant symbol of escape from the impotence Calvinism imposed. Interestingly, in his final speech Faustus invokes astrology ('You starres that raignd at my nativitie, | whose influence hath alotted death and hel' (14. 1474–5)). As C. S. Lewis observes in another context, 'The magician asserts human omnipotence: the astrologer, human impotence.'[57] The illusion in which magic deals, which gives it its other symbolic value, is no longer sustainable. In choosing magic, and in the language he uses, Faustus conveys his awareness of the circumscribing reality. His attempt to escape from orthodoxy actually affirms that orthodoxy's power. Rebellion is premised on despair.

Faustus's ironic tactics, which run from hilarious frivolity to dire blasphemy, seek to 'confound' knowledge he cannot ignore. He can be explicit about this at moments—when bereft of protection, for example, in the midst of his caperings with the Horsecourser:

> what art thou Faustus but a man condemnd to die?
> Thy fatall time doth drawe to finall ende,
> Dispaire doth drive distrust unto my thoughts,

---

[55] *Works*, p. 496. This was not an eccentric view for a puritan to hold. See also, for example, Sibbes, *The Bruised Reed and Smoking Flax* (1630), ed. P. A. Slack (Menston, 1973), 176: 'None are damned in the Church, but those that will.'

[56] See Thomas, *Religion and the Decline of Magic*, p. 567.

[57] *English Literature in the Sixteenth Century Excluding Drama* (1973), 6.

Confound these passions with a quiet sleepe:
Tush, Christ did call the thiefe upon the Crosse,
Then rest thee Faustus quiet in conceit.

(11. 1169–74)

Distraction suddenly fails him (and with him, no doubt, the audience), time-awareness returns; yet he has a technique of anaesthetizing his mind: contradictions are suspended in their ironic formulation. Here he denigrates as 'passions' what are from an orthodox standpoint glimpses of reason. With the reference to the penitent thief he both consoles himself and recognizes (pre-empting self-contempt) that the consolation is illusory—a 'conceit': he is conscious, unlike Philologus invoking the forgiven traitor Peter, of committing the sin of presumption.

Multiplying ironies, Faustus later begs Mephostophilis to intercede with Lucifer 'To pardon my unjust presumption' (13. 1337): he had 'presumed' on the forgiveness of Lucifer for his contemplated apostasy. B adds the statement 'I do repent' (B. 5. l. 1850), reinforcing the irony that he can assume theological attitudes towards Lucifer which, addressed to God, would save him. The perverse use of vocabulary transmits an underlying awareness of its proper application; yet to a reprobate, towards whom God's conduct was the inverse of that towards the elect, such displacement gives a kind of release, detaching the words from their conceptual moorings, disordering the relationship between signifier and signified. That this activity addles his intellect is a regrettable by-product of his compulsion to engage in it.

When repudiating the routine (though irrational) despairer's abject urge to commit suicide, Faustus asks:

Why should I dye then, or basely dispaire?
I am resolv'd *Faustus* shal nere repent.

(6. 660–1)

Rowland Wymer points out the oddity that 'repentance is here being *associated* with, rather than opposed to, despair and suicide'.[58] For Faustus, to repent would be to despair basely because he would be abandoning his fantasy to turn towards the objective Calvinist reality which condemns him. By associating

---

[58] *Suicide and Despair in the Jacobean Drama* (Brighton, 1986), 78.

repentance with despair (itself theologically reprehensible) he manages to turn the evaluative vocabulary he is stuck with against itself, so preserving his own arena of illusory freedom. The desperation which mobilizes this imaginative effort is indicated by his confession a few lines earlier:

> And long ere this I should have slaine my selfe,
> Had not sweete pleasure conquerd deepe dispaire.

$$(6.\ 653\text{--}4)$$

Since the pact was made in the previous scene this reveals Faustus's early consciousness of his predicament: his frenetic hedonism and linguistic games are techniques of survival.

Split consciousness enabling Faustus to monitor his own strategies is often conveyed by reference to himself in the second and third person. He can stand back and observe the construction of a self which believes illusions, positing a Faustus who will be 'quiet in conceit' to combat the intrusion of despair into 'my thoughts', or a Faustus frozen into a defiant posture who 'shal nere repent'. An early instance is his reply to Mephostophilis's declaration of interest in capturing his soul:

> This word damnation terrifies not him,
> For he confounds Hell in *Elizium*,
> His ghost be with the olde Philosophers,
> But leaving these vaine trifles of mens soules,
> Tell me . . .

$$(3.\ 303\text{--}7)$$

The flippant irony of the last phrase flows from the enunciated principle of 'confounding'. The humanist Faustus who is able to slide the idea of hell under the preferred image of Elysium, who can be dispatched at death to the company of pagan luminaries, lives in another possible world. The 'real' Faustus—that is the dominant self-understanding which is affirmed by its capacity to mobilize these strategies of evasion—is his creator: aware of the fabrication and that the world he inhabits is not confusible with such fictions. Yet the mental sleight buys him a temporary adjustment of identity, an imaginative, as well as imaginary, freedom.

Faustus's habitual self-address also arrests, like Donne ir-repressibly punning on his own name to tell God why 'thou hast not done', his sense of his own uniqueness, his 'selfe conceit'. In the first speech he tests various identities against his name and finds they do not match up: 'A greater subject fitteth *Faustus* wit' (1. 41); 'Why *Faustus*, hast thou not attaind that end?' (1. 48). Emphatically not Everyman, Faustus, primed for individualism by his career, lacking family, social or geographical roots, colleagues or companions on his own level in whom he can confide, or a job that absorbs him, is afflicted by the phoenix mentality Donne reprehends (and shares).[59] Tamburlaine (with more wilful self-aggrandizement and self-excuse) invoked his name as a totem he could only obey, not control; he was the vehicle of its destiny. Faustus has a similar sense of a unique script he must follow ('*Homo fuge*, yet shall not *Faustus* flye' (5. 522)), however fatal its mesmerism (Faustus is not just any *homo*). Surplus selfhood excludes him, as it is the product of exclusion, from the divine economy (in the ambiguous sense it is permissible to exploit).

Faustus's floating identity—expressed by his physical instability and geographical gyrations—condemns him to endless roleplay. 'Then in this shew let me an Actor be' (B. 3. 1. 877) is the most explicit acknowledgement (in the prelude to the Vatican scenes). This deepens the significance of Marlowe's dramatization of puritan opposition to aspects of the stage. Plato connected acting with rolelessness. 'It is unlikely', he thought, 'that anyone engaged on any worthwhile occupation will be able to give a variety of representations.' He would ban actors from his republic on account of their corrupting example as men who had no calling, for 'one man does one job and does not play two or a multiplicity of roles.'[60] Not only was Plato a major influence on the puritan attitude, evidence was wrung, too, from Aristotle. Stephen Gosson—an ex-playwright—derived from him the theory that acting, being a simulation of what is not, is 'with in the compasse of a lye, which by Aristotle's judgement is naught of it selfe and to be fledde'.[61] Marlowe makes the illusoriness of Faustus's and the devils' representations (in the raising of Helen for example) very transparent. That Faustus is an illusionist

[59] 'First Anniversary', *The Epithalamions, Anniversaries, and Epicedes of John Donne*, ed. W. Milgate (Oxford, 1978), 28, ll. 213–18.
[60] Plato, *The Republic*, trans. Desmond Lee, 2nd rev. edn. (Harmondsworth, 1974), 153, 156.   [61] Stephen Gosson, *Playes Confuted in Five Actions* (1582), 188.

suggests, too, a connection between necromancy and acting which Agrippa (wearing his pious hat) makes explicit in *Of the Vanitie and Uncertaintie of Artes and Sciences*: illusion, he observes, is the stock in trade of actors; both they and magicians do things 'onely . . . according to the outwarde appearance'. Both practise 'deceytes of the Divell'.[62] In the presence of so much illusion the audience could, paradoxically, hardly be surprised if the master of illusion made a real appearance for them as he does for Faustus when he turns to conjuring; and if not for them then for Edward Alleyn: according to report the actors shared the audience's jumpiness—they may not have been impervious to the view of some puritans that stage actions should be treated as tantamount morally to their real-life equivalents.[63]

It is scarcely possible to ignore the implication for, or of, Marlowe himself in all this. Gosson's discussion of Aristotle extended his stricture on acting to the poet's imagination. And Plato did likewise: artists make 'not "what is", but something which *resembles* "what is" without *being* it'. He 'makes a likeness of a thing' but 'knows nothing about the reality but only about the appearance'.[64] Faustus with his necromancy easily appears, then, to offer a surrogate for Marlowe with his art: an arena of illusion in which fantasies of human aggrandizement and freedom are played out. The elastic mind Calvin incautiously admired, exorbitantly vagrant, distends itself over the whole realm of the imaginable. But the playground of illusion is fenced round—as *Doctor Faustus* is by its Prologue and Epilogue and its eschatological conclusion—by a punitive, unignorable, collectively imagined 'reality'. William Perkins (whom I have often quoted in this chapter) entered Christ's College, Cambridge, two

[62] Agrippa. *Of the Vanitie and Uncertaintie of Artes and Sciences*, trans. Ja[mes] San[ford] (1569), fo. 62^r.

[63] Sasek, *The Literary Temper of the English Puritans* (New York, 1969), 95. J. Payne Collier, Alleyn's biographer, is derisive of Aubrey's report that Alleyn's foundation of 'God's Gift College at Dulwich' in 1613 was an act of contrition inspired by an occasion when (impossibly) playing a daemon in one of Shakespeare's plays, he saw an apparition of the devil (*Memoirs of Edward Alleyn* (1841), 111). Collier conjectures that the basis for 'the absurd report' was an incident recorded in Middleton's *The Blacke Booke* (1604) (sig. B4) when 'the old theatre [the Rose] cracked and frightened the audience' while a devil was on stage. The Middleton incident, sufficiently distinct from Prynne's story, strengthens the idea that audiences were twitchy. Alleyn's state of mind is irrecoverable, though the simplistic cause and effect indicated by Aubrey (even when the details are straightened out) attracts scepticism.

[64] Plato, *The Republic*, pp. 424, 429.

years before the 16-year-old Marlowe went up to Corpus. By 1590 Perkins was 'the most popular and the most impressive of the Cambridge preachers'.[65] Marlowe, who between 1580 and 1587 was in receipt of a Matthew Parker scholarship to train as a cleric, must have had his fill of sermons—if not preached by Perkins then by his theological clones—both on Calvinist dogma and the social and cultural outlook accreting to it. 'It is onely ridiculous dul Preachers,' said Nashe (who was himself accused of atheism), 'that have revived thys scornefull Secte of Atheists.'[66] Marlowe's desertion of his calling to the pulpit for, of all things, the theatre (and continental travel) could not but have reinforced his consciousness of the cultural polarization which had been developing in English society at large.

It is tempting—but it would be superficial—to say that if the Calvinist God did not already exist Marlowe might have found it necessary to invent him. He was attracted to ideas of omnipotence and impotence, and to the loser's choice between degrading submission and self-destructive rebellion. But then his mind may well have been disfigured by its concentrated exposure to Calvinism. However one interprets the origin of this fascination, the startling way in which it reveals itself in his work should be observed so that the idea that Marlowe positions himself in his own line of fire can lose its appearance of absurdity. Its starkest expression (it would be distracting to consider other examples) is in de Guise's manifesto speech in *Massacre at Paris*. The 'deep-engender'd thoughts' de Guise promises in his opening line 'burst abroad' in this dictum:

> Oft have I levell'd, and at last have learn'd
> That peril is the chiefest way to happiness.
>
> (1. 2. 34–8)[67]

Portentously announced by the first the second line is further publicized beyond its context in a mediocre half-written play by its—for Marlowe rare—Alexandrine metre. The idea that danger is a stimulant to intense experience fits well, of course, with the probable details of Marlowe's own life (his spying, streetfighting,

---

[65] See H. C. Porter, *Reformation and Reaction in Tudor Cambridge* (Cambridge, 1958), 287 *et passim*.

[66] *The Works of Thomas Nashe*, ed. R. B. McKerrow (1910), ii. 123.

[67] References are to *The Complete Plays of Christopher Marlowe*, ed. J. B. Steane (Harmondsworth, 1969).

homosexuality, and atheism) and with the kind of thrill his plays cultivate. But de Guise goes further than this:

> That like I best that flies beyond my reach.
> Set me to scale the high Pyramides,
> And thereon set the diadem of France;
> I'll either rend it with my nails to naught,
> Or mount the top with my aspiring wings,
> Although my downfall be the deepest hell.
>
> (42–7)

These lines expose Levin's concept of the overreacher (naturally encompassing 'the overreaching Guise')[68] as reductively moralistic. De Guise certainly does reach above himself but failure is built into his programme. The Icarus motif alters its meaning when the speaker is the Icarus figure. Grammatically and rhetorically the disjunctive proposition raises the expectation of triumph but comes to rest in hell. And while the last line appears to carry an ambiguity in its subjunctive mood the allusion to Icarus resolves the meaning as future not conditional.

For Faustus, too, prolepticized failure ('This night Ile conjure though I die therefore' (1. 199)) bizarrely conditions the excitement of his project. Quite evidently this extends, moreover, to aesthetic excitement. Aesthetic climax in *Faustus*—the apostrophe to Helen (13. 1357–63)—is fuelled by knowledge of the illusion on which it is based. Faustus ascribes to 'her', fantastically, the power to make him immortal, liberate his soul, and transport him to heaven; he conveys by his language (as by the odd insistence that she is more beautiful than God—'Brighter . . . then flaming *Jupiter*' (1372))—his aching sense of loss and exclusion, his preoccupation with what, now that time is up, is to engulf him. It is just because Helen is a surface illusion that the sense of beauty in the passage can be made exquisite. Marlowe and Faustus reach their poetic zenith at the moment of greatest menace; poignancy derives from the felt precariousness. The passage speaks for the freedom of Marlowe's imagination, a freedom he knows to be illusory.

For the individual imagination—'mine owne fantasie'—is overborne by the collective imagination. 'These black Opinions', to steal a phrase from John Smith, the Cambridge Platonist,

---

[68] *The Overreacher*, p. 107.

'shrink up the free born Spirit which is within us, which would otherwise be dilating and spreading it self boundlessly beyond all Finite Being.'[69] The shrinkage of Faustus's mind in his final speech is certainly drastic. The temptation for a critic to spirit away this atrocious finale is understandable. 'There is nothing', thinks Simon Shepherd, 'to confirm the truth of Faustus's visions beyond the power of his poetry: the scene is typically that of the deluded individual.'[70] But, leaving aside the devils who appear in both versions to claim him, the confirmation supplied by the Epilogue, and the absence of any sceptical device which might place his 'delusions', it may be asked what greater confirmation there could be than the power of Faustus's poetry of the truth—in the Jungian sense of psychological truth—of his vision. *Doctor Faustus* is, in Fredric Jameson's terminology, a 'Symbolic text' in which utopian desire includes 'with the utmost representative density' all the obstacles to its fulfilment without which its victory would be empty and delusive. 'It then sometimes happens', he says,

that the objections are irrefutable, and that the wish-fulfilling imagination does its preparatory work so well that the wish, and desire itself, are confounded by the unanswerable resistance of the Real . . . The real is thus . . . that which resists desire, that bedrock against which the desiring subject knows the breakup of hope and can finally measure everything that refuses its fulfillment.[71]

The ireful brow of God has the reality to Faustus that the vial of grace had to the Old Man: an imaginative reality supported by his culture and attested by the conviction carried by his poetry. The appearance of the devils is scarcely noticed, indeed, because they materialize so convincingly from Faustus's own visions ('O Ile leape up to my God: who pulles me downe?' (14. 1462)) and deepest expectations. It is if the crude machinery of damnation arrived *ab extra*, as a *coup de théâtre*, that one would accuse Marlowe of grotesque puppetry and question the 'truth' of his play.

The last speech—an amalgam in the psyche of divine hostility,

---

[69] John Smith, *Discoveries*, ed. John Worthington (1660), 124.
[70] Simon Shepherd, *Marlowe and the Politics of Elizabethan Theatre* (Brighton, 1986), 97.
[71] Fredric Jameson, *The Political Unconscious: Narrative as a Socially Symbolic Act* (Cornell, 1981), 183–4.

demonic intervention, and human resistance—brilliantly dramatizes the inability to repent. The habits of deferral and evasion are still running frantic circles in Faustus's mind when their rationale has been chopped off. He craves more time in which to repent when, were he capable of repentance, additional time would not be needed (1455–9). 'And as it often happeneth,' said Sir John Hayward, 'that whilest one thinketh too much of doing, he leaveth to doe the effect of his thinking.'[72] Trapped in self-consciousness and the conviction that God has rejected him—for which as we know he has ample cause—he is unable to project a prayer to Christ which does not swerve off course to address the impediment in his mind he thinks of as Lucifer (1464–7). The same conviction drives him to insult God's mercy and justice in one mouthful, assuming that the first is denied (and that Christ's redemptive death is insufficient to save him) and that the second might be satisfied by something less than eternal torment (1483–7). He commits two sins Donne was guilty of. wishing that his soul and body might take opposite directions (1476–80) and that he had been an undamnable creature without a soul (1489–90). Such heretical wishes are, in spite of their agreement with the theologians' anathemata, believably unavoidable ones when direct appeal for mercy is choked off by the conception of God contemporaries had developed. Throughout the play demonic power had asserted itself, as it did for Norwood, whenever Faustus's mind motioned towards repentance. The more he wants to repent the more strongly he runs up against the inhibiting mechanism at work in his mind: 'ah my God, I woulde | weepe, but the divel drawes in my teares . . . Oh he stayes my tong, | I would lift up my hands, but see, they hold them, they hold | them' (1416–20).

Calvin, at any rate, as I have observed, considered the writhings of the reprobate a vigorous confirmation of the truth of his religion; and Faustus enacts Calvinist psychology with obliging fidelity, not just at the end but throughout:

Yea therby is that whiche I travaile to prove more certainly gathered, that there is a felyng of godhead naturally graven in the hartes of men, forasmuche as the very reprobate them selves are of necessitie enforced to confesse it. In quiet prosperitie they pleasauntely mocke at god, yea

---

[72] *The Sanctuarie of a Troubled Soul* (1616), 21.

they are full of talke and pratyng to diminyshe the greatnesse of his power ['When at their ease, they can jest about God, and talk pertly and loquaciously in disparagement of his power']: but yf ones any desperation touche them, it stirreth them up to seke the same God, and mynistreth them sodeyn shorte prayers: by which it may appeare, that they were not utterly ignoraunt of god, but that the same whyche ought soner to have been uttered, was by obstinacie suppressed. [but should despair, from any cause, overtake them, it will stimulate them to seek him, and dictate ejaculatory prayers, proving that they were not entirely ignorant of God, but had perversely suppressed feelings which ought to have been earlier manifested]. (*Inst.* 1. 4. 4)

The contemporary most comparable with Marlowe and Faustus for his outrageous libertinism and scorn for religion was Robert Greene (who belonged, of course, to Marlowe's theatrical and social milieu). In his *Groatsworth of Wit* a remorseful Greene admonishes 'those Gentlemen his Quondam acquaintance, that spend their wits in making plaies': 'Wonder not,' he addresses Marlowe, 'that Greene, who hath said with thee (like the foole in his heart) There is no God, shoulde now give glorie unto his greatness: for penetrating is his power, his hand lies heavie upon me.' Attributing their shared atheism to Machiavelli, to whom he imaginatively assigns a 'conscience seared like Cain' and a remorseful death like those of Judas and Julian the Apostate, Greene presents himself to Marlowe, in the hackneyed puritan manner, as an exemplum: 'Looke unto me, by him [Machiavelli] perswaded to that libertie, and thou shalt finde it an infernall bondage.'[73]

While there is nothing to suggest that Marlowe was reduced to such cravenness before his death, there is no reason either to suppose him imaginatively impervious to the 'penetrating power' exercised over the mind, in the absence of a developed vocabulary of scepticism, by what were both state-authorized and collectively-assimilated beliefs. Although censorship and the threat of capital punishment can account for the absence of atheist publications, Greene's retraction, like the penitent works of Nashe, commands recognition of internalized pressures. So there is no reason to deny, as Empson does in his byzantine argument for extensive disfigurement of the play by censorship, what is consistently and powerfully apparent in the text of *Doctor*

---

[73] *The Life and Complete Works of Robert Greene*, ed. A. B. Grosart (1881–6), xii. 143.

Faustus: the discovery within the mind itself of the bondage of the libertine to a conviction of infernal identity.[74] It was a possibility Marlowe may well have apprehended for himself; it is clear from the play that there was excitement in touching it off in the minds of the audience. That he is able at the same time to dramatize how the reprobate is driven into the posture of rebel by the dullness, narrowness, and repressiveness of contemporary religious culture seems to me to give the play a truth to the possible consciousness of its time which accounts for the psychic charge it still transmits.

Repugnant as the thought is Calvin may well have been right regarding the culture out of which *Faustus* was produced. Atheism may have been almost unthinkable. The word entered the English language around 1568 and generally denoted godlessness, impiety, rather than philosophic unbelief. The title of D. C. Allen's book *Doubt's Boundless Sea: Skepticism and Faith in the Renaissance* is rather strongly qualified by its preface: 'None of the men in my present study called himself an atheist, none denied the existence of God.'[75] And G. T. Buckley constantly reminds the reader, in his *Atheism in the English Renaissance*, of the Elizabethan senses of the word; he finds little evidence of sustained disbelief in God's existence.[76] Unbelief began to be articulated in the seventeenth century, partly because of the very ruthlessness with which Calvinism had tried to screw down the lid: we saw how Bunyan had to deal with this countereffect of repression. But 'it is very hard', says G. E. Aylmer, 'to pin down a single Elizabethan unbeliever—as opposed to numerous popular scoffers and blasphemers.'[77] The more frontal the assault on religion, moreover, the more psychologically brittle it probably was. Francis Bacon thought atheists had to gabble about their opinions, even to themselves, in order to bolster them:

The Scripture saith, *The fool hath said in his heart, there is no God*; it is not said, *The fool hath thought in his heart*: so as he rather saith it by rote to himself, as that he would have, than that he can thoroughly believe it or be persuaded of it.[78]

[74] William Empson, *Faustus and the Censor* (Oxford, 1987).

[75] D. C. Allen. *Doubt's Boundless Sea: Skepticism and Faith in the Renaissance* (Baltimore, 1964), p. vi.

[76] George T. Buckley, *Atheism in the English Renaissance* (New York, 1965), *passim*.

[77] 'Unbelief in Seventeenth-Century England', pp. 22–3.

[78] Francis Bacon, *The Essays*, ed. J. Pitcher (Harmondsworth, 1985), 108–9.

G. E. Aylmer makes of Christopher Marlowe the one Elizabethan exception. Though Paul Kocher, who first published
Baines's note on which the charge of atheism against Marlowe
was based, thinks it records fragments of an atheist lecture, 'an
organized dissertation against Christianity', every statement is a
scoff or blasphemy plainly chosen for shock value, to court peril,
not a contribution to a reasoned atheist stance.[79] In the same
way Faustus's 'I thinke hell's a fable' (5. 573) which could look
like real scepticism is, in Mephostophilis's presence and in the
context of his generally pert tone, a bravuristic sally. Marlowe
too must have learned what de Guise levelled at and vicariously
carried the principle to its extreme in the experience of Faustus.
Blasphemy may be thrilling *because* it rouses the ferocity of the
persecutory imagination. As Jameson remarks: 'blasphemy not
only requires you to have a strong sense of the sacred quality of
the divine name, but may even be seen as a kind of ritual by
which that strength is reawakened and revitalized.'[80] If Marlowe
is the sole exception Aylmer can propose, it seems safe to
conclude that the rule has stood the proof. And it is hard to see in
the light of Marlowe's own career and the cultural milieu in
which it developed how his conception of God—assuming that he
had one—could have differed from that of Faustus. Both found it
impossible to cramp themselves into the narrow joyless culture
Calvinism and its puritan outcropping demarcated for them; and
the psychic punishment which results for Faustus no doubt
lurked in the mind not just of Marlowe but of all those
summoned to occupy the subject-position of the reprobate in an
ambience where scepticism was not a sustainable intellectual and
emotional posture.

The play turns scrutiny on the audience—embroiling it,
initially through the mechanism of the morality tradition, in
Faustus's predicament, forcing simultaneous cognition of cultural
polarities—and it is to this source of its vibrancy that I return the
concluding emphasis. 'The tension between what could be and
what actually takes place is', says David Bevington, 'the primary
source of conflict in Faustus' spiritual biography, and owes its
power to the morality heritage.'[81] But it is partly because
Marlowe differs from *Mankind* in this respect that *Doctor Faustus*

---

[79] *Christopher Marlowe*, pp. 34–6, 33.   [80] *The Political Unconscious*, p. 68.
[81] David Bevington, *From Mankind to Marlowe* (Cambridge, Mass., 1962), 251.

packs the power the moralities lack. *Doctor Faustus*, in company with, for example, *The Changeling* and *Macbeth*, convinces the audience that what takes place is necessary, and conflict and power derive from the illusion, cultivated by the protagonist, that it is not. The underlying conviction that optimism is an illusion is probably the essential attribute of despair and it is this, not as for example Lily Campbell thinks suspense, that the play offers the audience.[82] Far from suggesting that he is on the brink of success Faustus's efforts to repent, like his efforts to rebel, reinforce the actuality of the reprobate's psycho-theological prison. Audience members pit their irrepressible wishes against the outcome they foresee. Like Faustus they feel the undertow beneath the froth of the middle scenes which draws them towards a rendezvous with the persecutory deity. To the extent that they had internalized puritan discourse—and Norwood's record is a marker—they had a high price to pay for their entertainment. Confronting the persecutory imagination meant facing up to the impossibility of facing it down.

[82] Lily B. Campbell, '*Doctor Faustus*: A Case of Conscience', *PMLA* 67 (1952), 219–39, p. 224.

8
Calvin, Satan, and Milton's Purpose

MILTON is the natural terminus for my argument. He belongs both to the puritan tradition, to which the first half of the book was directly addressed, and to the classical humanist culture in which Burton, Donne, and Marlowe felt at home. Milton repudiated Calvinism's most distinctive tenets. Yet, in spite of the author's strenuous opposition to the theology which promoted them, human consciousness is still stalked, in *Paradise Lost*, by the Calvinist figments. Whatever Milton may have deliberately believed, and believed himself to be exhibiting in the poem, the full weight of imaginings in which his compatriots had acquiesced bears down on the experience the poem portrays. Had this pressure not registered, an imaginative poverty would have made itself felt. Attractive as a serenely consistent, morally superior, alternative system of values might be, it would feel like an evasion of, not an advance on, the theological and social ambience out of which the epic emerged. In fact, however, the poem assimilates the persecutory imagination, taking the measure of the beast at the same time as it shapes a fragile independence from it. A window opens, for reasons which can be linked to Milton's historical situation, on to a path towards sustainable freedom from the dispositions which gave Calvinism its purchase on the psyche.

The project of *Paradise Lost*, to 'assert eternal providence | And justify the ways of God to men', bespeaks a perceived need to justify God. While the word 'justify' could bear a simply declarative sense, contemporaries, as now, generally used it (as a glance through *OED*'s examples confirms) in contexts of accusation or defence. Since 'the ways of God to men' parallel 'eternal providence' one source of the felt need for justification could be the disappointment history had served up to Milton and the republican cause. But what on another (arguably related) level gave rise to it is conveniently clarified by Milton's use of similar phrasing in a prose work: 'As a vindication of God's justice [*Ad asserendam iustitiam Dei*] . . . some measure of free will should be allowed to man.' The idea that God rewarded 'the good' and punished 'the wicked' after first bending the will to his moral preference was bound, he said, to 'cause an outcry against divine justice from all sides'.[1] His project, then, is set against the backdrop of Calvin's denial of free will to mankind. While apologists for Christianity as a whole had of course abounded no one, I think, much before Milton had spoken of *justifying* God. The idea arose when it did because of the aggressive insistence of Calvinists, aimed at countering protest at the doctrine of predestined reprobation, that God should not be brought to the bar of human justice. Milton sees himself as opposing a theological norm: since, he argued, predestination is always presented in the Bible as an effect of God's mercy, 'we ought not attribute it, *as is usually done*, to his absolute and inscrutable will' (*CPW* vi. 175; my italics). In using the word 'justify' Milton at once announces his rejection of the Calvinist position that God's justice cannot be measured by human understanding and his determination to oppose those who had reacted to the God Calvinism had posited by questioning either tenets he considered fundamental to biblical Christianity or the justice of God itself.

Milton was not the only writer of his time in the business of justifying God's ways to men against a Calvinist backdrop. The chief aim of the Cambridge Platonists was, as D. P. Walker observes, the establishment of the 'priority of moral ideas over the divine will'; and they were asserting this aim 'against the Calvinism in which most of them had been brought up'.[2] Specifically anticipating the brief Milton set himself was a former pupil of Henry More, George Rust, who, in *A Letter of Resolution concerning Origen and the Chief of his Opinions* (1661), concluded his address 'To the Reader' by expressing himself '*confident thou wilt not be offended with any thing in it if thou beest of my humour, to think no Opinion formidable which does honour to God . . . which justifies the waies of his Providence, and reconciles them with his most precious Attributes,*

[1] *Complete Prose Works of John Milton*, ed. D. M. Wolfe (New Haven, 1953), vi. 397. Further references to this edition, abbreviated *CPW*, will be embodied in the text. (References to *Paradise Regained* will be abbreviated *PR*, *Samson Agonistes*, *SA* (*Poems*, ed. Carey and Fowler (1968)). In the case of *Paradise Lost* only book and line number need be indicated.) Calvinists would have quibbled with Milton's account of their position, but substantially the point is accurate: i.e. if God alone determined that some would turn to him he was responsible for the fact that the rest could not and did not, and for their unavoidable wickedness.

[2] *The Decline of Hell: Seventeenth-Century Discussions of Eternal Torment* (1964), 55–6.

Equity and Benignity. Farewell.' Such was Rust's confidence, it appears, in the favourable reception of his work that he adopted several layers of disguise. Signing himself C. L., he claimed to have received the letter from a friend in response to his theological queries; and the 'friend' used the cover of exposition of Origen so that he could speak, albeit with transparent irony, of 'an argument where the Sentiments of my own mind are not at all intended'.[3] His valediction points the reader to the section of the letter concerned with the restitution of all things, including the damned and even the devils. Rust's conception of what was required to justify God's ways can help to situate Milton's undertaking.

Like Milton, Rust derived impetus from Calvin's pre-emption of debate with the trump card of divine sovereignty:

I know there are many men who, part out of piety and humility, part from a Parrot-like talking such words as their Books and Education have taught them, would make no bones of this Difficulty of the *holy Father*, but can with very great ease and satisfaction of minde resolve all into the *pleasure* and *Sovereignty* of God, who being the Creator and Lord of all men, may (they say) dispose of them how and where he pleases. But it would be very well if they were as jealous Patrons of the more excellent *Attributes* of God, as they are peremptory Assertors of his *absolute Will* and *Power*. For then they would both render his Existence and Government in the world so desireable to all men, that none but the extremely guilty would wish either his *not being*, or his *non-concerning* himself in the Affairs of men; and also cut off many scandalous occasions of *Atheisme* and *Epicurisme*.

'Patrons of the more excellent *Attributes*' marks a new kind of detachment in talking about God. God's profile is being inspected from the consumer angle. An awareness is conveyed that the impositions of the Calvinist God are leading to deism ('*non-concerning* himself in the Affairs of men') and even atheism in the modern sense (a collective desire for 'his *not being*' could develop, Rust seems to sense, into a powerful cultural current). To Rust the rehabilitation of God required the idea of 'the liberation of the punished, whether men or *Daemons*'[4] as well as

---

[3] George Rust, *A Letter of Resolution concerning Origen and the Chief of his Opinions* (1661), facsimile, ed. Marjorie Hope Nicolson (New York, 1933), sig. A4ʳ, p. 136.

[4] *A Letter of Resolution*, pp. 31–2, 7. The connection between the experiential horrors of contemporary religion and movement towards deism was first evident in Lord Herbert of Cherbury's *De Veritate*, published in Paris in 1624: 'Universal

that of the pre-existence of souls (to make moral sense of the hard time God gave people this side of the grave).

Milton did not go nearly so far as Rust in his justification of God's ways. He adopted the Arminian position that faith in God was voluntary and that 'predestination' of the elect was on the basis of foreseen, not predetermined, faith. It does not seem, moreover, that he arrived early at this view. Arminianism achieved currency in England as part of a reactionary package, and this no doubt retarded its acceptance on its theological merits by opponents of Charles and Laud. As Richard Baxter observed of the English Arminians: 'And doubtless, one reason why they were so bad in England was, that the godly being first entered into another schoole, and so running one way (much by the force of example and affection and much by divine grace) the others were temporizers that took up the opinions for worldly respects'.[5] The theology was partly judged by the company it kept. But it would be too simple to say that Milton and other puritans clung to Calvinism merely because Laudians lined up behind Arminianism.

Influential recent critics such as David Norbrook and Christopher Hill have tended to talk down the theological substance of the stances adopted, sometimes presenting them as no more than counters in an essentially secular political struggle. Thus Norbrook: 'In abstract theological terms the debate between Calvinists and Arminians was abstruse and raised enormously complex philosophical issues. But it aroused deep passions amongst the laity because it had direct political connotations.'[6] Hill is more interested in the fuel Calvinism as a belief-system supplied to revolutionary action but he too cuts off

consent, then, will be found to be the final test of truth. It is of the highest importance to distinguish these Common Notions and to allot each of these indubitable truths to its proper position. This has never been so necessary as now. For men are now not only exhorted with every device that language can employ by arguments from the pulpit, but are tormented in spite of the protests of conscience and the inner consciousness, by the belief that all who are outside their particular Church are condemned, whether through ignorance or error, to undergo . . . eternal punishment after death. The wretched terror-stricken mass have no refuge, unless some immovable foundations of truth resting on universal consent are established, to which they can turn' (trans. and ed. M. H. Carré (Bristol, 1937), 117).

[5] Letter of 21 November 1653, quoted in W. M. Lamont, *Richard Baxter and the Millennium* (1979), 127.

[6] David Norbrook, *Poetry and Politics in the English Renaissance* (1984), 230.

when personal rather than social aspects of theology arise: 'academics', he says, 'tended to brood over abstruse problems like assurance of salvation and the visibility of the elect'.[7] We have, sadly, all the evidence we could need, including the testimony of favourites of Hill such as Lodowick Muggleton, Laurence Clarkson, and Jacob Bauthumley, that the problem of assurance was anything but abstruse or of academic concern to those who fell under the shadow of Calvin. Because the impact of theology on the structure of perception is largely disregarded the cross-over to Arminianism is too crudely understood.

For Hill, Milton 'justified God's ways to men by substituting for the Calvinist God of arbitrary power an Arminian God of goodness, justice and reasonableness'. George Rust plainly could not regard the Arminian God as good, just, and reasonable, however, because Calvin and his followers had, by their extremism, inadvertently raised to consciousness the moral horror of the doctrine of eternal torment. According to Hill, Milton's Arminianism 'means that salvation is potentially open to all, and is attained by good works'.[8] It was, however, on the voluntary nature of faith that Arminius insisted, while he retained the Lutheran principle that salvation was *sola fide*. As with Calvinists, works (or fruits) were the evidence of faith; but it was on perseverance in faith that salvation depended. And Milton, too, adopts this position. What was known as Arminianism in England in the build-up to the Civil War was the political anti-Calvinism of the Laudian party. But for those who graduated from Calvinism to Arminianism during or after the Civil War, the shift could amount, in effect, less to a theological conversion than to an adjustment of an existing outlook which had taken shape under Calvinist influence.

It may seem perverse to implicate Milton in a Calvinist cast of mind. He jettisoned the predestinarian teaching which was the direct source of the sense of being hunted down by a malevolent destiny. Seeing that human dignity came with the responsibility of unconstrained choice, he developed the perception into his

---

[7] *Milton and the English Revolution* (1977), 270.

[8] *Milton and the English Revolution*, pp. 275, 302. Hill refers the reader to *CPW*, vi. 166 for evidence of Milton's belief in salvation by works; while the passage certainly affirms free will the examples Milton gives (vi. 165–6) all concern abandonment of faith.

most consistent theme. Yet he held on to the doctrine of eternal punishment; and he did not restrict it to a comminatory function. Destinies in Milton's universe are still polarized. In order to justify the extreme divergence of lives of both types it was necessary to exhibit a plausibly drastic process of deterioration resulting from the lack of faith as well as a plausible process of sanctification of the elect. But doing this imposed a teleology not wholly distinct from Calvinist predestination. Satan, it is emphasized, chose freely; but once he had chosen the die was cast. Paradoxically Milton gives choice such awesome significance that it turns itself into a form of determinism. Satan shows how the reprobate are trapped by their choice, handcuffed to their consequential destiny.

The treatment of Satan does not contradict the Arminian stance; Arminians believed the devils were eternally damned. But what embarrasses this position, inasmuch as Arminians aspired to make God appear good, just, and reasonable by emphasizing free will, is the imaginative investment which is made in the hopelessness of Satan's predicament, the fluctuations in feeling towards the unrelenting deity, the self-alienation, and, above all, the lived-in experience of God's denial of repentance. Firmly ejecting Calvinism from statements of his theology both inside and outside *Paradise Lost* Milton readmits it by a back door by placing Satan in the predicament, and giving him much of the psychology, of the predestined reprobate. That Satan once had free will becomes as irrelevant to the psychic actuality which is portrayed from the opening of Book 1 as was Calvin's belief that Adam had been free before the Fall to the experience of his doomed progeny. It was Calvin's activation of the idea of reprobation as the condition of a species of psychological experience that made Satan possible. 'Only in a Calvinist system', says the historian Michael Walzer (thinking presumably of Milton), 'could Satan be viewed dramatically as a rebel against the arbitrary sovereign of the universe.'[9] Even if it could be shown that Satan's perception of God is deluded, the form of the delusion is determined by Calvinism; and from this delusion much of the poem's dramatic energy flows. It is extremely hard to dissociate God from a fantasy in which he plays a vigorous

[9] *The Revolution of the Saints: A Study in the Origins of Radical Politics* (1966), 154.

role. It is this fantasy, sharpening his identity as a person and actor rather than a sublime principle, that makes him unethereal enough for it to be tempting to speak of his more and less excellent attributes—though the kind of aloofness Rust seems to have acquired was historically preceded by guilt at an irrepressible resistance to the exigent patriarch.

It may appear that too much is being taken for granted. Satan is, after all, a principal actor in received accounts of the Fall. The fall of the angels is a natural precursor and had been developed into a routine component of the hexameral tradition. Grant McColley has painstakingly unearthed the antecedents.[10] Possible motives for Satan's rebellion (envy, pride, ambition) had been widely canvassed; and critics of *Paradise Lost* such as Merritt Y. Hughes and Arnold Williams have juggled with these, claiming this or that novel combination.[11] But the feeling persists that little has been explained. Helen Gardner saw that there was a critical lacuna: 'the question whether Satan had any ancestors has hardly been raised,' she observed, 'or has been dismissed by reference to the devil of popular tradition, or by allusion to the heroic figure of the Old English *Genesis B*.'[12] Milton's great continental predecessors do not help: 'Dante and Tasso', said Shelley, 'present us with a very gross idea of him.'[13]

A question remains as to why Milton should have conceived of the devil, in whose literal existence he believed, in the ways in which he projects him. It is apparent in the Bible, for example, what functions the character of Satan is introduced to perform. In the Book of Job he deflects criticism of God for torturing the protagonist. In the Gospel temptation story, the only other occasion on which he is given a speaking part, he serves a similar convenience of distancing evil thoughts from Christ's own mind. The Bible restricted Satan to the functions of a sketchy tempter figure. In the Old English *Fall of the Angels* Satan and the devils are militaristic and reflect that society's feudal concept of enmity

[10] Grant McColley, '*Paradise Lost*': *An Account of its Growth and Major Origins, with a Discussion of Milton's Use of Sources and Literary Patterns* (New York, 1940), *passim*.

[11] Merritt Y. Hughes, 'Myself Am Hell', *MP* 54 (1956), 80–94; Arnold Williams, 'The Motivation of Satan's Rebellion in *Paradise Lost*', *SP* 42 (1945), 253–68.

[12] Helen Gardner, 'The Tragedy of Damnation', reprinted in *Elizabethan Drama: Modern Essays and Criticism*, ed. R. J. Kaufmann (New York, 1961), 320.

[13] *The Complete Works of Percy Bysshe Shelley*, ed. R. Ingpen and W. E. Peck (1965), vii. 92.

and evil: Satan is a rival lord. In the medieval drama the devil is at once unspecified alien menace to the community, bogey man, and, as a means of controlling fear, a caricature. What stands out as new in Milton's treatment is not leadership, warriorship, or the salience of a particular sin or combination of sins. What is new is interiorization. This is obvious if one looks at Satan's response to the failure of his attempted coup in the Cædmonian *Genesis*, probably the most directly comparable analogue. Dismay is instantly translated into revenge plans; despair is bypassed or not considered; no strain is suggested between public bravado and private anguish. Similarly the Lucifer of the Mystery Plays reacts, when ducked into hell, without introspection.

It does not take us far towards explaining the new interiority of Satan to say that Milton conceived of hell as primarily a state of mind. McColley traces 'Myself am hell' back as far as Bonaventure in the thirteenth century: the devils 'carry the fire of hell with them wherever they go'.[14] And it was the standard patristic line that *poena damni*, exclusion from the presence of God, was yet more terrible to bear than *poena sensus*. But observations like Bonaventure's remain moralization from the outside. The same goes for the links Hill suggests with radicals such as William Walwyn, who declared that hell was nothing but the bad conscience of evil men. Hell is still for other people. And despite Hill's claim that he 'skirted very near to the radical doctrine which saw heaven and hell *merely* as internal states,'[15] Milton nowhere indicates the slightest scepticism as to the local actuality of hell. He situates it, consideredly, 'outside this world' on the grounds that it might otherwise be consumed in the great conflagration, a thought that would bring cheer to the people and devils who should occupy it for all eternity (*CPW* vi. 625). His belief that the psychological and spiritual anguish of the consequences of sin were more significant than the physical tortures was entirely conventional This view was strongly reiterated by the reformers after the crudity of much late medieval preaching. That Calvin thought those who spoke of a material hell had crass imaginations does not mean he questioned its existence.

[14] *'Paradise Lost': An Account of its Major Origins*, pp. 140–1.
[15] *Milton and the English Revolution*, pp. 309, 311; see also pp. 106–7.

The psychology of Milton's Satan speaks for a dramatic advance in the capacity to think about states of mind: in particular, despair and rejection and their connection with hatred and destructive behaviour. We need to ask why Milton should have wanted to get under Satan's skin and what it was in the contemporary scene that favoured such a development. Helen Gardner's essay, 'The Tragedy of Damnation', implicitly recognizes that it is the quality of being inside the villain, especially through soliloquy, that is most special to Milton's Satan. She believes that 'wherever Satan appears, what is said goes beyond the necessities of the narrative, because Milton was writing as a tragic artist obsessed by his imagination of a particular experience, and exploring it with maximum intensity. The experience might be called "exclusion".' She offered an entirely different kind of answer to the question of Satan's antecedents: 'if we ask where the idea of damnation was handled with seriousness and intensity in English literature before Milton, we can only reply: on the tragic stage.'[16] Milton, she argues, found in villain-heroes such as Faustus, Macbeth, and Beatrice-Joanna the inspiration for his fallen archangel, whose first soliloquy was originally to have introduced a tragedy. But questions remain. Why should Milton's imagination have been possessed by the idea of exclusion, and why should Satan have been chosen as the vehicle of its exploration? Helen Gardner's suggestive thesis, which is essentially a generic argument about the influence of a particular kind of tragedy, can, I think, be slanted in a different direction. It may be that the villain-heroes she speaks of are, as well as influences on Satan, products themselves of a similar extra-literary situation.[17] While it is true that the devil in his own person does not become a character, an ambiguity is maintained, in Macbeth and Faustus for example, as to whether they might not be demonic.

There are frequent incidental references to suggest this in

---

[16] Gardner, 'The Tragedy of Damnation', pp. 333, 331.

[17] I have explored this suggestion in relation to Macbeth and Beatrice-Joanna in 'Calvinist Psychology in *Macbeth*', *Shakespeare Studies* 20 (1988), 169–84, and 'Calvinist Psychology in the Tragedies of Middleton', in R. V. Holdsworth, ed., *Three Jacobean Revenge Tragedies: A Casebook* (1990). In using the term 'extra-literary' I do not mean to partition 'literature' off from other discourse; rather to suggest that such a walling-off of the non-literary is implied by the way in which earlier critics have directed their search for Satan's origins.

Doctor Faustus. In the farcical scenes Faustus is referred to as 'damned Hell-hound' and as the devil (B. 4. 3. 1404, 1421, 1443). The Epilogue speaks of his 'fiendful fortune'. Less casually, though, when the Bad Angel tells him, 'Thou art a spirite, God cannot pitty thee,' Faustus almost concedes demonic identity in his despairingly sophistical reply: 'Be I a divel, yet God may pitty me' (5. 642, 644). (The sense of this is suggested by Belial in *Paradise Lost* when he considers the possibility of God allowing the devils to pass into oblivion: 'How he can | Is doubtful; that he never will is sure' (2. 154–5).) Faustus has, after all, contracted with Lucifer to become '*a spirit in forme and substance*' (5. 541). The Signet editor is unhappy with this clause in the contract on the grounds that 'to see Faustus as transformed now into a devil deprived of the freedom to repent is to deprive the remainder of the play of much of its meaning'.[18] He presupposes, however, as many critics do, that having freedom to repent is more dramatically 'meaningful' than not having it. Yet the play's portrayal of Faustus's predicament as tantamount to a devil's enables exploration of an experience of alienation which is social as much as it is theological. It forces the audience to confront the experiential meaning of Calvinist reprobation. The inability to repent no more diminishes the psychological or dramatic interest in Faustus than in Milton's Satan.

By fostering uncertainty as to Faustus's human status Marlowe pitches his identity between the human and the demonic, an apt way of portraying the presumed reprobate. That the identity of the presumed reprobate and the devils could converge in this way may account for Rust's belief that it was not just all humanity but the devils too who must be redeemed. 'The terrible distinction between devils and men in popular theology lay', says Helen Gardner, 'in the irreversibility of the fall of the angels.'[19] At precisely the time about which she is writing, the meaning-fulness of this distinction broke down. The irreversibility of the fall of the angels became immediate to people when they began to learn, thanks to Calvin, what it felt like to be forever denied mercy, when the psychological state of devils became an object of empathy rather than shuddering recoil.

Reprobates were, said Calvin,

---

[18] Sylvan Barnet, ed., *Doctor Faustus* (New York, 1969), 42.
[19] 'The Tragedy of Damnation', p. 321.

noe better than the Devell. But that firste sorte of men are farre worse then the Devell, whiche do senslessly heare and understand those thinges for knoweledge whereof the Devells do tremble. And the other are in this point egall with the Devell, that the feeling suche as it is wherewith they are touched, turnet[h] only to terroure and discouragement. (*Inst.* 3. 2. 10)

Faustus manages to belong to both classes of reprobate. In response to his questions about hell, Mephostophilis piteously exclaims: 'O *Faustus*, leave these frivolous demands, | which strike a terror to my fainting soule,' and receives in reply an impassive jeer from Faustus:

> What, is great *Mephastophilis* so passionate,
> For being deprivd of the joyes of heaven?
> Learne thou of *Faustus* manly fortitude . . .
>
> (3. 326–30)

Terror and discouragement later inhibit any move towards repentance.

In addition to Faustus being thought, and suspecting himself to be, demonic, Mephostophilis is, of course, endowed with resonant humanity; and the possibility of mercy is withheld from him. Even if those who favour a so-called moderate Anglican reading of *Doctor Faustus* could show that its theology is not Calvinist, the humanization of Mephostophilis makes the effort pointless. Why allow Faustus the possibility of salvation and not the more soulfully remorseful Mephostophilis? While activation of the idea of reprobation brought the devils closer imaginatively to suffering humanity many people underwent, it appears, a radical self-alienation, often becoming objects of their own moral fury. In Elizabethan and Jacobean drama such self-alienation could be used to enrich punitive satisfaction, as when the inhuman Cardinal in *The Duchess of Malfi* sees in his fishpond 'a thing, arm'd with a rake | That seems to strike at me' (5. 5. 6–7). But sympathies are more confused when characters objectify themselves as moral exempla, as does Grimaldi in Massinger's *Renegado*: 'I am a divell already' (3. 2. 77), he moans when exhorted to repent. A pitch is made, as with Faustus, Macbeth, and Beatrice-Joanna, for the sympathy of anyone capable of understanding the feeling of irredeemable guilt. The villain-hero, structurally soliciting sympathy while morally reprobated, is, I think, a product, as much as anything else, of a new category of human identity to which Calvinist discourse, in concert with the conditions that provided its opening, gave birth.

In *Paradise Lost*, as in *De Doctrina*, Milton naturally links 'Bad men and angels' (3. 330–1; *CPW* vi. 165). This virtual equation seems to have become routine in Reformation writing. The tendency no doubt assisted demonization of political opponents (both sides in the Civil War saw Satan—Hebrew for adversary—as commanding general of the enemy troops), and was in turn reinforced by this practice. Typical is John Benbrigge's *Gods Fury, England's Fire* (1646), a book Milton had in his library:

Now, whence is it that the Devill and wicked men (wee may well joyne them together, for they are never asunder) have such an unquenchable fury against goodnesse and good men? . . . The antipathy that is in their natures against godlinesse; it is so offensive to them, as they cannot endure to see that man or that woman, wherein it appeares never so little.[20]

Milton appears, especially after disillusionment with the idea that the English people were the elect nation, to have accepted the division between the godly remnant and the rest which co-religionists expressed more crudely. John Goodwin's preface to *Anapologesiastes Antapologias: Or, the Inexcusablenesse of That Grand Accusation of the Brethren, Called Antapologia* (1646), another book Milton owned, protests against the attempt to include all in the church of God:

what do they (in effect) but sweare . . . that they will endeavour to bring day and night, light and darkness . . . Christ and Belial, into the nearest Communion and conjunction they can? Certainly Wolves and Tigers, Beares and Lions, are as capable of politick and civill conjunction with men; as loose, wicked, ungodly and prophane men are.

In the period of his disillusionment, culminating in the Restoration, Milton learnt that the crude act of side-taking under the banner of the good old cause concealed a multitude of malignant motives. So by the time he wrote *Paradise Lost* he was, not unlike the Presbyterians he despised, concerned to winnow the invisible saints from the rest. How do you know you are one of the elect? By testing yourself in the reading of the poem, a subtilized book of signs, to discover whether you belonged to the

---

[20] John Benbrigge, *Gods Fury, England's Fire* (1646), 40.

'fit audience . . . though few'.[21] One of Milton's chief concerns is with self-deception, or, in the puritan sense of the term, hypocrisy. This explains the trouble that is taken with Satan's thought processes.

Just as 'the faythfull', said Calvin, 'are hereby knowen to be the children of God because they beare his image: so they by the image of Satan into which they are gone out of kind, are properly discerned to be his children' (*Inst.* 1. 14. 18). Glossing the Bible's 'you are not of God', Milton asked: 'Does it mean "you are not elect"? No, indeed it is synonymous with "you are of the Devil," viii. 44, that is, you follow the Devil rather than God' (*CPW* vi. 201). The process by which this occurred was a source of fascination to Calvin: 'The heart of man hathe so many secrete corners of vanitie, is full of so many hidinge holes of lyeng, is covered wyth so guilefull hypocrisie, that it ofte deceiveth himselfe,' he writes in the section (*Inst.* 3. 2. 10) in which he demotes the reprobate beneath the devils. And in a passage that may have helped to inspire Milton's original exploration of Satan's psyche in soliloquy, he describes how 'hypocrites would obteyne by crooked compasses to seeme nye unto God, whome they fle from . . . At length they entangle theym selves with suche a heape of errours, that the darke myste of malice doothe choke, and at laste utterly quenche those sparkes, that glimmeryngly shyned to make them see the glory of god' (*Inst.* 1. 4. 4.). Inability to repent, thought Milton, resulted from 'your own obstinate and habitual incredulity or, at any rate, because of your pride, which stops your ears, or, finally, as the next verse puts it, *because you are of your father, the Devil, and want to perform your father's desires*' (*CPW* vi. 201). The unfit many, it may be inferred, could find their own mental processes mirrored in Satan's.

While Calvin coolly documented some observable effects of the psychological pressures to which his theology subjected people, Luther had supplied a passionate eloquence, bred of his own experience, which put readers in more intimate touch with the devil's feelings: 'If the Devil had not a bad conscience,' he confidently affirmed for example, 'he would be in heaven . . . the Devil would not be afraid of burning rocks or external torments:

---

[21] See Stanley Fish, *Surprised by Sin* (1967), *passim*, where the poem is seen as a sustained test on the reader.

it is from within that his tortures come, in his heart.'[22] Indeed for Milton Satan is 'never more in hell than when in heaven' (*PR* 1. 420). The ponderous materiality of the epic, as in its presentation of hell as a locality, generally operates to expose its triviality in comparison with what goes on in the mind: physical chains snap, heroic journeys put no distance at all between Satan and what he wants to escape, Satan feels worse the more his environment accentuates his rejection.

But the closest analogues for the interior life of Milton's Satan have been completely overlooked, presumably because they have little obvious political or literary or theological significance. The demonization of human characters was not just a theatrical device; there were actual people around whose social alienation was so preyed on by Calvinist preaching that they were convinced of their reprobation and sometimes, like Faustus, even took the small next step of thinking themselves demonic. Ex-Ranting Muggletonian Laurence Clarkson pointed to Calvinist despairers to reinforce his argument that people have 'A real devil within them, but an imagined devil without them'. Countering the objection to his 'Devil-man' concept that '*We are upon the earth not tormented*' and therefore cannot be devils, Clarkson pointed to the 'thousands of the brood that have an earnest peny of that they shall be hereafter; otherwise what causeth the hideous, doleful sighs, groans and cries of many of your seed in health, but much more on thy bed of sickness, concluding in thy self, I am damned, I am damned to all eternity . . . ?' He instanced the Baptist minister Thomas Gun, who shot himself with a pistol.[23] But it is the confessional accounts that provide access to the interior reality. So, for example, Richard Norwood was

tempted to doubt whether I was a man indeed endued with a reasonable soul, or whether I were not rather a devil incarnate in the likeness of a man, and a very enemy to God, and therefore did seem to wish that I had never been or that I might fly somewhere from God. ('Confessions', p. 95)

---

[22] Gordon Rupp, *The Righteousness of God: Luther Studies* (1953), 110.
[23] *Look about you, for the Devil that you Fear Is in you* (1659), 24, 23, 25–6, 27. Thomas Gun represented the fourth London Baptist Church in the 1644 *Confession* of the London Particular Baptists.

Like Satan in his soliloquies Norwood vacillates in his feelings about God. Rather than a believer who periodically falls from grace, he sees himself as a reprobate with occasional fits of remorse:

Yet so was my heart hardened that these and many other calamities could not move it to relent or take any pity or compassion on myself, only I think once or twice for a short time my heart did relent a little . . . (p. 27)

And later, when he had worked hard at persuading himself he was on God's side, he none the less relapsed into a Satanic perception of God:

and in that fit I was most suddenly and vehemently assaulted with a number of blasphemous and horrible thoughts and temptations or persuasions, as that God was not just and faithful in his word, that he was hard and unmerciful, etc. And that he had now certainly given me over to Satan and that I was now become a companion of the devil and his angels, and that I did hate God and rage against Him as the damned spirits do. And surely my heart seemed to be in a manner so disposed. (p. 96)

A local hell seems to have materialized out of the extremity of his psychic experiences: *Richard   Norwood.*

Oft-times I verily thought that I descended into Hell and there felt the pains of the damned, with many hideous things. (p. 26)

Methought as I looked back I saw myself far entered within the gates of hell, and now if the percullis should be let fall I should be kept in and could no more return, and I feared upon my offer to return the percullis would be presently let fall; such a kind of apprehension I had in my imagination. And indeed I found myself so weak, and so habituated and prone to despair, and Satan to have got such power over me by custom, that I much feared that as soon as he should perceive me about to return and to lay hold on the promises (which I had long neglected) he would assail me with all his power and be ready to overwhelm me with utter despair. (pp. 94–5)

Calvinism's reprobatory vocabulary did not, as is common in religious systems, merely bolster the in-group's sense of its special status; it penetrated deeply under the skin of many of its hapless objects, constructing them as subjects. Thinking oneself a devil was the ultimate self-ostracism it could inculcate. The state of mind displayed in Satan's soliloquies derives less from any picture of the devil which either theological or literary traditions had made available than from Milton's own contemporaries who themselves professed affinity with the devils.

George Trosse, in a mental asylum in Glastonbury, experienced a reckless vengefulness towards God and his creation which forced him into this self-description: 'They saw me as a *Bull*, kicking in the *Net* of GOD's *Judgments*; but they did not see me (as in Effect I was) a *Devil*, storming and roaring in my *Chains* of *Darkness*, and raging against GOD, Man and my Self.' 'My *desperate Hatred* of GOD,' he recalls in terms to which, leaving out the Belialesque cowardice, Milton's Satan could subscribe,

deriv'd itself upon *all* the *Creatures*, and that I might be *cruel* towards *Him*, I would be towards *them*. But at length I was perswaded that if I should do *so*, I should vastly *out-sin* the World of *sinful Men* and *Devils*, and so expose myself to *greater Degrees* of *Torments* than *any* I could inflict upon others: But neither would this allay my *Rage*, or blunt the Edge of my *Malice*, against GOD.

Like Satan looking up at the sun or at Adam and Eve making love, he 'carry'd as it were, my *Hell within* me, and therefore could see nothing *without* that was pleasing to me'. It was not the bestial level of appetite to which he had sunk: 'I sunk my self', he says, 'beneath the *Beasts* that perish, and levell'd my self (in effect) with the *Devils*, who are damn'd in their Despair, Rage, and Enmity against GOD, and in their Malice and Fury against Man.'[24]

The social reality of this mental condition informs the creation of Satan. But for such a condition to be plausible it was necessary for God to collaborate, or at least appear to collaborate, in its construction. Trosse puts despair before rage and enmity. Satan's soliloquies, we'll find, do the same; otherwise the logic of his emotions would fail to convince. The turmoil in his psyche is premissed on the idea of God's hatred and rejection. Richard Baxter saw the inescapable logic of response to the unremittingly hostile God Calvinism had tended to promote in the minds of many: 'They think he hateth them, and hath forsaken them; and how can they love such a God, who they think doth hate them, and resolve to damn them, and hath decreed them to it from Eternity?'[25] Victims were more commonly blamed for their

---

[24] *The Life* (Exeter, 1714), 71, 72, 60, 102.
[25] *Preservatives against Melancholy and Overmuch Sorrow* (1713), 12.

perception of God. Richard Capel described the problem without explaining how it could be averted:

> if wee once take a thought and it grow firme in us, that God doth hate us, and wil curse us, we will hate him againe and be ready to curse him . . . we all hate God by nature, but yet there is a further measure of hatred wrought in us to God, when we conceive, that out of very malice and spleene towards us, he doth use us as he never did nor doth use any other; and in this case our very stomacks will rise, and our bloud will swell against the LORD GOD Almighty.[26]

As a widespread phenomenon this was—it is worth considering afresh in relation to the originality of Milton's Satan—something new in spiritual experience. When Thomas More wrote his *Dialogue of Comforts* he was clear that it was the power of the devil, not of God, of which the victim of despair was terrified.[27] But for Luther it was God's more terrible enmity that crushed the despairer: 'For a heart completely cast down and in despair cannot open its mouth so wide, but it is dumb, or it slanders God and cannot think, believe or speak of God other than as a fearful tyrant, or as of the Devil, and only wants to flee and get away from him.'[28] The responsibility for this can be firmly laid at the door of protestant preachers. Luther himself, for all his genuine tenderness towards the spiritually afflicted, rejected the medieval church's belief that God loved the sinner while he hated the sin: 'God hates sin and the sinner,' he insisted, 'and necessarily; otherwise he would be unrighteous and a lover of sin.'[29] English Calvinists echoed this view: 'whome God rejecteth to condemnation,' said William Perkins, 'those he hateth.'[30] Carl Jung noted in a preface to R. J. Zwi Werblowsky's study of Milton's Satan: 'the Reformation thrust the figure of Satan once more into the foreground.'[31] The devil had to assume prominence in order to account for the poisonous picture of God which the reformers had themselves put abroad. 'The Design of the Devil,' said Baxter, 'is to describe God to us as like himself, who is a malicious Enemy, and delighteth to do hurt.'[32] Such was the

---

[26] *Tentations: Their Nature, their Danger, their Cure* (1633), 270–1.

[27] Thomas More, *A Dialogue of Comfort against Tribulation* (1534), 157–8.

[28] Rupp, *Righteousness of God*, p. 112.

[29] Quoted in J. S. Whale, *The Protestant Tradition: An Essay in Interpretation* (Cambridge, 1959), 23.   [30] *The Works* (Cambridge, 1605), 116.

[31] Carl Jung, preface to R. J. Zwi Werblowsky, *Lucifer and Prometheus: A Study of Milton's Satan* (1952), xi.   [32] *Preservatives against Melancholy*, p. 14.

terror of God the reformers instilled, above all when compounded by the fatalism Calvinism produced, that God and the devil came to share attributes. Thomas Edwards reported in his *Gangraena* on those who 'said God was as much in hell as in heaven'.[33] In fact God and the devil could even exchange attributes. Keith Thomas records a Mary Skipper's temptation to embrace witchcraft on the devil's promise to 'carry her to Heaven'.[34] And Lawrence Clarkson, in 1659, reported the corollary: 'I'le assure thee there is some this day in *London*, and Country also, that in my hearing hath said, God is a devil'.[35]

Satan and the other devils are presented subjectively in *Paradise Lost* because religious experience in Milton's day was characterized by alternative psychological postures which it was the tendency of protestant preaching to polarize. To understand properly why Satan is sympathetic in *Paradise Lost* we need to know how in the protestant imagination the devil had become less alien, more intimately involved in human thought processes, with a resulting confusion of spiritual values. Once God's hatred had become an imaginative reality the human response became indistinguishable from the formerly alien and shocking demonic response. Satan seeks 'league' and 'amity' with humanity. He does not so much intend to deceive Adam and Eve with what he knows, at the moment of using these words, to be a falsehood as seek to share with mankind his own perspective on God: a perspective which could be persuasively articulated as a temptation because it was one which would resonate with many of Milton's contemporary readers. It is somewhat misleading to say that hell was increasingly understood as the bad conscience of evil men when what was meant by that as a subjective experience was not an inability to live with oneself because of selfishness, cruelty to others, depraved appetites, and so forth, but rather the knot of negative emotions tied up by the conviction of rejection by the omnipotent father. It was routine for puritans like Perkins to say: 'a wicked man carrieth an hell about him in his life'.[36] But what is meant is not what a modern reader would at first take it to mean. John Sheffield brings us closer: 'all the torments and

---

[33] Quoted in Hill, *The World Turned Upside Down: Radical Ideas during the English Revolution* (1975), 176.

[34] Quoted in Thomas, *Religion and the Decline of Magic* (1971), 520.

[35] *Look about you, for the Devil that you Fear Is in you* (1659), 29.

[36] *Works*, p. 452.

miseries of Hel are *epitomised* in an unquiet, and self-tormenting Conscience. This man carries his Hell along with him where ever he comes or goes.'[37] The essence of the state is put time and again by victims: 'I now feel Gods heavy wrath,' said the notorious Spira, 'that burnes like the torments of hell within me'; 'I feel now an Hell in my conscience,' said the dying Oxford don Mr Peacock, who had led a life of earnest piety.[38]

Once damnation was subjectively apprehended perception of God underwent an irreversible imaginative shift. Under protestantism emotional rebellion, often involuntary, against the collectively postulated deity—what Milton calls 'Reluctance against God' (10. 1045)—was made more likely. Such recalcitrance was rationalized, and intensified, with the assistance of the Calvinist divines, as a symptom of reprobation. But the capricious authoritarianism and deterministic bind which induced this syndrome are exactly what Milton appears to reject. It therefore needs to be shown that the syndrome does gain access to *Paradise Lost*, and that Milton's God contributes to it.

On his arrival on earth, in Book 3, Satan comes upon the gate of heaven:

> far distant he descries,
> Ascending by degrees magnificent
> Up to the wall of heaven a structure high . . .
> The stairs were such as whereon Jacob saw
> Angels ascending and descending, bands
> Of guardians bright, when he from Esau fled
> To Padan-Aram in the field of Luz,
> Dreaming by night under the open sky,
> And waking cried, *This is the gate of heaven.*
>
> (3. 501–15)

Alastair Fowler observes of these lines: 'The relevance of the simile to Satan's situation is usually missed. Satan like Jacob has fled retribution and is at a parting of the ways where he could still repent.' Likewise for Louis Martz: the stairs 'symbolise the promise of God's everpresent grace'.[39] The belief that Satan 'could still repent' or that the promised availability of grace

---

[37] *A Good Conscience the Strongest Hold* (1650), 317.

[38] Robert Bolton, *Instructions for a Right Comforting Afflicted Consciences* (1631), 19, 84.

[39] Louis Martz, *Poet of Exile: A Study of Milton's Poetry* (New Haven, 1980), 103–4.

extends to him derives, I think, from two sources. One is the need to make Milton consistent in his portrayal of an Arminian God; the other is the recognition that it looks bad for God (and therefore compromises his justification) if he taunts Satan with the idea of grace while withholding the possibility from him. Fowler's embarrassment with Milton's text is particularly apparent when he confronts the ugly lines:

> The stairs were then let down, whether to dare
> The fiend by easy ascent, or aggravate
> His sad exclusion from the doors of bliss.

> (3. 523–5)

'Or perhaps,' suggests Fowler in lame support of his earlier note, 'to tempt the reader to fall into the satanic point of view ironically reflected in these conjectures?' There is no suggestion that these are Satan's thoughts (would Satan think of himself as 'the fiend'?). Nor is there, I think, any example elsewhere in *Paradise Lost* of blurred distinction between the thoughts of a character and the reflections of the epic voice. Both interpretations proposed by the epic voice tell the same story of vindictive divine intent, of an act of personal hatred. The lines provide a useful gloss on the later soliloquy on Mount Niphates where we share the psychological torture inflicted on the fiend by illusory possibilities of grace.

Jacob's ladder was commonly interpreted by Calvinists as a figure for the golden chain of salvation which William Perkins had popularized. Thomas Wilson, for example, wrote *Jacob's Ladder, Or a Short Treatise Laying forth Distinctly the Several Degrees of Gods Eternall Purpose, whereby his Grace Descends upon the Elect, and the Elect Ascend to the Predestinate Glory* (1611). The work was, he said, 'a practical outline of the process by which the elect and the reprobate respond to God's eternal and unchanging purpose'.[40] Milton is drawing on the double typology characteristic of Calvinists: biblical events had positive or negative application to individuals depending on their elect or reprobate identity. An occasion of progress to salvation to the one was a confirmation of rejection to the other. Satan's position is to be contrasted with

---

[40] Thomas Wilson, *Jacob's Ladder, Or a Short Treatise Laying forth Distinctly the Several Degrees of Gods Eternall Purpose, whereby his Grace Desends upon the Elect, and the Elect Ascend to the Predestinate Glory* (1611), 4–5.

that of Jacob. Jacob was awed by the vision, after he had cheated Esau out of his father's blessing, into (what was seen as) repentance. As we will see, Satan is shortly to be implicitly assimilated to Esau.

Christopher Ricks, hesitating over the dangerous facility of an approach to simile which sees point in disanalogy as well as analogy, is nevertheless driven by the apparent redundancy of the beauty and length of Jacob's relived vision of the gate to the view that 'Milton was interested in the gigantic difference between Satan and Jacob.' While 'Satan is the arch-enemy of God, Jacob was the chosen hand of God,' so Satan is pointedly not granted the same ravishing vision: the stairs were merely 'such as' Jacob saw under transfigured aspect.[41] Puritan typological practice helps to legitimize an interpretation which is hard to resist on other grounds: that in comparable circumstances God's grace visits one and not another. But though the specific vision symbolizing grace is denied to him Satan does exhibit full susceptibility to the magnetic beauty of divine creation. As Fowler points out, 'there is . . . a counterpart to Jacob's vision; for Satan is about to contemplate "all this world at once" (ll. 542 f.).' It is, though, a significantly different vision, so that it does not, as Fowler thinks, refute Ricks. The arch-enemy is being punished with the fullest possible feeling for what he has lost. Satan goes on, in surveying the world, to respond with the bitterness and deceptions of a reprobate, but the feelings build on the knowledge of disinheritance and divine rejection.

One understands critical reluctance to look steadily at this close-up on hell, and eagerness to make of it instead an instance of Satan's perverse imperviousness to God's goodness; but just as Milton, like Calvin, was hostile to attempts to soften or sophisticate the version of himself God had chosen to insert into the Bible there is good reason to suppose he would have disdained emollient interpreters of his own version (see *CPW* vi. 136; *Inst.* 1. 4. 3). *Paradise Lost* is an austere challenge to those who, in Calvin's words, 'worshyp not hym, but . . . their owne dreame in stede of hym' (*Inst.* 1. 4. 1). Milton's Arianism—no more than an intellectual tidying up of puritan emphasis on Old Testament national and personal parallels and the distinct personality of the Father—ensured, too, that the delineation of

---

[41] Christopher Ricks, *Milton's Grand Style* (Oxford, 1963), 127–8.

God's character was not soft-focused by an overlay of gentle Jesus meek and mild. Forgiveness and opportunities for repentance were, taking the Bible as a whole and eschewing Trinitarian mysticism, rather restricted.

At the beginning of Book 4 the possibility of repentance is once again claimed for Satan. 'Angels, like men,' says Christopher Hill, 'elect their own salvation. This is Arminian doctrine. Milton endowed Satan with conscience (IV. 23) and appears to envisage the possibility of his repenting (IV. 71–104). This too must be intended to stress the analogies between him and mankind.' Hill relegates to a footnote ('But cf. *PL* III. 131–2') God's perfectly clear statement: 'man therefore shall find grace, | The other none.'[42] Harry F. Robins admits, in his study of Milton and Origen, that Milton does not follow Origen on the eventual salvation of all rational creatures, but adds: 'Yet the idea of demonic repentance certainly interested Milton; for several times in the epic the fallen angels seem persuaded that it is possible.'[43] John Spencer Hill declares that 'Satan's damnation results from a series of refusals to accept offered grace and repent . . . In short, Satan damns himself'; and quotes in illustration: 'Is there no place | Left for repentance, none for pardon left?' (4. 79–80)[44]

Satan's question alludes to the reprobate type Esau, who, in contrast to Jacob, 'was rejected: for he found no place of repentance' (Heb. 12: 17). The allusion ensures that the question anticipates its answer. It is a cry of despair, a despair made more acute by knowledge of the inaccessible solution. In *Paradise Regained* Satan echoes all those presumptive reprobates who felt picked on by God:

> This wounds me most (what can it less) that man,
> Man fall'n shall be restored, I never more.
>
> (*PR* 1. 404–5)

It was the same text concerning Esau that trapped Bunyan in despair:

Now was I as one bound, I felt myself shut up unto the Judgment to

---

[42] *Milton and the English Revolution*, p. 367.
[43] Harry F. Robins, *If This Be Heresy: A Study of Milton and Origen*, Illinois Studies in Language and Literature, 51 (Urbana, 1963), 137.
[44] John Spencer Hill, *John Milton: Poet, Priest and Prophet* (1979), 12–13.

come; nothing now for two years together would abide with me, but damnation, and an expectation of damnation: I say, nothing now would abide with me but this, save some few moments for relief, as in the sequel you will see. (142).

It is the 'few moments for relief' that give credibility to Satan's despair. There are moments of distraction and moments of doubt about his irremediable state just as there were for his real-life doom-filled contemporaries. Flat despair is Satan's ambition, as it was sometimes his counterparts' to get to hell. When Christ, again in *Paradise Regained*, indicates to Satan that his destruction is imminent, Satan's reply is:

> Let that come when it comes; all hope is lost
> Of my reception into grace; what worse?
> For where no hope is left, is left no fear . . .
> I would be at the worst . . .
> The end I would attain, my final good.
>
> (*PR* 3. 204–11)

Irrational reflexes of hope refine his torture.

In stressing Milton's Arminian stance critics have distracted themselves from the historical religious imagination with which the poem is also lumbered. Doctrinal tenets assume different meanings in the different contexts to which they are assimilated. Milton's Arminianism modifies an understanding of God's relation to mankind which he inherited from puritan culture, clearing away the absurdity of holding people responsible for what they necessarily do. But he retained important traits of the Calvinist-puritan imagination, in particular its teleological and polarizing tendency. This imaginative characteristic was inculcated by belief in double predestination. It remained when its doctrinal prop was kicked away. In the passage where Arminian doctrine is spelt out God proceeds:

> The rest shall hear me call, and oft be warned
> Their sinful state, and to appease betimes
> The incensed Deity, while offered grace
> Invites; for I will clear their senses dark,
> What may suffice . . .
> This my long sufferance and my day of grace
> They who neglect and scorn, shall never taste;
> But hard be hardened, blind be blinded more,

That they may stumble on and deeper fall;
And none but such from mercy I exclude.

(3. 185–202)

Milton describes the development of reprobate experience (even though he insists it may be avoided) in a way that balances that of the elect. He also conceptualizes elect and non-elect experience as a progressive movement, a gradual but sure enlightenment or blinding.

The dramatic point of this debate in heaven is to make us aware that Satan's purpose is already foreseen and its success forestalled. We cannot, dramatically speaking, be interested as yet in the fate of mankind since we have not encountered the human pair except in disembodied argument. So the main effect is to convey the futility of Satan's mission. It is Satan who will 'stumble on and deeper fall' (3. 201). Moreover, because Satan is 'hard' in his rebellion against God we will see God inflict further hardness on him as a punishment. Doctrinal difficulty arose, thought Milton, because 'no distinction is made between a decree of reprobation and that punishment which involves the hardening of a sinner's heart' (*CPW* vi. 202). Once sinners were 'hard' and 'blind' God actively hardened and blinded them further, incapacitating belief (though the ambiguity of the passive mood may be used in the poetry to suggest that the hardening is simultaneously self-inflicted and inflicted by God). So just like Calvin's reprobates they entered, in this life, on the experience of hell. A moment was deemed to arrive when the day of grace was past, and what had impeded its reception was fortified into insurmountable resistance. Satan's reprobate experience is in the forefront of readers' minds as we arrive here after Books 1 and 2. We are still with him of course after the heavenly council (3. 418 ff.), when we witness the evidence of the punitive withholding of grace (which hardens Satan further); and then in Book 4 when we approach Adam and Eve through his eyes. So although it is often assumed that there is a fundamental difference between Satan and human beings, and that God's treatment of the one cannot be extrapolated to the other, the humanization of Satan, the vocabulary applied to him, and the engagement of the reader with his dramatic functions progressively undermine confidence in the distinction: Satan appears as a type of reprobate experience against which readers should measure themselves.

In the section of *De Doctrina* where Milton rejects predestined reprobation he phrases his conclusion somewhat oddly: 'It follows, therefore, that there is no reprobation except for those who do not believe or do not persist, and that this is rather a matter of consequence than of an express decree by God . . . None are predestined to destruction except through their own fault [ad interitum neminem (praedestinavit), nisi sua culpa].' These sentences indicate that beyond a certain point people are destined to be damned. God, Milton says, 'excludes no man from the way of penitence and eternal salvation, unless that man has continued to reject and despise the offer of grace, and of grace sufficient for salvation, until it is too late'. Human sin is the cause of reprobation and comes into effect 'when the sinner has either spurned grace right to the end, or has looked for it too late, and then only because he fears punishment, when the time-limit for grace has already passed' (*CPW* vi. 190, 194, 195). The guillotine comes down for Satan immediately he has transgressed, rather as for Calvin human free will was forfeited at the Fall. 'I formed them free,' says God of the rebel angels, 'and free they must remain, | Till they enthrall themselves' (3. 124–5). Milton's severe finality is inflected by Calvinism. It anticipates another famous Genevese, Rousseau, whose God said: 'I have made you too feeble to climb out of the pit, because I made you strong enough not to fall in.'[45]

The doctrinal departure from Calvin was less radical than might be supposed. 'If God decreed unconditionally that some people must be condemned,' allowed Milton, merely for the sake of argument, 'it follows . . . that God also decided upon the means without which he could not fulfil his decree. But the means are sin, and that alone' (*CPW* vi. 191). The point Milton stresses, therefore, is that the reprobate are not arbitrarily so in respect of their conduct. The argument opposes not so much Calvinists as those, on the one hand, who had adapted the idea of predestination to support an antinomian position, and those, on the other, who attacked it (on a similar understanding) as socially dangerous for removing motivation for moral restraint.

---

[45] Jean-Jacques Rousseau, *The Confessions*, trans. J. M. Cohen (Harmondsworth, 1953), 67.

In fact the whole Calvinist-puritan emphasis on signs of election and reprobation guarded against these distortions. 'If any be elect to eternall life,' said Perkins in answer to the Catholic charge that predestination was deleterious, 'they are also predestinate to the meanes by which they come to it.'[46] While Catholicism had tended to stress the cyclical nature of spiritual life—sin, confession, absolution, and sin again—Milton shared in the protestant, but especially Calvinist, tendency to see a linear progression, of which each experience marked a step, to heaven or hell. These experiences could be, moreover, as for more orthodox puritans, a succession, in large part, of mental states. It may be that with Milton you chose to climb on the train but there seems to have been little opportunity to get off once it had built up momentum. Satan is merely a stark instance of the fate befalling human beings.

Above all reprobates, like Satan, were characterized by the underlying conviction that they had no control over their destiny, that they were prisoners of powers greater than their will. This is the subtlest and perhaps most significant sense in which Milton suggests Satan and the reprobate enthrall themselves. In *De Doctrina* he implies a link between those who subscribe to the idea of a decree of reprobation aimed at particular individuals and those who see themselves as victims of external forces. He concludes chapter 4:

For those who believe in a decree of reprobation do, in fact, accuse God, however strongly they deny it. Even a heathen like Homer emphatically reproves such people in *Odyssey*, 1. 7:

> They perisht by their owne impietie.

—and again, through the mouth of Jupiter, 1. 32:

> O how falsly men
> Accuse us Gods as authors of their ill.
> When by the bane their owne bad lives instill
> They suffer all the miserie of their states—
> Past our inflictions and beyond their fates.
>
> (*CPW* vi. 202)

In Book 3 Milton has his God repudiate rigid predestination in a way that is designed at once to affirm his justice, anticipate exploitation of the false dogma in self-excuse and wrongful

---

[46] *Works*, p. 521.

accusation, and, implicitly, to criticize a theology which has
made him vulnerable. The devils could not, he says,

> justly accuse
> Their maker, or their making, or their fate,
> As if predestination overruled
> Their will.

(3. 112–15)

We certainly find this mental habit ingrained in Satan's
soliloquies (as it is in the spiritual autobiographies, and in the
speeches of Faustus). But Milton's success in discharging God is
made questionable by the determinist deadlock in which Satan is
admittedly placed and by the imaginative need to be faithful to
contemporary religious experience, which informs his portrayal.
For those who felt they did not control their lives the Calvinist
God remained in force. It was possible to be an Arminian only if
you felt free.

The Calvinist concept which will key us into Satan's
experience is that of double providence—the correlate, as we
have seen before, of double predestination:

for as muche as the will of God is sayd to be the cause of all thynges, his
Providence is thought the governesse in all purposes and workes of men,
so as it sheweth foorth her force not onely in the elect, whiche are
governed by the holye Spirite, but also compelleth the reprobate to
obedience.

This was an area where Calvin argued from the analogy of the
devil to human experience: 'if the devell whyche can not do but
evell yet willingly sinneth, who shall then saye that a manne
doothe therefore lesse wyllyngely synne for thys that hee ys
subject to necessitie of sinning.' The devil, it had always been
accepted, sins necessarily but this had not led theologians to
question the willed, and therefore culpable, nature of his sinning.
The reprobate, like the devil, were always fulfilling God's
purposes despite the nefarious intentions for which they were
rightly condemned:

This therefore he hath of hymselfe and of hys owne wyckednesse, that of
Desire and purpose he wythstandeth God. And by this wickednesse he
is stirred up to enterprising of those thinges that he knoweth to be most

against God. But because God holdeth him fast tied and restrayned with the bridle of his power, he executeth only those thinges that ar graunted him from God. And so doth he obey his creator whether he wil or no, because he is constrained to applie his service whether soever God compelleth him. (*Inst.* 1. 18. 2; 2. 3. 5; 1. 14. 17)

The extension of this thinking to human beings conferred observable reality on its psychological outworking. Before this, consideration of what it felt like to be the devil, squirming away from the realization that he was always playing into God's hands because unable to relinquish the role of adversary, could only take the form of abstract speculation. Its plangent dramatization could be read back into the devil only after the transfer of his predicament into the human domain, only, in other words, after his predicament had been inscribed in human experience.

Humanization of the demonic predicament may be seen in Milton's work: for example in *Samson Agonistes* where Samson speaks of 'swoonings of despair, | And sense of heaven's desertion' (ll. 629–32). His morose self-pity on Dalilah's departure ('God sent her to debase me, | And aggravate my folly' (ll. 999–1000)) indicates the alternative perception of divine providence: all things working together for ill to them that were *not* called according to God's purpose. No longer in the groove of divine favour Samson veers, in the interpretation of what befalls him, to the opposite idea of divine persecution. Dalilah's visit is still part of a divine plan, rather than an autonomous human act, but a plan to which vindictive intent is assigned (God 'aggravates' his woe as he does Satan's). Of course in his case the sense of divinely approved purpose returns, but the earlier part of the play gives access to the alternative state of mind. That alternative is not to become a free agent, for better or worse, but to be overwhelmed by a sense of rejection and persecution. The Father as Destiny looms over human lives but there is no presumption of benevolence.

That *Paradise Lost* opens on Satan enables us to live with him through the illusion of free agency and self-determination only to find that they have been nullified in advance. This progressive understanding, and therefore progressive despair, is what saps his vitality. It also discloses to us how Milton perceived the greatest possible suffering as well as the greatest possible evil. A good deal of attention has been given to the way in which the poem conceptualizes the latter; very little to how we might understand Satan as a portrait of the most painful experience imaginable. Satan's 'baleful' look, when we first meet him, intimates that the evil and the suffering are commingled in his psyche.

Satan describes himself in Book 1 as

>   one who brings
> A mind not to be changed by place or time.
> The mind is its own place, and in itself
> Can make a heaven of hell, a hell of heaven.
> What matter where if I be still the same,
> And what I should be, all but less than he
> Whom thunder hath made greater? Here at least
> We shall be free; the almighty hath not built
> Here for his envy, will not drive us hence:
>
>   (1. 252–60)

But Satan's freedom, Beelzebub explains, is a dream:

>   . . . while we dream,
> And know not that the king of heaven hath doomed
> This place our dungeon, not our safe retreat
> Beyond his potent arm, to live exempt
> From heaven's high jurisdiction,
>
>   (2. 315–19)

Shelley admired Satan because he 'perseveres in a purpose which he has conceived to be excellent, in spite of adversity and torture'.[47] In fact, though, he becomes enervated to the point when, in Sir John Hayward's words on the reprobate, 'his judgment is his Judge, when his owne knowledge conventeth him.'[48] He discovers, as post-structuralists could tell him, that his mind is not its own place but is traversed and constituted by a language he lacks the power to alter. This is particularly evident in the introverted aggression of the soliloquies (where, if ever, his mind is its own place). Though critics have complained of the shrinking Satan of *Paradise Lost* and the drained show he puts up in *Paradise Regained*, this owes less, I think, to a moralistic cutting down to size or a desertion by the author's creative juices, than to

---

[47] *The Complete Works*, vii. 91.
[48] *The Sanctuarie of a Troubled Soule* (1616), 10–11.

an imaginatively credible follow-through on his progressively disabling self-awareness.

God's denial of repentance to Satan and Satan's refusal to repent are presented, especially through soliloquy, in perfect equipoise. We are invited to understand that Satan consents to his damnation, that repentance is psychologically impossible to him and is not merely withheld by God; but the two attitudes are mutually dependent: 'as far | From granting he, as I from begging peace' (4. 103–4). Like Norwood, Satan censors his thoughts of repentance with the knowledge that 'Relapse' (a reprobate phase in Perkins's 'Table') after an apparent conversion which could not be sustained, or persevered in, could only worsen his position: attempted reconciliation 'would but lead me to a worse relapse | And heavier fall: so should I purchase dear | Short intermission bought with double smart' (4. 101–3). There is no self-delusion in Satan's realization that he must remain in hell. Were there any, his being there would not seem, as theologically it must, necessarily permanent. God's attitude to Satan is one of hatred and he has declared, in Book 3, that he will never relent. So Satan has no choice but to seek to overcome involuntary returns of the image of a loving God:

> Be then his love accursed, since love or hate,
> To me alike, it deals eternal woe.
>
> (4. 69–70)

Again Satan resembles the despairing autobiographers who had to live—except in rare moments (Bunyan's 'few moments for relief') when the mirage of mercy seemed to transform his character—with the conviction of God's hatred. And like them Satan has a mind which is conditioned, by an ineradicable obeisance to the authority of the father, to turn guilt inward: 'Nay, cursed be thou . . .' (4. 71). John Broadbent has rightly seen evidence in the soliloquies of the hardened heart; but again it helps to turn to the autobiographers for the interior experience Milton dramatizes, which drives one away from moralistic notions of a perverse persistence in evil.[49] While Norwood judges himself harshly for his hardened heart, for example, he supplies

---

[49] J. B. Broadbent, *Some Graver Subject: An Essay on 'Paradise Lost'* (1967), 76–8.

us, as we saw in an earlier chapter, with the evidence which
enables us to understand his impasse:

Yet so was my heart hardened that those and many other calamities
could not move it to relent or take any pity or compassion on myself,
only I think once or twice for a short time my heart did relent a little and
had some thoughts and purposes to return to England to settle myself in
I cared not how mean a calling so I might have the favor of God and
turn away his displeasure, which I conceived lay heavily upon me, but
these purposes were not constant but soon vanished again. (p. 27)

My second chapter explored Norwood's tacitly inhibiting
knowledge that he could not obey paternal imperatives. Satan,
too, knows he could not live contentedly under God's rule. What
we see of God's treatment of the angels, not to speak of the
provocative elevation of Christ, tends to support the devils'
perception of an authoritarian regime. God does appear, by
sending the angels on futile errands, to prompt query at least in
any self-respecting rational being. To Stanley Fish, 'God's
insensitivity to the angels' feelings is a compliment to them
because it assumes their firmness'; the more pointless a command
appeared the better the opportunity it supplied for demonstrating
obedience.[50] But if the poem were consistently addressed to
vindicating God's justice and reasonableness we could expect it
to imply (in Mary Astell's words some forty years later referring
to the exercise of male sovereignty in marriage) that such
obedience 'as is paid only to Authority, and not out of love and a
Sense of the Justice and Reasonableness of the Command will be
of uncertain Tenure'.[51] So it proved with the rebel angels, and
would, Satan realizes, prove again. Yet the failure to see reason
as the basis for God's fiats can only be considered culpable if one
holds with Fish that the demand for obedience is reason
enough—a position indistinguishable from the Calvinist tenet
that what God did must be thought just and reasonable because
he did it. The angels choose to believe, says Fish, 'that God has
their best interests at heart, no matter how inescapable a
contrary conclusion seems to be'.[52] It is inconceivable in the

[50] *Surprised by Sin*, p. 192.
[51] Mary Astell, *The First English Feminist: 'Reflections upon Marriage' and Other Writings*, ed. Bridget Hill (Aldershot, 1986), 33.
[52] *Surprised by Sin*, p. 192.

heaven Milton presents that any angel would seek an explanation, if none was volunteered, of the thinking behind any of God's
commands: prompt obedience or out-and-out rebellion (Satan
'durst defy the omnipotent' (1. 49)) are the only options, as is
characteristic of relationships with absolutist patriarchs. So we
are given a credible background of social experience to take the
emphasis off the pathology or gratuitous malignancy of Satan's
grace-resistant mind.

Isabel MacCaffrey takes Milton's description of hell as a place
where 'hope never comes | That comes to all' (1. 66–7) as a
reminder 'of the essential *difference* between ourselves and the
fallen angels'.[53] But I think the paradox aims to distinguish
rather between hope as a substantial state of consciousness and
the feverish impulses that start up to be frustrated both in
Satan's soliloquies and in some of the autobiographies. Satan
reveals indeed, in *Paradise Regained*, that his modest ambition is to
be at the end of his teleological journey—so that he can stop
being deluded, and tormented, by false hopes, false readings of
the historical process; and the devils' songs and debates
'excite | Fallacious hope' (2. 567–8). It is Satan's substratum of
understanding, resembling Faustus's, of the impossibility for him
of overcoming his resistance to God's authority that enables him
to check the sentimentality ('He deserved no such return | From
me' (4. 42–3)) and wishful thinking ('But say I . . . could
obtain | By act of grace my former state . . .' (92–4)) that rise
naturally to consciousness in a creature endowed with a full
complement of human feelings. He knows his repentance cannot
be 'endeavoured with sincere intent' (3. 192).

First seeing thanks and praise to God as 'easiest recompense'
(4. 47), Satan then exchanges this sentimental remorse for a
corrective reminder of his actual feelings at the time: he was
partly prompted to rebel by the need to 'quit | The debt immense
of endless gratitude' (51–2). 'Quit', usually meaning 'repay',
looks an odd choice when rebellion is the form repayment takes,
but it nicely expresses the thin line between adoring gratitude
and the, often unconscious, resentment engendered by that
attitude (to a social patron or patriarch): 'quit' can also mean
'avenge'—the ironic sense, for example, of Chaucer's Miller

---

[53] Isabel MacCaffrey, *'Paradise Lost' as 'Myth'* (Cambridge, Mass. 1959), 185.

when he promises to 'quyte the Knightes tale'.[54] The word slides
from the first meaning (Satan has already spoken of 'pay[ing]
him thanks | How due!' (47–8)) to the second. 'Thanks' may be
seen, as Christ sees it, as 'The slightest, easiest, readiest
recompense' (*PR* 3. 127–8); but it is not hard to understand the
intolerability of maintaining a permanent posture of gratefulness.

We can tell from the anguish of the soliloquy that it is no
simple matter of not wanting to feel the right things about God.
Donne found himself in a similar position when he tried to court
God with flattering speeches only to discover more authenticity
in his fear. Flattery of God, he explains in a sermon, aroused
God's anger: 'not that he can say more good, than is always true
of God; but towards God, as well as towards man, it is true, that
he that speaks more good than himself believes to be true, he
flatters, how true soever it be that he speaks' (*Sermons*, i. 278).
Satan, too, detects his own false notes. Milton had the typically
puritan understanding of hypocrisy as the pretension to unsustainable feelings, as his remarks on an emotionally exhausted
marriage suggest:

and where love cannot be, there can be left of wedlock nothing, but the
empty husk of an outside matrimony; as undelightfull and unpleasing to
God, as any other kind of hypocrisie . . . how miserably do we defraud
ourselves . . . by striving vainly to glue an error together which God and
nature will not joyne. (*CPW* ii. 256)

In Milton's own terms, therefore, there is an integrity in Satan's
recognition of the finality of his divorce from God. The defeat of
hope, and repentance, by self-knowledge is conveyed in terms
disturbingly unremote from human experience—especially,
when one thinks of autobiographies like Norwood's, contemporary
experience of the filial relation.

Increasingly Satan presents himself as a victim both of the
irreversibility of his fall from grace and of the oppositional stance
by which his identity is now constructed. Here again he
resembles the autobiographers. After posing the despairing
question ('is there no place | Left for repentance, none for pardon
left?' (2. 79–80)), its apparent hopefulness cancelled by the
knowledge informing it, Satan adds clauses ('and that word |
Disdain forbids me, and my dread of shame . . .' (4. 81–2))

[54] Geoffrey Chaucer, *Complete Works*, ed. W. W. Skeat (1912), 457.

which pile on the despair. Here we see him (in parallel to the spiritual autobiographers' typically passive constructions) positioning the self he identifies as his core ('me') as object rather than subject in the sentence. He feels himself to be the prisoner of reified postures into which his circumstances have precipitated him. This state of self-alienation, manifesting itself in a denial of responsibility for what he does and becomes, is near the centre of Milton's understanding of his evil-cum-suffering. When Satan seeks to exploit it for his advantage (by way of self-excuse, for instance, when resolving to pursue his mission) the epic voice condemns the ploy as 'necessity, the tyrant's plea' (4. 393). At the same time, however, it is true that Satan is an instrument of another's purposes, that destiny is not his choice. His repeated approaches to and jibbings at this realization constitute his anguish.

Satan is driven to conclude his soliloquy with the self-defeating, consciously despairing 'Evil be thou my good' (4. 110), a declaration which concedes to God the authority to assign values to words. It admits the objective status of 'good' and 'evil' as God has defined them and the merely subjective, necessarily self-delusive nature of the inversion. The impossibility of remaining neutral, of finding a self-definition independent of an attitude to God, is disclosed by the soliloquy:

> how I hate thy beams
> That bring to my remembrance from what state
> I fell, how glorious once above thy sphere.
>
> (4. 37–9)

The glory of the sun cannot be simply perceived; its sole significance is its relation to his own position. 'I carry'd, as it were, my *Hell within* me', said George Trosse, 'and therefore could see nothing *without* that was pleasing to me.'[55] Satan's mind commutes between two perspectives, the former celestial one and the present. The external world matters only in plotting his own position.

What first brought Satan to self-consciousness and thence to rebellion was a change (when Christ was elevated) in his social status which disclosed a fissure between his function and his presumed identity. His 'incessant autobiography' (complained of

[55] *Life*, p. 60.

by Lewis)[56] results from this fissure, for it introduces the idea of a personal history. As noted before, Paul Delany has demonstrated a strong correlation between the various kinds of self-conscious autobiography which developed in the seventeenth century and the authors' experience of social mobility.[57] The sense of oneself as a continuous entity is often posited by philosophers as definitive of personhood, and it is this historic shift in the devil from *being demonic* to self-consciousness that most humanizes him:

> conscience wakes despair
> That slumbered, wakes the bitter memory
> Of what was, what is, and what must be
> Worse.
>
> (4. 23–6)

The remembering conscience extrapolates a line of destiny from past to present on into the future. Introspection entails retrospection. This is why the devils seek to forget; but they are prevented from doing so because memory is integral to hell and to the performance of their teleological function. Satan again makes himself the object of mechanical processes: memory is controlled ('bring to my remembrance'; 'wakes the bitter memory') not by his will but by involuntary associations; conscience, or thinking about himself, is a semi-autonomous faculty which springs the logic of doom on him. God's power inside rebel heads confirmed its reality: 'there is graven in the mindes of men,' said Calvin, 'a certaine feling of the Godhead, which never can be blotted out' (*Inst.* 1. 2. 3).

Freedom of movement no more provides release from this temporal self-consciousness than did Norwood's bold excursions. Satan cannot escape from hell by travelling through space since he is still aware that he is enacting a destiny to which the journey contributes:

> within him hell
> He brings, and round about him, nor from hell
> One step no more than from himself can fly
> By change of place.
>
> (4. 20–3)

---

[56] C. S. Lewis, *A Preface to 'Paradise Lost'* (1942; paperback edn. 1960), 102.
[57] *British Autobiography in the Seventeenth Century* (1969). See above, p. 71 and n.

This is why he speculates (desperately, as again the phrasing indicates alienated awareness that he is not a producer of his own world) that 'Space may produce | New worlds' (1. 650–1), possible worlds of the mind to which the potent arm of God's empire does not extend. That Satan probably means more than physical worlds is suggested by the terms of praise given to Abdiel whose only care was 'To stand approved in sight of God, though worlds | Judged thee perverse' (5. 36–7). He is not entirely mistaken in venturing this hope, although Milton encourages us to think so; history was soon to bring about new thought-worlds from which God was banished.

Satan's portable hell is constructed primarily, then, by his awareness of how he stands towards God; and this is determined by his spatial and temporal co-ordinates—which God controls—and a theocentric discourse. His reaction to the sun indicates how little his mind is its own place, and he articulates the realization:

> Which way I fly is hell; my self am hell;
> And in the lowest deep a lower deep
> Still threatening to devour me opens wide,
> To which the hell I suffer seems a heaven.

> (4. 75–8)

Though a psychological pioneer, Satan finds no freedom in the new depths he discovers in himself. Like Norwood putting distance between himself and England, Satan thought 'furthest from him is best' (1. 247). The bid for independence is similar ('here at least | We shall be free' (1. 258–9)), as is its failure: 'the revengement of Gods majestie . . . doeth so much the more vehemently strike their consciences as they more labor to fly away from it' (*Inst.* 1. 3. 2.). Satan cannot find inner assurance so that, in Luther's words of those sensing God's persecution, 'the whole wide world becomes too narrow for him'.[58] Abdiel puts it too tritely when he dismisses Satan's claimed liberty ('Thy self not free but to thy self enthralled' (6. 181)); what Satan is in thrall to is the adversarial function from which it often seems he would like to retire. 'O then at last relent!' (4. 79), he exclaims; but retirement from purposive action, relenting, is not permitted.

---

[58] Rupp, *Righteousness of God*, p. 109.

Wherever he puts himself, history goes on extending and deepening his destiny. God has named him Adversary.

We looked before at the urge critics revealed to mollify Milton's God by having him extend to Satan the opportunity to repent so that a recidivist Satan could be effectively re-demonized in spurning it. The correlate of that piece of rewriting can be found in Louis Martz's perturbed response to the attribution to Satan, in this soliloquy, of a conscience:

Satan with a conscience? This seems not quite in accord with the theology that has just been explained, for Milton has given in book 3 the traditional view that Satan can never be granted grace and therefore, presumably, could never have a conscience. For conscience, we have been told, is the umpire that God will place within man's breast after the Fall, as a divinely given guide that may lead man from light to light toward his salvation . . . Milton is boldly raising here another of his ultimate questions: would not a just God prefer to see Satan repent, and give him the chance to repent? Milton seems to leave the question open by showing that Satan's pride would never have accepted the chance, and that therefore God has not offered it . . . Milton leaves us with the feeling that Satan somehow has the power, if only he had used it, to make a better choice.[59]

It is clear, however, that as regards Satan Milton has allowed himself to use the puritan understanding of conscience as articulated, for example, by William Perkins: it was 'a thing placed by God in the middest betweene him and man, as an arbitratour [Milton says "umpire"] to give sentence and to pronounce either with man or against man unto god'. It was the arbiter of spiritual identity, and could as well periodically illumine the reprobate's descent into darkness as confirm the elect's ascent into light. Conscience is like a sleeping beast, said Perkins, 'but when he is roused, he then awakes and flies into a mans face, and offers to pull out his throat'.[60]

Satan's experience is a type of those against whom conscience pronounced. As Luther said of the unregenerate: 'His conscience will be the greatest pain, because the soul cannot escape from itself, and yet it cannot avoid falling into horror.'[61] For puritans this could be a permanent condition: once awakened, the

[59] Louis Martz, *Poet of Exile*, pp. 106–7.
[60] *Works*, pp. 620, 660.
[61] Rupp, *Righteousness of God*, p. 110.

conscience will keep the soul, said Bolton, 'downe in the Dungeon of despaire for ever'.[62] Whether or not conscience acted as Martz imagines it must depended on which side of the great spiritual divide you occupied: 'If thou art an *Israelite*,' said John Sheffield, 'it [conscience] is the Red Sea, fear not to go into it, it will secure thee; if an *Egyptian*, thou art drowned if thou go into it.' Conscience could be, what it is to Satan, a '*Dungeon* to thee, yea, thy *upper Hell*'.[63] Though God's grace allows him to extricate himself Adam feels for a while, in the same determinist fix as Satan, and echoes his words:

> O conscience! into what abyss of fears
> And horrors hast thou driven me; out of which
> I find no way, from deep to deeper plunged!
>
> (10. 842–4)

We are given in Satan, then, a psychological equilibrium between the sense of God's rejection and resistance to him. The illusion of the freedom to repent tantalizes Satan (it is his most refined torment), but the near convergence of spiritual experiences does not alter the polarization of destinies. While those who got to heaven had to sail by hell, those who went to hell could have an anguishing taste of heaven.[64] Milton's God retains through his relation to Satan the capacity for flinty rejection while side-stepping its interference with human freedom. Milton takes such trouble with the psychology of Satan because of the human possibilities it dramatizes; and to the extent that that psychology is determined by the underlying conviction of divine rejection he acknowledges the social reality of the Calvinist God he ostensibly repudiates. The understanding the devils, like Calvinist despairers, possessed was 'a torment to them rather than a consolation; so that they utterly despair of their salvation' (*CPW* vi. 349)

There are moments in the poem when the experience of hell is, in Milton's word, 'suspended'. This is another Miltonic innovation which, theologically odd to say the least, owes itself to

[62] *Instructions for a Right Comforting Afflicted Consciences* (1631), 103.

[63] *A Good Conscience the Strongest Hold*, sigs. a3ᵛ, a2ʳ.

[64] Perkins, *Works*, p. 457; Thomas Goodwin, *A Childe of Light Walking in Darknes* (1636), 28–9; *Inst.* 3. 2. 11.

human analogues. Song is one form of imaginative escape. When Satan has left them some of the devils

> complain that fate
> Free virtue should enthral to force or chance.
> Their song was partial, but the harmony
> (What could it less when spirits immortal sing?)
> Suspended hell, and took with ravishment
> The thronging audience.
>
> (2. 550–5)

Lyricism can momentarily suspend historical awareness, as for Faustus it attempted to transcend personal destiny. The passage reads easily as an attack on the brittle lyricism of the cavalier poets, which was often transparently aimed at the suspension of temporal or historical awareness. Milton complained of the way songs could distort the past. In his *History of Britain* he condemned the '*British* Fables' of Geoffrey of Monmouth and dismissed achievements (glancing no doubt at the myth industry of the Caroline court) 'more renown'd in Songs and Romances, then in true stories. And the sequel it self declares as much' (*CPW* v. 156). The combination of assuming an inherent transcendent virtue and blaming hostile fate for its inability to show itself is held up as an object lesson in bad faith. The devils' frustrated longing is to drink from the river Lethe, which would erase their biting sense of the past and resulting extrapolation into the future; they want an escape route from the history they have, in Milton's eyes, made for themselves.

In this they resemble the despairing Samson:

> Sleep hath forsook and given me o'er
> To death's benumbing opium as my only cure.
>
> (*SA* ll. 629–30)

From the start it was the sense of history and his own part in it which punished him, though, as with the devils, lyricizing his suffering erects some defence against it. Like Satan, and the autobiographers, he is most attacked by the historical, or providential, sense in solitude which provides:

> Ease to the body some, none to the mind
> From restless thoughts, that like a deadly swarm
> Of hornets armed, no sooner found alone,

> But rush upon me thronging, and present
> Times past, what once I was, and what am now.
>
> (ll. 18–22)

Aesthetic rapture is another way, as we saw with Faustus, in which the pain of self-consciousness can be beguiled. All Satan's soliloquies are prompted, in a way presumably calculated to involve the reader with his consciousness, by a response to beauty: first sight of Eden, then of Adam and Eve, then of the young couple making love; lastly sense of the earth's beauty combined with memory of his own. The second is introduced:

> When Satan still in gaze, as first he stood,
> Scarce thus at length failed speech recovered sad.
> O hell! What do mine eyes with grief behold,
> Into our room of bliss thus high advanced
> Creatures of other mould.
>
> (4. 356–60)

Re-entry into language uncouples Satan's mind from his sensory responses, as happens again when

> the evil one abstracted stood
> From his own evil, and for the time remained
> Stupidly good, of enmity disarmed.
>
> (9. 463–5)

Here he reminds himself ('O hell!') of the perspective which must condition all his responses, the subject-position in which he seems bound to invest himself; and this poisons the response to beauty: considering the human pair, as the sun, in relation to himself plots his own degraded position.

To the extent that he 'could love' them he is self-alienated, as is evident from the sentimental description of the lovers as

> Ill fenced for heaven to keep out such a foe
> As now is entered; yet no purposed foe
> To you whom I could pity thus forlorn
> Though I unpitied.
>
> (4. 372–5)

The movement of his thought does him little credit when he slides into self-pity ('Though I unpitied') and dishonestly implies that mankind will benefit from a fall which, in his own case, he has just been bewailing. His initial solicitude for them may be regarded as authentic, based on his response to their beauty. It leads him, however, into unsustainable self-condemnation when he is forced to insert himself as a subject in language, equating himself with the 'foe' from which his dreamy, pre-linguistic mental processes have distanced him. The temptation to 'Melt' is consistent with the language of dissolution Satan uses elsewhere; 'relent' carries this sense (*OED* 1). Feeling himself genuinely to be 'no purposed foe', he wishes the teleology to which he is tied would dissolve away; his enmity is, he claims, reactive: 'Thank him who puts me loth to this revenge' (4. 386) (again presenting himself as the instrument of another's purpose). The only way he can realign himself with this foe he has, as if from the outside, described is by turning his mind from what is to be lost and towards an idea of solidarity with humanity in resistance to God: Satan seeks 'league' and 'amity' with mankind because he wants to occupy the province of the human mind with his own, albeit shifting, point of view.

This is not, then, a descent into the crudity of the hissable villain rubbing his hands with malign glee; at worst it is another effect of sentimentality. His mind slides past the Fall as though it were a *fait accompli*. Since from the reader's point of view it is just that, and since for many readers the poem has been confirming their own emotional estrangement from God, Satan does no more than echo their own sense of loss and 'reluctance against God'. Naturally puritan divines attributed mistrust of God to the devil: 'It was his art from the beginning,' said Sibbes, 'to discredit God with man, by calling Gods love into question.'[65] But it was the Calvinist picture of God that created the need for such assurances. And it was with this unrelenting God that Satan contended; so the talk of amity and league is not simple hypocrisy. Satan ends his soliloquy by returning to a straight-forward statement of his inner contradiction:

> And should I at your harmless innocence
> Melt, as I do, yet public reason just,
> Honour and empire with revenge enlarged,
> By conquering this new world, compels me now
> To do what else though damned I should abhor.

> (4. 388–92)

[65] *The Bruised Reed and Smoking Flax* (1630), ed. P. A. Slack (Menston, 1973), 164.

He expresses himself again as the servant of abstract forces outside himself.

Satan's soliloquies bear out Calvin's meaning when he said that to introspect was to be damned: 'If thou consider thy self, there is certaine damnation' (*Inst.* 3. 2. 24); even 'The Christian, when he beholdeth hym selfe, seeth nothing but cause of feare and of dispayre.'[66] Looking to himself confirms Satan's inability to eradicate God, or the moral unilateralism by which he is always prejudged, from his mind. His writhings perform the function of confirming the strength of contemporary belief in the Christian God, as did those of the reprobate for Calvin:

Yea that this perswasion, that there is a god, is even from their generacion naturally planted in them and depely roted within their bones, the very obstinacy of the wicked is a substantiall witnesse, which with their furious striving yet can never winde themselves out of the feare of God . . . when the dul hardnes, which the wicked do desirously labor to get to despise God withall, doth lie piningly in their hartes, yet the same feling of God, whyche they woulde moste of al desire to have utterly destroied, liveth still, and sometyme doeth utter it self. (*Inst.* 1. 2. 3)

When Satan manages to sidestep the internal punitive mechanism (which soliloquy lays bare) and persist in his rebellious mission, he runs into the external one—which then reinforces his despair and increases the effectiveness of his own inhibitions. Richard Sibbes exhorts the believer: 'we must joyn with God in bruising our selves; when hee humbles us let us humble our selves, and not stand out against him, for then hee will redouble his strokes.'[67] Milton read the history of Britain in the light of this back-up punitive providence where self-correction failed. At one time the 'instruments of divine justice' vie with each other to 'destroy a wicked Nation': 'the Pestilence forestalling the Sword left scarce alive whom to bury the dead' (*CPW* v. 141). God may be seen to 'redouble his strokes' in the brutal incident, about which Waldock and others complain, of the metamorphosis into snakes.[68] The incident merely fulfils earlier prediction:

[66] John Calvin, *A Commentarie upon St. Pauls Epistles to the Corinthians*, trans. T. Timme (1577), 1 Cor. 1: 9.   [67] *The Bruised Reed*, p. 33.

[68] A. J. A. Waldock speaks of a 'cartoon scene' in *'Paradise Lost' and its Critics* (Cambridge, 1947), 91.

> so bent he seems
> On desperate revenge, that shall redound
> Upon his own rebellious head.

(3. 84–6)

The devils remain, whatever they do, subject to the Father's punitive caprice:

> for what peace will be given
> To us enslaved, but custody severe,
> And stripes, and arbitrary punishment
> Inflicted?

(2. 332–5)

In fact it is to provide a perpetual object of God's wrath, as Empson points out, that the devils are kept in being.[69] Milton's God, unlike say Rust's, appears to have a permanent need to punish, just as Satan appears to be trapped in a posture of self-defeating rebellion. The reprobate, too, were punished, thought Calvin, not with a view to bringing them 'to a better minde: but only that, to their great hurt, they should prove God to be a judge and revenger'; they too were 'raised up to set forth his glorie with their damnation' (*Inst.* 3. 4. 33; 3. 24. 14).

The Satan of *Paradise Regained* exhibits a flatter despair; he is inhibited by the knowledge that enmity to God is a mode of self-destruction. No longer able even temporarily to convince himself of his illusions he has a dull masochistic curiosity as to how his destiny is to be accomplished. The Arch-fiend is pathetically quick, when challenged by Christ, to discard his rustic disguise: ' 'Tis true, I am that spirit unfortunate' (*PR* 1. 358). His own interest now is in who Christ is, and what is meant by the son of God; and his performance of the role of tempter seems half-hearted enough to anticipate the contemptuous rebuffs it meets. There seems at least some truth in his chastened consciousness of 'doings which not will | But misery have wrested from me' (*PR* 1. 469–70). Again Milton's determination to connect evil with a disavowal of autonomy, and thus responsibility, is apparent; but again, too, his psychology is

---

[69]　*Milton's God* (1961; paperback edn. Cambridge, 1981), 38.

faithful enough to the situation he dramatizes to show the pain of this alienated acting out of somebody else's script.[70]

Satan's momentary wish to believe that in tempting Job and executing other malicious schemes he was serving God has pathos in its very dishonesty. He has learnt that he does God's bidding willy-nilly and is wearied by the processes of self-deception his position forces on him. Christ merely confirms an existing awareness with his chilled reply:

> do as thou find'st
> Permission from above; thou canst not more.
>
> (*PR* 1. 495–6)

Satan continues to set himself up for further humiliation without ever conveying the exhilaration of scented success; his role has become a tired masochistic routine inviting such responses as:

> Satan, I know thy strength, and thou know'st mine,
> Neither our own but given; what folly then
> To boast what arms can do, since thine no more
> Than heaven permits, nor mine . . .
>
> (*PR* 4. 1006–9)

Nothing could be worse, to Milton, than playing into the hands of your enemy and being aware of the fact, or finding yourself trapped into pursuing a cause you knew to be wrong. Calvin may again have prompted this understanding of the experience of hell: 'if a man marke it,' he said, 'he shal easily see that the extremitie of all miseries is the ignoraunce of Gods Providence, and the chief blessednesse standeth in the knowledge therof' (*Inst.* 1. 17. 11). Satan expresses what Milton saw as the antithesis of the kind of life he wanted for himself; it consisted essentially in alienation from one's actions and apparent choices, the compulsion to commit one's intellectual gifts to the defence of an existence one knew at bottom to be inauthentic, and the ineluctable conviction that all voluntary manœuvring snarled one up further in a destructive destiny. The closest Milton himself appears to have come to the experience he portrays in

---

[70] A parallel could be drawn between Satan and Macbeth in this respect. Macbeth's apprehension of his duped performance of another's script informs his 'Tomorrow' speech: he finds that he is merely an actor in a tale which is meaningless to him. This discovery is related to his own disavowal of responsibility for his actions. See my 'Calvinist Psychology in *Macbeth*'.

Satan was the sense of the finality (under the law) of the choice of marriage partner; at least there appears to be a confessional rawness in the following passage from *The Doctrine and Discipline of Divorce*:

And the solitarines of man, which God had namely and principally orderd to prevent by mariage, hath no remedy, but lies under a worse condition than the loneliest single life; for in single life the absence and remoteness of a helper might inure him to expect his own comforts out of himselfe, or to seek with hope; but here the continuall sight of his deluded thoughts without cure, must needs be to him, if especially his complexion incline him to melancholy, a daily trouble and paine of losse, in some degree like that which Reprobates feel. (*CPW* ii. 246–7)

But freedom always lay for him in claiming it: 'God sends remedies, as well as evills,' he said typically, speaking of divorce, 'under which he who lies and groans, that may lawfully acquitt himself, is accessory to his own ruin' (*CPW* ii. 341). He defied the thraldom of marriage by legitimizing divorce.

It is vital to understanding Milton's puritan imagination and why he conceives of Satan's suffering as he does that we notice the prominence of teleological thinking in his work, as in his life. To be without a calling, without a purpose, or strapped to one's destiny by wrong choice was the worst imaginable thing. Samson's despair is of this kind; so too is Satan's. Yet active choice, to be fulfilling, had to be exercised in accordance, paradoxically, with a sense of destined purpose. 'I was his nursling once and choice delight,' Samson recollects the feeling, 'His destined from the womb' (ll. 633–4). Milton and Christ (in *Paradise Regained*) are motivated by their quest for an existing purpose. Even in the 'Nativity Ode' Milton cannot bear to think of Christ other than teleologically, seeing the frail babe already embracing what is scripted for him:

> The babe lies yet in smiling infancy
> That on the bitter cross
> Must redeem our loss.
>
> (p. 108, ll. 151–3)

The future floods the present.

From childhood Milton seems to have had a strong sense of his life's purpose. In 1641 he recalls that, until 'Church-outed by the Prelats', to the service of the Church of England 'by the intentions of my parents and friends I was destin'd of a child, and in mine own resolutions' (*CPW* i. 823, 822). The habit of considering the present in the light of the future persisted. This comes out in gratuitous bits of *Paradise Regained*: gratuitous in that what they ascribe to the consciousness of Christ is not suggested by the gospels or by tradition:

> When I was yet a child, no childish play
> To me was pleasing, all my mind was set
> Serious to learn and know, and thence to do
> What might be public good; myself I thought
> Born to that end.
>
> $\qquad$ (*PR* 1. 201–5)

Milton and his Christ appropriate their calling as their own mission. They are swept forward by the idea that they have a great purpose to fulfil. 'My time I told thee . . . is not yet come' (3. 396–7), says Christ; and 'All things are best fulfilled in their due time' (3. 182). Even in sterile periods, as in Restoration England, this habit of thought could be—as ~~Paradise Regained is no doubt meant to show~~—profoundly fortifying. Just as Laudianism had obliged Milton to rediscover his purposed way outside the expected institutional structure (the institution rather than the purpose had changed) so the Restoration called for a self-realignment to the difficult purpose history was disclosing.

At the age of 23, while evincing frustration, Milton is persuasively calmed by a sure sense, emphasized by the ponderously measured stresses, of a divinely appointed future controlling the development of his substituted poetic calling:

> Yet be it less or more, or soon or slow,
> $\quad$ It shall be still in strictest measure even,
> $\quad$ To that same lot, however mean or high,
> Toward which time leads me, and the will of heaven;
> $\quad$ All is, if I have grace to use it so,
> $\quad$ As ever in my great task-master's eye.
>
> $\qquad$ (pp. 147–8)

When he turned to polemical prose in the 1640s we find again that he had assumed a future vantage point from which to judge himself in the present:

neither envy nor gall hath entered me upon this controversy, but the enforcement of conscience only, and a preventive fear lest the omitting of this duty should be against me when I would store up to myself the good provision of peaceful hours.[71]

He was sufficiently in the stream of puritan feeling to construct a mental autobiography governed by the idea of final judgement. More narrowly conceived, this concern to avoid being 'accursed by god in old age' informs autobiographies like Oliver Heywood's.[72] Milton was habituated, he knew, to strenuous self-monitoring: 'For if I be either by disposition, or what other cause, too inquisitive or suspicious of myself and mine own doings,' he shrugged, 'who can help it?'[73] But unlike Satan he was never looking at himself in isolation, as an essence separate, or alienated, from the sense of purpose that impelled him. So tautly controlled was his life by the purposes governing it that he obviously had difficulty relaxing. Diodati wrote to him teasingly in Cambridge:

Live, laugh, make the most of Youth and the hours as they pass . . . In everything else inferior to you, I seem to myself—and am—your superior in one thing: that I know a measure to my labours.[74]

But Milton, like his unrelenting deity, was adamantine:

My own disposition is such that no delay, no rest, no thought or care for anything else, can divert me from my purpose, until I reach my goal and complete some great cycle of my studies.[75]

The contrast with Satan could not be starker. Satan sees himself either as under a necessity to act as he does; or, less convincingly, he sees himself and others as blown about by chance: 'Sir what ill chance hath brought thee to this place?' he asks Christ self-incriminatingly when posing as a shepherd (*PR* 1. 321). Destiny and chance ('force or chance' (2. 551)) work paradoxically in tandem to enable disavowal of responsibility. As Christopher Hill observes, for Milton, and protestants generally, 'God, after all, is not only King of the English Commonwealth, he is also the historical process: what he wills is fate.'[76] In God's

---

[71] John S. Diekhoff, *Milton on Himself* (1966), 5.

[72] *His Autobiography, Diaries, Anecdote and Event Books*, ed. J. H. Turner (Brighouse, 1882), i. 151.   [73] Diekhoff, *Milton on Himself*, p. 4.

[74] W. R. Parker, *Milton: A Biography* (Oxford, 1968), 60.

[75] *Milton's Private Correspondence and Academic Exercises*, trans. P. B. Tillyard, ed. E. M. W. Tillyard (Cambridge, 1932), 11.

[76] *Milton and the English Revolution*, p. 368.

words 'necessity and chance | Approach not me, and what I will is fate' (7. 172–3). Necessity and chance are both to be distinguished from the sense of purpose or providence, in which what is destined and what beckons your assent and energies are felt to be one and the same.

Satan and some of the autobiographers were self-obsessed, but obsessed primarily by their entrapment—and this way of thinking about themselves was a self-fufilling prophecy. Milton sees the propensity to fatalism (and specifically belief in predestination) as a moral failing. The root of evil and of self-destruction was acceptance of precisely the passivity Calvinism tended to induce. God created the devils, as mankind, free to fall because he would have derived no pleasure from their obedience

> When will and reason (reason also is choice)
> Useless and vain, of freedom both despoiled,
> Made passive both, had served necessity,
> Not me.
>
> (3. 108 11)

When will and reason fail to conduce to serving God these free beings 'enthrall themselves' (3. 125). Part of that thraldom consisted in acceding to a necessitarian outlook. Which, after the primal disobedience, came first—the irresistible logic of reprobation or the fatalism of those to whom it applied—is not considered.

Milton adumbrates in *De Doctrina* and appears to dramatize in *Paradise Lost* a novel idea that pays its dues to Calvinism and yet represents a psychologically credible development from it. It is that liberation of the will is a progressive experience. The more you claimed and exercised your narrow freedom the more it opened up—like a previously unsuspected faculty—and strengthened itself. The view expressed in *Areopagitica*, that strenuous exertion was vital in order to consolidate any spiritual gains, anticipates this insight: 'Well knows he who uses to consider, that our faith and knowledge thrives by exercise, as well as our limbs and complexion.' Thus Milton created a position between determinism and free will:

when God determined to restore mankind, he also decided unquestionably (and what could be more just?) to restore some part at least of man's lost freedom of will. So he gave a greater power of willing and running (that is, of believing) to those whom he saw willing or running already by virtue of the fact that their wills had been freed either before or at the actual time of their call. (*CPW* ii. 543; vi. 187)

Freedom of the will was cumulative. Conversely, for the unregenerate, disuse would gradually close the faculty down irrecoverably: in the end the passivity and impotence, and victimization by fate, which were claimed in self-excuse, became real. It is because this self-disablement takes real effect that Milton speaks of a point when 'it is too late,' when 'the time-limit for grace has already passed' and the incapacity to repent has become a divine punishment (*CPW* vi. 194, 195). The fatalistic frame of mind was 'Th' effect and cause, the punishment and sinne'.

'The essence of all alienation', says Peter L. Berger in *The Social Reality of Religion*, 'is the imposition of a fictitious inexorability on our humanly constructed world. Activity becomes process. Choices become destiny.'[77] This is the condition of the spirit 'alienate from God' (6. 877) of Milton's epic. If Satan were the traditional devil, menacing mankind with a tireless automatic evil, there would be no reason to suppose he suffered. Suffering comes in through his sense of hostile destiny, his double vision of himself and of every action he undertakes. He resembles the spiritual autobiographers in seeing every detail of experience in the light of a teleology to which the will is wholly subordinate: 'Activity becomes process.' This is why, like them, he has constant resort to passive locutions. He is a reluctantly exploited instrument whose experience is the inverted image Milton projects from his sense of the purposiveness of life.

Berger's useful definition of alienation simplifies, as perhaps does Milton himself at times, by implying that it is a form of moral weakness. While it is clear enough that the world people inhabit is humanly constructed it is also fully understandable that large numbers of Milton's contemporaries felt unable to contribute to its construction; excluded from political participation, even at local level, and subject to economic forces over which they exercised little or no control, people like Norwood and Bunyan naturally succumbed to an instrumental perception of themselves. For them the inexorability was real. For Milton, and other securely middle-class puritans with growing political

---

[77] Peter L. Berger, *The Social Reality of Religion* (1969), 95.

power, construction of the world along chosen lines was just imaginable. Yet it may be seen as an expression of moral strength on Milton's part both that he held on to that vision when circumstances appeared to shatter it and that he resisted the facile drift of his class, on the tide of economic self-interest, towards an accommodation with monarchy. The urgency with which Milton insists that the idea of freedom should be grasped, combined with the moral muscularity he was constantly toning up, measures his sensitivity to its precariousness—as does the vivid presentation in a hell-bound Satan of its irretrievable loss.

To understand the purpose to which you could voluntarily contribute required determined scrutiny of history. But the historical purview which assisted escape from the feeling of subjection to capricious fate (the agent of Adam's liberation) could only hearten those who belonged to a social group or class which could reasonably believe itself to be capable of exercising influence over the direction of the historical process. This belief was not available to the likes of Norwood and Bunyan. It is generally true, I think, that peoples or social groups who have no credible opportunity to change their worlds adopt fatalistic philosophic or religious beliefs (the strong belief in *Kharma* among the Indian poor is an example), and this goes along with indifference to history. It is no more an object of thought than the geological strata on which one happens to stand. Milton belonged to an ascendant social power, the bourgeoisie; yet he recognized the need to fight to clear and expand the opening for independent, purposeful, influential choice which he was able to see and to convert economic strength into political freedom. He grew up in a world of well-to-do merchant families where, says Hill, he 'must have absorbed the "protestant ethic" with the air he breathed. It would be taken for granted that hard work was a religious duty, that bargains were made to be kept, and enforced by law against those who could or would not keep them, that the weakest went to the wall, that God helped those who helped themselves.'[78] It is as likely that, coming from such an industrious and prosperous background, Milton would feel invigorated by Calvinism to embrace the idea of himself as elect as it is understandable that Bunyan, in his social circumstances, would be prone to feeling himself its victim.

[78] *Milton and the English Revolution*, p. 23.

The argument for Calvinism's back-door access to *Paradise Lost* gains prima-facie plausibility not only from the general historical pressure it exerted over the imagination but also from the personal-historical pressure of mental habit. 'We do not know', says Hill, 'how early Milton abandoned Calvinism. In 1641 he assumed that Pelagianism was a heresy, but refused to accept Calvin as an authority; in *Areopagitica* he referred to Arminius with respect but apparent disagreement.' In *De Doctrina* Milton was still impressed by the support the Bible appeared to give Calvinism (which Hill rather implausibly, in view of the private purpose for which the work was written, wants to attribute to the hope of reuniting supporters of the revolutionary cause).[79] There is no doubting Milton's Arminianism; but there remains good reason to suppose that the structure of perception fostered by Calvinism continued to play a role. Given the belief in individual responsibility and the value of vigorous use of one's opportunities which attended affluent Calvinist societies, the assertion of spiritual freedom was a natural development (one that occurred in Holland and even Geneva as well as England); but the shadow of its opposite, passive entrapment within an uncontrollable destiny, remained to heighten vigilance over such privileged freedom.

Milton aimed at a society in which authoritarianism, and 'servile crouchings', would be replaced by 'a cheerful and adoptive boldness' (*CPW* i. 616); and, in keeping with the late seventeenth- and eighteenth-century trend towards meliorist social thought (of which Locke was the most impressive and influential exponent), he wanted the criterion of value to be whether things 'render this life of ours happy (or at least comfortable and pleasant, without dishonor)' as well as whether they 'lead us to the other, happier life' (*CPW* iv. 601). Even within *Paradise Lost*, as William Empson brilliantly argued, one sees the superannuation of the Calvinist God occurring.[80] Hill sees something similar: 'In *Paradise Lost* the Father was kicked upstairs—formally accepted, but not felt. In the later books of

---

[79] *Milton and the English Revolution*, pp. 275, 218. As late as 1673, when he published *Of True Religion*, Milton remained impressed by the biblical support for Calvinist doctrinal emphases, as the sagacious double negative at the end of this statement indicates: 'The Calvinist is taxt with Predestination, and to make God the Author of sin; not with any dishonourable thought of God, but it may be over zealously asserting his absolute power, not without plea of Scripture' (*CPW* viii. 424).

[80] *Milton's God*, pp. 130–46.

the poem he recedes, and is replaced by the Creator-Son.'[81]
While justice is done to the collectively inherited picture of God,
omission of which would weaken the work's claim to epic
inclusiveness, mankind is given an opportunity to slip the
authoritarian bind, taking its destiny, or history, into its own
hands: growing up psychically in a way that allows the looming
patriarch to recede. The change occurs when Adam and Eve
actively resolve not to follow the passive route of Satan, 'from
deep to deeper plung'd' (10. 844), take a conspectus of human
history for which they acknowledge responsibility ('I yield it
just,' says Adam (11. 526)), and accept that their future lies in
their own hands (departing Eden, they will 'choose | Their place
of rest' (12. 646–7)). They close the gap, in effect, between
Destiny, or the Father, and their own doings—their own,
human construction of the world. So the authoritarian projection
ceases to be necessary. More accurately, of course, it is Adam,
the domestic patriarch, to whom this relative autonomy is
granted. Like Milton, in his bourgeois household, he has become
his own patriarch.

What must be added to the growing economic confidence of
the social groups to which Calvinism had typically appealed in
more anxious times is the action, sometimes delayed, of the Civil
War as solvent for the authoritarian structure of religious, as of
social, experience. Inasmuch as it was for a religious principle
that the Civil War was fought it was the principle that if two
authorities are in conflict, the Bible and the bishops, God and
King, it is the higher that must be obeyed. While God remained
a patriarchal giant this bespoke no liberation at all. But in the
process of opposing the most sacred and powerful of secular
patriarchs (and invoking history as well as sacred writ in
justification) people to whom self-determination had been
inconceivable savoured the exhilarating possibility that they
might take control of their own lives and communities, submitting
themselves only in name, if indeed at all, to a talismanic deity.
Hobbes's choice between serving an existing authority and
submitting oneself to a greater could be transcended by
republican or egalitarian ideals. And the more the idea of
communal self-sufficiency grew on the mind the more the
patriarchal giant faded on the imagination. This is how

[81] *Milton and the English Revolution*, p. 357.

Winstanley and some of the other radicals enabled themselves to reject deterministic, authoritarian Calvinism.

The legitimacy of unconditional patriarchal power would, once the war's seismic repercussions were gauged, no longer be socially embedded as an ideological given. Hobbes, after all, had to argue strenuously for it. Obedience to authority not based on a sense of its justice and reasonableness, it would now have to be recognized, was of uncertain tenure. Satan's rebellion addresses that awareness, whether or not one believes God is justified. Needless to say this historical lesson did not transform social relations and spiritual experience overnight (or, indeed, for large numbers of people, at all). Mary Astell, for example, sees the inconsistency between rejection of a monarchy that tended towards absolutism and unquestioning condonement of a similar unappealable sovereignty in marriage. '*If all Men are born free,*' she was soon to ask, 'how is it that all Women are born slaves? as they must be if the being subject to the *inconstant, uncertain, unknown, arbitrary Will* of Men, be the *perfect Condition of Slavery?*'[82] Yet that she, a conservative thinker, can, by the turn of the century, avail herself of an analogue which exposes this so coolly evidences an advance from self-authorizing patriarchy towards ideas of rational contract. A new vocabulary has become available and infiltrates contiguous areas of experience.

But it should not be supposed that authoritarian habits of mind could be easily sloughed off. The God–Satan axis in *Paradise Lost* is there to remind us of this. Milton is doing more in *Paradise Lost* than dramatizing the theology to which he consciously subscribed, the theology of *De Doctrina*; he is imaginatively heightening aspects of the spiritual experience of his day, aspects which had no less social reality for having sprung from doctrines he rejected. He had concluded that it was entirely on the opinion that the will was powerless to do good in the sight of God 'that the outcry against divine justice is founded'. And it was unquestionably his aim to clear God on this count, simultaneously restoring responsibility to mankind. Yet unconscious theological dispositions (to transfer to Milton a phrase T. S. Eliot restricts to his critics;[83] and they chose Satan as their vehicle.

[82] *The First English Feminist*, p. 76.

[83] T. S. Eliot, *Milton*, Annual Lecture on a Master Mind: Henrietta Hertz Trust of the British Academy (1947), 3.

APPENDIX

A note on the recent questioning of the Marx, Weber, Tawney belief that the sixteenth and seventeenth centuries were a period of transition in England from feudalism to capitalism.

An extreme revision of the Marx, Weber, Tawney views of the development from feudalism to capitalism which agree in locating the transition mainly in the sixteenth and seventeenth centuries has been advanced by Alan Macfarlane in *The Origins of English Individualism* (Oxford, 1978). It has made historians reconsider the assumption that England, in the Middle Ages, resembled European peasant economies. His thesis is summarized thus:

> It has been argued that if we use the criteria suggested by Marx, Weber, and most economic historians, England was as 'capitalist' in 1250 as it was in 1550 or 1750. That is to say, there were already a developed market and mobility of labour, land was treated as a commodity and full private ownership was established, there was very considerable geographical and social mobility, a complete distinction between farm and family existed, and rational accounting and the profit motive were widespread. (p. 195)

The dust of the debate about Macfarlane's contentions has not yet settled so it is hard for an outsider to make definite judgments. I should like, however, to make one or two observations to justify adhering to the older, strongly persisting, view (that this period is transitional and characterized by insecurity) though without committing myself on how property was conceptualized, and so forth, in the Middle Ages.

First, weaknesses in Macfarlane's use of his sources of evidence have been exposed. For instance, Miranda Chaytor ('Household and Kinship: Ryton in the Late 16th and Early 17th Centuries', *History Workshop* no. 10 (1980), 25–60, p. 59 n. 31) points out that the documents of the two villages on which Macfarlane does his closest work are examined in different periods. While the Ryton listings, indicating kinship ties, survive for the late sixteenth and early seventeenth centuries, the listing for Kirkby Lonsdale is for 1695. Christopher Hill comments wryly: 'Perhaps 100 years made a difference and changes did take place in the 16th and 17th centuries as Marx, Tawney, and the many historians Alan Macfarlane is concerned to refute, thought they did' ('Note: Household and Kinship', *P&P* 88 (1980), p. 142).

Secondly, historians who agree that market forces were vigorously in play at least in the fifteenth century have argued that circumstances altered in the sixteenth to make these seem less beneficent. Thus John Hatcher in 'English Serfdom and Villeinage: Towards a Reassessment', (*P&P* 90 (1981), 3–39, p. 39):

When in the sixteenth century population and prices rose, when land became ever more scarce and expensive, and real wages fell, those tenants unprotected by ancient custom were acutely vulnerable to eviction and rack-renting. The demise of custom gave a freer rein to market forces: in the fifteenth century this was beneficial, but the adversity of market forces in the following century ensured that, viewed in the broad perspective, the decline of serfdom produced for a sizeable proportion of the peasantry only short-term benefit and long-term harm.

Robert Brenner too ('The Agrarian Roots of European Capitalism', *P&P* 97 (1982), 16–113) includes in his analysis of sixteenth- and seventeenth-century change a number of features which would, according to my argument, strengthen the plausibility of the negative doctrines of Calvinism. There was for instance a massive decline of small farmers, elbowed out by big capitalists who, owing to large investment funds, could afford to sit out market fluctuations. Lands were turned over to arable; enclosures meant depopulation (except where small industries were able to absorb the surplus labour). Big tenants were also trapped by market forces since they had to pay high rents when they were getting low prices. 'They ended up in many cases', says Brenner, 'handing over to the lords every last bit of accumulated capital in order to hold onto their leases before going under' (p. 104). High unemployment was also experienced in areas affected by crisis in the cloth industry.

It seems to me that it was not so much the novelty of salient features of the sixteenth-century economy that registered in the religious imagination as their scale and the way they were viewed. Indeed, according to Macfarlane's own argument (he is dismissive at the end of his book of historians who slight the testimony of contemporaries about themselves), the two ought to be related. It would be strange for instance that so much fuss was made about the need for a Poor Law if the scale of vagrancy was not unprecedented. Descriptions of masterless men would scarcely abound if expropriation and depopulation from the land had not driven homeless and jobless people to the towns in alarming numbers. Likewise clamour over distinctions of status provides contemporary testimony to a new perception of disruptions caused by social mobility.

Even if, right back to the thirteenth century, individualized ownership was the norm in England, so that younger sons and daughters often moved away from their family village in order to obtain work, this ethos, since shared, need not have produced great personal insecurity (when work was available and wages for labourers were fairly high). A communal ethos in villages where, as Zvi Razi argues ('Review Article: The Toronto School's Reconstruction of Medieval Peasant Society: A Critical View', *P&P* 85 (1979), 141–57), there was co-operation between richer and poorer villagers could have obtained without a strong kinship basis. It is perhaps only when the scale of capital investment grows that the use of money becomes largely detached from ideas of social responsibility (of which custom had been the custodian) with the resulting 'spiralling accumulation', to use Macfarlane's phrase, 'whereby the rich continue to get rich and the poor to get poorer' (p. 69). Many historians still seem to believe that the pace and scale of changes in the sixteenth and seventeenth centuries were sufficient to create a general sense of insecurity and bewilderment in pre-industrial England (to which Calvinism could address itself with eloquence). Strangely enough, Macfarlane himself makes the anti-Weberian point that Calvinism should be seen 'as a consequence, rather than as a cause of the patterns' (p. 199) he has described; strangely, because this can only really be so if the patterns had achieved a new clarity or prominence.

INDEX

Note: Subject entries for which the only sensible reference would be *passim* have been excluded from this index.

THE
PERSECUTORY
IMAGINATION